# Foundation Adobe Edge Animate

For HTML5, CSS3, and JavaScript

**Tom Green and Michael Clawson**

friendsof

DESIGNER TO DESIGNER™

*an Apress® company*

# Foundation Adobe Edge Animate

ISBN 978-1-4302-4350-2

ISBN 978-1-4302-4351-9 (eBook)

Distributed to the book trade worldwide by Springer Science+Business Media New York, 233 Spring Street, 6th Floor, New York, NY 10013. Phone 1-800-SPRINGER, fax (201) 348-4505, e-mail orders-ny@springer-sbm.com, or visit www.springeronline.com.

For information on translations, please e-mail rights@apress.com or visit www.apress.com.

Apress and friends of ED books may be purchased in bulk for academic, corporate, or promotional use. eBook versions and licenses are also available for most titles. For more information, reference our Special Bulk Sales–eBook Licensing web page at www.apress.com/bulk-sales. APress Media, LLC is a California LLC and the sole member (owner) is Springer Science + Business Media Finance Inc (SSBM Finance Inc). SSBM Finance Inc is a Delaware corporation.

Any source code or other supplementary materials referenced by the author in this text is available to readers at www.apress.com. For detailed information about how to locate your book's source code, go to www.apress.com/source-code/.

# Credits

**President and Publisher:**
Paul Manning

**Lead Editor:**
Ben Renow-Clarke

**Technical Reviewers:**
shaRon sachse, Doug R. Winnie

**Editorial Board:**
Steve Anglin, Mark Beckner, Ewan Buckingham, Gary Cornell, Louise Corrigan, Morgan Ertel, Jonathan Gennick, Jonathan Hassell, Robert Hutchinson, Michelle Lowman, James Markham, Matthew Moodie, Jeff Olson, Jeffrey Pepper, Douglas Pundick, Ben Renow-Clarke, Dominic Shakeshaft, Gwenan Spearing, Matt Wade, Tom Welsh

**Coordinating Editor:**
Anamika Panchoo

**Copy Editor:**
Mary Bearden

**Compositor:**
Bytheway Publishing Services

**Indexer:**
SPI Global

**Artist:**
SPI Global

**Cover Image Artist:**
Corné van Dooren

**Cover Designer:**
Anna Ishchenko

*To another 35 years with the main passion in my life . . . my wife, Keltie.*

*—Tom Green*


*To the three people in my life that mean more to me with each passing day—my wife, Patty, my daughter, Tessa, and my son, Nicholas. Thanks for putting up with me during the course of this book.*

*—Michael Clawson*

# Contents at a Glance

# Contents

# About the Authors

**Tom Green** is currently a professor of interactive media in the School of Media Studies at the Humber Institute of Technology and Advanced Learning in Toronto, Canada. He has written 12 previous books on Adobe technologies and many articles for numerous magazines and web sites, including *Layers* magazine, webdesign.tutsplus.com, the Adobe Developer Center, and Computer Arts. He has spoken at more than 40 conferences internationally, including Adobe MAX, National Association of Broadcasters (NAB), FITC, MX North, Digital Design World, TODCon, D2W, and SparkEurope. You can contact Tom at tom@tomontheweb.ca.

**Michael Clawson** is the "Chief Fish" at Big Fish Creations, an advertising and digital media company in the Sierra town of Graeagle. His background began in Silicon Valley when Apple Computer and Adobe Systems first made their mark in desktop publishing. He was introduced to interactive media early in his career, transitioned to production artist, and later, creator and lead principal of an interactive department at a major Nevada advertising agency. Specializing in branding across multiple media platforms, his diverse repertoire includes a hybrid combination of designer and developer with emphasis on graphic design, branding, photography, and communication. As a speaker, Michael has presented at several industry-specific conferences, including Adobe Max and MacWorld. You can contact Michael at michael@bigfishcreations.com.

# About the Technical Reviewer(s)

 **shaRon sachse** is a front-end web animation geek and Adobe-certified expert who creates art and expressions for the digital canvas, motion, and Web using a suite of Adobe tools + open source. She does front-end web development incorporating video, HTML 5, Web Fonts, animation, and rich interactive experiences on multiple screens. shaRon also builds apps, extending creativity to the new handheld devices. Clients include AMC Siggraph-LA chapter, Santa Monica College, Charles Drew University, Friends of Yad Sarah, King of Queens, Time Warner Cable, and Rainbow Book Mobile. You can see her work at http://sharon-folio.com.

An Edge Animate enthusiast, shaRon continually focuses on the cutting edge and beyond, concentrating on new technologies to stay at the forefront of the industry. She started working with Edge Animate close to its conception and has seen multiple preview releases and enjoys working with this technology everyday. You can find her Edge Animate blog at http://edgeanimate101.wordpress.com.

shaRon loves to share technology and design with her community. She is the organizer of HTML5LA (a Los Angeles group focusing on open source technologies: HTML 5, CSS3, JavaScript, and other web and mobile technologies) (http://www.html5la.org/). She is also the manager of DDLA, the first Adobe Edge Animate user group (http://ddla.groups.adobe.com), the organizer of the LA Tech event, MobileCampLa, and a speaker at conferences and user group meetings.

When she is not animating or bringing a vision to life on the web, she can be found pursuing her other passions; she is an avid bicyclist, foodie, Drupaler, and creator of education apps.

 **Doug R. Winnie** has worked in the computer industry as a designer, developer, trainer, product manager, and community professional for over 15 years. During his time as a designer and developer, Doug built web applications for numerous companies, including Safeway, Toyota, Lexus, Hewlett-Packard, and Industrial Light and Magic. Through his work, his projects have been nominated multiple times for industry awards, including two Webby Award nominations.

Courtesy Gladys Jem Allen

At Adobe, Doug worked for many years on bridging the gap between the needs and requirements of designers and developers, which resulted in many projects and applications, the most recent of which was Adobe Edge Animate.

In addition to his full-time work, Doug is an instructor at San Francisco State University focusing on HTML 5 and other interactive technologies. He is the author of two books, a regular speaker at industry conventions, and is an avid mobile application developer in his spare time.

Doug currently is the director of content for web and developer courses at lynda.com and lives in San Francisco, California. He is @sfdesigner on Twitter and has a blog at http://sfdesignerdw.wordpress.com/.

# About the Cover Image Designer

**Corné van Dooren** designed the front cover image for this book. After taking a break from friends of ED to create a new design for the Foundation series, he worked at combining technological and organic forms, with the results now appearing on the cover of this and other books.

Corné spent his childhood drawing on everything at hand and then began exploring the infinite world of multimedia—and his journey of discovery hasn't stopped since. His mantra has always been "the only limit to multimedia is the imagination," a saying that constantly keeps him moving forward.

Corné works for many international clients, writes features for multimedia magazines, reviews and tests software, authors multimedia studies, and works on many other friends of ED books. If you like Corné's work, be sure to check out his chapter in *New Masters of Photoshop: Volume 2* (friends of ED, 2004). You can see more of his work (and contact him) at his web site www.cornevandooren.com.

# Acknowledgments

As I once said in a previous friends of ED book, "Working with a coauthor can be a tricky business. In fact, it is a lot like a marriage. Everything is wonderful when things are going well, but you never really discover the strength of the relationship until you get deep into it." I have known Michael for a few years and had always admired his simple approach to design, his sense of humor, and his dogged determination to solve problems. When we started work on this book, those three qualities became critically important as we contended with the Agile product development process instituted at Adobe and editors who, quite rightly, kept wondering what was holding up the book. As we moved through the process of creating this book, our friendship became a partnership.

What makes this partnership work is that we are both passionate about what we do and are unwilling to settle for the path of least resistance. Many are the times Mike yanked me off that path, gave me a good shake, and shoved me forward.

As we dug into this book, we realized that we could tell you what to do, but as things changed over the course of the Preview Release, we realized the scope of the book and design and development techniques around using Edge Animate were in flux. We reached out to a number of people to help us understand this emerging technology. We deeply appreciate the help we got from the Animate team, Mark Anders, John Dunning, Chris Georgenes, Darryl Heath, Dave Hogue, Sarah Hunt, Joseph Labrecque, Rich Lee, Doug Winnie, and many more for their insights and guidance.

Another important influence during this process was our tech editor shaRon Sachse. shaRon is an amazing motion graphic professional based out of Los Angeles who has been involved with Edge Animate from slightly before the Preview release. The work she turned out using the early builds of Edge Animate was jaw dropping, and her influence with this book can't be understated. That she was our tech editor meant we had to rise to her standards. We hope we did.

Next up is our editor, Ben Renow-Clarke. This is the fourth book I have written with him. Ben stayed out of the way but was always there when we got stuck and needed a kick in the pants or a "Have you thought of this . . . ?" idea.

Finally, writing a book means I hole myself up in my office and become generally moody and difficult to be around as I mull over a technique or try to identify why something isn't quite working. It takes a very unique individual to live with that, let alone understand why—and my wife, best friend, and life partner over the past 35 years, Keltie, has somehow put up with it.

Tom Green

When I was first asked to coauthor a book with Tom Green, it was at Adobe Max 2011 during a casual conversation over drinks. For several years I had been friends with Tom and our mutual friend, Jim Babbage, and had admired their speaking and writing skills. Not to mention, they both have a great sense of humor.

But, here was Tom asking me if I was interested in writing a book with him that would feature the recently introduced Adobe Muse and the up and coming Adobe Edge, which was Edge Animate's name at the time. Since I had spent time beta testing Muse and had produced several web sites for my clients, I was more than happy to take on the challenge of writing a book and sharing my knowledge about the program. I mean, how hard could that be? But, shortly after, it became apparent for reasons not really in our control that the focus of the book shifted to feature only Edge Animate, and thus began the so-called wild ride that I happily climbed aboard with the help of Tom's experience, encouragement, and guidance.

Now, Tom will not admit it, but in our industry, he's a celebrity. He gathers an audience wherever he talks and is well respected by his colleagues. He was even able to fend off an attack by the comedian of the same name who tried to take his Twitter handle away, which Tom had possessed way before Twitter was even chic. His story made the national news in fact. So, here I was writing with the best of the best, totally expecting to be treated as a complete rookie author. But you know what? It never happened. Sure, I made some rookie mistakes, and, Tom helped me through them. But, throughout the course of our book, I was treated like a colleague and a friend, which was indeed refreshing. Tom really helped me understand how to communicate my ideas in a simple, concise manner, mixed with a bit of humor. Writing this book with Tom was a great experience, and I would do again in a heartbeat.

Through Tom, and on a camping trip to Canada, I met Doug Winnie. The first thing I learned about Doug, apart from the fact that he is a highly technical and smart guy, is that you should never under any circumstances go up against him in a Star Trek trivia contest. You will lose. End of story. But, as Tom explained, it was Doug who showed him "the magic" of Edge Animate and pointed him toward the path of our book. For that, I owe Doug a big thank you, since it paved the way for this great writing partnership I forged with Tom.

Further acknowledgment must go to the Edge Animate team, Mark Anders, Sarah Hunt, Rich Lee, and the other members and fellow authors responsible for beta testing the application: Darryl Heath, David Hogue, Chris Georgenes, Joseph Labreque, and Doug Winnie, to name a few. Our tech editor shaRon Sachse offered some super valuable insights and ideas that helped make our book that much more succinct combined with the practical brilliance of our editor, Ben Renow-Clarke, who ensured we had all our exercise steps covered with sound logic and overall flow. And, I can't forget senior coordinating editor Anamika Panchoo, who really helped keep me on deadline throughout my chapter submission and review process.

In closing, I believe this experience has really opened new doors for me, and I truly look forward to where it will take me. Though it seems I sweated blood at times while figuring things out or coming up with solutions for things that needed solving, I could not have completed this effort without the love and support from my wife, Patty, and my two kids, Tessa and Nicholas. They were my cheering team who kept me going and focused throughout the ups and downs of the feature changes in the program, release delay, and so forth. In the end, I think the timing was perfect, and now I have an opportunity to thank them for their support and belief in me by achieving something that I know will not be my last.

Michael Clawson

# Foreword

When I was about eight, I got a book from my step-dad. We had a PC at home, in fact, it was one of the first IBM PC clones that was made by Sperry, an old mainframe company that was entering into the new PC market. The book was made by IBM and it was a computer programming book aimed at kids to learn BASIC.

The book was illustrated with dragons, robots, and spaceships, and appropriately so. The world of programming was fantasy. It was a world where if you imagined it, you could turn it into reality. I went through that book from cover to cover multiple times, going through the examples and tweaking them to do all kinds of crazy stuff. But what really transformed me was when I finally embarked on my own projects from scratch.

My first projects were little games, but eventually I wanted to do more. As a kid, and as my friends would tell you even more so as an adult, I was a big Star Trek fan. I loved the show, but wanted to make it more real. Since it was my imagination, then programming was the best way to bring it into reality, so I created an application that simulated all of the functions of the bridge of the Enterprise. It had sounds, graphics, I could go to warp speed and fight Klingons, I was able to create something from scratch with only my imagination and the confidence I built through that book.

It was through that book, and the possibilities it exposed me to, that gave me the confidence to take my own ideas and turn them into reality. That same knowledge and world of possibilities is in your hands right now. The Web, animation, and interactivity let you take what you imagine and turn it into reality.

But as with any technology, there are changes and evolutions that happen over time. HTML 5 is the latest of these, but as HTML 5 started to grow, it was a bewildering mess of languages, coding, and concepts to understand. This made it almost impossible for someone to see the beauty that it actually enabled and the opportunity it provided to web professionals.

Something that I have always appreciated about Adobe is how it is able to take complex technologies and bring them to the masses. They first did this with desktop publishing and most recently with digital publishing for tablets. Now, with Edge Animate, this same philosophy has been brought to HTML 5. The same magic I had years ago I now have available to me again. Edge Animate combines the creative drive in all of us with modern technology that allows the world to see it and for us to express ourselves in new ways. It allows our imagination to become reality.

When I was working on the Edge Animate team, it was clear that we were doing something special. Combining the technologies of HTML, CSS, jQuery, and JavaScript together while maintaining the same level of expressiveness and ease of use as older technologies like Flash was a challenge, but also extremely rewarding. Through my work on Edge Animate, I was able to meet some amazing people in the community, including my good friends Tom Green and Michael Clawson. Their passion for combining beauty, design, technology, and expression makes them perfect mentors for anyone who is diving into the Web for the first time or for those who are learning new ways to express themselves after years of working on the Web in the past.

My time with the Edge Animate team provided some of the most rewarding and challenging days of my life, but I am proud of what Edge Animate has become, but even more so—what it is enabling millions of people like you to do: Combine beauty with the Web and let your imagination become reality.

I hope you enjoy Edge Animate as much as I did helping it along in its early days. As Tom said when I first showed him Edge Animate, "The magic is back."

Have fun.

Doug Winnie
Former Edge Animate Product Manager

# Introduction

It is somewhat ironic that I am writing this on November 9, 2012, which is one year, to the day, after Dan Winokur, vice president and general manager of interactive development at Adobe, turned the Flash community inside out and rearranged its molecules when he posted this to his blog:

> We will no longer continue to develop Flash Player in the browser to work with new mobile device configurations (chipset, browser, OS version, etc.) following the upcoming release of Flash Player 11.1 for Android and BlackBerry PlayBook. We will of course continue to provide critical bug fixes and security updates for existing device configurations. We will also allow our source code licensees to continue working on and release their own implementations.

Though the Flash community reacted rather predictably to this announcement, I wasn't really surprised. I was having fun with Flash—teaching it, writing tutorials, producing three Flash books for friends of ED—but I had concluded Flash was a mature product, and that the sense of wonder and joy that had marked the Flash community from the first version of Flash to Flash CS5 was disappearing.

About seven months earlier in April 2011, I happened to be wandering the floor at FITC, one of the more important Flash conferences, when Doug Winnie, an Adobe product manager, asked me to sit in a corner of the exhibitor area with him while he showed me something he was working on. That something was an app he called "Edge." Rather than walk me through what I could do with the app, he simply plunked his computer on my lap and told me to play around with it. For the next 20 minutes, as I shoved boxes and text around the screen, nothing existed in my universe other than this interesting app. When I passed the computer back to him, rather than tell him what he wanted to hear—Nice product—I simply looked at him for a second and said, "The magic is back."

So much of what intrigued me and others in the early days of Flash 2 and Flash 3 was there in Edge, and I made it quite clear to Doug, "I want in." Three months later, I was at Adobe headquarters in San Francisco with six others and spent three of the most incredible days of my association with Adobe huddling with the Edge team, creating amazing HTML animations, and discovering this was not going to be the usual product development cycle. The community and the team were going to be working together to develop Edge. For the next 18 months, that is exactly what happened, and the result of that partnership is Edge Animate. It will become an important tool in your web design and development toolbox, and I hope you have as much fun with this application as I am having.

This book is also a bit different from any Edge Animate book you may have read or considered purchasing. From the very start of the process, Mike and I put ourselves in your shoes and asked a simple question: What do you need to know and why? This question led us into territory that we didn't quite expect. As we were grappling with that question early in the process, we kept bothering our network of Edge Animate friends to be sure we were on the right track.

One other aspect of this book is that we had a lot of fun developing the examples and exercises. The fun aspect is important, because if learning is fun, what you learn will be retained. Anyone can show you how to shrink and rotate objects in space. It is more effective when you do exactly that by dropping an anvil on a rabbit. Anyone can dryly explain type, but it becomes less techie when you apply text formatting and Web Fonts to a single word sitting on a horizon line. Nested symbols are a "yawner" at best, but when they are related to a starfield and a shooting star in a twilight sky, the concept becomes understandable. Need to experience how to create image flips with hyperlinks? Why not move into the Swiss Alps?

As you may have guessed, we continue to exhibit a sense of joy and wonder with Edge Animate, and we hope a little of our enthusiasm rubs off on you as well.

# Book Structure and Flow

To start, this is not a typical Foundation book. There is no common project that runs throughout the book. Instead, each chapter contains a number of exercises to help you develop some "Edge Animate chops," and every now and then we turn you loose in a "Your Turn" section.

We start by dropping you right into the application to create a small Edge Animate movie we call "Big City Cuisine" (told you we were having fun). This chapter familiarizes you with the Edge Animate workspace and the fundamentals of using Edge Animate. Chapter 2 introduces you to working with the interface and finishes with dropping that anvil on a rabbit.

Chapter 3 introduces you to symbols and nested elements in Edge Animate. In this chapter, you learn how to create and use symbols, and we even create a series of planets and moons to show how nesting elements works, and a sports car is used to show how nested symbols work. Along the way, you travel from the Swiss Alps to the Toronto subway, discovering how to create some rather powerful effects in your Edge Animate compositions.

After Chapter 3, you have pretty well mastered the fundamentals of motion in Edge Animate. Chapter 4 focuses on how content for Edge Animate is created in Illustrator, Photoshop, Fireworks, and Flash. The rest of the book builds on what you have learned. Chapter 5 walks you through the typographic aspects of Edge Animate, including how Web Font technology can be used in Edge Animate.

Chapter 6 picks you up and throws you into the Edge Animate coding pool. Don't worry if you're not a programmer! Edge Animate is designed to appeal to all programming skill levels from neophyte to "give me a blank page and I'll write some magic." Chapter 7 is one of the more important chapters in the book. Its focus is on the end game: getting your compositions ready for everything from web pages to DPS. We even walk through how you deal with browsers that can't display your compositions and wind up by showing you how easy it is to add YouTube and Google Maps content to your compositions. Here's a hint: if you can copy and paste, you are in the game.

With all of the fundamentals out of the way, we know you are just itching to take your new skills out for a test run. Chapter 8 is designed to do just that. You will be creating assets in Fireworks and putting them in motion in Edge Animate. You will be creating magnets and letters in Illustrator and having the letters zip up to the magnet heads in Edge Animate as the magnet passes over them. You will create an Edge Animate preloader in Flash and finish up by creating a pop-down menu created solely in Edge Animate.

Chapter 9 shows you how to add Edge Animate content to DPS publications and iBooks, and we finish the book by showing you how to create Edge Animate compositions destined for a mobile and responsive universe.

Finally, Michael and I are no different from you. We are learning about this application—what it can and cannot do—at the same time as you are learning about it. Though we may be coming at it from a slightly more advanced level, there is a lot about this application we're still discovering. If there is something we have missed or something you don't quite understand, by all means, contact us. And here are our final words of advice for you:

The amount of fun you can have with this application should be illegal. We'll see you in jail!

# Layout Conventions

To keep this book as clear and easy to follow as possible, the following text conventions are used throughout:.

- Important words or concepts are normally highlighted on the first appearance in italics.
- Code is presented in fixed-width font.
- New or changed code is normally presented in bold fixed-width font.
- Menu commands are written in the form Menu > Submenu > Submenu.
- Where I want to draw your attention to something, I've highlighted it like this:

*Ahem, don't say we didn't warn you.*

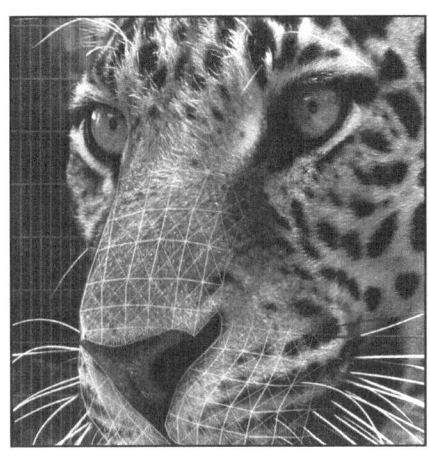

# Chapter 1

# Learning the Edge Animate Interface

Welcome to Edge Animate! We suspect you are here because you have heard a lot about the product, may have tried Edge Animate during its preview release on the Adobe Labs web site, or seen some of the tutorials that have been popping up on the Web. Regardless of the reason you're here, it is now your turn to get into the web-based motion graphics game. Whether you are a web developer, web designer, motion graphics pro, or simply have an interest in motion and interactivity on the Web, you are about to discover there is a serious amount of power under Edge Animate's hood. Whatever brings you to Edge Animate, be assured that both of us have been in your shoes and know that learning a new piece of software and adding it to your skill set or workflow can be both mystifying and, at times, overwhelming. With that in mind, instead of jumping right into the application, let's go for a walk.

In this chapter we are going to cover:

- Exploring the Edge Animate interface

- Using the Edge Animate Stage

- Working with panels

- The Edge Animate menus

- The various areas of the Edge Animate timeline

- The value of the Properties panel

- The Edge Animate tools

- How to use the In-App lessons

If you haven't already downloaded the chapter files, they can be found at:

http://www.apress.com/9781430243502
In this chapter we will be using these files:

- BigCity.an

What we are going to do during our walk is to explore the authoring environment—called the *Edge Animate interface*—pointing out its key features and letting you try them out. By the end of our tour, you should be fairly comfortable with Edge Animate and have a good idea of how the various bits and pieces of the interface combine to help you bring your ideas to life.

Along the way we will stop and have a few conversations with you that will help you grasp the fundamentals of creating an Edge Animate project. Having this knowledge at the start of the learning process will give you the confidence to proceed through this book and develop the Edge Animate skills you need to become productive. Like any walk, we need to start somewhere, and a great place to start is the Edge Animate Start page.

# Getting Started

When you double-click the application to start Edge Animate, the first thing you may notice is how fast it loads compared to such Adobe applications as Illustrator, Dreamweaver, and Flash. When Edge Animate does launch, you are immediately taken into the Edge Animate interface shown in Figure 1-1. This is a bit different from what you may be used to with other Adobe applications.

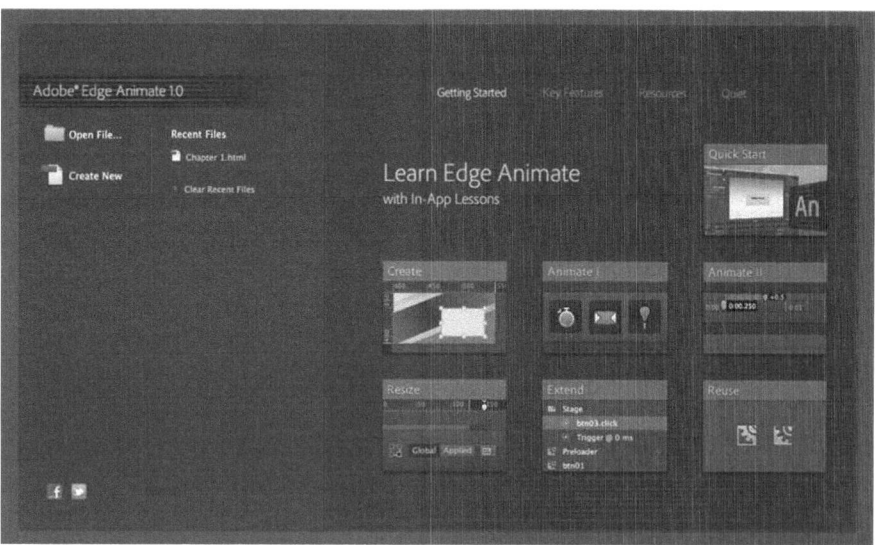

**Figure 1-1.** The Get Started panel is built into the interface.

- *Create New/Open File*: This area, on the far left, allows you to create a New Edge Animate document. If the file you are looking for is not in the Recent Files listing to the right, then click the Open File button. This will allow you to navigate to the Edge Animate file you are looking for.

> *A nifty feature of Edge Animate is you don't necessarily have to open the .an file. Edge Animate will also open an HTML file.*

- *Recent Files*: A list of the recently opened files will appear. Click one in the list and that file will open. If you want to clear out the list, click the Clear Recent Files button.

- *Facebook/Twitter Icons*: At the bottom of this section are two icons that, when clicked, will take you to the Edge Animate Facebook page or the Edge Animate Twitter feed.

- *Getting Started*: When you click this link, a series of "In-App" lessons will open. This feature is unique to Edge Animate and contains a series of step-by-step tutorials that review the basics of using Edge Animate.

- *What's New*: As a Cloud application, Edge Animate will be regularly updated, and these updates will be "pushed" to your computer. Click this and you can see what new features have been added to your version of Edge Animate.

- *Resources*: Clicking this button will open a list of resources available to you, including documentation, training videos on AdobeTV, samples of Edge Animate work, and the Edge Animate JavaScript API (Application Programming Interface) that gives you many details regarding the Edge Animate runtime that is created when you publish an Edge Animate document.

- *Quiet*: This button is quite unique to the Adobe Start Page line up. Click it and everything on the right side of the page—Getting Started, Key Features, or Resources—disappears. To bring a topic back, simply click its button.

## Creating a New Edge Animate Document

Let's continue our walk through the Edge Animate interface and create a new document. To do this, click the Create New button on the Get Started panel. The interface will change to the one shown in Figure 1-2.

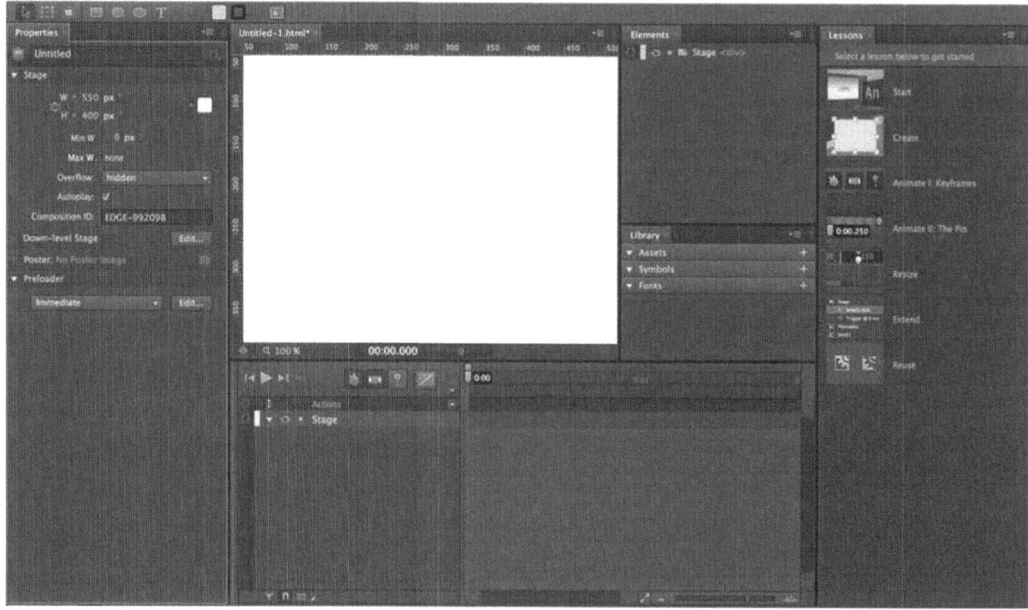

**Figure 1-2.** A new empty document is created.

When the interface opens, you will see a number of panels. From left to right they are:

- *Properties*: All objects, in Edge Animate they are referred to as elements, have properties ranging from location on the Stage to the color of the object.

- *Timeline*: This is the heart and soul of Edge Animate. This is where motion is created, interactivity is added, and the duration and order of effects are set.

- *Elements*: Every object added to Edge Animate is added to the Elements panel. Their order is determined, initially, by the order in which they were added or imported into Edge Animate.

- *Library*: This is where Assets, Symbols, and Fonts are located. The difference between items in the Elements panel and items in the Library is subtle but important. Elements are all of the items within the Edge Animate project, and a great way of looking at Elements is to regard them as divs in an HTML document. The Library contains the assets used in the project, and they don't necessarily need to live in the composition because they will most likely be reused throughout the project.

- *Lessons*: The in-app lessons appear in this panel.

That big white area you see is the Stage. This is where the action happens and a good rule of thumb, when it comes to the Stage, is: "If it is on the stage, the user sees it. If it isn't on the stage, the user doesn't." When it comes to Edge Animate, this is not exactly true. Here's why.

Edge Animate's purpose is to create web-based animations and interactivity in HTML 5, CSS3, and JavaScript without the use or assistance of plug-ins or players when viewed in a browser. With that in mind, a great way of regarding the Stage is as one great big Cascading Style Sheet (CSS) div and all the action occurs within the physical confines of that div. The gray area surrounding the Stage is not the pasteboard you may be used to in Flash, Illustrator, Fireworks, or InDesign. In those applications, content on the pasteboard is not always visible.

In Edge Animate, that gray area is the Overflow area, meaning you have a number of options as to how Edge Animate will manage what the user sees. In fact, your Properties panel now sports an Overflow pop-down menu with the four choices shown in Figure 1-3.

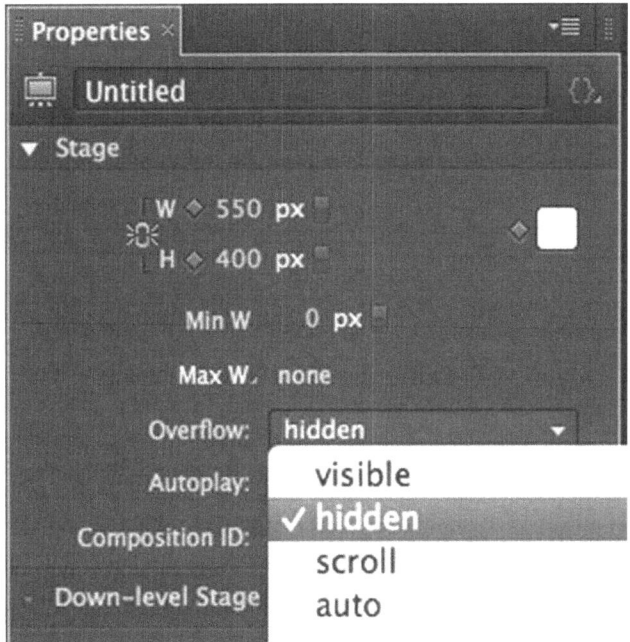

**Figure 1-3.** The Edge Animate Stage is nothing more than a CSS div.

If you are familiar with CSS, the Overflow property specifies what happens if content overflows an element's box. It can be visible, hidden, sport scroll bars, or, in the case of auto, overflow is left to the discretion of the browser. The default value for the application is hidden. In fact, if you look at the Elements panel, you will see the Stage, as shown in Figure 1-4, is not only there but is also regarded as a div with color, width, height, and overflow properties as shown in the Properties panel. The inference you can draw from this is the Stage is the "box" where the action occurs.

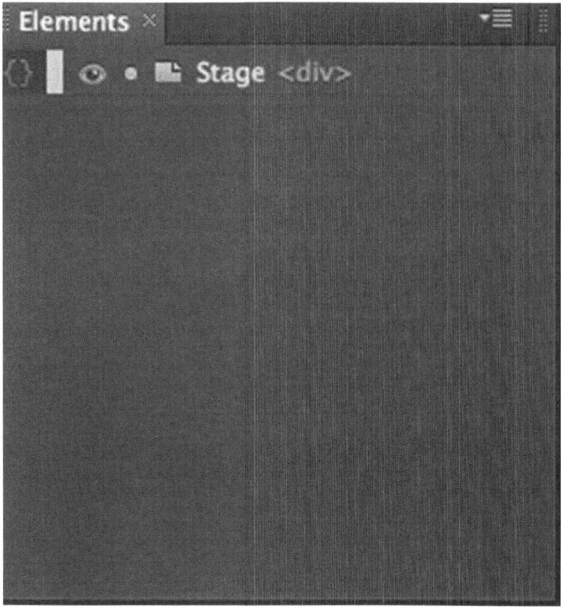

**Figure 1-4.** The Stage is also a CSS element, which is why it appears in the Elements panel.

## The Edge Animate Timeline

Though we have drawn your attention to the Stage, Elements, and Properties panels, something else happened when you created a new document: the Timeline panel, as shown in Figure 1-5, came to life.

**Figure 1-5.** The Edge Animate timeline

The major feature of the Edge Animate timeline is that it is time based, not frame based. This may not mean much if you spend time editing video, but if you are coming to Edge Animate from Flash, this is a fundamental difference between the two applications.

Time on the Edge Animate timeline is measured in minutes:seconds.milliseconds, and the time divisions on the Edge Animate timeline follow that measurement system. This may not be evident at first glance because the first major division is 0.01, which could reasonably be expected to be expressed as 1/100 of a second. It isn't. It is the 1-second mark—0 minutes: 01 second. The increments on the timeline are, therefore one-quarter-second increments.

The yellow pointer with the red line draped over the timeline is called the *playhead*. Its purpose is to show you the current time in the timeline. If you drag the playhead to the right—a process called *scrubbing*—the timecode changes as you move the playhead. Another way of moving the playhead is to scrub the timecode at the bottom of the Stage panel by clicking and dragging across it. As you move your mouse left or right, the numbers change and the playhead moves accordingly.

> *Here's a little teacher trick: Scrubbing the timecode increases or decreases the time by milliseconds. Hold down the Shift key while scrubbing and the timecode will increase or decrease in units of 1/100 seconds. If you are an absolute control freak, double-click the timecode and enter a precise time.*

The various icons, shown in Figure 1-6, along the top and the bottom of the timeline serve very specific purposes. You will be using them a lot as you move through the various exercises in this book. Here's a brief explanation of what each one does:

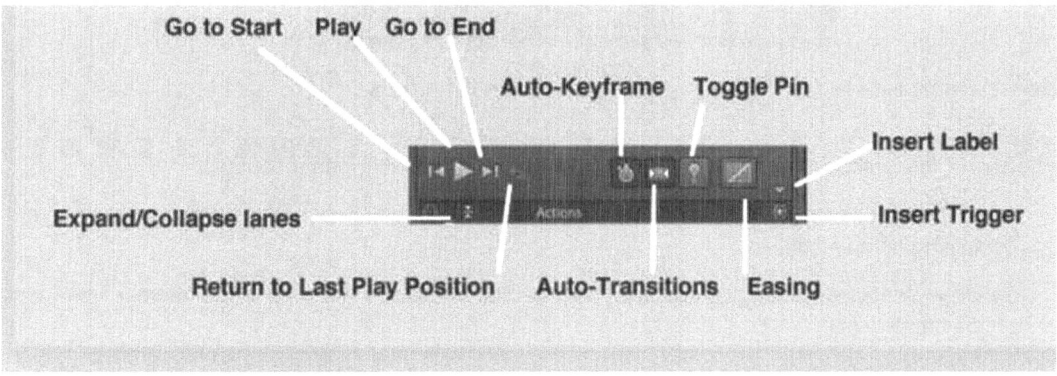

**Figure 1-6.** The timeline controls.

The icons shown in Figure 1-6 are at the top of the timeline. They are:

- *Playback Controls*: Press Rewind and you are sent to the start of the timeline. Press Fast Forward and you are sent to the last frame. Press Play and the composition plays from the position of the playhead. The Return to Last Play Position control, when clicked, returns the playhead to the last position on the timeline where you played the composition.

- *Auto-Keyframes*: If the icon is red, any property change made to an object will add a keyframe to the timeline.

- *Auto-Transitions*: If this icon is green, transitions will occur between keyframes. If it is gray, the transition occurs at the keyframe.

- *The Pin*: This feature is unique to Edge Animate. The Pin locks ("pins") a property in place. When selected, the icon is blue and the "box" above the playhead will also turn blue.

- *Eases*: Edge Animate contains a series of JavaScript transitions. Click this box and the list of Eases that can be applied will appear.

- *Add Frame Label (Chevron)*: Click this to add frame labels to the timeline. These are really important navigation aids when working with the code feature of Edge Animate.

- *Open Timeline Action (Brackets)*: Click this and a list of code snippets that apply to the timeline will appear.

- *Expand/Collapse Lanes*: Click this and all of the property changes in all of the Layers will be shown. Click it again and they collapse.

- *Insert Trigger*: Click this icon—a curly brace with a diamond inside—and a list of actions that will be "triggered" when the playhead reaches the frame will appear.

**Figure 1-7.** There are three more important controls at the bottom of the timeline.

At the bottom of the Timeline, as shown in Figure 1-7, are three more important controls:

- *Show Animated Elements*: The "Martini glass," when clicked, will open or close any timeline layers containing an animation.

- *Timeline Snapping*: When you click the "magnet," all transitions will snap to the nearest increment on the timeline grid.

- *Show Grid*: Click this and the timeline will be divided into the increments indicated. If you click the Options button beside it—the button looks like a triangle—you are, as shown in Figure 1-8, presented with some rather interesting decisions. The items in this pop-up let you determine the grid increments on the timeline.

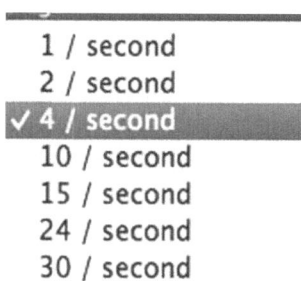

**Figure 1-8.** The Grid Options give you quite a bit of granularity with the timeline.

If you are coming to Edge Animate from Flash, choosing 24/second turns the Edge timeline into a very familiar place. Your timeline will divide into the increments chosen, which gives you a high degree of precision when placing objects on the timeline and manipulating their properties. Does this mean you are also changing the playback speed of the Edge animation? No. An Edge Animate project, with lots of bitmaps, animation, and interaction, will be rather zippy when played back on a computer. View that same project on Smartphones or tablets, with different processors and network speed, and there could be a noticeable performance "hit." Edge Animate takes all of this into consideration and adjusts the playback speed to accommodate the device.

## Managing Your Workspace

There are going to be times where you want to close panels, make them smaller, or even move them around to suit your personal way of doing things. You will also discover, as you start creating Edge Animate projects, that screen real estate is a precious commodity. The solution to these issues is an understanding of how to work with the various panels. Here's how:

- *Widen or shrink a panel*: Place your cursor between any two panels. The cursor, as shown in Figure 1-9, changes to the Splitter icon. Click and drag the mouse to widen, lengthen, or shorten a panel. Release the mouse when you are satisfied.

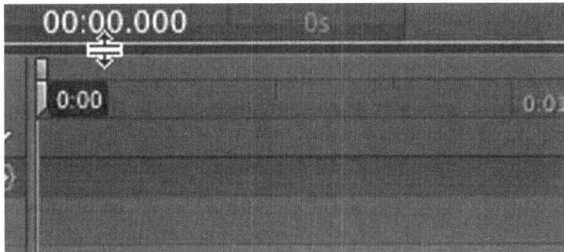

**Figure 1-9.** The Splitter icon allows you shrink, widen, or lengthen panels.

- *Dock and undock panels*: This is commonly done when you want to rearrange your panels. For example, let's assume you want to move the Elements panel to the left side of the Stage. What you would do is click the Panel tab and drag the panel to the left side of the Stage. The first thing you should notice is the panel doesn't move. What you are doing is telling Edge Animate where the panel should be. As you are dragging, you should see various areas of the Stage panel, as shown in Figure 1-10, turn purple as your mouse rolls over them. These are the areas where the Elements panel can be placed, including the Stage itself. When you reach the left side of the Stage, release the mouse and the panel appears in its new location.

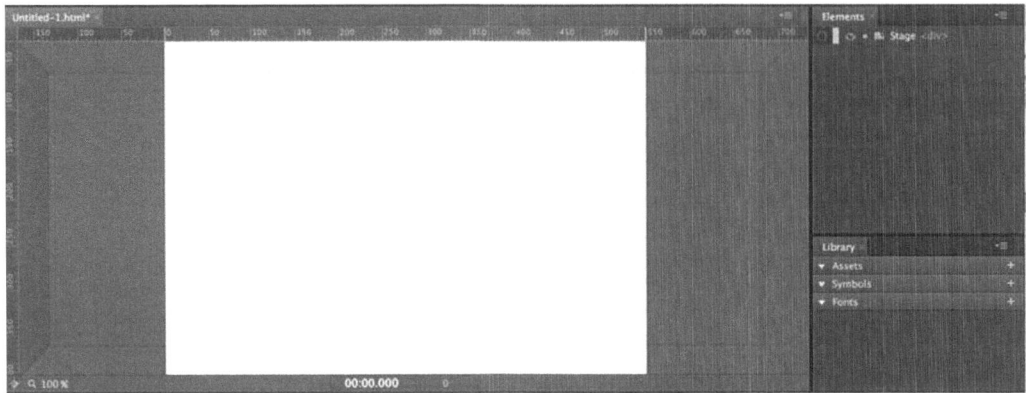

**Figure 1-10.** The Elements panels is about to be moved to the left side of the Stage.

If you drag a panel over the black line under the Tools panel or to the bottom of the Timeline panel, a green bar appears. Release the mouse and the panel moves to that location and its width increases to the width of the interface.

> *Once a panel is moved, the new location becomes the default position for that panel.*

• *Nest panels*: Panels can be turned into groups—the term is *nesting*—of panels in a single frame. If you click and drag the Library tab over the Element**s** tab, you will see a dark line appear across the top of the Elements panel. Release the mouse and the Elements and Library tabs, as shown in Figure 1-11, will be beside each other. You have just nested the Library panel with the Elements panel.

**Figure 1-11.** The Elements and Library panels have been nested.

- *Float a panel*: The panels are normally docked, meaning their positions in the interface are fixed. There are going to be occasions where you need every inch of the screen for the Stage but still need access to, say, the Properties panel. In this case, you can "float" the panel above the interface. To do this either right-click (PC) or Option-click (Mac) the name of the panel or click the Panel Options button to open the Panel Options menu, as shown in Figure 1-12. Select Undock Frame, and the panel will appear in its own window above the interface.

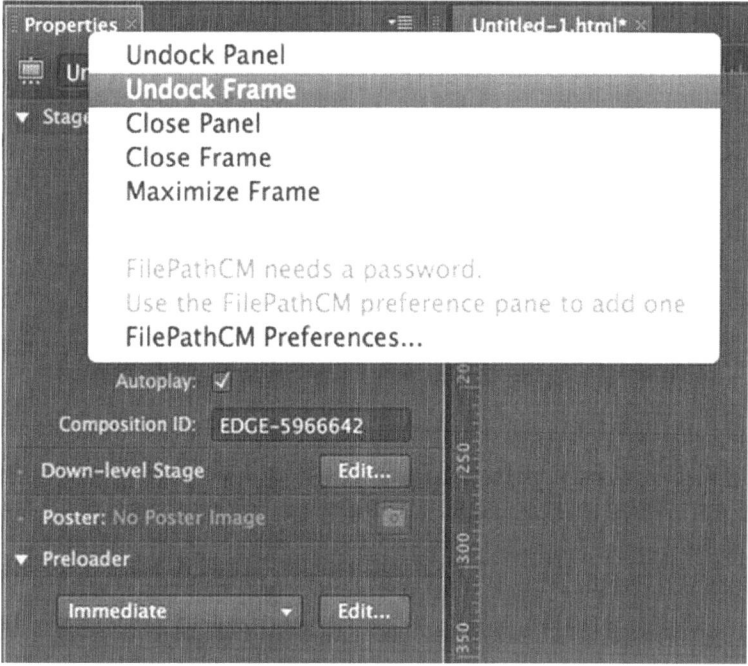

**Figure 1-12.** Use the Panel options to "float" a panel.

> *Undock frame . . . huh? Isn't that a panel we just floated? You are both right and wrong. A panel contains the interface items that pertain to the panel. A frame is screen real estate used by a panel or group of nested panels. It's a fine distinction and we didn't make the rules.*

- *Close a panel*: You have a couple of choices. Click the panel's Close button or select Close Panel or Close Frame from the Panel Options pop-down.

- *Open or add a panel*: To open a panel you have closed or to add a panel you may need, open the Window menu and select the panel name from the menu.

There is another aspect of managing your workspace, and it has to do with how you view the Stage. In the bottom left corner of the Stage panel, as shown in Figure 1-13, are two icons. Here's what they do:

- *Center the Stage*: Click the button that looks like a star and the Stage will move directly into the center of the panel.

- *Zoom the Stage*: Scrub across the panel value and you can zoom in or out of the Stage. This is a lot handier than the Zoom In and Zoom out menu items found in the View menu.

**Figure 1-13:** There are two ways to control the Stage view.

Now that you have learned to become the master of your work environment, let's wander over to the Tools panel.

## The Tools Panel

The Edge Animate Tools panel may, at first glance, appear to be . . . shall we say . . . lacking. There isn't much there. The tools, from left to right as shown in Figure 1-14, are Selection, Transform, Clipping, Rectangle, Rounded Rectangle, Ellipse, and Text. The three icons on the right allow you to change the Fill and Stroke colors of selected objects created with the tools and to apply custom default values to the current composition in the Properties panel.

**Figure 1-14.** The Edge Animate lineup of Tools.

In fact, they are practically the only tools you will need. Edge Animate is not a drawing application. Artwork and images come from elsewhere. It is not a web site design tool, although you can use Edge Animate to put content in web pages into motion. It is an HTML 5 CSS3 layout application whose sole purpose is to give you the ability to make content move or make it interactive. That means you really only need the ability to:

- Select items using the Selection tool.

- Quickly rotate and scale selections using the Transform tool.

- Hide content in an Element using the edges of the element's div Clipping tool.

- Create primitive shapes using the Rectangle, Rounded Rectangle, or Ellipse tools.

- Add text blocks using the Text tool.

- Manipulate shapes and change their Fill and Stroke colors. Of course, being Elements, the fill and stroke are the CSS background and CSS border colors.

- Set the CSS Layout properties of selections or objects.

Rather than get into a long explanation of the use and value of each tool, let's create a navigation tab using the tools. Here's how:

1. Open a new document.

2. Select the Rectangle tool and move the cursor to the Stage. The cursor will change to a cross-hair.

3. Draw a rectangle. Don't worry about size or color. As soon as you release the mouse, the Properties panel lights up. Being context sensitive, the Properties panel presents you with all of the properties for a rectangle, as shown in Figure 1-15.

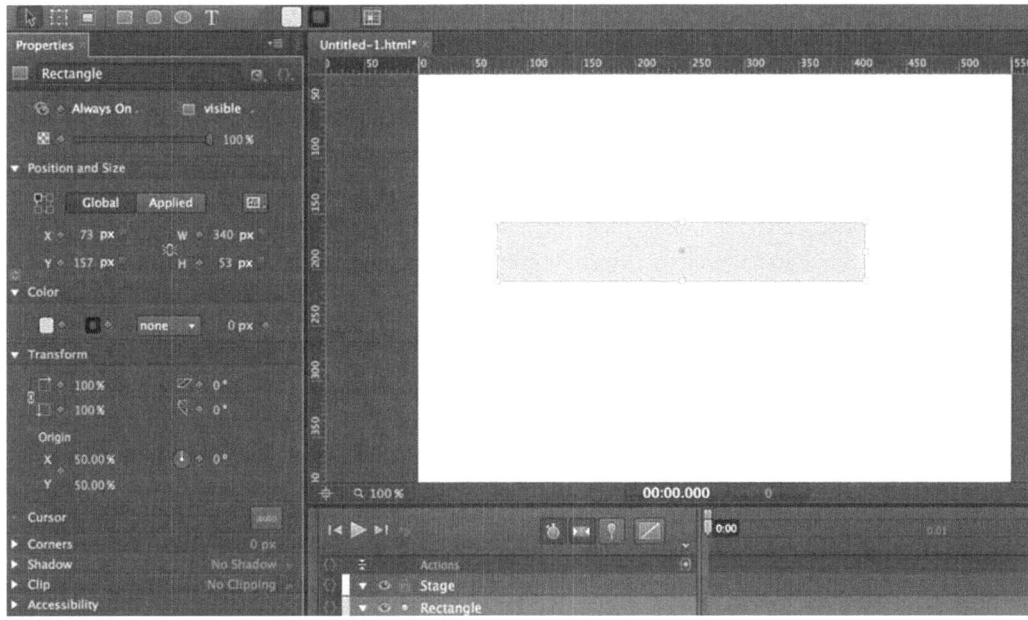

**Figure 1-15.** When an object is added to or drawn on the Stage, the Properties panel lights up.

> *Your Stage is going to look a lot different from the one shown in Figure 1-15. In order to keep you focused, we will, on occasion, undock a panel and move it closer to the object we are talking about.*

This is an important relationship you are looking at. Any time an object is added to the Stage, the Properties panel lights up to present you with the properties that are unique to the object just added or drawn. This is why the Properties panel is regarded as "context sensitive." Let's stop and take a look at the Edge Animate Properties panel.

# The Edge Animate Properties Panel

The six areas of the Properties panel, from the top to the bottom, are:

- *Element name*: Always use a name that means something. In this case, we can get away with Rectangle, but if there is more than one rectangle, change the name.

- *Display*: There are three choices here: Always On, On, and Off. This property essentially sets the visibility of an element on the timeline.

- *Overflow*: Everything added to Edge Animate is a <div>, and you can determine how content moving outside the <div> is managed in the browser.

- *Opacity and Position and Size*: Their purpose is self-evident.

- *Color*: Click the color chip to open the Color Picker to set the Stroke and Fill colors for the selection. You can also set the thickness of the stroke, and the pop-down beside the stroke color lets you choose the line style. Your choices are none, solid, and dashed.

- *Transform Properties*: Use this area to set the origin point of a transformation, Rotation, Skew, and Scale values. If you look at your rectangle on the Stage, the blue dot in the middle is the origin point and any transformations use that point. For example, if you were to rotate the rectangle, it would rotate around that origin point.

- Cursor: This Fly Out menu is rather neat. What it does is to set the type of cursor the user sees when the cursor is over the object on a web page.

- *Corners*: It sounds like a mouthful but, in actual fact, this is where you set the roundness values for the corners of a selection. The three numbers at the top—1, 4, 8—determine how the roundness for each corner can be set. For example, 1 simply applies the roundness to the entire object. To see this, click the 1 and scrub the roundness value. As you change the number, the shape changes equally on all four corners. Click the 8 and you see that each corner contains two values, which allow you to create some interesting shapes.

- *Shadow*: Use this area to add a drop shadow to selections.

- *Clipping*: We'll get into using this in greater depth later in the book. For now, regard it as setting the values for a mask.

Now that you know what each section of the Properties panel does, let's change the shape of the rectangle. Here's how:

1. Click once on the Red stopwatch in the timeline. This will turn off Auto Keyframing, and the Stopwatch will turn gray and allow you to focus on the task at hand rather than wondering: "Why did those diamonds appear?" We'll talk about that later in this chapter.

2. With your shape selected, click the chain link beside the Width and Height values in the Properties panel. By turning off the link, you can change the values independent of each other.

3.  Change the width value to 400 and the height value to 50, as shown in Figure 1-16. Remember, you can either scrub across the values to change them or double-click a value, input the exact number, and press the Return/Enter key to accept the change.

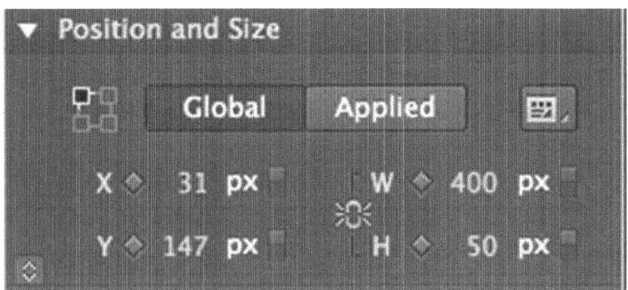

**Figure 1-16.** The Width, Height, Stage Location, and Opacity of a selection are set in the Properties panel.

Note how the selection instantly changes as you scrub the values. If you find this to be a bit challenging, hold down the Shift key while scrubbing, and you will increment or decrement the values by 10 rather than 1. Also the diamonds you see in all of the properties indicate the ability to add keyframes. Keyframes determine how stuff moves on the Edge Animate Stage.

> The horizontal—x—or vertical—y—values you see in the **Properties** panel or elsewhere are measured from the top left corner of the Stage. You can't, as in other applications, set the 0,0 point to another location.

Now that we have a rectangle on the Stage, let's round off the right side of the shape. Here's how:

1.  Click the number 4 in the Corners properties. Each corner now sports a value that can be changed.

2.  Change the upper right and bottom right values, as shown in Figure 1-17, to 25. Your shape now looks like a tongue depressor.

**Figure 1-17.** Setting the corner roundness value in the Properties panel.

Now that you understand how to use the Properties panel to manipulate shapes, let's use it to manage text by setting the font, weight, size, color, and alignment of text. This is also a great place to discover that the Properties panel is "context sensitive." We are going to add your name to the project and you will see the Properties panel change to reflect the fact you are adding text. Follow these steps to add your name to the project:

1. Select the Text tool and click once on the Stage. When you do this, the Properties panel—shown in Figure 1-18—changes to show you the Text properties and a small gray box appears on the Stage where you clicked the mouse. That text box is, in many respects, a text entry box. Type in your first name.

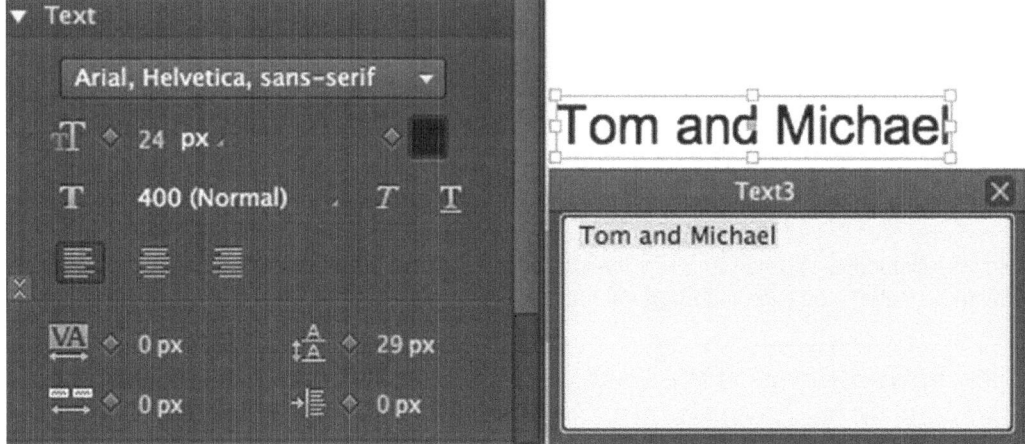

**Figure 1-18.** Click once on the Stage with the Text tool and the Text properties light up.

The Text properties may, at first, appear to be somewhat lacking, but this would be a huge misconception on your part. Remember, Edge Animate is a web application, and many of the common CSS properties that can be applied to text are contained in this area. From top to bottom the properties include:

- *Font*: This pop-down list presents you with the standard list of web fonts and their alternates. As you will discover later on in this book, you can even use the @font-face rule that has started regaining the attention of web designers and developers as they start exploring HTML 5 and CSS3. What this rule does is allow font embedding into web pages.

- *Type size*: Depending on how you work, you can set the size using either pixels, percent, or ems as your measurement standard.

- *Color*: This pop-down lets you choose the text color.

- *Style*: You have nine common font weight choices ranging from the choices 100(Thin) to 900(Black).

- *Alignment*: There are three choices: Left, Center, or Right.

- *Letter Spacing*: Adjusts the space between the letters in a line of text.

- *Line Height*: Sets the spacing between the lines of text.

- *Word Spacing*: Adjusts the space between the words in a text block.

- *Indent*: Change the value to indent a block of text.

> *You can't use the Type tool to enter more than a small block of text. Edge Animate is not a web-design tool and is simply unable to manage multiple columns of text.*

## Document Layers and the Elements Panel

If you look at your Elements panel, you will see, as shown in Figure 1-19, two divs—a Text div and a Rectangle div—have been added to the panel. This is a key aspect of Edge Animate: anything added to the Stage will appear in its own div in the Elements panel. The other aspect of the Elements panel is that the contents of the div are represented by an icon. This gives you a quick visual representation of the content in each element.

> *You may have noticed that the two divs are indented under the Stage div. What this tells you is that any element added to your project will be a "child" of the Stage div or is "nested" within the Stage element. This is indicated by the indent.*

This is a "good thing," but as your projects become increasingly complex, the Elements panel can become a source of great frustration as you try to figure out which element is which on the Stage. There is a solution, and it is a habit every Edge Animate designer or developer should use: *Name the Elements*.

**Figure 1-19.** Anything added to the Edge Animate Stage will be contained in its own div.

Follow these steps to rename an Element:

1.  Double-click the Text element. The text will be highlighted.

2.  Replace the selected text with the word "Name" and press the Return/Enter key to accept the change.

3.  Change the name of the Rectangle div to "Shape_01." You now have two elements with unique, not generic, names.

Not only can you change the name of the elements, but you can also change their layering order. Here's how:

1.  Click once on your name on the Stage.

2.  If you look at the Elements panel, you will notice the Name element is selected.

3.  Twirl up the Stage element by clicking the triangle beside the element name in the Elements panel. The Name and Shape_01 elements disappear. Twirl down the Stage element. You will notice those two elements seem to be indented in the panel. What this tells you is these two elements are contained, or "nested," in the Stage element.

4.  In the Elements panel, click the Name element. Your name is now selected on the Stage. This is a handy way of selecting items on the Stage.

5.  With the Name element selected in the Elements panel, drag the strip under the Shape_01 strip. When you release the mouse, your name, as shown in Figure 1-20, is now behind the shape. This is how you change the layering order in an Edge Animate project.

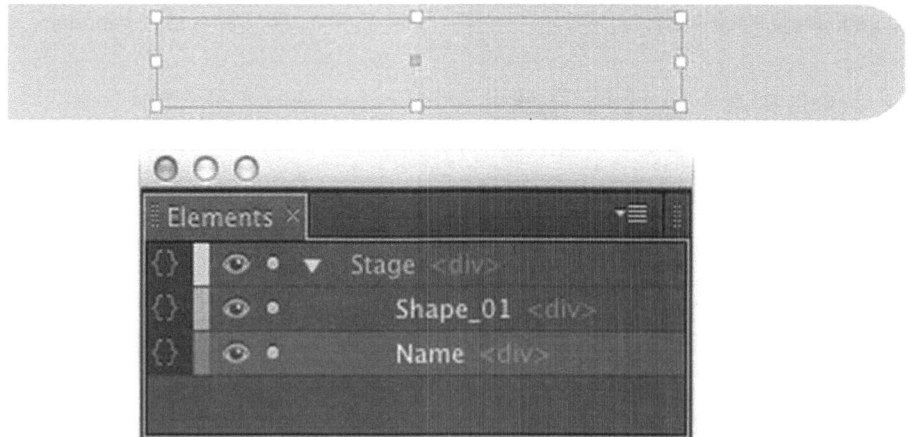

**Figure 1-20.** Change the layering order of the elements by dragging them to new positions in the Elements panel.

Apart from managing the Layering order of the elements, the Elements panel allows you to, as shown in Figure 1-21, lock an element and/or turn off its visibility. Here's how:

1. To turn off the visibility of an element or layer, click the eyeball, called the Visibility icon. This is a great way of isolating content on the Stage and allowing you to manipulate it without the distraction of accidentally selecting the wrong item or worrying about any content in the vicinity of the item you are manipulating. When you are finished, simply click the Visibility icon to turn on the item's visibility.

2. To lock an element or layer, click the dot to the right of the Visibility icon. The dot will be replaced with a Lock icon. Locking layers or elements is a critical habit to develop. What it does is keep it visible on the Stage but prevents you from accidentally selecting it. To unlock the element, just click the Lock icon.

3. Close the document and don't save the changes.

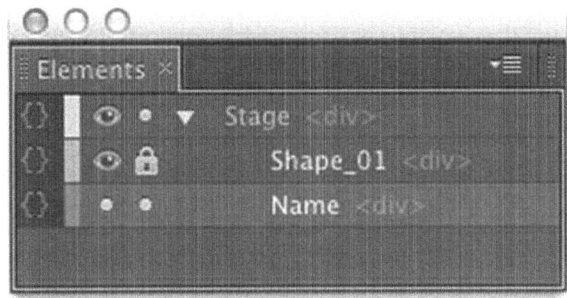

**Figure 1-21.** The Shape_01 layer is locked and the Name layer is invisible.

# Importing Content into Edge Animate

Now that you have an idea of what most of the panels in the interface do, it would be a good time to review how artwork is added to Edge Animate.

The formats that can be used by Edge Animate are:

- GIF

- JPG

- PNG including 32-bit PNG images with transparency

- SVG

- Animated GIF

We'll get deeper into their creation and use in Edge Animate in Chapter 4. The purpose of this exercise is to simply learn how to bring these images into Edge Animate. Let's get started:

1. Open a new Edge Animate document and set the Stage size to 800 pixels wide by 400 pixels high.

2. Select File > Import. When the Import dialog box opens, navigate to the Import folder located in the Exercise folder.

3. When the folder opens, as shown in Figure 1-22, you will see there are three images: JPG, SVG, and PNG. Select them and click the Open button.

> *File naming is important when importing content into Edge Animate. Make sure the file names contain no spaces or characters that won't be read by CSS 3.*

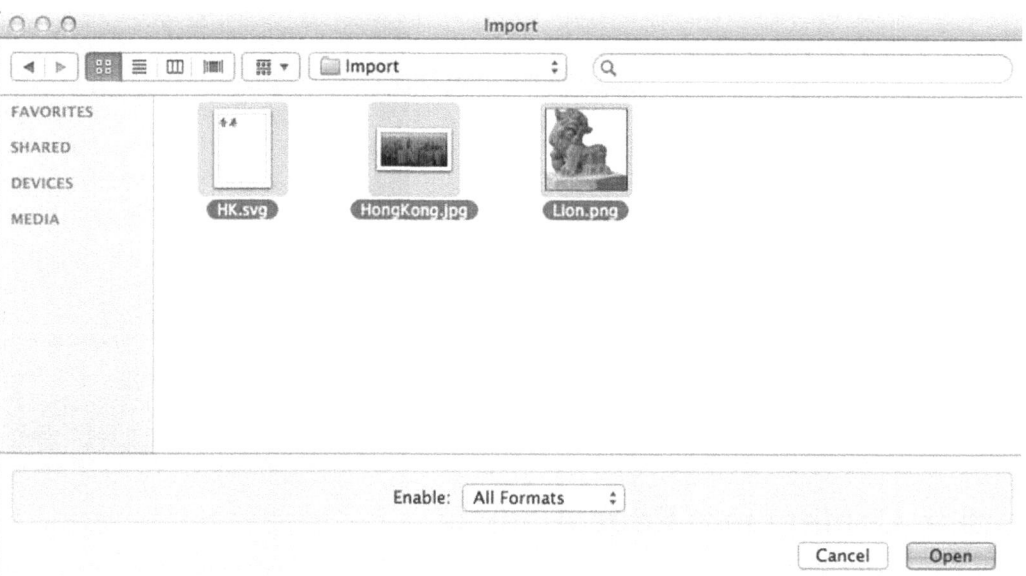

**Figure 1-22.** The three main files types that can be imported into Edge Animate.

4. The images are placed on the Stage and, if you look at the Library, they will be in the Images folder as well. They are also placed on the timeline and in the Elements folder.

5. Click the Lion element on the Stage and move it to the bottom right corner of the Stage. The Lion image is a PNG image, which is the only bitmap format used by Edge Animate that supports

transparency. Although transparent GIF's are supported in Edge Animate, their limited color palette is rarely used for photographic images.

6.  Move the HK layer in the timeline between the Lion and Stage layers. This image is an SVG (scalable vector graphic) image and is the only vector format used by Edge Animate. When you finish, as shown in Figure 1-23, you have created a postcard for Hong Kong.

**Figure 1-23.** The images are imported into Edge Animate.

There is an even cooler way of bringing content into Edge Animate, and, in fact, it is unique to Adobe: drag and drop the images right onto the Stage from the desktop. Here's how:

1.  Open a new Edge Animate document and set the Stage size to 800 pixels wide by 400 pixels high.

2.  Navigate to the Import folder on your desktop and open it.

3.  With the shift key held down, select the three images and, as shown in Figure 1-24, drag them directly from the folder to the Stage. When you release the mouse, the images appear on the Stage and in the Library and Elements panels.

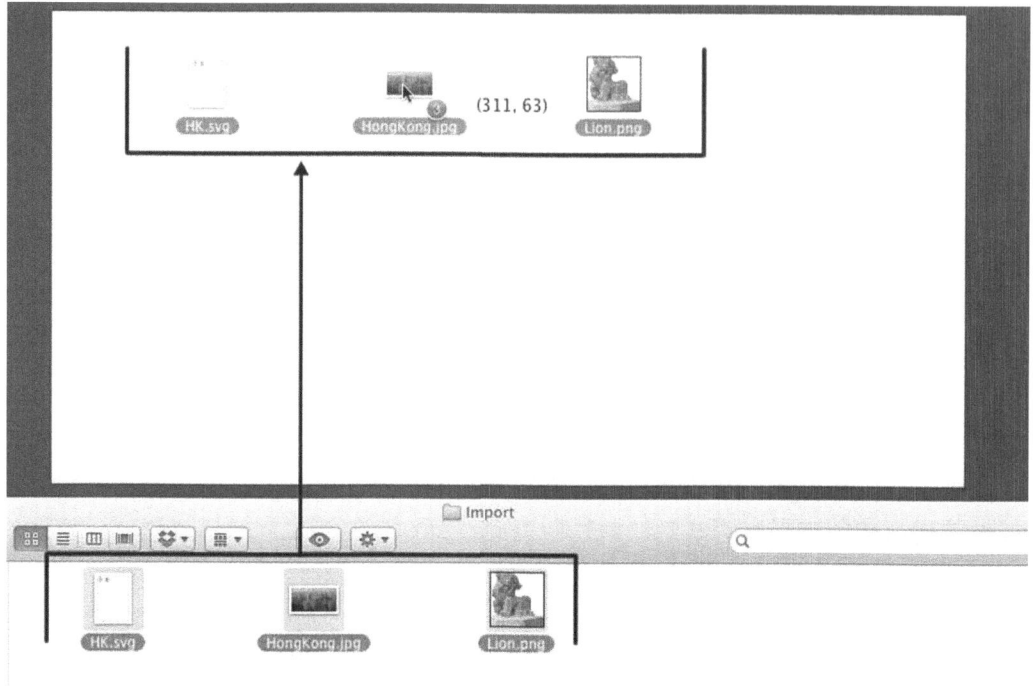

**Figure 1-24.** Drag and drop content from desktop folders directly into Edge Animate.

# The Edge Animate Menus

The menus in Edge Animate really aren't that different, regardless of whether you are using a Mac or a PC. The major differences, which we will bring to your attention throughout the book, are the keyboard commands. Still, let's stop for a minute and take a quick look at the menus. In order they are:

- *File*: The major items in this menu are Publish Settings, Publish, and Preview in Browser. The first two options will be covered extensively in Chapter 7. They essentially determine how Edge Animate files are prepared for inclusion in a web page. The final option, which we will briefly review at the end of this chapter, is how you can test your work without leaving Edge Animate.

- *Edit*: The usual menu items—Cut, Copy, and Paste—are found here. The new item is Paste Special, as shown in Figure 1-25, which allows you to reuse effects and transitions in the timeline.

- *View*: This menu lets you zoom the page, work with rulers and guides, as well as look at the Stage used for a preloader or older browser, called a Down-level stage.

- *Modify*: This menu can be used to arrange, align, and distribute selections on the Stage. It is also used to create and edit symbols.

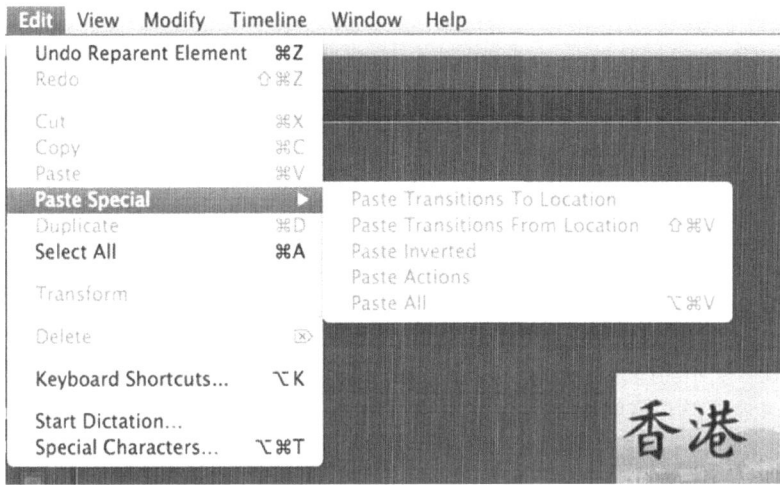

**Figure 1-25.** The Edit menu lets you reuse effects and transitions.

- *Timeline*: Use this menu to navigate across the timeline, add keyframes, triggers, and labels, and to collapse the layers on the timeline. Many of the commands in this menu are also found in the Timeline panel.

- *Window*: As is common with Adobe applications that use panel-based interfaces, you open and close panels in this menu.

# Your Turn: Building an Edge Animate Presentation

In this exercise we are going to build on what you have learned to this point. We have spent a lot of time reviewing the interface, and the time has arrived to give you an opportunity to try out Edge Animate. Over the course of this exercise you will :

- Open an Edge Animate file

- Select objects on the Stage and change their properties

- Explore the timeline

- Create a simple animation through the use of a tween

- Save an Edge Animate movie

- Test an Edge Animate movie

By the end of this exercise, you will have a fairly good understanding of how an Edge Animate movie is created and tested. You will also start learning the workflow involved in creating a simple Edge Animate movie. Let's get started.

## Opening the .an File

You may have read the heading to this section and thought, "You idiots, of course I know how to open a file." Regardless of what you may think, opening an Edge Animate file is one of the most important lessons you will learn when it comes to using Edge Animate. To start, open the `BigCityCuisine` folder in your Exercise folder.

> All exercises in this book will be contained in folders found in each chapter's exercise folder. Unless told otherwise, we will be working with the **.edge** files found in the folders. Why? Read on.

When the folder opens, there is, as shown in Figure 1-26, not a single file but what looks like an entire web directory. In fact, that is exactly what an Edge Animate file is . . . a web directory.

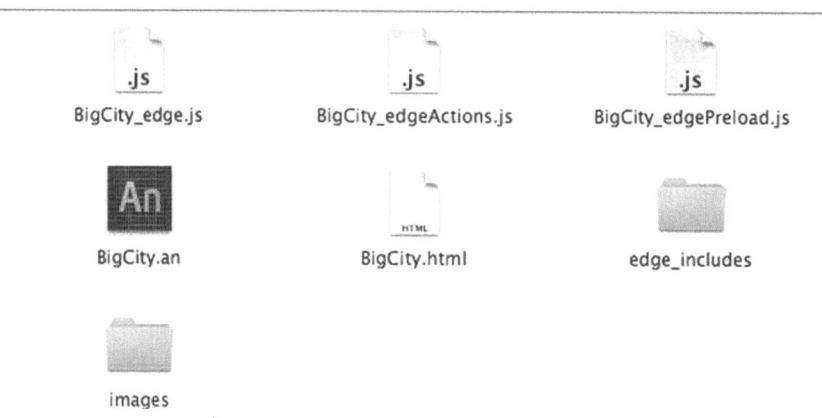

**Figure 1-26.** An Edge Animate "file" is a web directory.

Edge Animate generates each of the files and folders in this directory, and they are all used in the `BigCity.html` file that Edge Animate creates when a file is saved. If any one of these files or folders is missing, you will have problems. The reason is found in the HTML document. If you were to open it in Dreamweaver or another editor program, you will see the following code:

```
<!DOCTYPE html>
<html>
<head>
<title>BigCity</title>
<!--Adobe Edge Runtime-->
<script type="text/javascript" charset="utf-8" src="BigCity_edgePreload.js"></script>
<style>
.edgeLoad-EDGE-16215073 { visibility:hidden; }
</style>
<!--Adobe Edge Runtime End-->
```

```
</head>
<body style="margin:0;padding:0;">
<div id="stage" class="EDGE-16215073 edgeLoad-EDGE-16215073">
</div>
</body>
</html>
```

As you peruse the `<script>` tag, note how it calls a .js document found in the `BigCityCuisine` folder. The files used by the Adobe Edge Animate Runtime are also found in the `edge_includes` folder. If any of those files are missing or changed, you will get a variety of error messages or a blank screen. Thus it is extremely important that you keep all of the files in a single folder.

> *When you create a new Edge Animate project, it is a common best practice to create a directory to hold the project even before launching Edge Animate. If you don't, the files will be saved to your desktop.*

There is one other important nugget you need to know: you can open either the HTML or the .an file in Edge Animate.

You may not have noticed it when you first created a new document, but, if you look at the tab for the `Stage` panel, as shown in Figure 1-27, you will note the file name is `untitled.html`. This is because the Stage uses the WebKit browser—the same browser used in Dreamweaver's Live View feature—to display the content and animations. What you can gather from this is you can open either the HTML or .an version of the project in Edge Animate, sort of.

**Figure 1-27.** Edge Animate opens both .an and HTML files.

You can, indeed, double-click the .an file in the project folder to launch the project in Edge Animate. Do that with the HTML file and the odds are pretty good you will open your computer's default browser. Instead, you need to launch Edge Animate and then navigate to the HTML file by clicking the Open File button on the Start page or by selecting it in the list of Recent Files if you have had it open at some earlier date.

## Changing the Order of Layers

To get yourself started with this exercise, open the `BigCity.an` file. When it opens, as shown in Figure 1-28, you might think you are looking at a magazine advertisement. It is only when you examine the `Elements` and `Library` panels that you realize this ad is a bit more complex than you thought. Let's examine what we have, and a good place to start is actually the `Properties` panel.

**Figure 1-28.** It looks like Big City Cuisine is dishing up some goodness.

You may notice the document seems to have the `Composite ID` name of `EDGE ANIMATE-16215073`. This isn't the name of the document. It is, in fact, the Class name, and you can choose to either change it or leave it alone. The numbers are actually random numbers. This is done to ensure the `ID` does not conflict with other compositions. Why? A typical scenario would be a web page that has three Edge Animate animations located at various places on the page. If the class names and Composite ID's were the same, the Edge Animate files would conflict with each other, and that is not a good thing.

Over on the `Elements` panel, you now have your first look at how the layering order of the divs or elements in the project works in Edge Animate. Each div in this project is exposed and the layering is the typical "bottom/up" order you are used to in other applications. In this case, the `Background` div is at the bottom of the stack and the `Logo` div is at the top. The Elements panel is where layers can be reordered. Follow these steps to move the `Logo` div to a new position in the Layering order:

1. Click once on the `Logo` div. Not only does the selected element light up in the panel but, if you take a look at the Stage, you will see the logo has also been selected. This feature makes it very easy to select objects buried in dozens of layers.

2. Drag the Logo layer under the Background layer. When you see the black line, release the mouse. As shown in Figure 1-29, the Logo layer is now at the bottom of the stack. Move the Logo layer back to the top of the Elements.

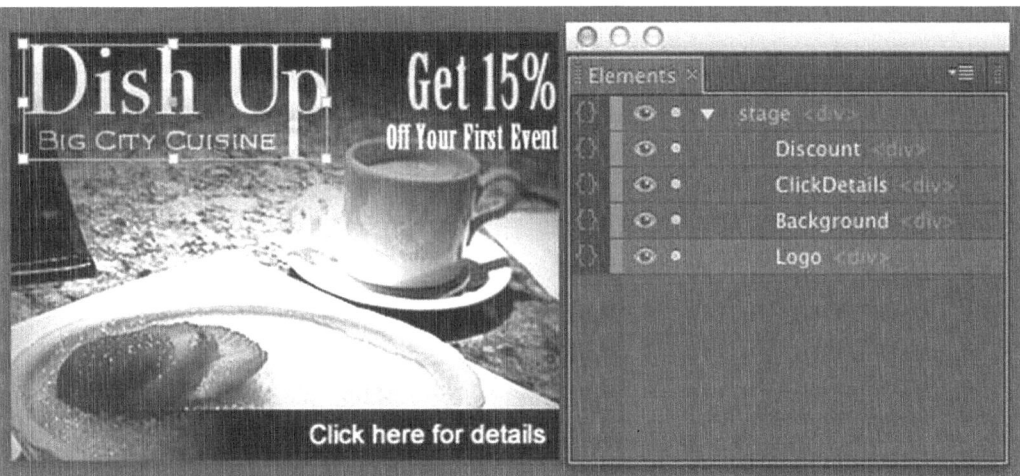

**Figure 1-29.** The Logo layer has been moved under the Background layer.

## SOME ELEMENT PANEL GOTCHA'S

We chose this subhead to get your attention because when it comes to Elements/Layers, there are some things you need to know:

- The name of each Element should be unique and mean something.

- Elements can be nested. That means the Logo layer can be nested inside the Background layer. This is a really neat technique, and we'll get deeper into it in Chapter 3.

- If an Element/Layer is not being manipulated at any point in the project, lock the layer.

- There really is no limit, other than common sense, to the number of Layers that can be contained in a project

- In multilayer documents, get into the habit of turning off the visibility of Elements/Layers you don't need for the task at hand.

## Using the Library Panel

Let's now turn our attention to the Library panel. As you may have guessed, as shown in Figure 1-30, this is where the artwork, symbols, and fonts are stored for reuse.

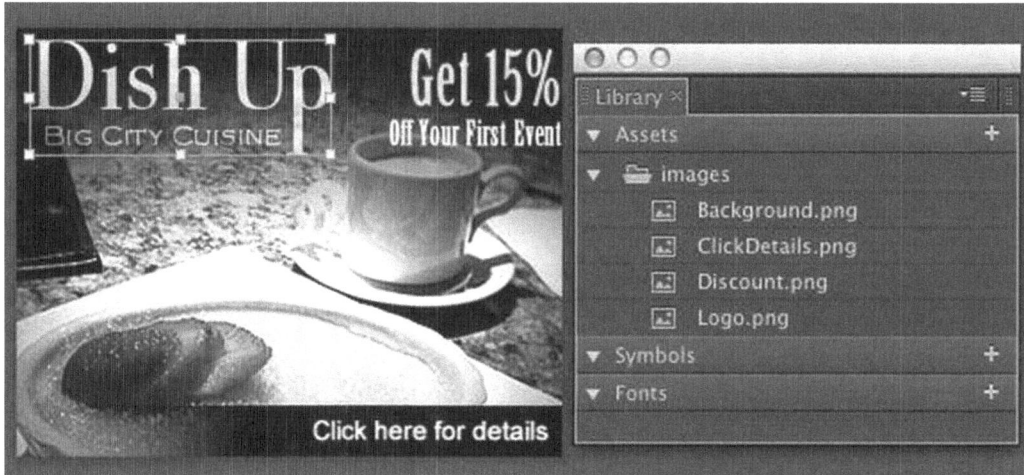

**Figure 1-30.** The Library panel stores assets for subsequent reuse in the project.

The Images folder actually contains the line art and photos that get moved to the images folder when the Edge Animate file is saved. They are listed alphabetically, not in their order of use or layer, and can be added to the Stage at any time. Here's how:

1.  Turn off the visibility of all of the items in the Elements panel by turning off the visibility of everything but the stage element. We need you to concentrate on what you will be doing with no clutter.

2.  Click once on the stage element and, in the Properties panel, change the stage color to White—#ffffff—by clicking on the White color chip in the Color Picker. You should now have a blank white Stage.

3.  If it isn't open, twirl down the assets area of the Library panel.

> *Nobody is quite sure what the formal name is for those triangles in the various panels. Being After Effects users we tend to call them "Twirlies." When a Twirlie is to be clicked to open or collapse an area, we will use the term Twirl Down to open the hidden features or Twirl Up to collapse the features.*

4.  Select the Background.png file in the images folder and drag it to the Stage. When you release the mouse, the image appears on the Stage.

When you dragged the image to the Stage, you saw, as shown in Figure 1-31, an angle bracket and two numbers enclosed in brackets. Those numbers are the x and y coordinates for the image you are adding to the Stage and, where the angles intersect—the cursor points to it—is where the image will be placed when you release the mouse.

There was another event that occurred while you weren't looking. If you check out the Elements panel, you will see the image is sitting in its own, new, div. This means that items dragged from the Library can be manipulated independent of the other instances of the object on the Stage.

5.  Delete the change you just made or undo the last step to revert back to the original state of the movie.

6.  Turn on the visibility of the elements in the Elements panel and reset the Stage color to black.

*We aren't going to get into the Symbols and Fonts area of the Library at this point in time. They are important and will be discussed in much greater depth in Chapters 3 and 5.*

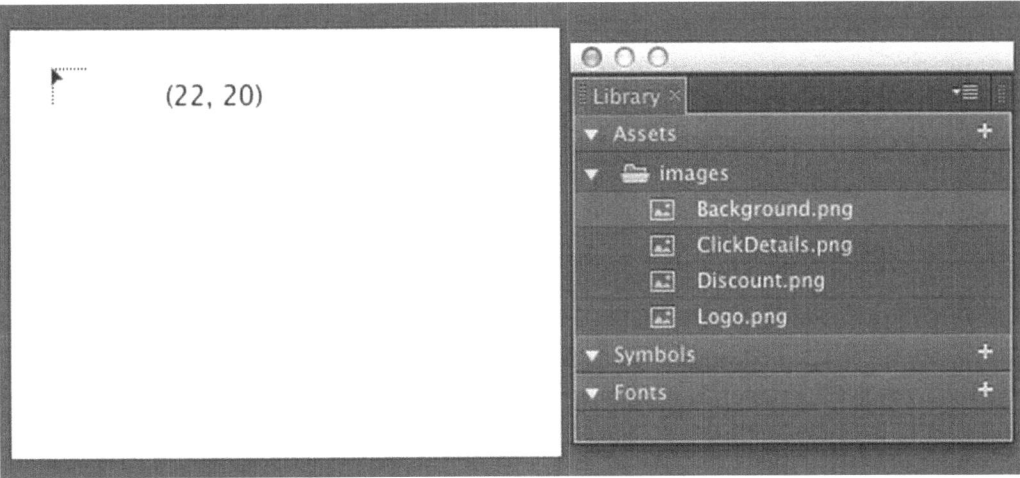

**Figure 1-31.** Dragging an image from the Library to the Stage actually adds a lot more precision placement than you might expect.

# Putting Elements in Motion

The plan is very simple. The discount offer will fade up on the page, and when it finishes the "Click here for details" banner slides into place. Follow these steps to create a simple animation:

1.  Click once on the Discount element to select it on the Stage.

2.  Making sure the playhead is at time 00.00.000, click the diamond beside Opacity in the Properties panel. When your mouse rolls over that diamond, it changes to a gold color to indicate you are about to add a keyframe and, when you click it, you will notice, as shown in Figure 1-32, the Discount element has been added to the timeline and a white diamond, indicating a keyframe, is placed under the playhead.

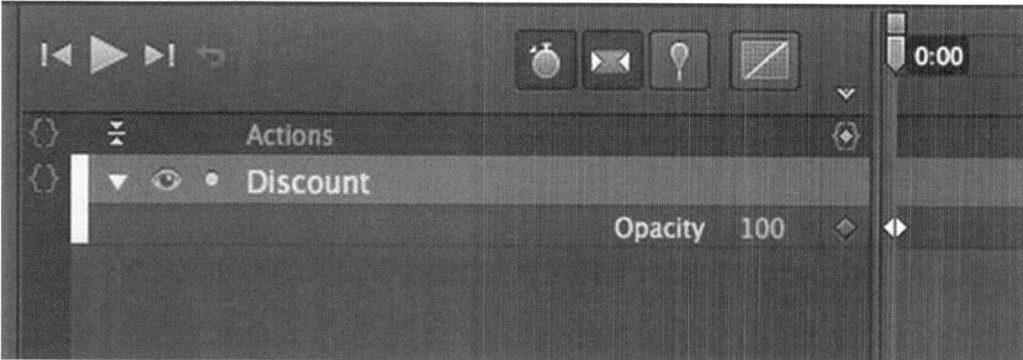

**Figure 1-32.** When a change is made to a selection on the Stage, that Element is add to the timeline and a keyframe is added to the property just changed.

3.  The number 100 in the Opacity area of the timeline indicates full opacity. Click the number and change it to 0. Press the Return/Enter key to accept the change and the selected text block will disappear.

4.  Move the playhead to the half-second mark of the timeline—it is the second mark to the right or, if you pay attention to the timecode, it will read 00.00.500—and change the opacity number to 100. As you can see in Figure 1-33, the Opacity area now sports two keyframes, and the Opacity value at each keyframe is shown. The solid strip over the keyframes is called the Transition strip and it shows the duration of the transition. If you scrub the playhead, you will see the text fade in.

**Figure 1-33.** A Transition strip indicates transitions and keyframes can be found in a layer in the timeline.

*Here's a handy tip that will preserve your sanity. Twirl up the **Discount** layer on the timeline and the properties will disappear and just the strip remains. Complex Edge Animate animations can involve dozens of layers and multiple property changes for each item in the timeline. This means the timeline can be a rather busy place. Twirling up the layers to just show the Transition Strip results in a very tidy workspace.*

We have dealt with the fade, let's now turn our attention to the text at the bottom of the Stage. The plan here is to have the text move from the right side of the Stage to its current position. Not only that, but when it reaches its final position it will bounce. Here's how:

1. Select the ClickDetails element to select the text on the Stage.

2. Move the playhead back to the 0 point of the timeline. You can do this by either dragging the playhead back to time 00:00.000, clicking the Rewind button in the top left corner of the Timeline panel, or pressing the Home key on your keyboard.

The plan here is to have the selection move from right to left to its current position. Although your initial approach will be to add a Location keyframe from the Properties panel, you will, in fact, be complicating your life. Adding a Location keyframe actually adds x and y position keyframes to the timeline. This text only needs to move across the x axis. Here's how to do accomplish this task:

1. Right-click (Control-click [Mac]) on the selected text block on the Stage. This will open the Context menu, as shown in Figure 1-34.

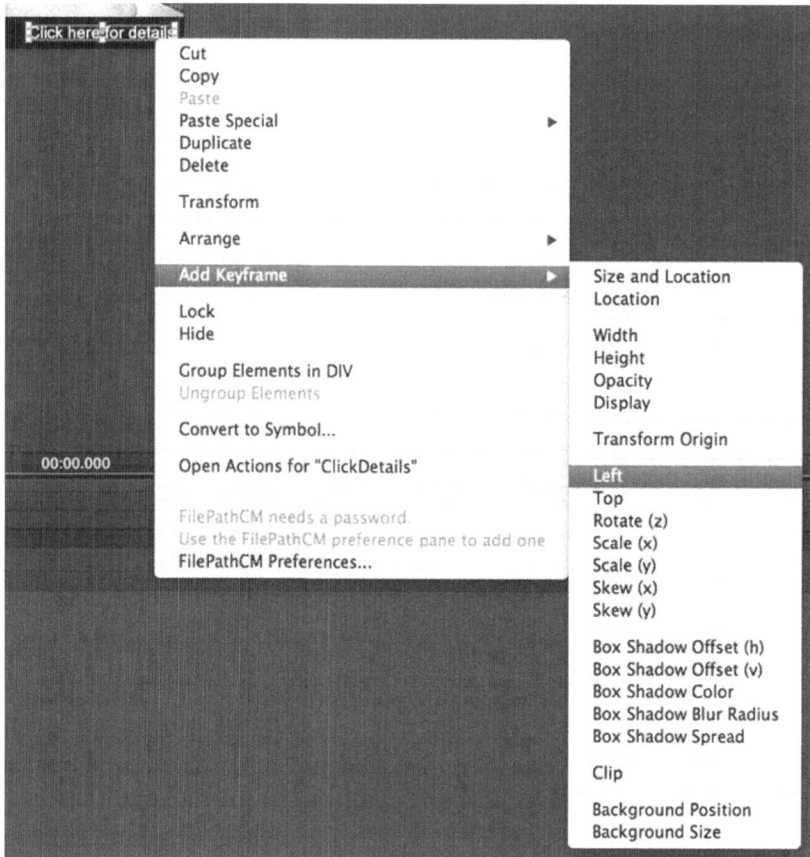

**Figure 1-34.** Keyframes for individual properties can be added through the Context menu.

2. Select Add Keyframe > Left. A Left strip and a keyframe appear on the timeline.

> *Hang on! What's with the word "left"? Let's not forget that motion in Edge Animate is accomplished by moving divs from here to there. In this case, the object is 16 pixels away from the left edge of the Stage. Conversely, you could have simply added an x keyframe in the Properties panel.*

3. Move the playhead to the one-half-second mark of the timeline and change the Left value to -136. The text moves off of the Stage. Drag the playhead across the timeline, and you will see the text move.

Of course there is a small problem. The text moves from right to left, which is the wrong direction. Time to let the software do the work and change the animation. Here's how:

1. Click once on the ClickDetails transition strip—it has the solid color with no values—to select it.

2. Select Timeline > Invert Transitions. The values for the Left keyframes change on the timeline, and if you scrub the timeline or press the Spacebar, the movie plays and . . . problem solved. You might also want to set the Stage's overflow value to "hidden" in the Properties panel.

## Using Easing

If you are a Flash user, you are quite familiar with easing. It is the gradual acceleration or deceleration during an animation that makes motion appear more realistic or natural. In Edge Animate, easing is accomplished through the use of JavaScript. In this example, we are going to add a bounce effect to the text. Here's how:

1. To add the "bounce," click once on the ClickDetails transition strip to select it.

2. Click the Easing Linear button, it looks like a graph, at the top of the timeline. The Ease panel will open.

3. Select Ease Out > Bounce from the list shown in Figure 1-35. The graph shows the effect.

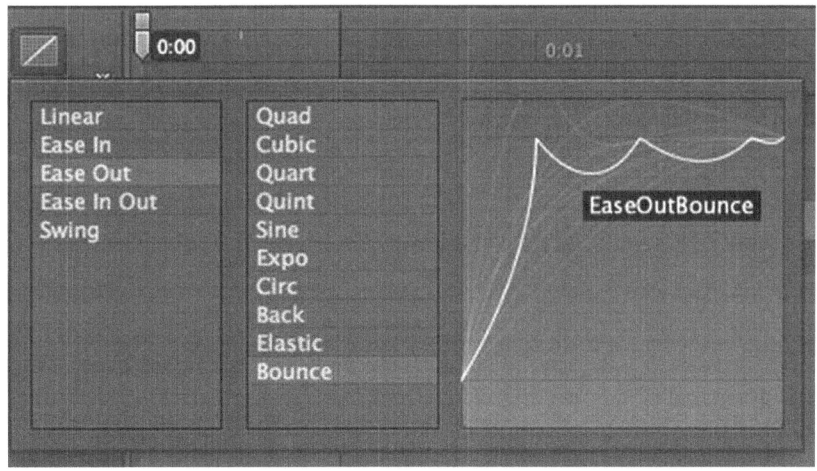

**Figure 1-35.** The eases are a collection of JavaScript effects installed with Edge Animate.

4. Press the spacebar and the text "bounces" into place.

## Browser Testing Your Project

Being an HTML-based application, you would expect that you would be able to test your work in a browser. You can test your work both within Edge Animate and outside of Edge Animate. Let's look at both ways.

1. To test within Edge Animate, simply select File > Preview in Browser. For those of you familiar with Flash or Dreamweaver, Edge Animate uses the same keyboard command—Command > Return (Mac) or Ctrl > Enter (PC)—to accomplish this task. When you select the menu item, the browser opens, and, as shown in Figure 1-36, your project starts to play. When you quit the browser, you will be returned to Edge Animate.

**Figure 1-36.** Your projects can be browser tested from within Edge Animate.

The problem with testing in Edge Animate is you only get to use your computer's default browser. If you want to test in other browsers, you will need to save your file and open the project's HTML file in another browser. In this example, were we to want to view the project in Firefox and not the computer's default Chrome, we would simply open the BigCity.html file in Firefox.

# You Have Learned

- The purpose of many of the panels and menu items in Edge Animate
- How to customize your Edge Animate workspace

- How to dock, undock, and float panels in the Edge Animate workspace

- How to reorder items in the Elements panel

- How to create a simple timeline-based animation in Edge Animate

- How to browser test an Edge Animate movie

That is a lot of stuff you have learned during our casual stroll. In the next chapter, we are going to explore how to make "magic" happen on the Edge Animate timeline by fully exploring keyframes, transitions, and a tool unique to Edge Animate: the Pin. We'll see you there.

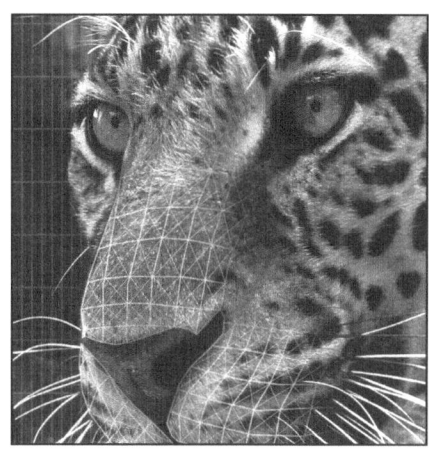

# Chapter 2

# Creating Timeline Animations: Part 1

When you really think about it, animation is nothing more than simply getting things to move from here to there. Prior to Edge Animate, motion graphics using CSS3 required mastering a lot of rather complex code and spending an inordinate amount of time testing to see if the object really did move from here to where you wanted it . . . over there. Edge Animate makes this process transparent by giving you a visual approach—you can actually see things move—to web animation.

In the previous chapter, we gave you a faint whiff of how the timeline creates animation in Edge Animate. In this chapter, the process gets quite a bit more complex because Edge Animate has a lot of tools and features aimed precisely at animation. In fact, if you are a Flash or After Effects user, you are going to feel right at home because the Edge Animate tweening model is pretty darn close to that used in those two applications.

Although animation is a pretty complex subject, we are going to deal with it in much the same way we always deal with complexity: from a starting point of simplicity. As you progress through the chapter, you will learn a variety of new animation workflows that you can mix and match to create some pretty neat timeline animations

Here is what we will cover in this chapter:

- Auto-Keyframing

- Manual keyframing

- Smooth transitions

- Using the playhead and the Pin

- Tweening element properties

- Turning off transition smoothness

- Adding easing

- Using overflow on the Stage

- Using the Elements and Timeline panels to manage layers

- Using transition strips to automate repetitive tasks

- Animating on a curve

If you haven't already downloaded the chapter files, they can be found at http://www.apress.com/9781430243502. In this chapter, we will be using these files:

- Autumn.an

- ThePin.an

- Clip.an

- Rabbit.an

- Matrix.an

- Easing.an

- Dragons.an

- Splat.an

This chapter is going to contain a lot of information, so let's skip the pleasantries and jump directly into animating with Edge Animate.

# Auto-Keyframing

Depending on how you look at it, Auto-Keyframing in Edge Animate is either a blessing or a necessary evil. It sure does speed things up when there is a lot of motion to be added to the project but it can also be a hindrance when you want to move things from here to there but aren't sure where "there" is going to be. Let's look at both scenarios:

1. Open the Autumn.an file located in your Chapter 2 Exercise folder. When it opens you will notice there are only two elements: Bush and Leaf. The plan is to have the leaf fall off the branch and gently tumble off the Stage.

> *You will notice that we have locked the Bush element. A great habit to develop is to lock elements that either won't move or have already been animated. This way they can't accidentally be selected and manipulated.*

2.  Click once on the Leaf element to select it. We deliberately added a Leaf element to show you that sometimes it is difficult to find objects on the Stage. The easiest way of picking what you need out of the crowd is to select the Element rather than clicking all over the Stage to hunt down what you are looking for.

3.  Click the red Stopwatch, as shown in Figure 2-1, at the top of the timeline. The stopwatch will change color. That stopwatch is Auto-Keyframing. When it is red, the Edge Animate default, the feature is turned on and when it is gray, Auto-Keyframing is turned off.

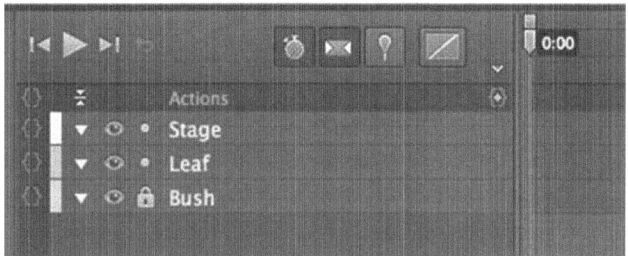

**Figure 2-1.** A red stopwatch, Auto-Keyframing turned on, is the Edge Animate default.

4.  Click the Stopwatch to turn on Auto-Keyframing. With the leaf still selected on the Stage, click the diamond beside the X and Y properties in the Properties panel, as shown in Figure 2-2. Let's take a brief pause here to discuss what just happened on the timeline.

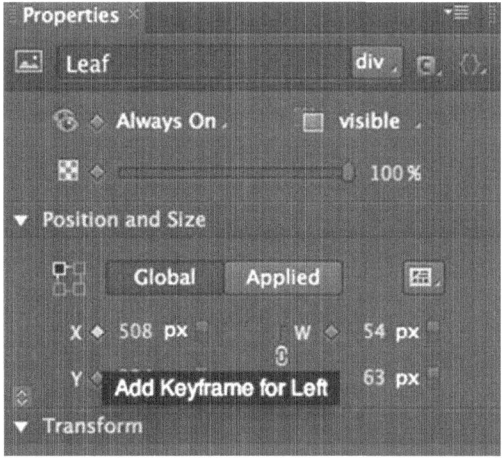

**Figure 2-2.** Keyframes can be added in the Properties panel.

When you add a keyframe to identify the start point of an animation, a white diamond appears under the element on the timeline. Not only that, but all of the properties associated with the keyframe light up under the element, as shown in Figure 2-3. In this case, the location of the selection on the X and Y or Top and Left axis are shown.

> *Why* Top *and* Left *and not* X *and* Y *on the timeline? Those two CSS properties set the position of an element within its containing element, which, in this case, is the Stage. You can gather from this that these values are part of the CSS generated by Edge Animate.*

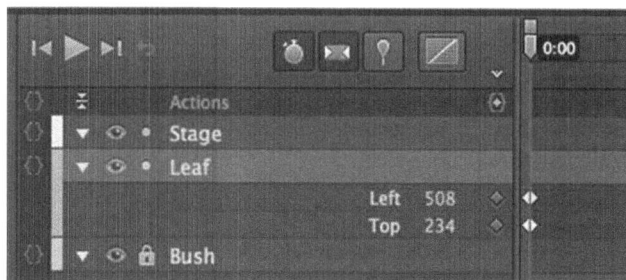

**Figure 2-3.** *Elements only appear on the timeline when keyframes are added.*

If you are coming to Edge Animate from Flash or some other animation application, this is a rather novel concept because timelines traditionally show everything in the animation on the timeline. Edge Animate doesn't because things can get rather complicated in a hurry. By using this approach, you are able to concentrate only on the object being manipulated. If you want to see how all of the Elements, including the Stage, stack up with one another, click the Only Show Animated Elements button—it looks like the Martini glass icon in the bottom left corner of the timeline—and everything, as shown in Figure 2-4, appears in the timeline. Click again and only the Leaf element appears because it is the only element containing keyframes. If you have a complex project containing a number of elements, clicking the Martini glass icon will preserve your sanity.

**Figure 2-4.** Clicking the Only Show Animated Elements button turns it off and exposes all of the elements on the current timeline.

5. Move the playhead to the 1-second mark (0.01) of the timeline. You are now telling Edge Animate what the duration of this animation will be.

6. In the timeline, scrub the Top value to 400. The leaf is now off the Stage and, if you drag the playhead backward and forward, you can follow, as shown in Figure 2-5, the motion of the leaf.

7. Select File > Revert to return the exercise file to its original state.

**Figure 2-5.** Scrub the playhead to preview the leaf's motion.

*As is so typical of the digital studio, there are other ways of doing the same thing. Scrubbing the* Top *value is one way. Another is to hold down the Shift key and, with the Shift key held down, drag the leaf to its final position. You could change the* Top *value on the* Properties *panel and even select the leaf and move it downward using the down Arrow key on your keyboard. What's the best way? Who cares? Is the leaf where you wanted it to finish?*

# Manually Adding Keyframes

In this exercise we are going to have the leaf fall but, this time, we won't use Auto-Keyframes. Here's how:

1. Turn off `Auto-Keyframes` by clicking the `Stopwatch`. If it turns from red to gray, Auto-Keyframing is turned off.

2. Select the leaf on the Stage and add a `Location` keyframe using the `Context` menu that appears.

3. Move the playhead to the 1-second mark on the timeline and drag the leaf off the Stage. When you release the mouse, take a look at the timeline. As shown in Figure 2-6, the keyframe icon is missing. How did that happen?

**Figure 2-6.** Missing keyframes are your first indication Auto-Keyframes has been turned off.

When you turn off Auto-Keyframes, you are essentially telling Edge Animate you don't want any sort of motion or transition. You are simply changing the selection's properties. Let's fix that.

1. Undo your change to return the leaf to its starting position and move the playhead to the 1-second mark of the timeline.

2. With the leaf still selected, click the keyframe icon for the Top property. You have just manually added a keyframe.

3. Drag the leaf off the Stage.

4. Scrub the timeline and the leaf falls off the branch.

## Adding Extra Keyframes

Our leaf falls straight down and you could stop there and congratulate yourself for creating an Edge Animate animation. Not so fast. The trick to animating objects is mimicking real life, and leaves don't fall from trees in a straight line to the ground. Let's have our leaf follow a lazy zig-zag pattern downward and, at the same time, learn a rather cool technique for using keyframes.

1. Turn on Auto-Keyframes and move the playhead to the half-second mark of the timeline. Add a Left keyframe on the timeline. Do the same thing at the 1-second mark. You should have three Left keyframes.

2. Move the playhead to the quarter-second mark (00:00.250 on the Timecode) and scrub the Left value to move the leaf a short distance to the left.

3. Repeat step 2 at the 00:00.750 mark of the Timecode, only this time move the leaf a short distance to the right.

4. Click once between any pair of the keyframes just created and look closely at your timeline. You should see, as in Figure 2-7, a half keyframe and the other one is a solid keyframe. What you are seeing is a feature unique to Timeline animations: the split keyframe. What you are being told is the selected segment starts with one value set earlier but ends with a different one.

> You will also see a hollow keyframe right at the start of the animation. A hollow keyframe indicates the value hasn't changed.

5. Scrub the timeline or press the Spacebar to review the motion of the leaf.

**Figure 2-7.** Split keyframes are unique to Edge Animate.

# Adding Transitions to an Element

The motion looks good, but one key animation principle—anticipation—hasn't been added. Anticipation is that visual "extra" that kicks off motion. In this case, the leaf is going to "jiggle" and then begin its downward descent.

This is accomplished through a rather nifty feature of Edge Animate. The solid bar you see for the Leaf element is called the *transition strip*, and all of the transitions applied to that element, or object, are listed under the strip. If you add another transition, it will appear in the list, not as a separate layer on the timeline. Let's see how this works and "jiggle" a leaf. First, though, we need to prepare the timeline:

1. Click once on the Transition strip for the Leaf element and drag it to the quarter-second—00:00.250—mark of the timeline. What you have done is to delay the start of the leaf's downward motion by that amount of time.

2. Turn off Auto-Keyframes and pull the playhead back to the 0 point of the timeline. Add a Left keyframe. This "locks in" the Left position until the animation starts.

Our animation is delayed, and we can now turn our attention to the "jiggle."

> The importance of the ability to move entire transitions and their keyframes to different times in the timeline can't be understated. With this feature, you can "tweak" effects until their timing and duration are just right. You can also select individual keyframes and move them on the timeline as well.

The effect we need will use rotation to create the back and forth motion. This is fine, but you also need to consider "where" the rotation is going to occur. By default, all effects in Edge Animate are based on the location of the selected object's transformation origin or pivot point, which is the blue dot found at the geographic center of any selection you make on the Stage. This won't work here unless you want to treat the leaf as the minute hand of a watch.

When a leaf falls from a tree, its "pivot" is the point where the leaf's stem is attached to the branch. Here's how to change a selection's transformation point, called an *Origin point* in Timeline animations:

1. Select the Leaf on the Stage. The blue dot, as shown in Figure 2-8, is the Origin point.

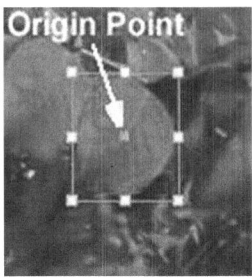

**Figure 2-8.** The Origin point is used to set the point where transformations occur.

2. Select the Transform tool, as shown in Figure 2-9, and the blue dot is replaced with a small registration point. Place the cursor over the Origin point. The cursor will change from the Compass to an arrow.

**Figure 2-9.** The Transform tool

3. Click and drag the Origin point to the top center point of the image.

> *If you are a total control freak, you can also do this by the numbers. Simply change or scrub the X and Y values in the Transform Origin area of the Properties panel. The Origin point will move as the values change.*

# Creating Anticipation

With the Origin point for our animation in place, we can now concentrate on the leaf's rocking. Here's how:

1. Making sure the playhead is at the start of the timeline and the leaf is selected, click the Rotation keyframe icon in the Properties panel to add a Rotation keyframe in the timeline.

2. Turn on Auto-Keyframes and drag the playhead a short distance on the timeline. Set the Rotate value in the timeline to –15.

3. Move the playhead a short distance on the timeline and change the rotate value to 10.

4. Add three more Rotate changes along the timeline (Figure 2-10) to have the leaf gently rotate as it falls.

5. Return the playhead to the start of the timeline and press the Spacebar. The leaf briefly jiggles and falls off the branch.

**Figure 2-10.** A gentle rocking effect is created by using the Rotate property of an object.

That may seem to be a lot of work to animate a simple leaf falling off a branch. In fact, it is. As you have learned, motion involves more than simply moving an object from "here" to "there." It involves paying attention to the world around you and using the tools available to you to mimic how a leaf really falls from a tree.

# Animating with the Pin

Edge Animate has a feature that is unique to the Adobe animation tools lineup. It is called *the Pin*, and, once you get used to using it, you will start wondering why no one else has previously thought of this rather sweet tool. The problem with the Pin, that little box over the playhead, is getting used to it. Once you do, you will find yourself using it religiously.

The first thing you need to know about the Pin is that it works with the playhead. It can't be used alone. The next thing you need to know is that changes occur *from* the Pin *to* the playhead. Once you grasp those two concepts, your workflow will speed up. Let's check out what we are talking about:

1.  In your Exercise _02 folder is a file named ThePin.an. Open it. When it opens, as shown in Figure 2-11, you are placed in the Swiss Alps and the text invites you to "Explore Switzerland." Also note we have locked the image Element because the plan is to have the text "zoom in" over 2 seconds.

**Figure 2-11.** What better place to learn how to use the Pin than the Swiss Alps.

2. Select the `Text` element on the Stage and, in the `Properties` panel, add `Scale X` and `Scale Y` keyframes. The Text element will light up on the timeline and sport a Scale keyframe.

3. Click the `Toggle Pin` button—it looks like a push pin—at the top of the `Timeline` panel. Not only does the Toggle Pin button turn blue, but the Pin itself, right above the playhead, as shown in Figure 2-12, turns blue. It also turns on Auto-Keyframes.

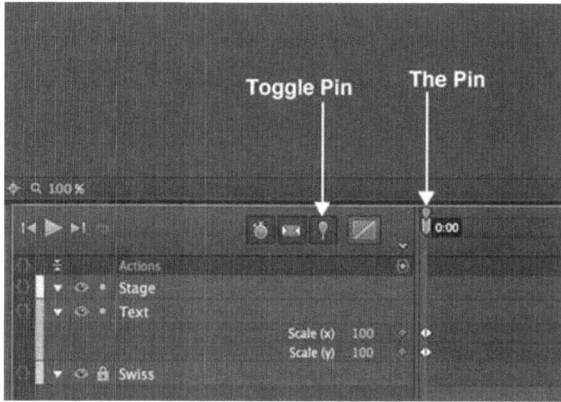

**Figure 2-12.** The Pin is activated by clicking the Toggle Pin button.

*Another way of activating the Pin is to simply double-click it in the Timeline panel. Double-click it again, and it will turn off.*

4. Drag the Pin to the 2-second point (0.02) on the timeline. As shown in Figure 2-13, a blue line indicating the "direction" of the transition—back to the playhead—appears on the timeline. The numbers beside the Pin and the Timecode indicate the distance between the Pin and the playhead.

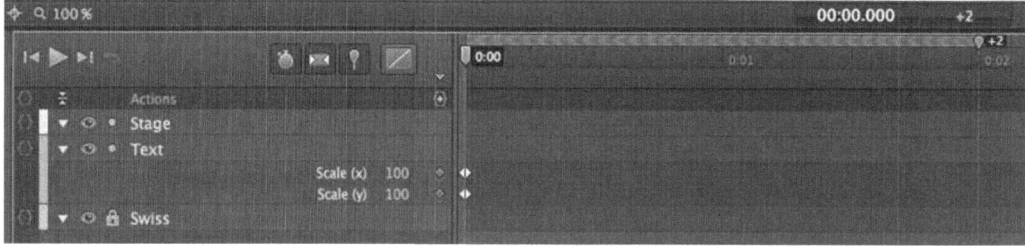

**Figure 2-13.** The Pin is moved to the 2-second point of the timeline.

5. In the `Timeline` panel, change the `Scale` values to 10%. The text shrinks and, if you scrub the playhead from the start of the timeline to the Pin, the text will grow. In this case the resize occurred from the placement of the Pin. If you look at the Scale values, as shown in Figure 2-14, in the Transition strip, you will see the scale value for the selection is 10% right at the start of the animation and 100% at the end. What you did was essentially tell Timeline animations: "Grow from 10% to 100% size at this point in time."

**Figure 2-14.** Everything happens from the Pin to the playhead.

6. This time let's have a change occur in the other direction: from the Pin ahead to the playhead. To get started, drag the playhead to the 4-second mark on the timeline. Note how the chevron in the direction strip points toward the playhead and that the strip changes color.

> *Why does that blue timecode change to −2 when I am at the 4-second mark? Excellent question. That timecode indicator tells you how far the Pin is from the playhead. In this case it is 2 seconds behind the playhead, which explains the negative number.*

7. In the `Properties` panel, change the text color from white to black.

8. Scrub the timeline and the text changes from white—where the Pin is located—to black, as shown in Figure 2-15, at the 4-second mark.

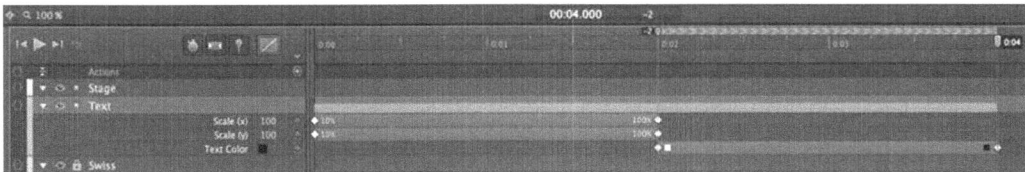

**Figure 2-15.** A transition that runs from the Pin to the playhead.

> *To turn off the Pin, simply double-click the playhead or click the Toggle Pin button.*

# Clipping Elements in Edge Animate

Although Edge Animate does not include a masking feature, there is an item on the Properties panel—Clip—that does a pretty good job as a rudimentary stand-in. Essentially, *clipping* is a form of reveal or wipe effect. In actuality, the clip property from CSS3 lets you specify the dimensions of an element that should be visible, and the parts of the element not within those dimensions are clipped.

In this example, we are going to use it, and the Pin, to reveal the "Explore Switzerland" text from the previous exercise. Here's how:

1. Open the Clip.an file located in your Exercise folder.

2. Activate the Pin, select the text, and drag the Pin to the 2-second point on the timeline.

3. At the bottom of the Properties panel is a Clip area. Click the toggle switch beside the words "No Clipping" to activate the panel and add a Clip keyframe to the timeline.

The four numbers you see in the Clip area, shown in Figure 2-16, determine the direction of the clipping. The directions are based on the Top, Bottom, Left, and Right edges of the selection. The numbers show you the width and height of the selection based on the location of the bottom and right edges of the text block. In this exercise, the intention is to revel the text—from left to right—over 2 seconds.

**Figure 2-16.** The clipping values show you the locations of a selection's edges.

4. Scrub **the** Clip (right) value, left, toward 0. As you scrub, you will see, as shown in Figure 2-17, the text disappears as you change the Clip (right) values.

**Figure 2-17.** Clipping an element on the timeline.

5.  Keep scrubbing until the E in Explore is completely invisible—the Clip (right) value should be about 0—and then release the mouse. The Clip area of the timeline now has two keyframes and, if you press the Spacebar, the text will reveal itself over 2 seconds.

# Using Transitions to Swap Images

To this point in the chapter, you have been using smooth transitions to make stuff move from here to there or to change a selection from one state to another. As the term implies, the transition between, say, 0% opacity and 100% opacity over a series of frames is a gradual and smooth process. Smooth transitions is the default setting in Edge Animate, but there are going to be occasions where you simply want an image to suddenly appear or "pop" into place . . . like when an anvil lands on a rabbit's head.

Let's get in touch with our "inner Looney Tunes" and start dropping anvils. Here's how:

1.  Open the Rabbit.an Animate file located in your Chapter 2 Exercise folder. When it opens, you will see, as shown in Figure 2-18, a cartoon rabbit sitting in a field and, if you review the Library panel, you will notice the graphics for the anvil and another rabbit head are part of the project.

**Figure 2-18.** The assets are assembled.

Although the plan is rather simple—drop an anvil on the rabbit—there is an "issue." When an anvil is dropped on a Looney Tunes character's head, the character reacts. If we were to simply drop the anvil on the rabbit, nothing would happen to the rabbit and the anvil will fall off the screen. What should happen is, when the anvil lands on the rabbit's head, the rabbit would react. In this case, the Head_Up image is replaced with the Head_Down image when the anvil hits and, when the anvil bounces off, the Head_Down image is replaced with the Head_Up image. Let's make that happen.

2. Drag the Anvil.png image from the Assets folder to the upper right corner of the Stage. The anvil is going to roar out of that flock of birds in that location.

3. With the anvil selected, add Location keyframes in the Properties panel at time 0.

4. With the anvil still selected, add Scale keyframes in the Properties panel and set the Scale x **and** y values to 6%. The anvil shrinks and looks like it is a part of that flock of birds.

5. Move the playhead to the 00:00.250 mark of the timeline and add Left, Top, Scale X, and Scale Y keyframes in the anvil properties in the timeline. What you have just done is to "hold" the anvil in place for a short period of time.

6. Still at the 00:00.250 mark of the timeline, add a Rotate keyframe to the anvil and change the Rotate value to –300. With the assets prepared, it is time to drop an anvil on an unsuspecting rabbit.

## Animating Multiple Properties

The plan is simple, the anvil falls out of the flock of birds. As it does, it rotates and gets larger as it approaches the rabbit's head. When it hits the rabbit, the anvil bounces and rotates as it moves off the Stage. To accomplish this task, follow these steps:

1. Move the playhead to the 1-second mark of the timeline. This is the point in time where the anvil hits.

2. With the Anvil layer selected on the timeline, use these values:

   - Scale X: 75
   - Scale Y: 75
   - Rotate: 0
   - Left: 7
   - Top: 230

If you scrub the timeline, you will see the anvil rotating as it moves out of the flock of birds. When it lands on the rabbit, the bottom of the anvil is in the proper position. Let's finish off the anvil's animation:

3. Move the playhead to the 1.5-second mark of the timeline and, with the Anvil layer still selected on the timeline, use these values:

- Scale X: 60

- Scale Y: 60

- Rotate: -70

- Left: -250

- Top: 30

4. Scrub the timeline and, as shown in Figure 2-19, you will see you have created a nifty little anvil drop.

5. Twirl up the Anvil layer and lock the layer. We are now finished with it.

**Figure 2-19.** Multiple properties of the anvil are animated.

# Swapping Assets

Having created the anvil drop, we can now turn our attention to the rabbit. As pointed out earlier, the current animation is a bit lame because the rabbit doesn't react to an anvil landing on its head. What needs to happen is, when the anvil arrives, we need to "swap out" the Head_Up element with the Head_Down image in the Assets panel. Here's how:

1. If they aren't visible, click the Martini glass icon to reveal all of the layers on the timeline and click the Stopwatch—it turns white—to turn off Auto-Keyframing.

2. Click the Auto-Transition Mode button—the icon beside the Stopwatch as shown in Figure 2-20— to turn off Auto-Transitions. By disabling Auto-Transition Mode you are enabling the "swap." An auto-transition is simply a smooth transition. Turning it off makes the transition abrupt.

**Figure 2-20.** Deselecting Auto-Transition Mode allows you to make abrupt changes on the timeline.

3. Move the playhead to 00:00.981 on the timeline—the point where the anvil is closest to the character's head—select the Head_Up layer, and add an Opacity keyframe.

4. Move the playhead to the 1-second mark on the timeline, add an Opacity keyframe, and change the opacity to 0. Two things happen. The first is the head disappears. The second is that a hollow keyframe, shown in Figure 2-21, is added to the timeline. That hollow keyframe is your visual indicator that there will be nothing smooth about the transition from 100% to 0% opacity.

**Figure 2-21.** Hollow keyframes indicate there is nothing smooth about the transition.

5. Move the playhead back to .981 and drag the Head_Down image from the Assets panel to the Stage. Move it into position over the rabbit's body, add an Opacity keyframe, and set the value to 0%.

6. Move the playhead to the 1-second mark and change the Head_Down opacity to 100%.

7. Move the playhead to 00:01.188 and change the opacity in the Head_Down layer to 0% and in the Head_Up layer to 100%.

8. To finish up, select the Stage element on the timeline and, in the Properties panel, ensure the Overflow property is set to hidden, as shown in Figure 2-22.

9. Play or scrub the movie.

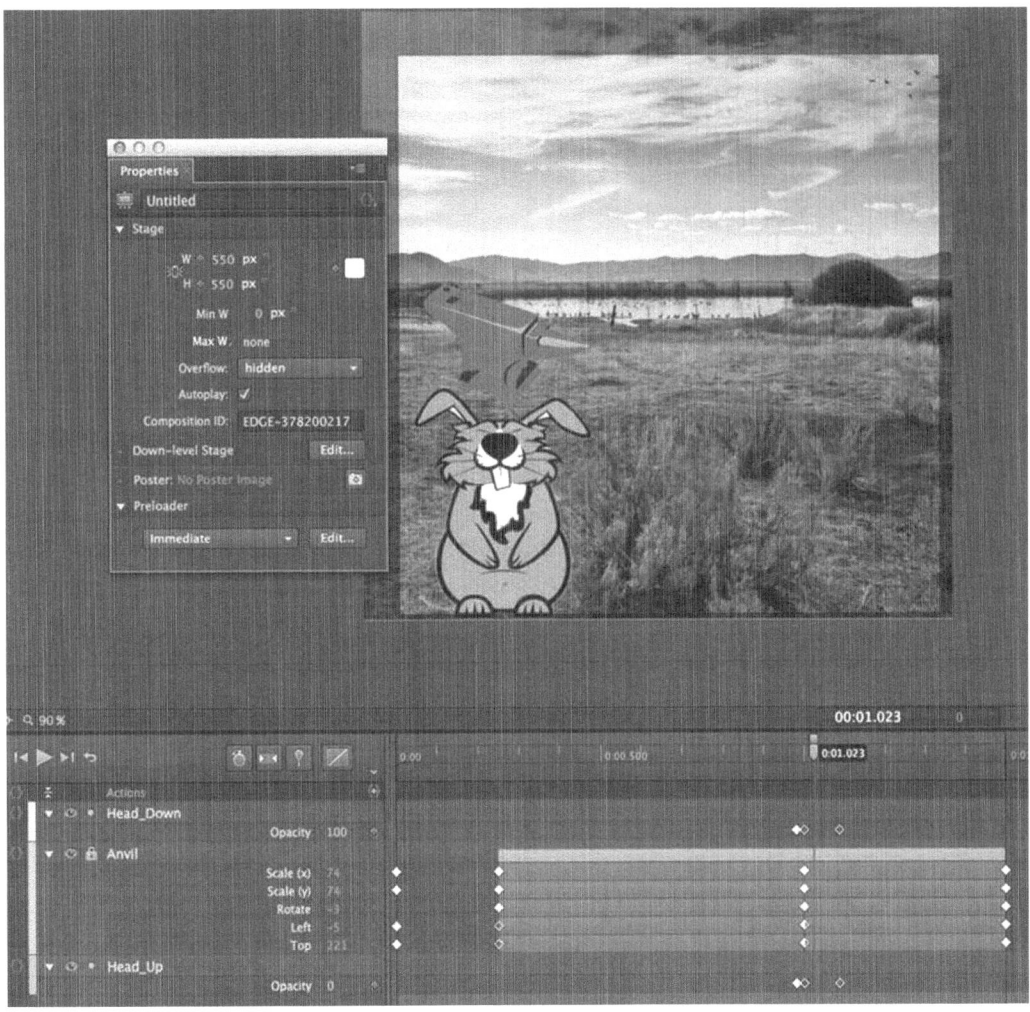

**Figure 2-22.** Multiple transitions, hidden overflow, and no smooth transitions make this animation work.

*This exercise demonstrated a little-known fact about animations in Edge Animate. You will notice only the Anvil layer has a transition strip. The two Head layers don't. This is because there are no smooth transitions in those two layers. Keep this in mind when your projects contain changes or motion you may not be able to find. The odds are really good that those changes are in layers not containing a smooth transition.*

# "Recycling" Edge Animate Transitions

Workflow in the digital studio, especially when it applies to motion graphics, always revolves around a key word: efficiency. If repetitive tasks can be done faster, your workflow improves as you suddenly discover you can actually do more in less time. There is a feature in Edge Animate that underlines that concept in bright red neon. It is the ability to apply multiple effects to an element in the timeline and with, it seems, the click of a mouse, you apply that same effect to a few dozen elements in the timeline. Although there is no official term for the technique we are about to present, we regard it as "recycling transitions." Let's get busy and efficient.

1. Open the `Matrix.an` file located in your `Exercise` folder. When it opens you will see the words "Edge Animate" sitting above the Stage. The plan is to have an effect like the titling sequence in the movie *The Matrix*, where a bunch of letters randomly fall onto the Stage.

2. Right-click (Control-click for Mac) on the letter `E in Edge`. When the context menu opens, select, `Add Keyframe > Top`.

3. Making sure Auto-Keyframes is turned on and move the playhead to the half-second mark—00:00.500—of the timeline and scrub the Top value to move the letter to the bottom of the stage. When you release the mouse, a transition strip will appear showing you the motion.

4. Pull the playhead back to the 0 point of the timeline and add an `Opacity` keyframe. Set the value to 40. At the end of the transition set the `Opacity` value to 100.

5. Pull the playhead back to the 0 point on the timeline. Add a `Rotation` keyframe and set the initial value to `-15`. At the end of the transition strip set the `Rotation` value to 360. What you have just done, as shown in Figure 2-23, is to have the letter come tumbling into its final position.

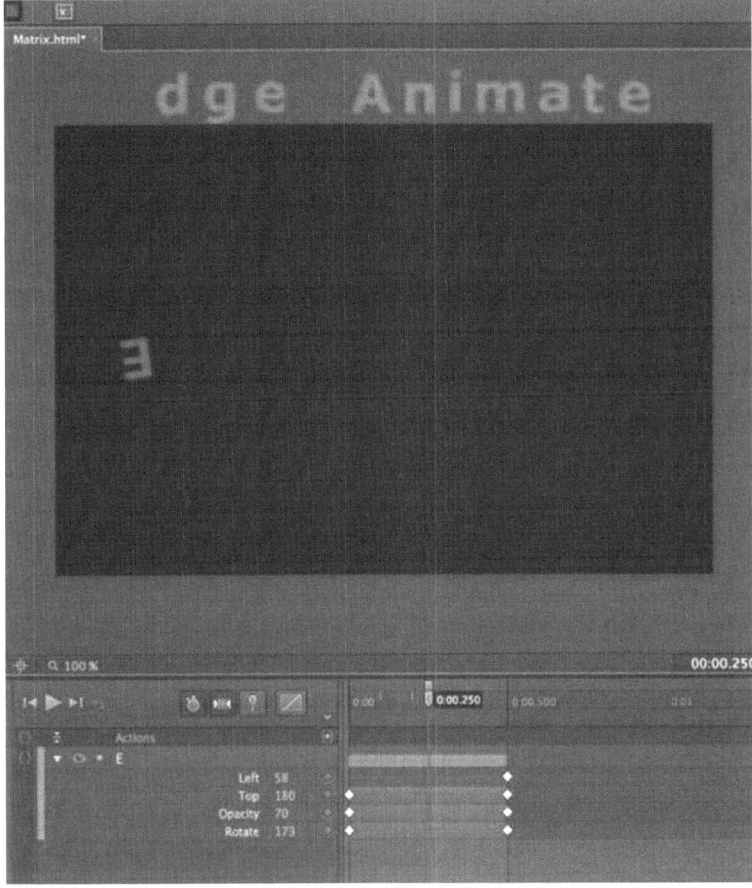

**Figure 2-23.** The letter E moves, fades in, and tumbles into place.

Now repeat steps 2 through 5 for each of the ten remaining letters. We hope your reaction is, "Say what???" If it was, then you are going to love the rest of this exercise.

6. Twirl up the `Transition` strip and move the playhead to the start of the timeline. Things are about to get busy on the timeline, and you are going to want to reduce the clutter.

7. Click once on the `Transition` strip to select it. Selecting a Transition strip also selects the effects associated with it.

8. Copy the selection to the clipboard and select all of the remaining letters at the top of the Stage.

9. With the letters selected, select `Edit > Paste Special > Paste Transitions From Location`. The letters move to the bottom of the Stage and, best of all, they appear on the timeline and, as shown in Figure 2-24, they all have the same effects as the letter E.

**Figure 2-24.** The Paste Special item from the Edit menu puts productivity on afterburner.

*Be careful with those two choices:* Paste Transitions From Location *and* Paste Transitions To Location. *The first choice adds the transition from the letter E to the selected items, and they do exactly what the letter E does and move from the top of the stage or their current location on the Stage to the bottom of the Stage. The second choice adds the transition to the selected objects but, and this is critical, the transition assumes the selections are in the finish position. If you were to apply this choice to the selected letters, they would fall from a distance above their current location that is equal to the distance the letter E falls and finish right where they are currently located.*

Let's finish this up and add some randomness to the animation.

10. Twirl up all of the elements on the timeline. When you finish, you should see only a Transition strip for each layer in the timeline.

11. Drag the strips to various staggered locations on the timeline. You can have them overlap, happen later than others, earlier, or whatever. You can even increase their duration by dragging an edge of

the Transition strip. When you finish, your timeline will somewhat resemble the one shown in Figure 2-25. Rewind and play.

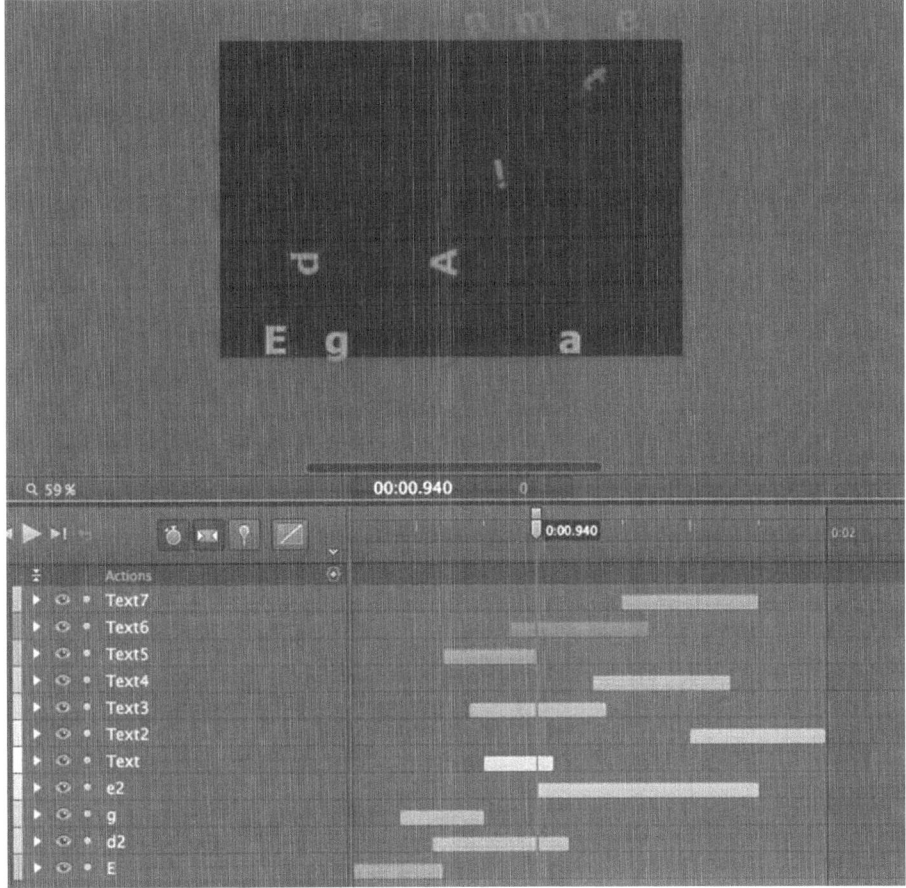

**Figure 2-25.** Random motion based on one element applied to a number of elements in under 10 minutes.

# Animating with Eases

The key to any animation is answering a question you should always ask: Does this look real? Think of a bouncing ball. When it bounces, unless it is in a place where gravity is not present, it never reaches its original height. A ball's bounce height gets smaller, thanks to physics, as it loses energy. Although we can't mimic physics in Edge Animate, easing makes the process of a bounce, for example, more realistic and believable.

Easing is usually applied in two ways: easing in and easing out. Easing in, when applied to the ball, actually accelerates the motion when it is released. Easing out is the exact opposite: speed is reduced. In this exercise, we are going to explore the fundamentals as they apply to Edge Animate. To get started:

1. Open the Easing.an file in your Exercise folder. As you can see, we are going to apply easing to a falling hammer.

2. Click once on the Hammer and drag the Origin Point of the hammer to the bottom of the hammer, as shown in Figure 2-26. The plan is to bounce the hammer head off the bottom of the Stage. Moving the Origin Point puts the "pivot" point at the proper place on the hammer. If we didn't move it, the hammer would rotate from the original location, making the animation look rather cheesy.

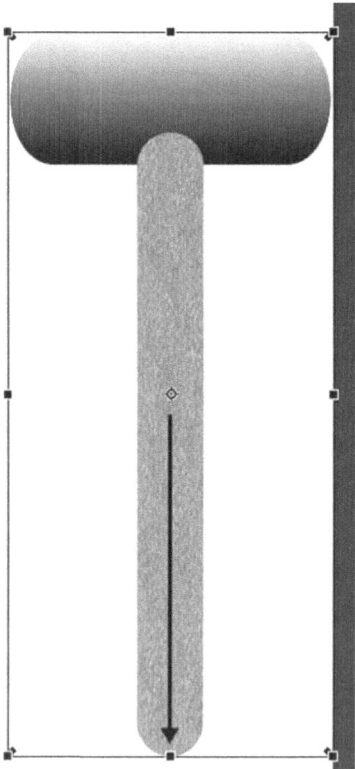

**Figure 2-26.** The first step is to move the Origin Point to a more "believable" location.

3. With the hammer still selected, add a rotation keyframe at the 0 point on the timeline.

4. Move the playhead to the 00:01.500 point of the timeline and, with the hammer still selected, change the Rotation value to −78. The hammer will rotate downward to the left and finish at the bottom of the Stage.

5. If you rewind and play the movie, you will have a slowly swinging hammer. The timing is deliberate. It is important that you see what easing can do, and over longer durations the eases are pronounced.

6. Select the hammer's `Transition` strip in the timeline and click the Easing button to open the Easing panel. When you do, the `Easing` area of the `Transition Properties` panel will appear.

7. Select `Ease Out > Bounce`, as shown in Figure 2-27, in the panel. If you rewind and play the movie, you have just added a realistic bounce to the hammer's falling motion.

> *How do you know which ease has been applied to a Transition strip? Select the strip and the graphic shown in the Eases panel appears as the Easing button's icon on the timeline.*

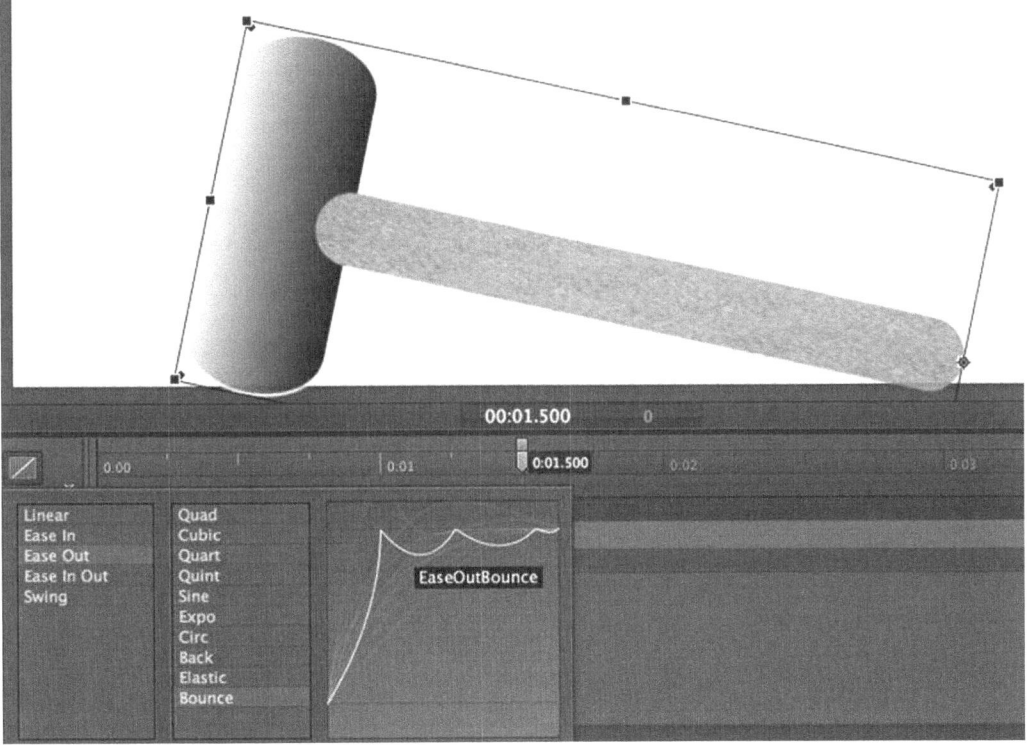

**Figure 2-27.** Eases are added to transitions, not elements.

The eases that come packaged with Edge Animate are contained in a JavaScript library, which means, unlike Flash, you get what you get because they can't be edited within Edge Animate. The other thing you need to know about easing is only one ease can be applied to a Transition strip. Having one `Ease In Effect` for the start of a strip and a different Ease Out at the end is not allowed. Finally, as we pointed out at the start of this exercise, any ease with the word "In" contained in its name is applied at the start of the transition. Any with "Out" in their name will apply the effect at the end of the transition.

> *If you are curious as to what each of the 32 eases packaged with Edge Animate actually do, point your browser to* http://hosted.zeh.com.br/mctween/animationtypes.html. *Not only is each ease explained, but there is also an animation showing what each one does. One thing to keep in mind is the eases packaged with Edge Animate are found in the* jquery.easing.1.3.js *file in the Edge Animate composition's* edge-includes *folder. Unless you know exactly what you are doing, it is strongly recommended that you don't touch or otherwise edit this file.*

## Your Turn: Animating Web Page Elements with Eases

Bouncing a hammer is a great way to learn how to use eases, but it is not a real-world application of the feature. We agree, and in this exercise we are going to let you do just that. Follow these steps to add some zing to a static design:

1.   Open the Dragon.an file located in your Exercise folder. When the file opens, as shown in Figure 2-28, you are presented with a design around the topic of dragons. It contains the usual elements: text, a main picture, and a gallery of images. The plan is simple: add some motion to catch the user's attention.

**Figure 2-28.** We start with a traditional static layout.

2. Making sure Auto-Keyframing is turned on, select the first text block "dragon myths in our culture" and drag the Pin to the half-second mark in the timeline.

3. With the Shift key held down, drag the selected text to the top of the Stage.

4. Click once on the resulting Transition strip and apply an EaseOutBack effect. If you scrub the timeline, you will see this effect gently drops the text into its final position.

5. Copy the Transition strip to the clipboard, select the next text block, and select Edit > Paste Special > Paste Transitions To Location. As shown in Figure 2-29, the transition is added to the selection at the half-second mark of the timeline and, when you play the movie, the text blocks gently drop into place.

> This is an important technique to note. Paste Special can be applied to selections on the Stage and, if you caught it, the transition is applied to the selection at the playhead's location.

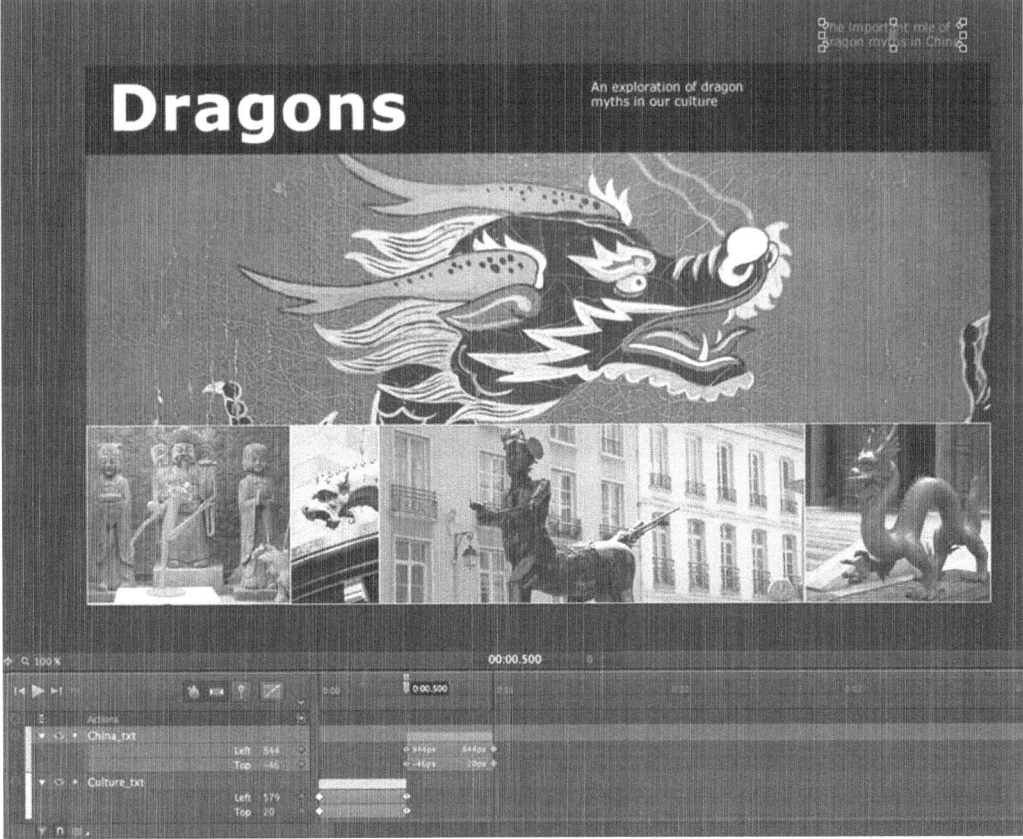

**Figure 2-29.** The text blocks are put into motion.

Having dealt with the text, let's turn our attention to the four images at the bottom. The plan here is to have them slide over one another from the left side of the Stage into their final position. Here's how:

1.  The first thing you need to be aware of is that the order of the Elements containing those four images currently has them sliding under one another. Rearrange the Elements in the Elements panel, as shown in Figure 2-30, into the following order from the top:

    *   ForbiddenCity

    *   Paris

    *   Gargoyle

    *   Dancer

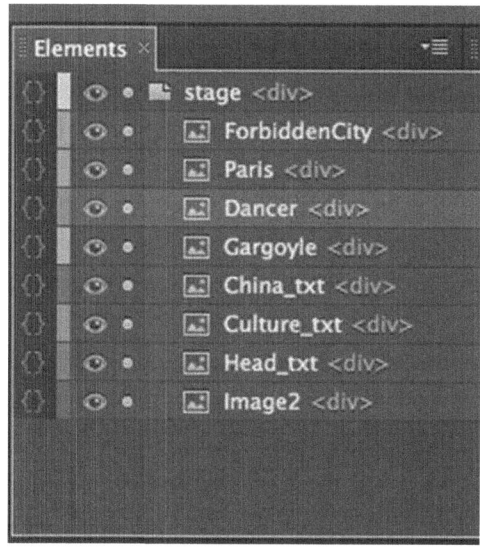

**Figure 2-30.** The order of the Elements first needs to be rearranged.

2.  Move the playhead to 00:01.500 and the Pin to 00:02.000. Click once on the Dancer image and, using the left Arrow key, move it to the left side of the stage.

> *If you find using the left Arrow key to move the dancer to be somewhat slow, speed things up and hold down both the Shift key and the Arrow key. The dancer will move in 10-pixel increments.*

3.  Apply an Ease Out > Elastic to the Transition.

4.  Leaving a quarter second between the animations and apply steps 2 and 3 to the remaining three images.

5. Rewind and play the movie. As shown in Figure 2-31, you have a nicely "stepped" timeline and a series of images that come sliding in and bounce into place.

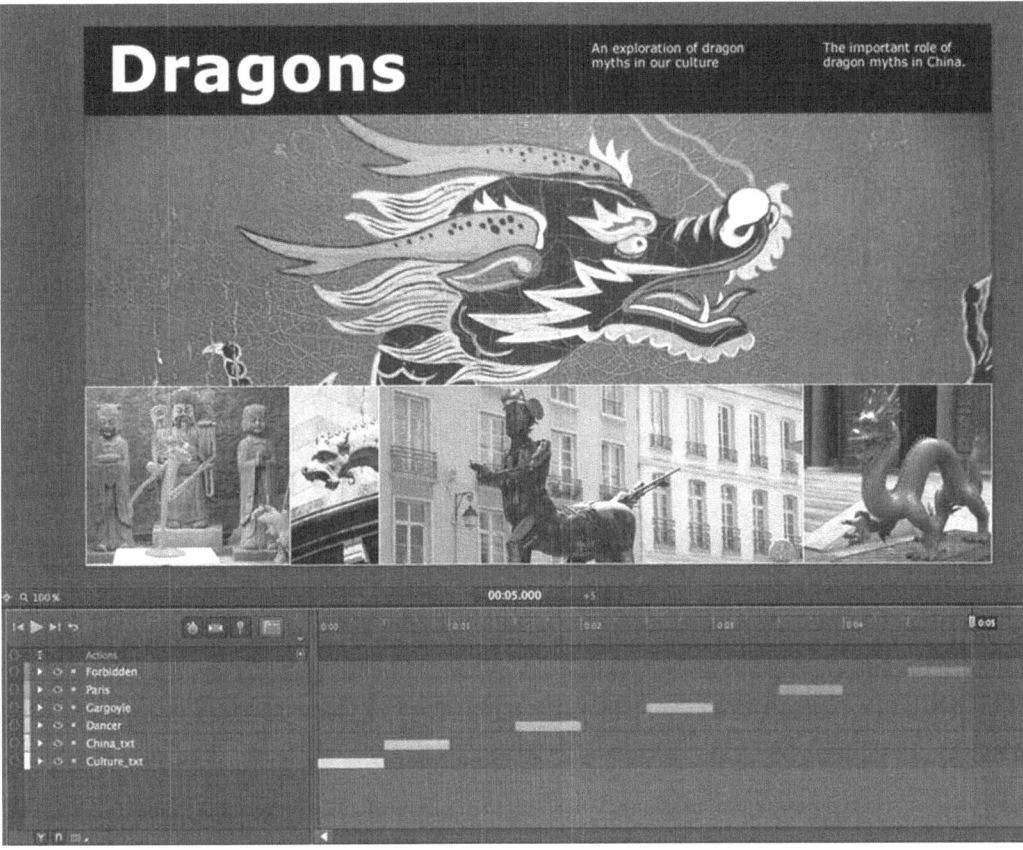

**Figure 2-31.** The final timeline.

---

## BONUS ROUND

---

That was a rather simple example. Here are some ideas you might want to try to change it up a bit:

- Extend the duration of the animations.

- Stagger the duration where some animations are longer than others.

- Overlap the transitions on the timeline.

- Try applying a different ease type. We are partial to Ease Out > Expo, which starts at 0 velocity, accelerates until the halfway point, and then decelerates to 0 velocity.

Once you've taken time to play with the animation settings, it's time to move on and look at animating an object along a path.

# Curved Paths in Edge Animate

Unlike Flash or other animation applications, there is no ability to have an object follow a curved path as it moves along the Edge Animate Stage. There is a way of creating a curved path, and what it requires of you is to be aware of a simple rule: Follow the geometry.

We know all basic motion in Edge Animate follows a straight path from "here" to "there." As the object follows that path, its X and Y positions, Left and Top on the timeline, are constantly changing. That change is the key to creating a curve. If you change both the duration and axis direction of an object as it moves from here to there, a bump or curve is created because it takes less time to travel along one axis than the other.

Here's a short exercise that demonstrates that concept:

1.  Open the Curve.an file in your Exercise folder. When it opens, you will see an icon that moves in a straight line from the top of the Stage to the bottom, the Top property on the timeline, over the space of 2 seconds.

2.  Move the playhead to the 00:00:250 point on the timeline and click the Left keyframe icon on the timeline to add a keyframe.

3.  Move the playhead to the 1-second mark and change the Left value to 20. You have just created the "bump."

4.  Move the playhead to the 00:01.750 mark on the timeline and set the Left value to 40.

5.  Rewind and play the movie. The Mailbox icon, as shown in Figure 2-32, follows a somewhat curved path.

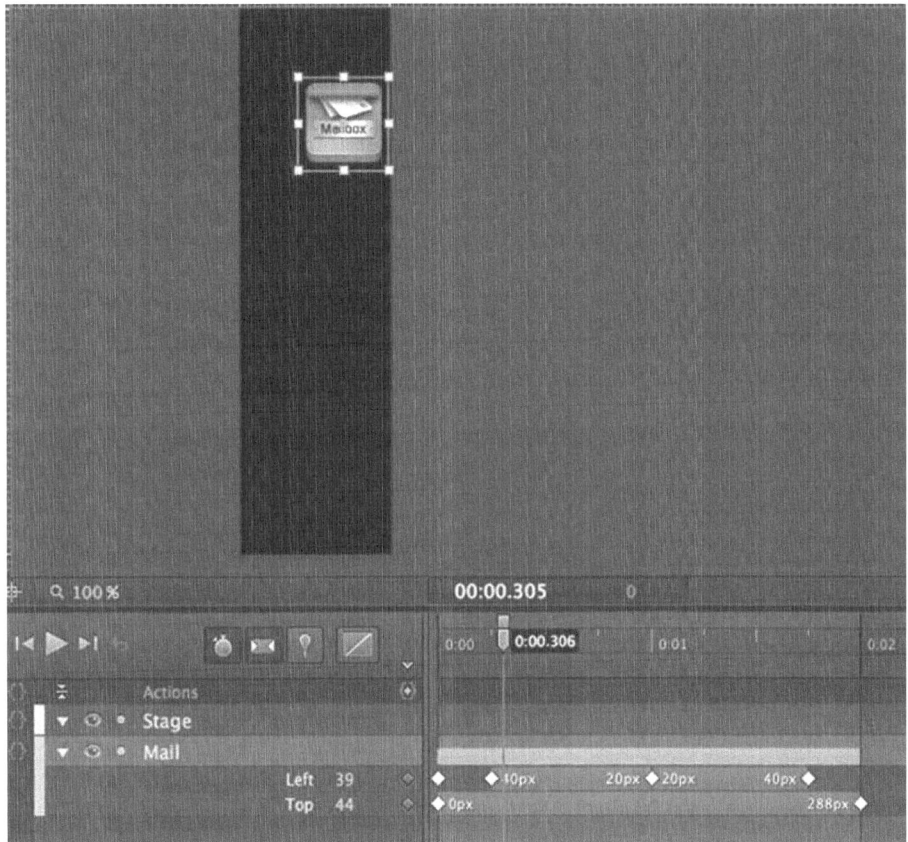

**Figure 2-32.** "Curved" paths are created by changing the duration and position on the X or Y axis of an animated object.

# Your Turn: More Anvil Dropping

We admit it. We are huge Looney Tunes fans, and our favorite character is Wile E. Coyote, who inevitably manages to fall off a cliff and land on the valley floor in a puff of dust. In this exercise, our rabbit friend from earlier in this chapter is going over the cliff, followed by the anvil, and when they both hit the valley floor, there will be the inevitable puff of dust to indicate the arrival of the anvil on the rabbit.

Although the purpose of this exercise is to have some fun, it will also use many of the techniques presented in this chapter and give you a good grounding in the process of creating animations in Edge Animate. Let's give that pesky rabbit a shove:

1.  Open the Splat.an file located in your Exercise folder. When it opens, you will see all of the assets to construct this project have been added. Your job is simple: put them to work.

2. Lock the `Valley` element.

3. Drag a copy of the `Rabbit.png` file from the `Assets` folder to the Stage and add `Scale` and `Rotation` keyframes to the selection.

4. Move the playhead to the 4-second mark of the timeline and use these values:

   - `Scale X: 3`

   - `Scale Y: 3`

   - `Rotate: 250`

5. Scrub the playhead and, as shown in Figure 2-33, the rabbit rotates as it descends to the valley floor.

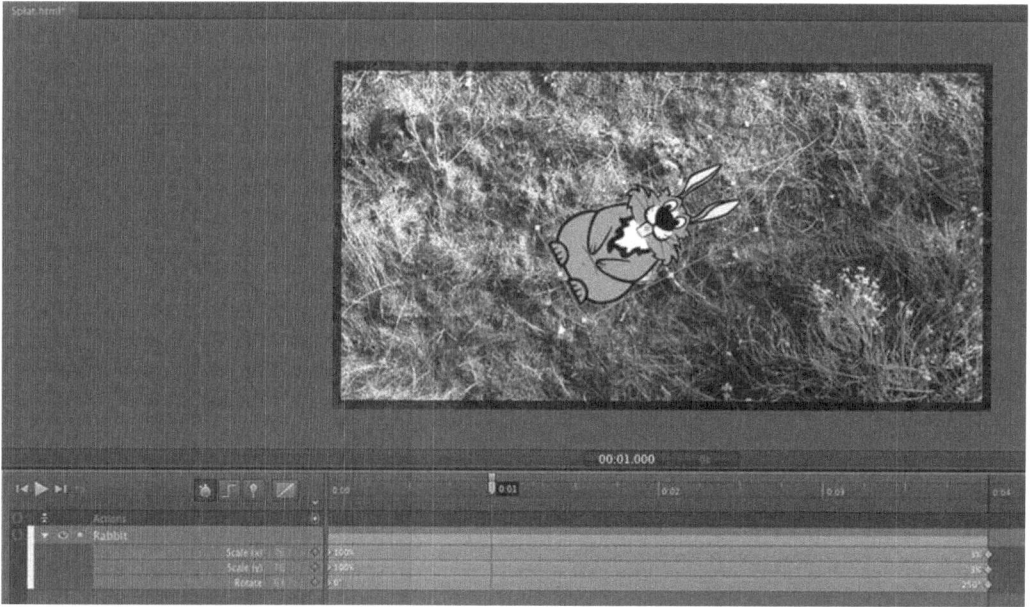

**Figure 2-33.** The rabbit is in motion.

With the Rabbit animation in place, we can turn our attention to the anvil. Let's add a bit of surprise:

6. Click once on the `Rabbit` element in the timeline to select it. If the horizontal and vertical rules aren't visible, select `View > Rulers` to turn them on. Drag guides to mark the rabbit's transformation point. We are going to drop an anvil on the rabbit and the guides let us know where the rabbit landed.

7. Drag a copy of the Anvil.png file to the Stage from the Assets folder. Place the image just off the bottom left corner of the Stage and add a Location keyframe to the anvil.

8. Move the playhead to 00:00.500 and, on the timeline, add Left and Top keyframes to the anvil. This will hold the anvil in place for one-half second.

9. Move the playhead to the 1-second mark on the timeline and add Rotate and Scale keyframes to the anvil.

10. Move the playhead to the 4-second mark and make the following Property changes to the Layer:

   • Left: 207

   • Top: 92

   • Scale X: 3

   • Scale Y: 3

   • Rotate: 140

> *The Left and Top numbers are what we used and may not match yours. Your final location for the anvil may be different depending on where your rabbit landed.*

11. Rewind and play the movie. You should, as shown in Figure 2-34, have the anvil look like it was tossed out after the rabbit starts its descent and then follow the rabbit down to the same landing point.

**Figure 2-34.** Hey! Somebody just tossed an anvil after the rabbit.

## Details Make the Difference

The base animation is in place and it is time to seal the deal. To do this, let's add a puff of dust to indicate something just happened. Here's how:

1. Drag the playhead to 00:04.000, which is the point where the anvil and rabbit animations finish.

2. Drag the Puff.png image from the Assets folder to the stage and place it over the rabbit and anvil location.

3. In the `Properties` panel, set the `Display` property, as shown in Figure 2-35, to On. You will see a hollow keyframe.

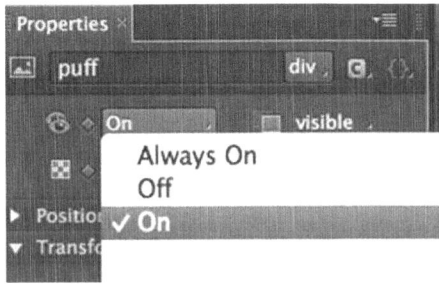

**Figure 2-35.** Use the Display property to control visibility of a div on the Stage.

If you scrub the mouse across the Display keyframe, you will see the puff turn on when the playhead passes over the keyframe. What you have done is to use the CSS3 `display:none` property to toggle the visibility of the puff element. By changing the Display property to On, you are telling Edge Animate the puff will be there, but invisible, until the playhead crosses that keyframe.

4. Add `Scale` keyframes to the Puff element at the 4-second mark and set the Scale values to 3%.

5. Move the playhead to 00:04.500 and use the following values:
    - `Scale X: 70`
    - `Scale Y: 70`

6. Add an `Opacity` keyframe to the Puff element at 00:04.500.

7. Move the playhead to 00:05.000 and use these values:
    - `Scale X: 3`
    - `Scale Y: 3`
    - `Opacity: 0`

8. Rewind and play the movie. The puff, as shown in Figure 2-36, just adds that extra bit of detail that the viewer won't be expecting.

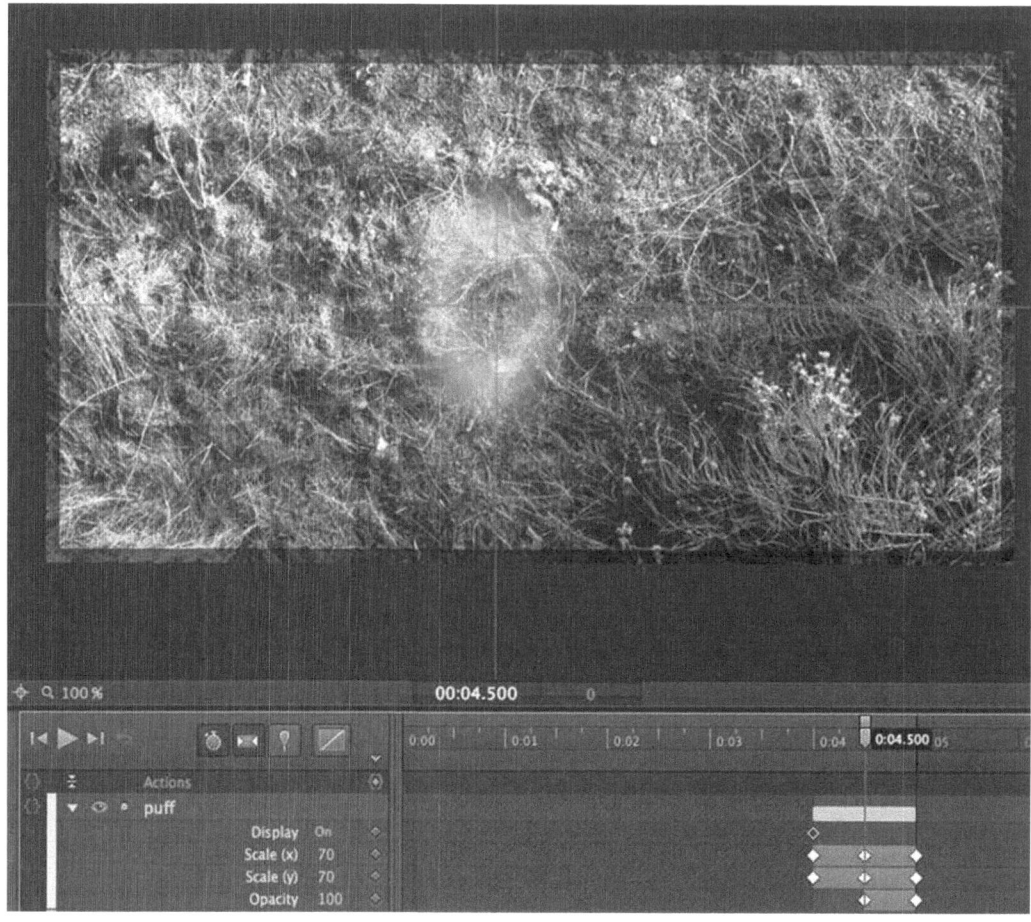

**Figure 2-36.** All that's left is a small puff of dust.

# You Have Learned

In this chapter, you have learned the following:

- How to create timeline animations in Edge Animate

- A variety of animation techniques using the various properties in Edge Animate

- The importance of keyframes and how to use them

- How to reuse transitions to give your workflow a speed boost

- The importance of easing and how to apply the Edge Animate eases

This has been a rather busy chapter, which started with falling leaves and ended by tossing an anvil over a cliff. Along the way you picked up a number of fundamental animation techniques that you will use on a regular basis as you start exploring even more complex animations in Edge Animate. If there was one unspoken rule that reverberated through this chapter it is: Pay attention to the details. The shake of a leaf before it falls . . . the puff of dust when an anvil lands on a rabbit . . . an object that bounces and comes to rest. These are the details that separate okay animations from really great animations.

Is there more you can do with animation beyond these fundamentals? Glad you asked. That is the subject of the next chapter.

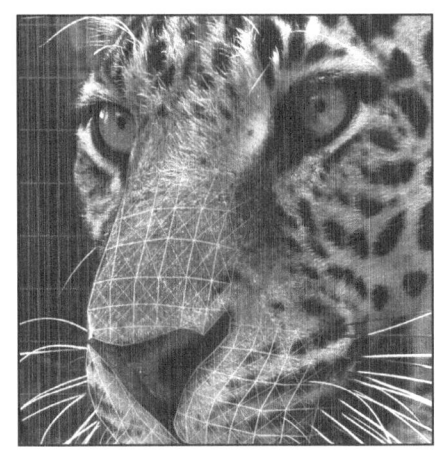

# Chapter 3

# Creating Timeline Animations: Part 2

In the previous chapter, we covered the fundamentals of timeline animation in Adobe Edge Animate. We say "fundamentals" because these are the animation starting points for anyone new to Adobe Edge Animate. Naturally there are other, more efficient, ways of doing things, and the choice of which to use—the fundamentals or what we are about to talk about—is up to you.

Here is what we will cover in this chapter:

- Shape tweens

- Shadows and gradients

- Nesting

- Symbols

- Using PNG sequences to create animation

If you haven't already downloaded the chapter files, they can be found at http://www.apress.com/9781430243502. In this chapter, we will be using these files:

- Gondola.an

- Planets.an

- BasicSymbol.an

- Nesting.an

- Assets > PNGSequence

# Shape Tweens

One of the more common, eye-catching animation techniques is a shape change. It could be something as simple as a rectangle whose corners round off or a circle that changes into a teardrop shape. Used judiciously, shape changes are a great way of drawing a viewer's attention to a particular spot in an Edge Animate composition.

In Edge Animate, shape changes are accomplished using the drawing tools. At the top of the toolbar are three tools: the Rectangle tool, the Rounded Rectangle tool, and the Ellipse tool. They do exactly what their names imply, and you can create a couple of interesting effects by changing their shapes using a tween. Follow these steps to create a simple shape tween:

1. Create a new Edge Animate document and set the Stage color to black. Select the `Rectangle tool` and draw a rectangle on the Stage. When you release the mouse, the rectangle's properties light up on the `Properties` panel.

2. With the Rectangle selected, use these settings, as shown in Figure 3-1, in the `Properties` panel:

   - **Click the `Link` icon in the `Width` and `Height` areas. This allows you to create individual values.**

   - **`Width`: 100**

   - **`Height`: 50**

   - **`Background color`: #FF0000**

   - **`Border`: None**

With the shape created, the plan is to have it extend outward, change color, and have the corners on the right edge round off as the shape grows.

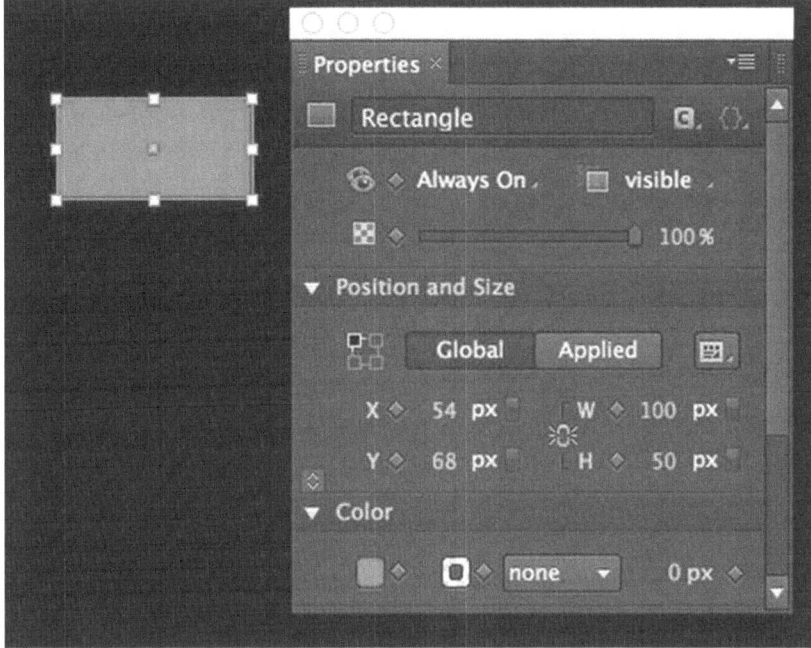

**Figure 3-1.** We start with a red rectangle.

3.   With the playhead at 00:00.000, add keyframes for the properties you just set.

One of the really interesting features of CSS3 is the ability to create rounded corners on boxes. This capability has been "baked into" Edge Animate. Let's have this box morph.

4.   As shown in Figure 3-2, add a Corner Radius keyframe at 00:00.000.

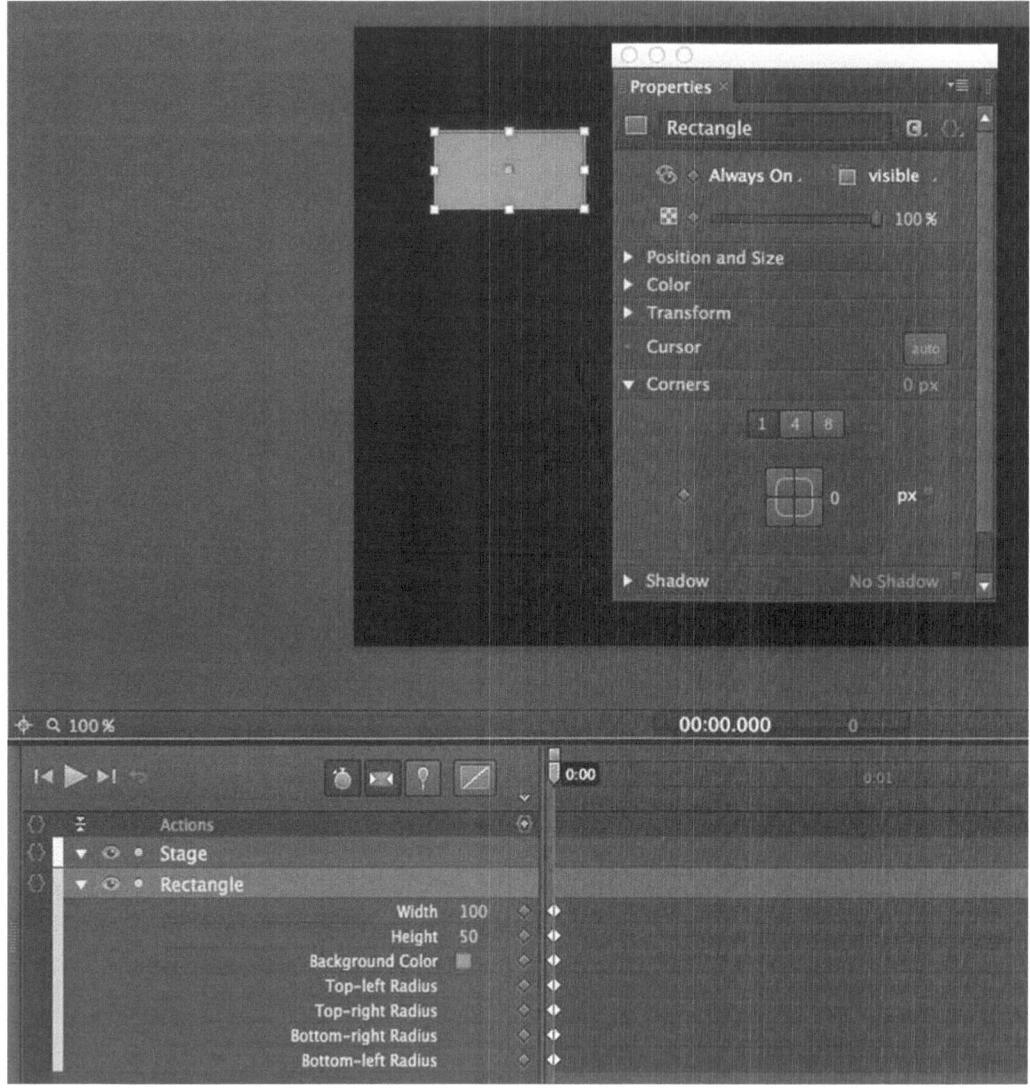

**Figure 3-2.** Rounded corners use the Corner Radius property in Edge Animate.

This area of the Properties panel, on the surface, looks confusing but once you understand its bits and pieces, it becomes rather simple to understand.

The numbers along the top—1, 4, and 8—refer to the number of control points available at the corners of the rectangle. Although the official CSS3 term for these numbers is border-radius, Adobe calls this the *Corner Radius*. If you select 1, only one number will appear and, if you scrub across that number, all four corners will round off equally. This is great for turning a rectangle into a circle. If you select 4, you will see four numbers appear, meaning each corner can have an independent radius value. Select 8 and each corner can have two independent values applied to it, which lets you create some rather interesting shapes.

> *At the bottom of the area is a small pop-down that lets you set the units in pixels (px) or percentages (%). If your work is destined for a Responsive Design layout, choose the percentage option.*

For this exercise we are only concerned with absolute values and the right edge of the rectangle. We want it to round off. Here's how:

5.  Making sure Auto-Keyframes are turned on, move the playhead to the 2-second mark of the timeline, and click the 4 in the `Corner Radius` area of the `Properties` panel.

> *Corner Radius values are one of the very few property values that can't be changed directly on the timeline. You need to use the Properties panel.*

6.  Change the two right values—Top Right and Bottom Right—to 20. The right edge of the rectangle becomes rounded.

7.  Change the `width` value in the timeline to 300.

8.  If you rewind and play the movie, you will see the rectangle grow across the Stage and, in the process, the right edge starts becoming distinctly rounded.

> *You don't have to "do it by the numbers" to change the Corner Radius. If you select the shape on the Stage and click the Transform tool, the object will sprout two sets of handles: squares to control the shape and diamonds to control the Corner Radius property. The diamond-shaped handle, as shown in Figure 3-3, can be dragged in or out to change the border radius of an object and a dotted line indicating the amount of the change also appears as you drag the handle. Just be aware that dragging one handle changes all of them. You can fix that by changing the values to 4 or 8 in the Corners area of the Properties panel.*

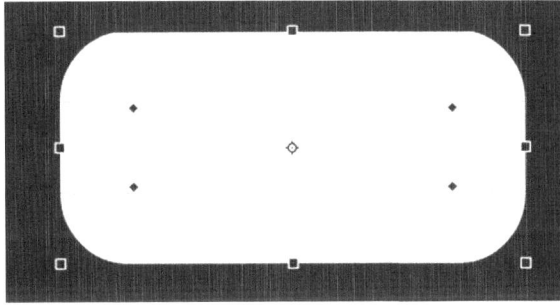

**Figure 3-3.** You can drag a black diamond handle to change the radius.

# Shadows and Gradients

An integral part of the CSS3 specifications is the box-shadow property. If you were to write it out, the syntax would be something along these lines:

```
div#aBox
{
background-color:yellow;
width:200px;
height:100px;
box-shadow:50px 50px 20px black;
}
```

Edge Animate, being a visual editor, actually writes this code for you, which allows you to concentrate more on design than valid code. This means you can use the Rectangle and Rounded Rectangle tools to create some interesting shapes and then slide a drop shadow under the shape for extra emphasis. Here's how:

1. Open a new document, select the Rectangle tool, and deselect the width and height link in the Properties panel. This allows you to customize the dimensions of the shape.

2. Set the width value to 200 and height value to 100. Set the fill color to yellow—#FFFF00—and set the stroke to None. We have now created the box, without the shadow, from the above code block. Let's add the shadow.

The box-shadow properties are found in the Shadow area of the Properties panel. The Shadow feature is turned off by default. Click the switch and, as shown in Figure 3-4, the properties light up. They are:

- *Drop Shadow/Inset Shadow*: Click either one to set the placement of the shadow.

- *Color*: Click this chip and the color picker opens. The color picker contains two color models: RGBA and Hexadecimal. The RGBA model allows you set the Red, Green, Blue, and Alpha or transparency values of a color. Hexadecimal allows you to apply web colors to an object. One really neat feature is the ability to apply a color using either model and then to add transparency to the object.

- *Horizontal and vertical offset*: Change the X and Y values here to determine the location of the shadow.

- *Blur radius*: The value sets the distance of the blur applied to the shadow.

- *Spread*: The value used here determines the size of the shadow.

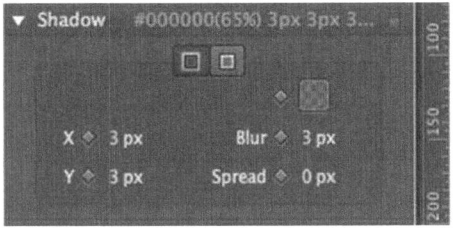 

**Figure 3-4.** The Shadow properties are switched on in the Properties panel.

3. Use the following box-shadow values:

   • Color: Black (#000000)

   • Vertical and Horizontal Offset: 50

   • Blur Radius: 20

4. Press the Return/Enter key and the Shadow, as shown in Figure 3-5, appears under the yellow box.

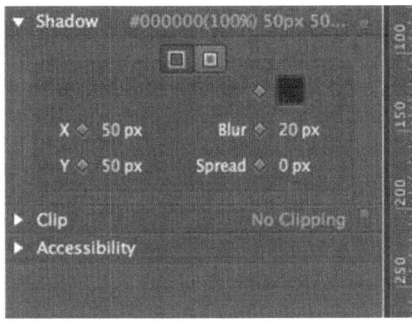 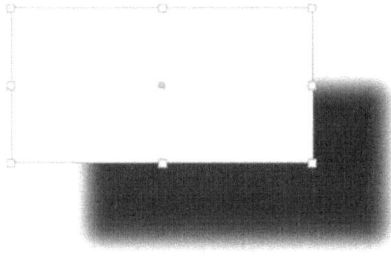

**Figure 3-5.** Applying a drop shadow to an element on the Edge Animate Stage.

This works well for a rectangle, what about one that is a nontraditional shape?

5. Select the box on the Stage and, in the Corner Radius area, use these values:

   • Number: 4

   • Upper Right: 40

   • Bottom Left: 40

The box and the shadow sport rounded corners.

6. Change the Shadow parameters to:

- Horizontal Offset: 10

- Vertical Offset: 15

As shown in Figure 3-6, the shadow is tucked in closer to the shape and reflects the shape change.

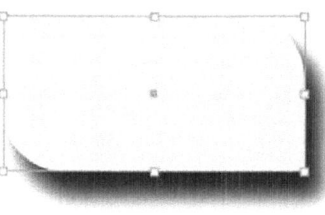

**Figure 3-6.** Shadows change to reflect the Box Radii properties.

You are probably thinking, "Cool, I can slip drop shadows under imported artwork." No you can't. This CSS3 property is applied to the element, not the contents of the element. If, for example, you import an SVG graphic into Edge Animate and apply a drop shadow to the graphic, the Shadow is applied to the shape of the element not the graphic in the element. Let's take a quick look at what we are talking about:

1. Open the Gondola.an file in the Exercise folder. When it opens you will see the drawing of a Cable Car on the Stage. Note that the windows of the cable car are transparent and you can see the Stage color through them.

2. Click once on the element and apply these drop-shadow parameters:

    - Color: Black

    - Horizontal Offset: 10

    - Vertical Offset: 10

    - Blur Radius: 20

    - Spread: 5

3. Press the Return/Enter key and you will see, as shown in Figure 3-7, the shadow has been applied to the outside edges of the element.

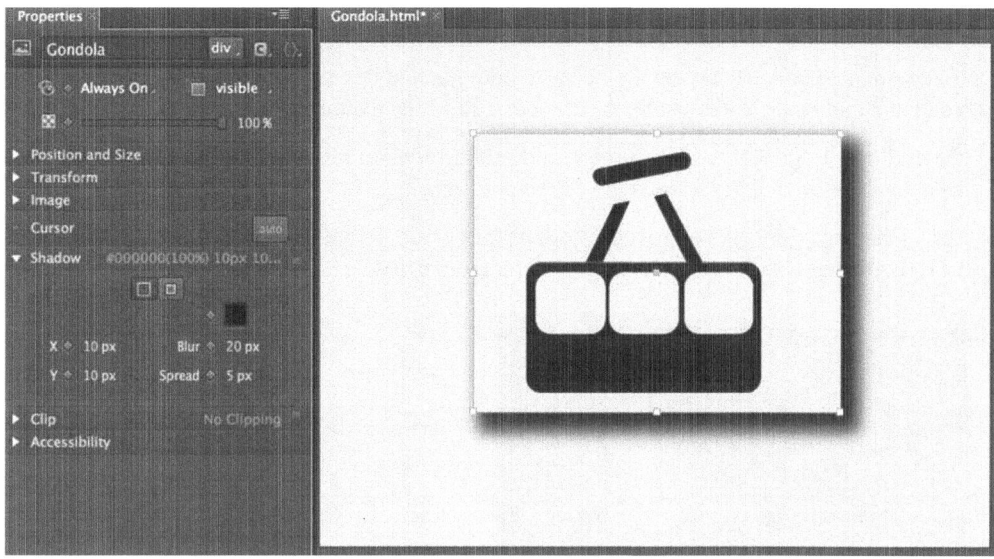

**Figure 3-7.** Drop shadows are added to the element, not the contents.

The same thing applies if you select the Inset choice. The shadow, as shown in Figure 3-8, is applied to the inside edges of the element.

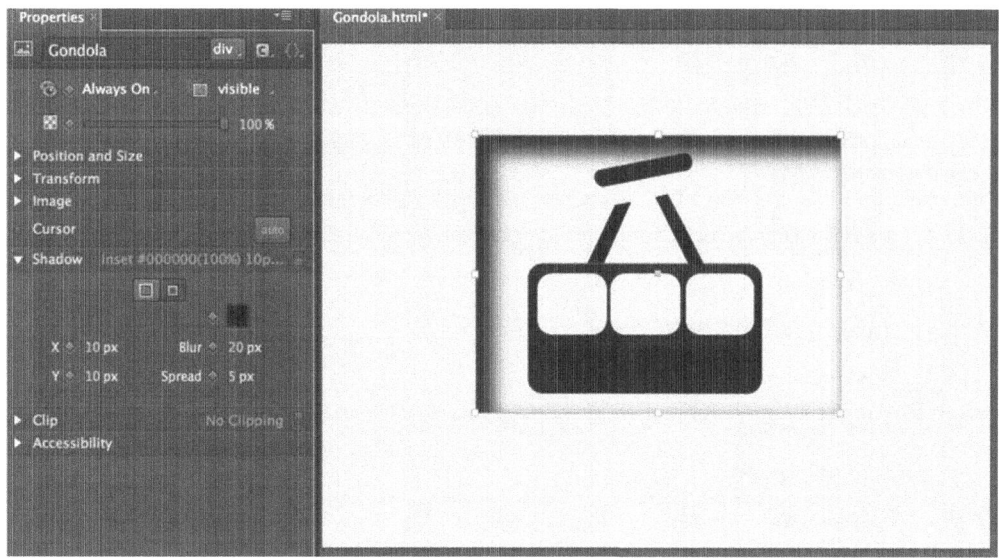

**Figure 3-8.** Selecting Inset simply moves the shadow to the inside edges of the element.

# Using Drop Shadow Parameters to Create Gradients

Although Edge Animate doesn't contain the ability to add gradient fills to your elements, Figure 3-8 dropped a pretty broad hint that this is somewhat possible. Let's do a little exploring:

1. Open a new Edge Animate document and add a rounded rectangle to the Stage with width and height values of 150. We'll leave the Fill color to you.

2. Select the shape and, in the Corner Radius properties, select the 4 and change the corner values to 100. As shown in Figure 3-9, you have created a circle.

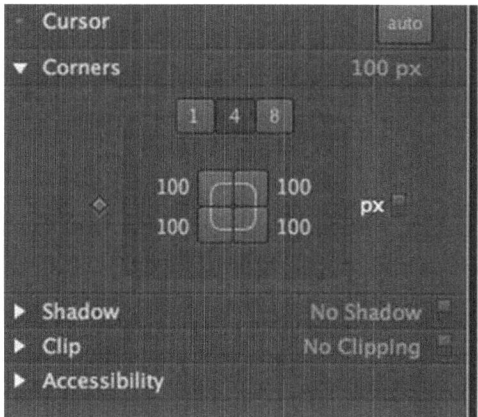 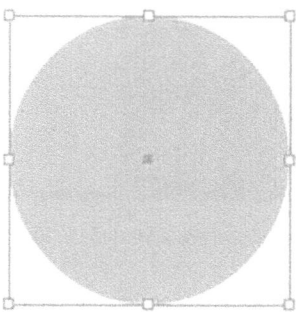

**Figure 3-9.** We start with a circle.

> Yes, we could have used the Circle tool or we know we could have left the **Corner Radius** at 1 and just applied the value of 100. Think of it as either being another way of creating a circle or us showing off.

3. With the ball still selected, change the drop-shadow parameters to:

   - Type: Inset

   - Color: Blue (#0000FF)

   - Horizontal and Vertical Offset: 25

   - Inset: Selected

   - Blur Radius: 60

   - Spread: 30

Notice how you now have a gradient, as shown in Figure 3-10, in place of the solid fill, and this gradient looks like a radial gradient. Not only that, but you can "switch up" the look of the object by changing the Offset, Blur, and Spread properties.

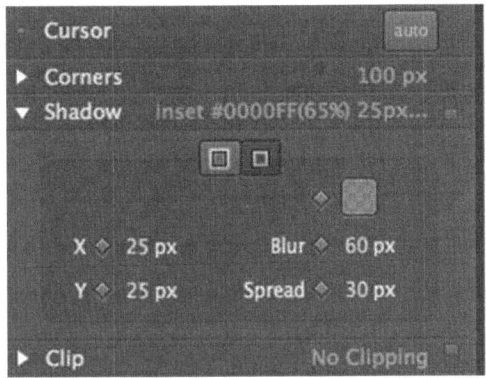 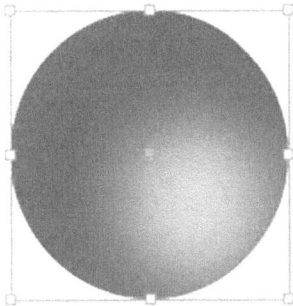

**Figure 3-10.** Using the drop-shadow parameters to create a gradient.

The interesting aspect of this exercise is that you can actually control the gradient colors. The highlight color is the ball's fill color, while the second gradient color is the shadow color.

You can also put all of these properties into motion. Here's how:

1.  Open a new document and, using the Circle tool, create a circle that is 300 by 300 pixels. Leave the Corner Radius at 1 but set the value to 400. You have created a circle.

2.  With the circle selected, fill it with black, add a Background Color keyframe, and use these drop-shadow values:

    - **Type:** Inset

    - Color: White (#FFFFFF)

    - Horizontal Offset: 11

    - Vertical Offset: 57

    - Blur Radius: 98

    - Spread: 15

3.  Move the playhead to the 1-second mark and apply these values to the drop shadow:

    - Color: Blue (#0000FF)

    - Vertical Offset: −28

    - Blur Radius: 180

- Spread: 78

As you may have noticed, the drop shadow is directly tied to the circle. The changed drop-shadow properties now appear on the timeline with their corresponding keyframes. If you scrub back to the 0 point, you will see that the new drop-shadow values have been applied. We aren't sure why you can't add drop-shadow keyframes, but there is a quick fix:

4.  Move the playhead back to the 0 point and use the drop-shadow properties from Step 2. Keyframes appear, and if you scrub, the shadow moves upward.

5.  Move the playhead to the 2-second mark and use the fill and drop-shadow values from Step 3. Scrub the timeline and, as shown in Figure 3-11, the shadow moves up and down.

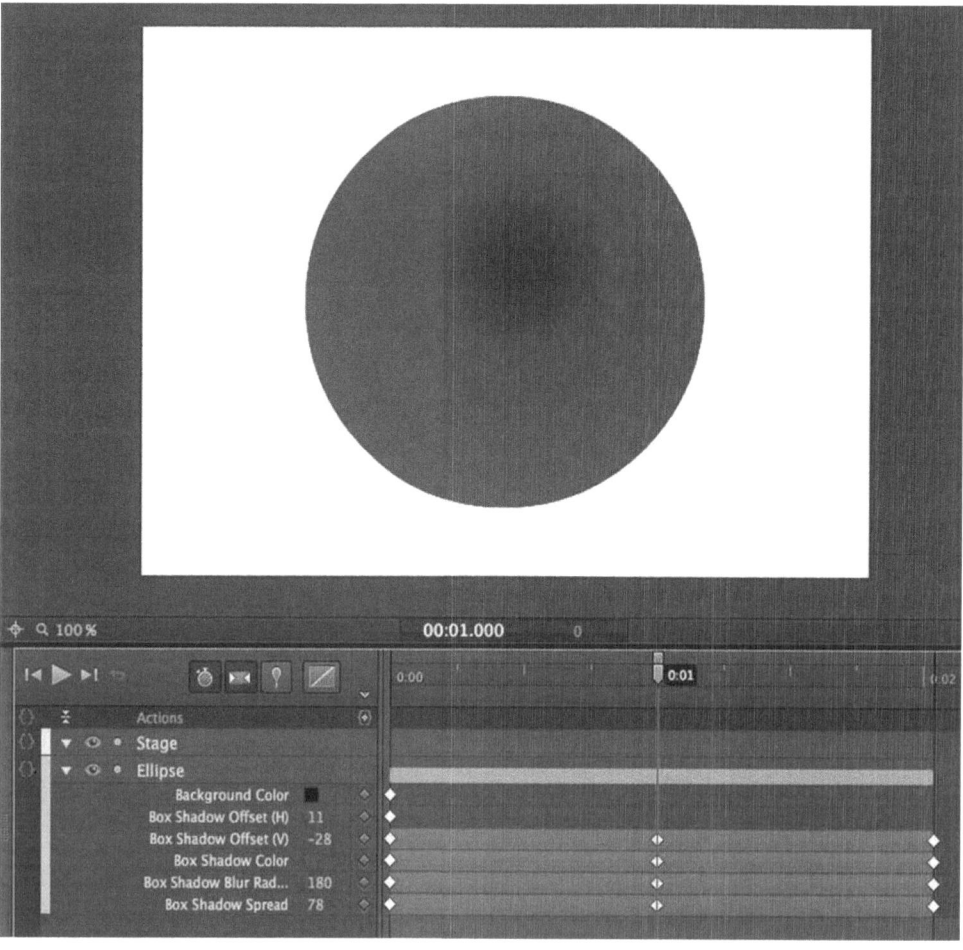

**Figure 3-11.** Shadow properties can be tweened.

# Nesting Elements

Earlier you used a rectangle with a rounded corner to create a fly-out menu item. Although the technique is pretty cool, there is another use for rectangles that is not immediately obvious. Rectangles can have animation properties applied to them, and those properties can be applied to objects on the Stage by using the rectangle's properties as the parent of the object. This is accomplished through a technique known as *nesting* elements.

In this exercise, you are going to have a planet orbit around another planet and, at the same time, you are going to a have a moon orbit around the second planet. Let's get started:

1.  Open the Planets.an file located in your Exercise folder. When it opens, as seen in Figure 3-12, you will see two planets and a moon.

**Figure 3-12.** Two planets and a moon are ready to be put in motion.

2.  Select the Rectangle tool and draw a rectangle over the orange planet. Set both the Background and Stroke color for the rectangle to transparent.

3.  With the rectangle still selected, make sure the playhead is at 00:00.000 and add a Rotation keyframe.

4.  Move the playhead to the 3-second mark on the timeline and set the Rotation value for the rectangle to 360. If you scrub the playhead, the rectangle will rotate.

Obviously we want the orange planet, not the box, to rotate. By nesting the orange planet inside the rectangle and making the rectangle the "parent" of the orange planet, the planet will inherit the rectangle's rotation properties. Here's how to accomplish this task:

5.  The orange planet is named Jupiter in the Elements panel. Drag the Jupiter element on top of the Rectangle element. When you release the mouse, as shown in Figure 3-13, the Jupiter element is under the Rectangle element and it is indented. That tells you the object is now a child of the Rectangle. If you scrub the timeline, the planet will now rotate.

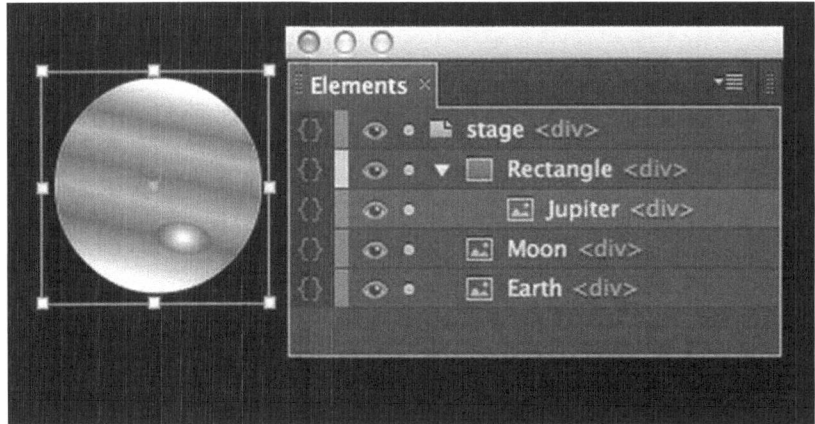

**Figure 3-13.** Jupiter is now a child of the Rectangle element and will inherit the rectangle's motion.

Now that you understand how to create parent–child relationships, let's build on that knowledge. The plan is to have the Earth element orbit the Jupiter element. While that is occurring, the Moon element is going to orbit the Earth element. This is where the concept of nesting elements comes into play.

When you created the first relationship between the Rectangle and Jupiter you, for all intents and purposes, placed the Jupiter element inside the Rectangle element. What you did was "nest" one element inside another. We are going to create the same relationships with the Earth and the Moon elements but you are going to nest the Moon element inside the Earth element. You can infer from this that it is possible to nest elements inside nested elements. To learn how this is done, follow these steps:

6.  Select the Rectangle tool and draw another rectangle, slightly bigger than the planet, over the Earth element. Name this element EarthRect.

7.  Turn off the visibility of the Earth element in the Elements panel. We only want to work with the EarthRect element, not the Earth.

8.  With the Rectangle selected, move *its* Origin Point to the middle of Jupiter. Remember, all transitions are tied to the object's Origin Point. By moving the Origin to the center of Jupiter, the box will orbit the planet.

9. Move the playhead to 00:00.000 and apply a Rotation keyframe to the EarthRect element. Move the playhead to the 3-second mark and set the Rotation value to −360 to have EarthRect rotate in a counterclockwise direction around Jupiter.

10. Turn on the visibility of the Earth element and make EarthRect its parent. Scrub the timeline and Earth now orbits Jupiter. Let's turn our attention to the Moon element.

11. Repeat steps 6 through 9 for the Moon element, only this time name the element MoonRect and change the Rotation value to 720.

12. If you press the Spacebar to preview the animation, something is not quite right. The moon seems to have its own orbit. Drag the MoonRect element on top of the EarthRect **element** in the Elements panel to nest the Moon inside the Earth element, as shown in Figure 3-14.

13. Rewind and play the movie.

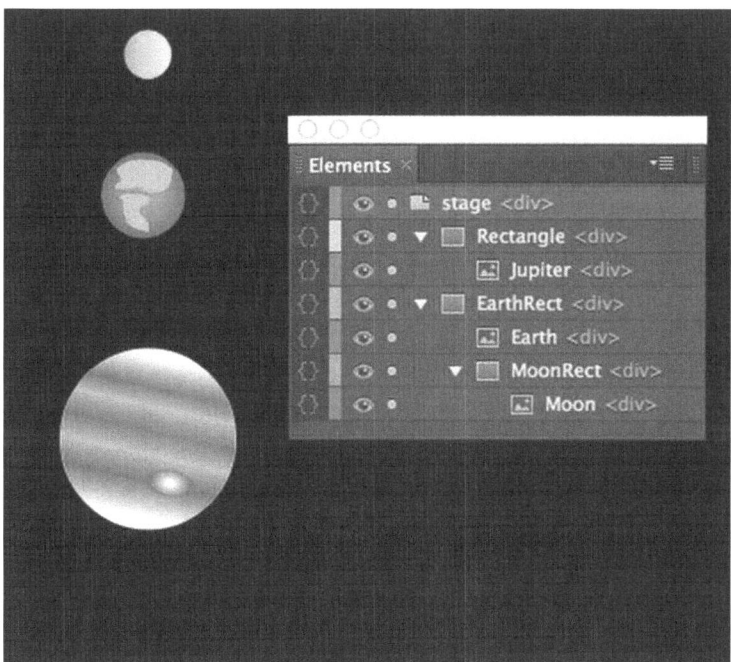

**Figure 3-14.** The Moon element is "nested" inside the Earth element.

> *There is another way of creating nested elements. Right-click on an element and select* **Group Elements in DIV.** *A new element named* **Group** *will appear and you will notice the original element is nested in the Group. Apply transitions to the Group Div and everything in the group will be affected. You can also change the group element's name to something more meaningful.*

# Symbols in Edge Animate

Symbols in Edge Animate are one of the most powerful features of the application. This is because they allow you to create reusable content. You only need one copy of a symbol. Once it is on the Edge Animate Stage, you can then transform it or otherwise manipulate it without affecting the original content sitting in the Library.

Symbols will rapidly become a critical component of your Edge Animate workflow. This will occur when you come to the realization that an animation or other piece of content will be used several times throughout the project. In fact, as you will discover, symbols in Edge Animate can be used in multiple Edge Animate projects and, if you work in a team-based production environment, they can even be shared among the members of the team.

Reduced to its basics, an Edge Animate symbol is nothing more than a piece of content or animation, with an independent timeline, used on the main timeline. When a symbol is created, it is placed in the `Symbols` folder of the `Library` and a copy of that symbol on the Stage at any point in the timeline is said to be an *instance* of the symbol.

> *Symbols not only have independent timelines, but any code inside a symbol will execute independent of the main timeline as well.*

Let's create a symbol to start understanding how these things work. Here's how:

1.  Open the `BasicSymbol.an` file located in your `Exercise` folder. When it opens, you will see that the `background.jpg` image is sitting in the `Assets` folder and that image is contained in an element named `Clouds`. Click once on the image to select it.

> *If you need to create <alt> tags for your images, you need to change the selection's HTML tag from **div** to **img** in the Tag Selector found in the Properties panel. When you make the change, the Alt text input area of the Image section, shown in Figure 3-15, in the Image area of the property panel lights up.*

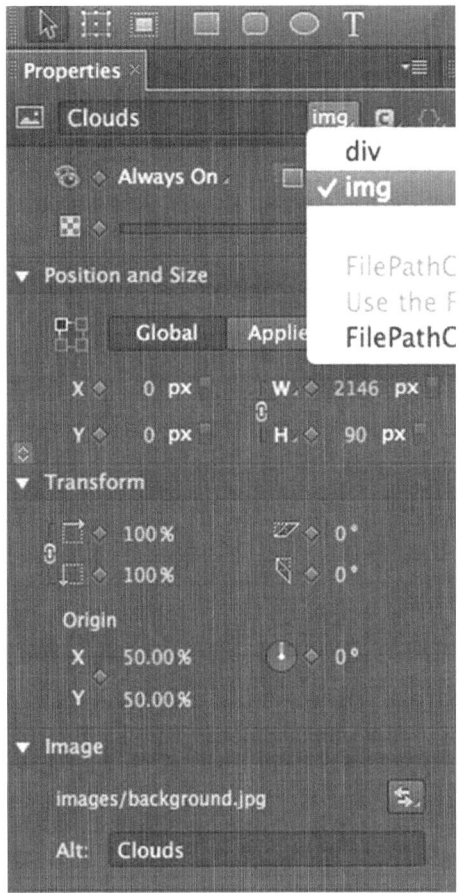

**Figure 3-15.** Alt text is added to images by changing the tag from div to img in the Tag Selector pop-down.

2.  With the image selected on the Stage, select as shown in Figure 3-16, Modify > Convert to Symbol. This opens the Create Symbol dialog box.

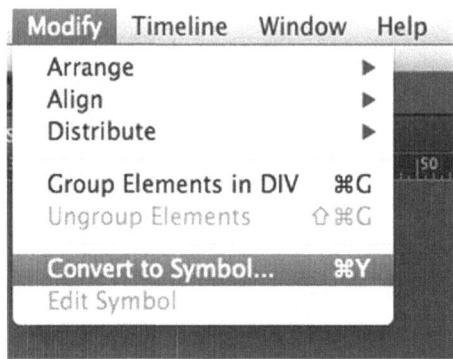

**Figure 3-16.** Symbols can be created using the Modify menu.

> *There are a couple of other methods you can use to create a symbol. Select the Element on the Stage and press **Ctrl+Y** (PC) **or Command+Y** (Mac) or simply right-click (PC) or Control-click (Mac) on the Element and **Choose Convert to Symbol** from the Context menu that opens.*

3.   In the Create Symbol dialog box, shown in Figure 3-17, name the symbol Clouds_bkgrnd, select Autoplay timeline, and click OK. The dialog box closes and the symbol appears in the Symbols area of the Library.

**Figure 3-17.** The Create Symbol dialog box.

> *Unlike Flash, there is only one type of symbol, and its Flash equivalent is a movie clip. In fact, when a Symbol is created, it has the same icon as the common Flash movie clip in the Edge Animate Library. Also, when you create symbols, get into the habit of giving them a name that describes what they do.*

4. Select the new symbol on the Stage and delete it. Notice how the instance was removed but the symbol itself is still in the Symbols folder in the Library.

5. Select the symbol in the Library and drag it to the Stage. As you drag the instance onto the Stage, you should see an angle bracket and the numbers you see are the X and Y coordinates for the symbol on the Stage.

6. When the coordinates are 0,0, release the mouse and the symbol drops into position.

What you have just learned are the absolute fundamentals of creating symbols and placing them on the Stage. Now that you have those skills mastered, let's dig a bit deeper into symbols and learn how to edit them.

## Editing Symbols

Edge Animate symbols can be thought of as movies-within-movies. They run independent of the main timeline and can contain code that determines how they react to events on the main timeline or how they play in their own timeline. Symbols can even be placed inside other symbols, which is where the real power of symbols becomes evident.

The current symbol on the timeline really doesn't do much. Let's fix that and put the clouds in motion. Follow these steps to accomplish this task:

1. Double click the symbol on the Stage. Three things will happen:

   • The pasteboard area of the Stage darkens.

   • If you look at the upper left corner of the Stage panel, you will see, as shown in Figure 3-18, a breadcrumb trail telling you that you are inside the Clouds-bkgrnd symbol, which is on the Stage.

   • The timeline changes, and you will see that the element on the Stage is no longer the symbol but the Clouds element.

Each of these changes is a visual clue that you have entered "Edit In Place" mode in Edge Animate. When you double-click a symbol, everything but the symbol on the Stage darkens.

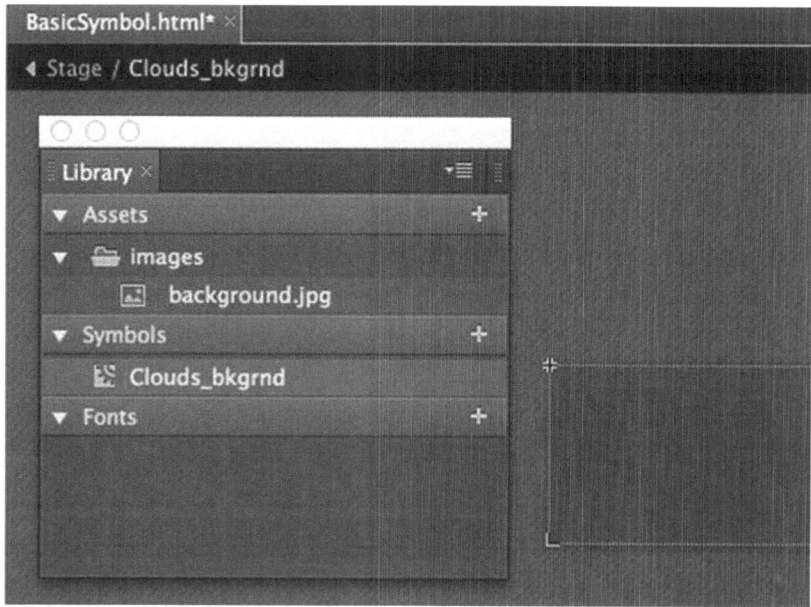

**Figure 3-18.** Symbols are edited using Edit In Place mode.

2. Click once on the Cloud element and turn on the Pin.

3. Drag the playhead to the 2-second mark on the timeline and move the cloud image to the left until its right edge is aligned with the right edge of the Stage.

4. Turn off the Pin, rewind the movie, and press the Spacebar. The clouds, as shown in Figure 3-19, move across the Stage between the keyframes on the timeline.

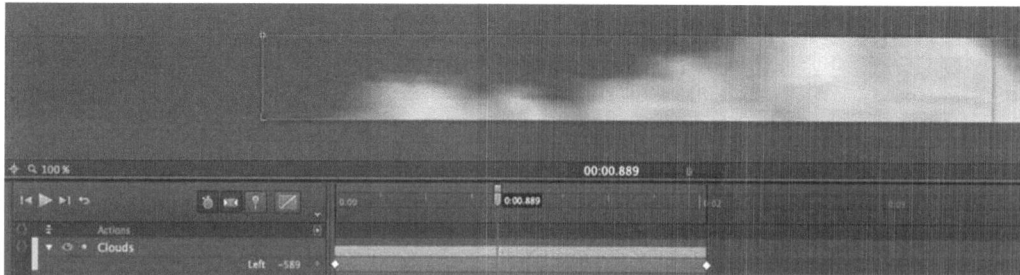

**Figure 3-19.** Adding motion inside a symbol.

5. Click the Stage link in the breadcrumb trail to exit Edit In Place mode and return to the main timeline.

6.  When you arrive back at the main timeline, twirl down the symbol. You will notice that the symbol, as shown in Figure 3-20, has sprouted chevrons that march across the timeline and end at the same time, 2 seconds, as the animation in the symbol. Those chevrons are a visual clue there is an animated symbol on the Stage and the symbol's duration.

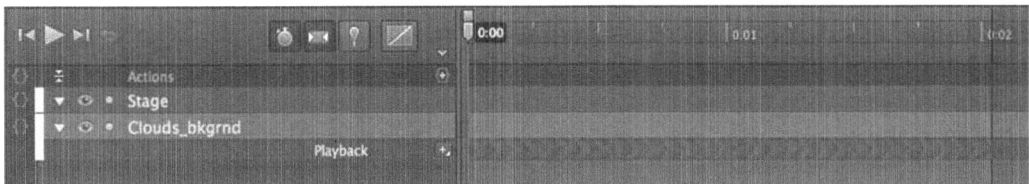

**Figure 3-20.** The chevrons on the timeline are a visual clue of a symbol's duration.

7.  If you twirl up the Element on the timeline, you no longer have a clue that you are looking at a symbol. Change the element name in the `Elements` panel to `Clouds_sym`.

8.  There actually is one last visual clue that the selected element on the timeline is indeed a symbol. If you take a look at the top of the `Properties` panel, the familiar symbol icon, as shown in Figure 3-21, is visible. At the bottom of that area you will also see `Symbol: Clouds_bkgrnd`. This tells you that even though you can change the element name, Animate will show you the name of the original symbol in the Library.

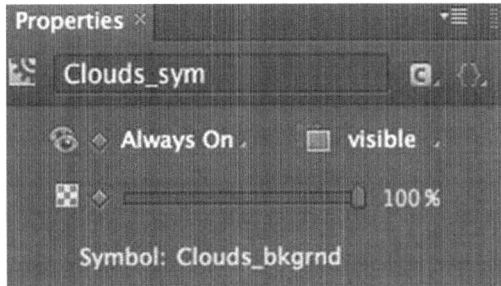

**Figure 3-21.** Select an element on the main timeline and the Properties panel will tell you if the selection is a symbol and which symbol it is.

You can also modify symbols right in the Library. Here's how:

9.  Right-click (Control-click on a Mac) on the `Clouds_bkgrnd` symbol in the Library. This will open the Context menu shown in Figure 3-22. Your options are:

    •   *Edit*: Select this and you move into Edit In Place mode for the symbol.

    •   *Delete*: Deletes the symbol from the Library.

    •   *Rename*: Use this if you want to rename a symbol.

- *Duplicate*: Select this option to create a duplicate of the symbol in the Library, not on the timeline.

- *Export*: Selecting this option allows you to share a symbol to multiple Edge Animate projects or with other members of the team.

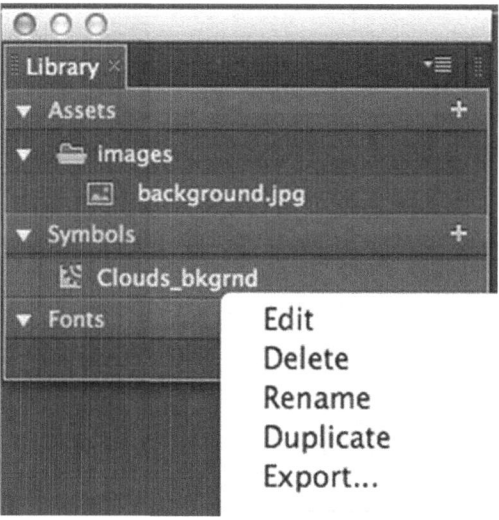

**Figure 3-22.** The Edge Animate symbol options from the Context menu.

## Exporting and Importing Symbols

Unlike its Flash cousin, Edge Animate does not include the ability to create a Shared Library. Instead, you can export a symbol out of Edge Animate as its own document and use it in other projects or share it with your team. Follow these steps to export an Edge Animate symbol:

1. Select the Clouds_bkgrnd symbol in the Library and open the Context menu. Select Export . . .

2. When the Export Symbols to File dialog box, shown in Figure 3-23, opens, navigate to the folder where you would like to save the file. We chose the Complete folder in this lesson's Exercise folder.

3. Deselect the Hide extension check box, name the file ExportClouds, and click the Save button.

> When you deselected the **Hide extension** check box an extension—**ANSYM**—was added to the file name. This is a contraction for Animate Symbol and is the extension used for all exported symbols.

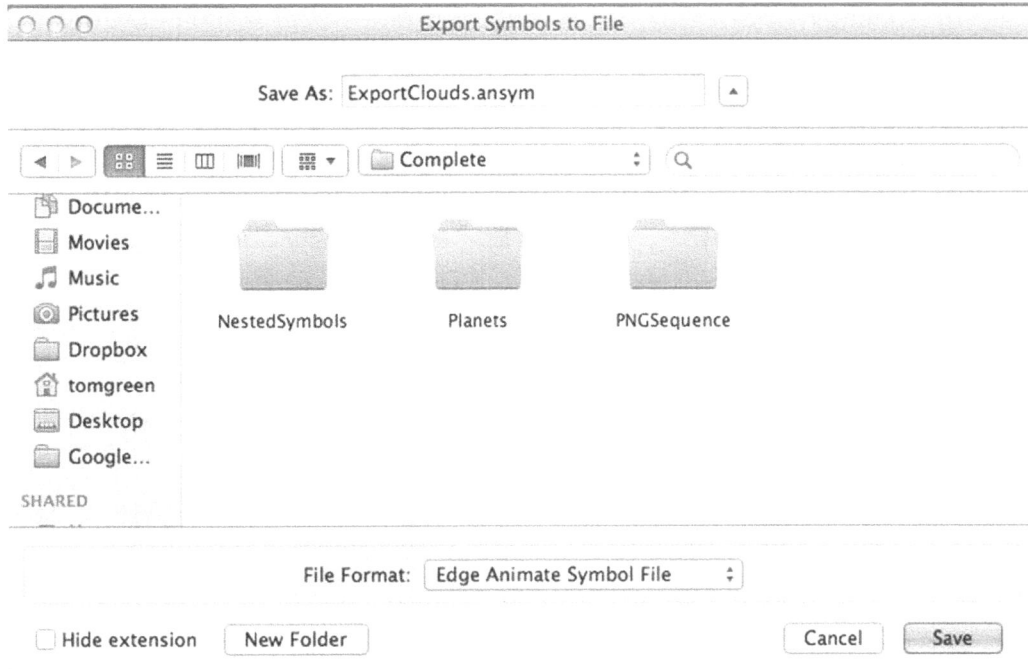

**Figure 3-23.** Exported Edge Animate symbols all use the ANSYM extension.

To add the ANSYM file extension to an Edge Animate project, what you don't do is select File > Import. Instead:

4.  Click once on the Add Symbol button (the + sign) in the Symbols area of the Library. As shown in Figure 3-24, when the dialog box opens, click once on Import Symbols.

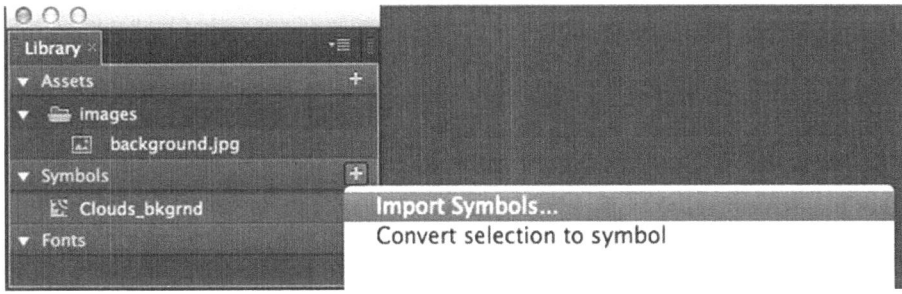

**Figure 3-24.** Symbols are imported into Edge Animate by clicking the Add Symbol button in the Library.

5. When the Import Symbols from File dialog box opens, navigate to the folder where you saved the ExportClouds.ansym file, select it, and click the Open button. The symbol, shown in Figure 3-25, is added to your Library.

> *An interesting aspect of importing a symbol is the fact that the symbol retains its original name, not the name of the ANSYM file, when it is imported into Edge Animate. To avoid confusion you might consider renaming the symbol.*

**Figure 3-25.** An Edge Animate symbol imported into a project's Library retains the original symbol name.

# Nesting Symbols

Earlier in this chapter, we showed you how to nest elements inside each other. The process is a bit different when it comes to nesting symbols. Follow these steps to learn how:

1. Open the Nesting.an file in your Exercise folder. When it opens, you will see we have put the background in motion and there are two graphics in the Images folder. The plan is to assemble the car and have it drive across the screen.

2. Drag the carbody.png file to the Stage and convert it to a symbol named Racer.

3. Double-click the symbol on the Stage to enter Edit In Place mode.

4. Drag the carwheel.png image from the Library, as shown in Figure 3-26, and place it in the rear wheel well of the car. Convert the wheel image to a symbol named Wheel.

**Figure 3-26.** The rear wheel is in place and converted to a symbol.

5. Double-click the Wheel symbol to open it. Note how the screen darkens and the breadcrumb trail shows you the path to the Wheel symbol.

6. With the playhead at the 0 point of the Wheel symbol's timeline, add a Rotation keyframe.

7. Drag the playhead to the 1-second mark of the timeline and change the Rotation value of the wheel to 1080. If you scrub across the timeline, the wheel will rotate three times in 1 second.

8. Click the Racer link in the breadcrumb trail to return to the car.

9. Drag another copy of the Wheel symbol from the Symbols panel to the timeline and place it in the front wheel well of the car. If you scrub the timeline, both wheels will rotate. The critical point here is, as shown in Figure 3-27, you have placed two instances of the Wheel symbol in the Racer symbol. This is how symbols are nested within each other.

**Figure 3-27.** Instances of the Wheel symbol are added to the Racer symbol's timeline.

10. Click the `Stage` link in the breadcrumb trail to return to the main timeline.

> When you scrubbed the timeline the wheels turned because two copies of the Wheel symbol are nested inside the Racer symbol. This demonstrates a key aspect of symbols—they have independent timelines—at play.

11. Turn off Auto-Keyframes, select the Racer symbol on the Stage and, using the `Scale` property in the `Properties` panel, set the scale amount to 25%. Note how both the car and the wheels scale in proportion. This is one of the advantages of nesting symbols within each other.

12. Move the symbol to the left edge of the Stage.

13. With the symbol still selected, turn on Auto-Keyframes and add a `Left` keyframe at the 0 point of the timeline.

14. Move the playhead to the 2-second mark of the timeline and move the car off the Stage to the right by scrubbing the `Left` value in the timeline. Test the movie. The car, with wheels turning, zips off the Stage.

## Your Turn: Animate a PNG Sequence

When Flash was in its infancy—between Flash 3 and Flash 5—the holy grail of Flash was video. Designers and developers just *knew* it could be done. How to do it was the big question. In the autumn of 2000, one of the authors just happened to be there when video in Flash was first demonstrated to a room full of people at Apple headquarters in New York City.

That evening, Hillman Curtis got up in front of the inaugural gathering of the New York Macromedia Users Group and played a short 2-second video clip in Flash. What he did was "go for the obvious." By that, we mean he ignored fancy and complex code or a customized approach and, instead, showed a very simple and elegant solution that had a bunch of us saying at the end of the presentation: "Of course . . . why didn't we think of that?"

The solution was to strip video down to its basic components: a series of images on a timeline and an audio track. To accomplish this, Hillman simply took a short video clip, exported it out as an image sequence, and laid those images out, in order, on the Flash timeline.

Thanks to competing video codec standards among the browsers used in the HTML 5 space, Edge Animate really can't incorporate video without a lot of heavy lifting through JavaScript. Still, if you take Hillman's approach and apply it to Edge Animate, you can add short "video" sequences to your Edge Animate projects or use a sequence of images to create a "flip book" effect. Here's how:

1. Open a new Edge Animate document and set the stage size to 320 pixels wide by 240 pixels high.

2. Open the PNGSequence folder in your `Exercise` folder and select all of the images in the folder. Making sure your cursor is over the `Subway 01.png` image, drag and drop all of the images in that folder on to the Edge Animate timeline. Be sure the X and Y coordinates are 0,0 before you release

the mouse. When you release the mouse, the images will all drop onto the timeline, as shown in Figure 3-28, in order and in register. Save the file as SubwayVideo to your Exercise folder.

**Figure 3-28.** A series of images in a PNG sequence hit the Edge Animate timeline in order and neatly tucked up against the 0,0 point.

*We used QuickTime to output the PNG sequence. This technique is pretty well a common output standard with video editing software. Also you can output either a JPG or PNG sequence. Edge Animate can handle either one.*

At this point you need to break out your calculator because you want to mimic the playback of the video. The original video was output at 30 frames per second (fps). This means a PNG sequence of the 2-second clip would create 60 images. This, as it was in the early days of Flash, is a lot of images for a short time span. What we did was to reduce the frame rate to 12 fps, which explains the more manageable count of 28 images. At that rate, one frame of the sequence is visible for roughly 0.083 seconds, which is the result of this calculation: 1/12. That's a lot of math and, frankly, busy work. There is an easier method that uses the timeline.

Using a couple of features in Edge Animate, Show Grid and the Grid Size in the Timeline panel, we can create a "flip book" that will mimic the playback of the video. To create the animation, follow these steps:

3. In the timeline select the Subway_02 to Subway_28 elements and in the Element Display area of the Properties panel set the Display value, as shown in Figure 3-29, to Off.

4. Select the Subway_01 element in the timeline and change its Display value to On.

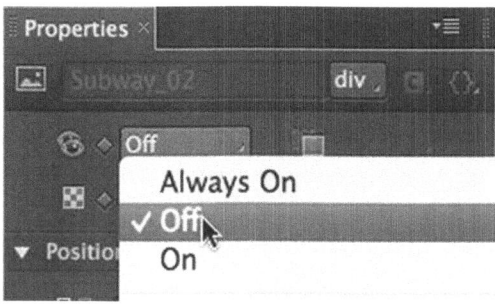

**Figure 3-29.** You only need the images visible when they need to be.

With the elements prepared, you can now concentrate on the actual flip book. One of the really useful features of Edge Animate is the ability to break the timeline into more familiar units than milliseconds. Here's how:

5. At the bottom of the timeline is the Show Grid button and beside it is a small arrow that lets you set the grid size on the timeline. Click the Grid Size arrow and, as shown in Figure 3-30, a dialog box with some pretty familiar time increments appears. Select 24/second.

*These values have absolutely nothing to do with frame rate or playback speed. They simply divide the timeline into the increments selected.*

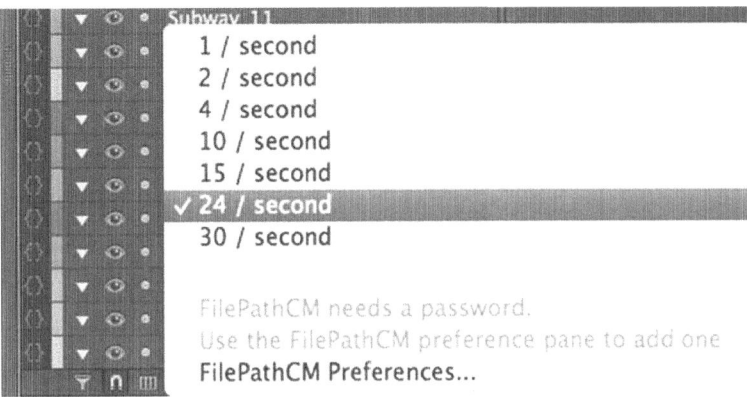

**Figure 3-30.** Changing the timeline increments.

6. Click the Show Grid button and the timeline is now divided into "frames." Each frame is 1/24 of a second, which means that each image in the flip book is visible for two frames.

7. Move the playhead to Frame 2. Select the Subway_02 element in the timeline and set its Display property in the timeline to On. The image becomes visible.

8. Select the Subway_01 element in the timeline and, as shown in Figure 3-31, set its Display property to Off.

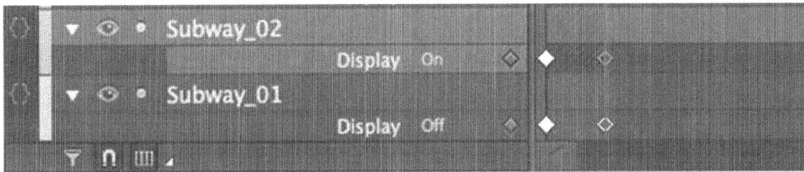

**Figure 3-31.** Using the Display property for a PNG sequence lets the "software do the work" and turn off the Display property of the element.

9. Repeat steps 7 and 8 for the remaining elements in the timeline.

10. When you finish, rewind and press the Spacebar. You have a "video" playing on your timeline.

## You Have Learned

In this chapter, you have learned the following:

• How to create shape tweens in Edge Animate

• How to add a drop shadow to an Edge Animate element

- A way to use the drop shadow property to create gradients in Edge Animate

- Using nested elements to create animations

- How to create, nest, and share symbols in Edge Animate

- A method of animating a video PNG sequence.

This chapter has focused on expanding your animation skills in Edge Animate beyond the basics outlined in the previous chapter. From the nesting of elements to create animations to the use of Display properties to create an animated PNG sequence, you have discovered there is more to animation in Edge Animate than simply moving stuff from "here" to "there."

Speaking of "stuff," you may be wondering how images and line art are prepared in a variety of Adobe applications for use in Edge Animate. Turn the page to find out.

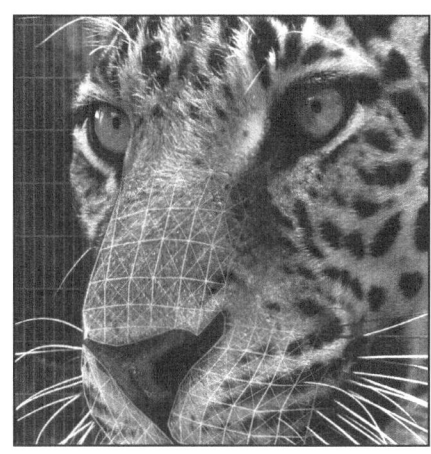

# Chapter 4

# Creating Graphics for Edge Animate

As we mentioned in Chapter 1, Adobe Edge Animate is not a drawing application. Line art and images come from elsewhere. Edge Animate's job is to give you the tools to put that content in motion or make it interactive. In order to do that, we first need to create content for Edge Animate in a drawing, imaging, animation, or video-editing application. The content can then be exported in a number of graphic formats and then imported into Edge Animate. The question, of course, is what type of files can be imported into Adobe Edge Animate?

Adobe Edge Animate can import the following graphic file formats: SVG, JPG, PNG, and GIF. Fortunately, this gives us some creative freedom regarding the graphic applications we choose, since many of them can export files in these formats. Also, one thing you might notice, if you are at all familiar with web design, is the fact that three of these formats—JPG, PNG, and GIF—are well-known web graphic formats. This is what makes Animate so special—it works with web standard graphics rather than requiring a proprietary graphic format.

But wait! What about SVG you ask? It's not a format you are familiar with? Don't worry. SVG is a standard format designed specifically for working with vector graphics on the web. We will explain more about this later in the chapter.

Here is what we will cover in this chapter:

- Understanding the graphic formats Adobe Edge Animate supports

- Choosing which format to use for specific Adobe Edge Animate content

- Creating and exporting graphics in Adobe Photoshop

- Creating and exporting graphics in Adobe Illustrator

- Creating and exporting graphics in Adobe Fireworks

- Adding GIF animations to Adobe Edge Animate movies

- Creating PNG sequences in Flash Professional CS6

- Creating Sprite Sheets in Flash Professional CS6

If you haven't already downloaded the chapter files, they can be found at: `http://www.apress.com/9781430243502`. In this chapter, we will be using these files:

- `Banner.an`

- `balloon.png`

- `BannerAd.svg`

- `bannerAd.ai`

- `background.png`

- `Batch`

- `Hougou.png`

- `Vidsequence`

- `Ant.fla`

- `Ant.an`

This chapter will work with a few Adobe design applications. If you don't own a copy of a specific design program that we mention, you can download a 30-day trial version of the application from `http://www.adobe.com/downloads/`.

# Understanding Graphic Formats

Standard web graphic formats have been around for a long time. Although there are many types of web graphics, a few have become the ones that have shaped the web as we know it. It comes as no surprise that these formats are the ones available for use in Edge Animate. They are as follows:

- GIF (Graphic Interchange Format) is a format designed originally by CompuServe in the late 1980s. This graphic format uses an indexed color format (referred to as a palette) that contains no more than 256 colors and can be optimized down to a minimum of two colors. In the early days of the web, designers would use the GIF format—a "lossless image compression format"—to drastically reduce their graphics file sizes with practically no visual loss for faster delivery through modems. The GIF format can also store multiple images (frames) in a single file, thus producing an animated GIF file. It also has the ability to assign a transparent color to a GIF file. Because every browser supports the GIF format, it has long been a go-to format for web graphics and photos.

However, with the introduction of the JPEG, and later PNG, file format, as well as Adobe's Flash animation format, SWF, the GIF format is not as commonly used as it was in the past.

> *Originally, the creators of the GIF format pronounced the word with a soft G, as in the word jiffy. But, such as it is with technology acronyms, the word was later pronounced with a hard G, as in the word get. Luckily, the Oxford English Dictionary and American Heritage Dictionary agree that both pronunciations are actually correct.*

- JPG (JPEG) (Joint Photographic Experts Group) format was first developed by the committee of the same name as a codec (COMpressor/DECompressor). The format was designed to optimize compressed photographic images on the web in a "lossy" format. One clear advantage the JPG format has over the GIF format is the ability to handle a larger color palette—up to 16.7 million colors to be exact. This explains why the JPG format is commonly used to display photographs and highly detailed graphic images on the web. However, built into the file format is a lossy compression algorithm that adjusts (in a sliding scale) the visual quality of the image at the expense of the overall file size of the image. The more you adjust the compression in a JPG file, the more quality you lose in the final image output. The reverse is also true. When you apply less compression in a JPG file, the visual quality of your JPG image will look better but the file size will increase. In fact, if you compress a JPG image to the point where areas of color are completely gone, those areas will look like halos. The term for this is effect *ringing*, and it is to be avoided at all costs.

- PNG (Portable Network Graphics) format is similar to the GIF format, supporting "lossless image compression" as well as color palettes. However, unlike the GIF format, PNG supports more than 256 colors. In fact, the format can support up to 32 bits of data information. What does that actually mean? Simple. The JPEG format supports 16.7 colors, which translates to 24 bits of data information. The extra 8 bits available in a PNG-32 file are reserved for what is called an *alpha channel*. This is a separate channel specifically designed to hold transparency information. The PNG format, pronounced "ping," was originally developed as a replacement for the GIF format, primarily because GIF is not open source and royalties are still paid to CompuServe to this day.

- SVG (Scalable Vector Graphics) is an open standards file format based on XML (Extensible Markup Language) that has been under development by the World Wide Web Consortium (WC3) since 1999. SVG files entered the web motion graphics world when Adobe, in 2000, launched a Flash competitor—now defunct—named Live Motion. The difference between SVG and its bitmap counterpart is the fact that the image is constructed using XML code rather than mapping color values to the location of individual pixels. This is exactly how vector drawing applications like Illustrator create their images and it also explains why the word vector is used in the format name. In addition, the SVG format supports gradients, colors, paths, text, clipping paths, filter effects, interactivity, linking, fonts, transparency, and metadata. When you put all of this together, you can see why SVG graphics are used by Edge Animate!

What's with "lossy" and "lossless"? When you compress an image using the JPG format, you can't help but notice the file size reduces. This is due to that algorithm that looks for similar colors and removes the ones that are really close to each other. This information is "tossed out" of the image and, if information is tossed out, it can't be put back. It is lost and thus the term lossy.

# Choosing the Right Format

Now that you have a better understanding of the graphic formats that Adobe Edge Animate supports, let's shine some light on how to choose the best format for your Edge Animate project. The easiest way we can explain this is by using a very simple example. To get yourself started, follow these steps:

1.  Open the Banner.an file located in your Chapter 4 Exercise folder. When it opens, you will notice, as shown in Figure 4-1, there are five elements on the Stage—LA_Adobe_Max, GIF, JPG, PNG, and SVG. What we will be demonstrating is the difference between raster graphic images and vector graphic images.

**Figure4-1. The** main screen of the Banner.an file.

The image you are looking at was taken during the annual Adobe Conference called Adobe Max. The huge banner draped over the outside of the building provides us with a great starting point for this exercise. There is very little color—just red and white—which makes it easy to pull the banner out of the image to use in this exercise.

The first thing we did was to convert the banner to each of the four formats. You can see them used as elements in the Animate Elements panel and in the Library. The first thing you need to pay attention to is the file size of each image. When it comes to the web, small is beautiful because small image files load rather quickly. The size of each image is:

- JPG: 21k
- GIF: 7k
- PNG: 65k
- SVG: 3k

Looking at those numbers, you would immediately opt for the SVG image. Not so fast. You need to first ask yourself: "Why is there such a stark range of sizes for each file type?" The answer lies in lost information, specifically color information.

The JPG image has been compressed and, in doing so, subtle gradations of the red have been lost. The GIF image has been reduced to a limited palette of colors, meaning all of the subtlety in the red is gone. The PNG image keeps the fidelity of the original, which explains why its file size is roughly three times that of its JPG cousin. The SVG image is so small because it has been reduced to code. Based on this, one would think SVG is the way to go. Not quite. You need to look a little deeper.

2. Turn off the visibility of the SVG, PNG, and JPG layers in the timeline. The GIF image is visible.

3. Scrub the timeline to the 1-second mark and the GIF image scales to 200%. As you can see, as shown in Figure 4-2, there are issues. There are artifacts in the red due to GIF's inability to manage subtle color shifts, and the text looks jaggy because it is a bitmap image. What you can infer from this is GIF is best suited to physically small graphics with solid colors.

**Figure 4-2.** Just because a GIF image is small, doesn't necessarily mean it is better.

4.  Turn off the visibility of the GIF  layer and turn on the visibility of the SVG layer. If you scrub the timeline, the image, as shown in Figure 4-3, grows, the color is great, and there is hardly any distortion.

**Figure 4-3.** The SVG image scales nicely with none of the distortion and color issues of the GIF image.

The downside to SVG is Internet Explorer (IE). Although IE9 supports this format, earlier versions will require a plug-in to display SVG graphics. Still, HTML 5 supports the embedding of SVG in HTML, which makes this format especially attractive in the mobile space.

The remaining two layers—PNG and JPG—will have few color issues, but quality is affected when they are scaled. What you need to gather from this exercise is that use and file size determine the format to be used. If the graphic is to be scaled beyond its current size or is a vector graphic created in Illustrator, such as this one, then your only choice is to output the SVG graphic from within Illustrator. If you need alpha transparency, your only option is PNG. If color fidelity is critical, use JPG or PNG and, finally, if the item is physically small and uses solid fill colors, GIF might just be the format for you.

# Adobe Edge Animate and Photoshop

Now that you understand the difference between the graphic formats that Adobe Edge Animate supports, let's take a look at how we use Photoshop to create graphics for Animate.

One area where Photoshop excels is in the creative application of masking to raster images. It has an array of tools that help isolate specific objects from complex backgrounds. When we animate elements within Edge Animate, the last thing we want getting in the way of our beautiful design is so-called noise in the background. We need a clean and transparent "floating" object that we can move around the Animate canvas with ease. One powerful tool, unique to Photoshop, is the Quick Selection tool. If the Magic Wand tool is magic (overuse of the Magic Wand tool has some Photoshop power users referring to it derisively as the tragic wand), then the Quick Selection tool is truly the wizard's staff! Let's see how this works:

1. Open the `balloon.psd` file located in your Chapter 4 `Exercise` folder. When it opens, you will see a hot air balloon floating above a quiet town on a sunny day. The plan is to put the balloon in motion. To accomplish this, we need to first isolate the balloon from the image in order to put it in motion in Edge Animate.

2. To begin, select the `Quick Selection Tool` (Figure 4-4) from the `Tools` menu on the left.

**Figure 4-4.** Choosing the Quick Selection Tool.

3. With the Quick Selection Tool activated, click on the Brush Picker menu in the top Tool Options bar and, as shown in Figure 4-5, set the brush size to 10 pixels, the hardness to 100%, and spacing to 25%. You select the balloon by clicking within the colored area of the balloon and, with the mouse button held down, dragging the brush inside the balloon.

What you will notice, as you move the mouse, is the Quick Selection Tool calculates your selection and begins adding to it based on the contrast in your image, in this case, the blue sky.

> *If you accidentally make a selection outside of the balloon area, don't worry, you can reverse that selection by holding down the option/alt key, which activates the Subtract from Selection tool. With the option/alt key held down, click over the selection you don't want and it will be removed from your existing selection.*

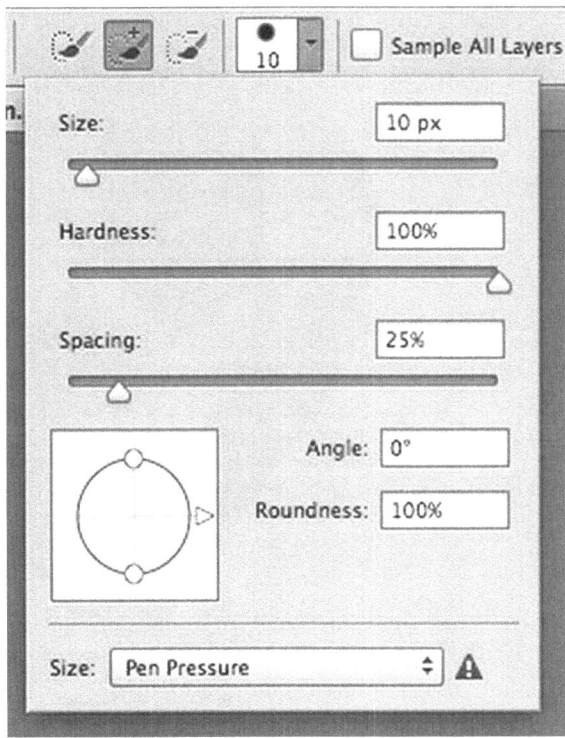

**Figure 4-5.** Adjusting brush size options for the Quick Selection Tool.

4. Now, add the balloon's basket to the selection by clicking inside the basket.

5. Once you are satisfied with your selection, click the Refine Edge button to open the Refine Edge options menu. The background is hidden (turned white), and we can now focus on refining our balloon selection.

6. Click the Smart Radius option in the Edge Detection section and enter a radius of about 2 pixels. You'll notice right away that the balloon begins to blend better with the white background.

7. To sharpen the selection edge even further, adjust the contrast to 50% under the Adjust Edge section.

8. Finally, under output, check the Decontaminate Colors option and set it for 50%. This will further separate the blue sky from the balloon's outline. If your Refine Edge settings resemble those in Figure 4-6, click OK to close the dialog box.

Photoshop now hides the original layer and creates a new layer with our mask. We need to apply this mask to the new layer to complete our isolation of the balloon.

**Figure 4-6.** Refining our selection in the Refine Edge dialog box.

# Floating a Balloon

With the balloon isolated in the image and on its own layer, we have a small problem. If you turn on the visibility of the Background layer, the balloon is still there. It has to go. Here's how:

1.  Select Layer > Layer Mask and choose Apply. The mask will be applied to the layer and the balloon will be floating in transparent space on its own layer.

2.  Turn off the visibility of the Background copy layer and turn on the visibility of the Background layer. We are now ready to remove our original balloon image from our background layer using another Photoshop feature called Content Aware Fill.

3.  First, we need to quickly select our balloon. With the Background layer selected, hold the Command/ Ctrl key down and click the tiny balloon Layer thumbnail image (Figure 4-7), not the Layer itself, on the Background copy layer. What this does is load the Background copy layer as a selection mask, which is exactly what we need to quickly select the balloon in our original image.

**Figure 4-7.** Clicking on the Layer thumbnail image creates the selection.

4.  To expand our selection, choose Select > Modify > Expand. When the Expand selection dialog box opens, enter 5 as the Expand By value and click OK. What you have done is given Content Aware Fill some room to work. Expanding the selection by 5 pixels ensures the Content Aware Fill feature will smoothly remove the image from our background and seamlessly blend the existing background into our image. With this slightly expanded selection, we can now remove the balloon from our original image.

5. Select Edit > Fill to open the Fill dialog box. Select Content-Aware (Figure 4-8) from the Use pop-down and click OK. The balloon disappears!

**Figure 4-8.** Removing the original balloon from our background with Content Aware Fill.

6. Choose Select > Deselect to remove the "marching ants" surrounding the balloon. Turn on the visibility of the Background copy layer, double-click the layer name to select it, and rename the layer to Balloon.

7. To preserve your work to this point, save your file as a Photoshop file and give it a new name, something like balloon_final.psd.

## Creating a PNG File in Photoshop

The balloon is now on its own Photoshop layer and the intention is to put the balloon in motion in Edge Animate. This tells you the balloon needs to be on its own transparent layer in Animate, and the only bitmap format that gives you accurate color while supporting transparency is the PNG format. Follow these steps to prepare a PNG image in Photoshop:

1. Hide the balloon layer again by clicking the eye icon.

2.  Select File > Save for Web... to open the Save for Web dialog box, as shown in Figure 4-9.

**Figure 4-9.** Exporting the background image with the Save for Web dialog box.

> *If you are using a CS6 version of Photoshop, nothing has changed here other than the name. The Save for Web and Devices dialog has changed to simply Save for Web.*

3.  We want to be as efficient as we can with our file size yet still maintain the quality of our image. So we will select the JPEG High option under the Preset menu, which will compress our exported image by 60%. Click the Save button to open the Save Optimized As dialog box.

4.  Name the file Background.jpg and click Save and save it to the SaveForWeb folder in your Exercise folder.

We can now turn our attention to the task of exporting the balloon. The goal here is to crop the balloon before we export it to get rid of the extra transparent information once we import it into Adobe Edge Animate. As with many tasks within Photoshop, there are several ways you can accomplish the same goal. Here's one method:

1.  Select the Image menu and choose Duplicate. Make sure the Duplicate Merged Layers Only is NOT checked. Click OK. By doing this we are working on a copy of the original image, meaning if we make a huge mistake, we still have access to the original image.

2.  Turn on the visibility of the balloon layer to show the balloon.

3. Select the Background layer, click the Trash Can icon, and click Yes when asked if you want to "Delete the layer background?" We don't need it, so it is best to get rid of it.

4. Choose the Crop tool in the tools menu or type c to switch to the crop tool.

5. With the Crop tool selected, draw a tight box around the balloon (Figure 4-10) and press Return/Enter to crop the balloon image. With the balloon isolated and the excess information trimmed off, we can turn our attention to creating the PNG file.

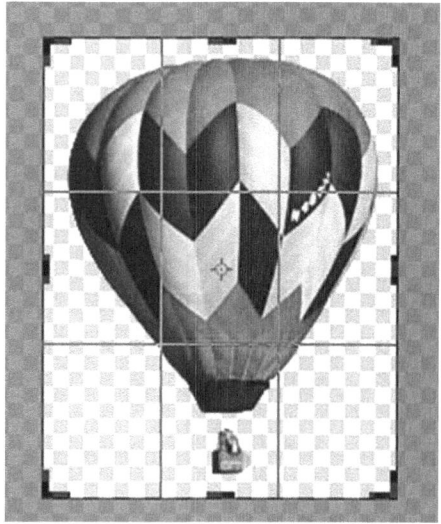

**Figure 4-10.** Cropping the balloon image.

6. Return to the Save for Web menu. In the dialog box, you should notice the balloon image floating over a white background. The reason this is happening is because Photoshop remembers your last export format, which, in this case, was JPEG. All we need to do is tell Photoshop to export this graphic out as a PNG file.

7. Select PNG-24 from the Preset menu and the white background disappears. Click Save and, in the dialog box, name the file Balloon.png and save it to the SaveForWeb folder.

8. Quit Photoshop.

# From Photoshop to Adobe Edge Animate

The images are prepared and we are set for lift off in Adobe Edge Animate. The plan is to have the balloon slowly waft into view and gently land on the shore of the lake. Here's how:

1.  Open a new Adobe Edge Animate document and set the Stage dimensions to 1,000 pixels wide by 542 pixels high. These are the dimensions of the background image.

2.  Import both the background.jpg and balloon.png images created in Photoshop into Animate.

3.  Lock the Background element in the Elements panel. It won't move, so it makes sense to lock it into position.

4.  Click the Balloon element on the Stage and, in the Properties panel, set its X position to 450 and its Y position to 282, as shown in Figure 4-11. The balloon should be sitting on the shore.

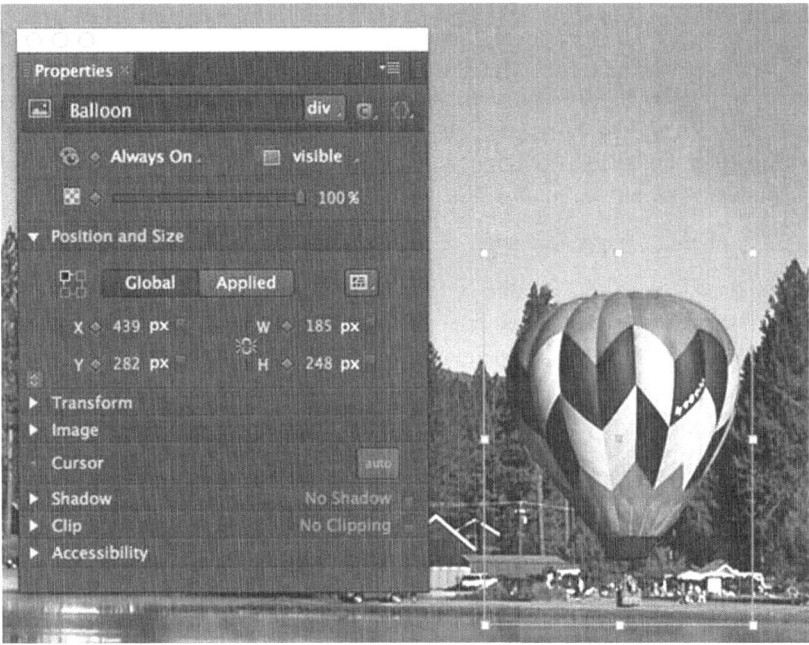

Figure 4-11. We start with the balloon hovering a few feet off the ground.

5.  With the balloon selected on the Stage, add Location and Scale(x) and Scale(y) keyframes at the 0 point.

6.  Click the Pin to activate it and drag the playhead to the 5-second mark on the timeline. Use the following values for the balloon:

- Top: −135

- Left: 924

- Scale(x): 1%

- Scale(y): 1%

- Ease: Ease Out > Quad

7. Scrub the timeline. The balloon floats off into the sky.

8. If you are a real stickler for realism, balloons don't move in a straight line or pass through trees. Move the playhead to the 0:00.650 point of the timeline and change the Left position of the balloon to 482 and the Top position to 69. If you rewind and play the movie, the balloon will clear the trees and float off of the screen.

# Creating Graphics in Illustrator

One of the clear strengths of Adobe Illustrator is its ability to create vector graphics. Since vectors are drawn mathematically rather than on a pixel-by-pixel basis, their scalability is practically limitless and their file size is considerably smaller. As we explained earlier in the chapter, Adobe Edge Animate supports vectors in the form of SVG, which just happens to be a format that Illustrator supports. So, let's import an SVG graphic into Adobe Edge Animate and create a banner ad for a cruise. Let's get started:

1. Open Edge Animate and create a new Edge Animate document with a Stage size of 300 x 600.

2. Import the BannerAd.svg file located in your Chapter 4 Exercise folder. Voila! As shown in Figure 4-12, our enticing travel banner ad appears. The plan here is to animate the waves, bob the ship up and down, and then drop the anchor arrow to reveal the price discount. There is one problem— Edge Animate has imported the banner ad as a single flattened graphic, which means we will not be able to animate separate objects. Not to worry, we'll fix that in Illustrator.

**Figure 4-12.** We have a problem. The SVG image has been flattened.

*Asking you to work with a flattened SVG file was done deliberately. It is all too easy to simply save out an Illustrator graphic as an SVG file and "assume" that all of the layering will be retained. This isn't the case. You need to know exactly how the file and its layers will be used in Edge Animate and then prepare your Illustrator file for SVG import into Edge Animate. To do that let's open the original AI file and examine an emerging workflow.*

## Cruising the Original Banner Ad

The plan for this banner ad is simple:

- Animate the waves.

- Have the ship bob up and down.

- Drop the anchor.

What this tells you is there is a need to have separate elements in Adobe Edge Animate and that the bits and pieces from the Illustrator document need to be in those elements, not a flattened document.

1. If you have Illustrator CS6, open the `BannerAd.ai` file located in your Chapter 4 `Exercise` folder and follow along.

> *We are using Illustrator CS6, which is the latest version of the application. The techniques we present here work just as well in the CS5 versions of the application. You won't be able to open a CS6 AI file in Illustrator CS5. To make life easy for you, we have placed a CS5 version of the BannerAd.ai file in the CS5 folder.*

2. Locate the Layers palette and, as shown in Figure 4-13, review the layer organization. One great tip to keep in mind when designing graphics in Illustrator for Edge Animate is to use layers to organize the objects you plan to animate or add interaction to within Edge Animate. As you can see, we have already done this for you. Your job is to extract these layers as separate SVG graphics, delete the unused layers to reduce the file size, and then import each graphic into the Animate environment.

**Figure 4-13.** The `BannerAd.ai` file's layer organization.

3. We will start at the bottom of the Layers list and work our way up. First, we want to hide everything except the current top-level layer that we are working on (the top-level layers are the layers marked with triangles). A quick way to hide the other layers is by holding down the Option+Alt key and clicking the eye icon next to the layer we want visible. When we do that, Illustrator reveals only the layer whose eye icon we clicked on.

4. Now that we have visually isolated only the layer named Background, we can export it out of Illustrator as an SVG file. Choose File > Save As to open up the Save As menu.

5. We want to organize our saved SVG graphics into a separate folder. Click the New Folder button and create a folder named SvgExport.

6. Under the Format menu choose SVG(svg).

7. Under the Save As field, enter the name Background.svg.

8. Click Save. The SVG Options menu opens. This menu allows you to specify certain aspects of your saved format that can be accessed through code. In this case, we are going to accept the defaults shown in Figure 4-14 and click OK.

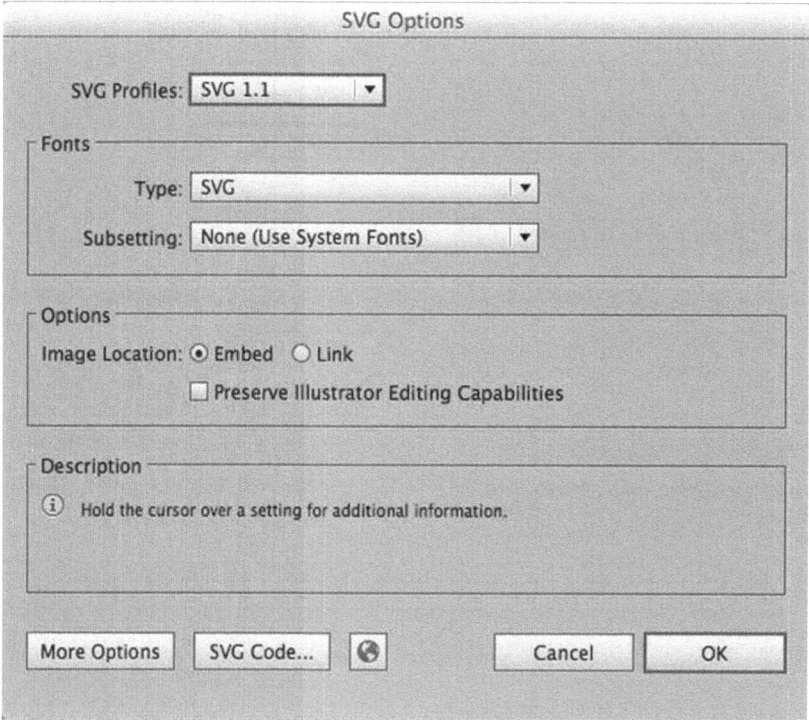

**Figure 4-14.** The SVG Options window.

9. When you click OK, you will notice the file extension has changed to SVG and the Illustrator layers still show in the Layers panel. This is a common pitfall because the document name has been changed in the application. What you need to do now is to close this document and reopen it in Illustrator to get a true representation of the document's layer structure.

# Removing the Hidden Layers from Our SVG File

One might assume that we are done working with our exported SVG file after we click the OK button. In fact, if you import the Background.svg file into Adobe Edge Animate, you'll notice that it is only the background file that we see. Although that appears to be the case, the truth is the hidden layers are actually still inside the exported SVG file, which means our file is larger than we really need.

1. Locate the Background.svg file you just exported in the folder SvgExport and open it in Illustrator.

2. Open the Layers panel. What you'll notice is we now have a single top layer named Layer 1. If we click the triangle next to the layer, it reveals all our layers from the original BannerAd.ai file but displays only the Background layer as visible, which is what we did before exporting to SVG in our previous exercise. As a result, our background file is now 20k. You are probably saying "Hold on a minute. What's the big deal with a 20k file in this day and age?" Actually, it's not the size that matters here, but file efficiency. If you aren't using the layers, get rid of them.

> *The layers that we have hidden are still there in the XML code generated from Illustrator when we exported our file to SVG. Illustrator has simply added a display = none description in each XML <g id> tag that describes our hidden layers. If we turn a layer back on and then reexport the file, Illustrator will remove the display = none option and display the graphic described within the <g id> tag. Because the generated code is text based, we could theoretically edit the code by hand and remove the display = none designation in the SVG/XML file. But that means we would have to design in code. It is much easier using Illustrator for this task.*

3. Let's get rid of the extra hidden layers. Shift-click to select a group of layers adjacent to each other or Command/Ctrl-click to select a group of nonsequential layers. The idea here is we want to select the hidden layers, not the background layer, and delete them from our SVG document.

4. Click the trash can icon (Figure 4-15) to delete the selected layers.

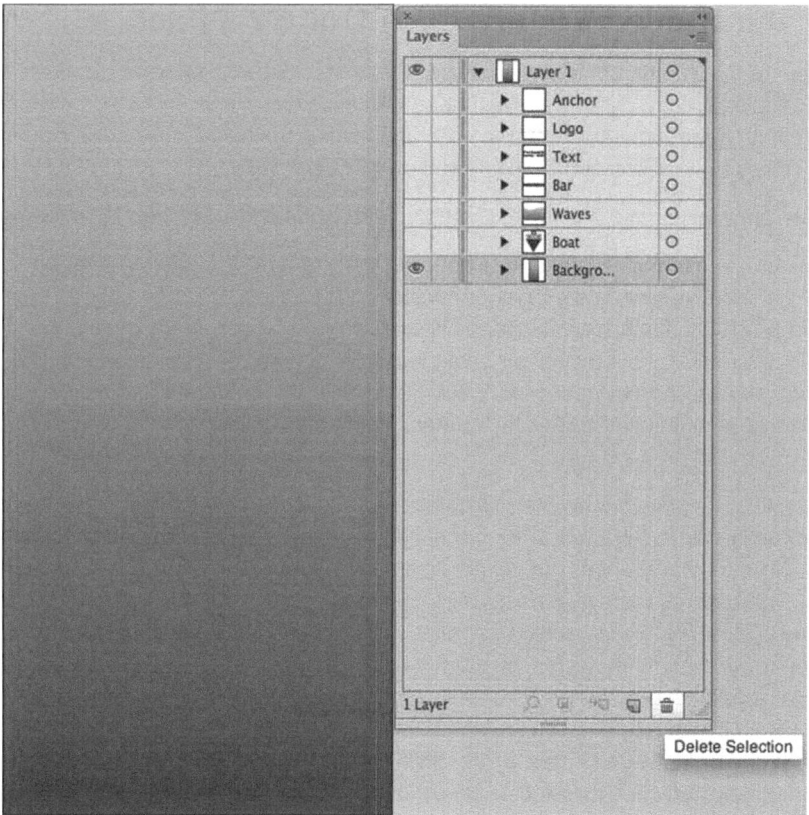

**Figure 4-15.** Delete unused layers from the Background.svg document.

5.  When you have deleted all of the unnecessary layers, click File > Save to overwrite the Background.svg file. Close the file.

6.  Our Background.svg file is now 4k. But, more important than that is we have removed the unused XML code, making our final file more efficient.

## Lather, Rinse, Repeat

At this point, we have walked you through the process of exporting an Illustrator layer to the SVG format and removing hidden layers to further file efficiency. What you will essentially do next is repeat these steps to isolate each layer in the BannerAd.ai file, saving them into the SvgExport folder you created earlier. We will help you get started with the first one.

1.  Open the BannerAd.ai file.

2. Hold down the Option/Alt key and click Visibility next to the layer named Boat to hide every layer except for the Boat layer.

> Hold on . . . why not just delete the unwanted layers and do a quick "Save as"? Good question. The reason is you are going to be constantly reopening the Illustrator file and deleting unwanted layers. This way you isolate the layer you need in the SVG graphic and export just that layer.

3. Choose File > Save As to open the Save As menu. Locate the SvgExport folder, choose SVG for the format and name the file Boat.svg, click Save, and accept the defaults in the SVG Options menu by clicking OK.

4. You are returned to the Illustrator desktop and are now working on the saved SVG file, so as a shortcut, select the hidden layers and delete them from the Boat.svg document.

5. Choose File > Save to overwrite the Boat.svg file. The final file will have the single layer shown in Figure 4-16.

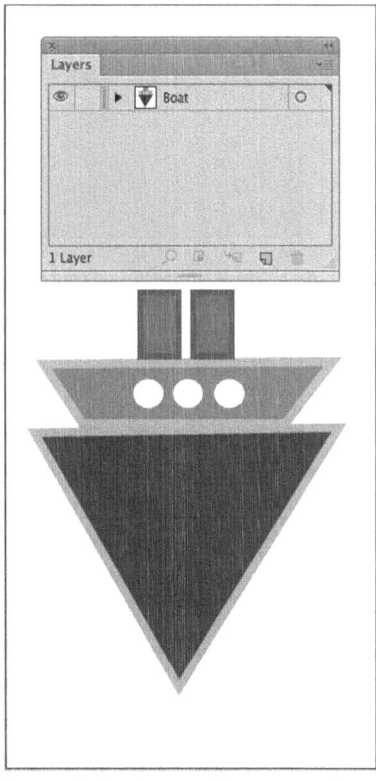

Figure 4-16. The edited Boat.svg file with hidden layers removed.

> *We are going to animate each of the sublayers in the **Waves** layer. Make sure they are converted to SVG images and named **Waves12**, **Waves22**, and **Waves33**.*

## A Word About Text Inside an SVG File

We can create a design in Illustrator with editable text and then export it out in SVG format. The editable text will then be embedded into our SVG file using the `font-family` embed code. However, the gotcha here is users will need to have the font installed on their system, otherwise they will see a substitute font, which may be very different from the original font in our design. Of course, we could add the text in Adobe Edge Animate, which you will see how to do in the next chapter. What we want to do in this case is to convert our editable text to outline vector format on the fly right before we export it to SVG.

1.  Open the `BannerAd.ai` file.

2.  Hold down the Option/Alt key and click on the eye icon next to the layer named `Text` to hide every layer except the layer named `Text`.

3.  Choose `File > Save As` to open the `Save As` menu, locate the `SvgExport` folder, choose SVG for the format, name the file `Text.svg`, click Save but, in the `SVG Options` dialog, locate the pull-down menu named `Type` (Figure 4-17) inside the `Fonts` area and change the option from `SVG` to `Convert to outline`. This will convert the fonts to vectors. Click OK.

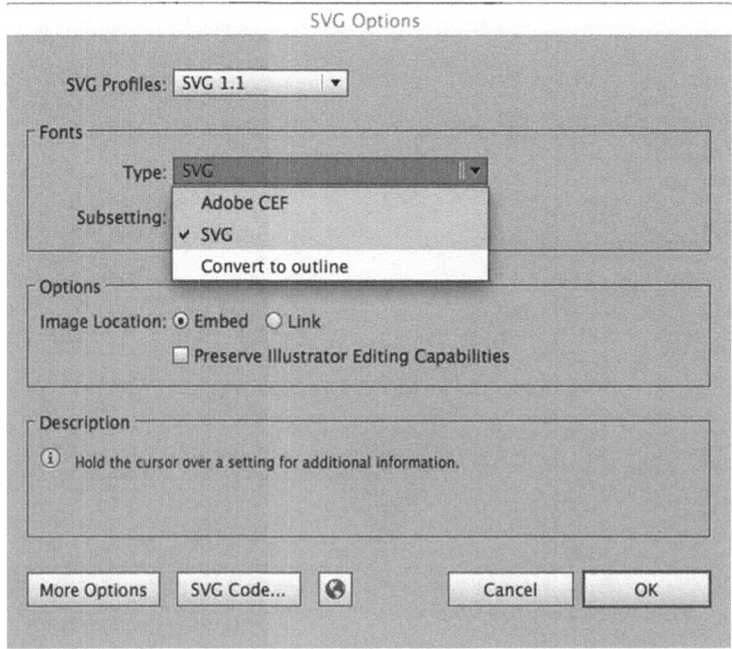

**Figure 4-17.** Converting fonts to outline vector formats prior to export.

# From Illustrator to Adobe Edge Animate

Before we start work, one of the cardinal rules of digital design is to assemble your assets. At this point you should have created the following files:

- Anchor.svg
- Background.svg
- Boat.svg
- Logo.svg
- Text.svg
- Waves12.svg
- Waves22.svg
- Waves33.svg

With the inventory completed and the assets all converted to the necessary SVG format, it is time to assemble the ad and get things moving. Here's how:

1. Open a new Adobe Edge Animate document and set the Stage dimension to 300 pixels wide and 600 high to match the dimensions of the ad.
2. Import the Background.svg image and lock it into place.
3. Import the Boat.svg image and move it into place.

We have three wave graphics that are going to simulate the ocean's motion. To do that, the plan is to have one wave graphic move up and down; the other will move down and up; and the final wave graphic will be stretched in and out to simulate lateral movement.

4. Import the Waves12.svg image to the timeline. Notice how it just drops into position thanks to the SVG export from Illustrator.
5. Add a Location keyframe and drag the playhead to the 1-second mark. Change the Top value on the Timeline to 20.
6. Pull the playhead to the 2-second mark and set the Top value back to 0. You now have a wave that moves down and up.
7. Import the Waves22.svg image to the timeline and add a Location keyframe.
8. Drag the playhead to the 1-second mark. Change the Top value to −15.
9. Pull the playhead to the 2-second mark and set the Top value back to 0. You now have a wave that moves up and down.
10. Drag the Transition strip for this Layer to the half-second mark.

11. Import the Waves33.svg image to the timeline and add a Scale(x) keyframe.

12. Drag the playhead to the 1-second mark. Change the Scale(x) value to 120%.

13. Pull the playhead to the 2-second mark and set the Scale(x) value back to 100. You now have a wave that expands and contracts.

14. Drag the Transition strip for this layer to the 1-second mark.

15. Select the Transition strips for the Waves layers and copy them to the clipboard.

16. Move the playhead to the 3-second mark and paste the transitions into place. If you scrub the timeline, you have a boat on the ocean waves, as shown in Figure 4-18.

**Figure 4-18.** A little SVG wave action courtesy of Adobe Edge Animate.

The last part of the exercise is to add the anchor and the text. Here's how:

1. Using File > Import, bring the `Anchor.svg` image into Adobe Edge Animate. You need precise placement of the anchor from the original image, and using the menu item will accomplish that objective.

2. Add the `Logo.svg` and the `Text.svg` images to the project and either scrub the playhead or test the movie in a browser. For bonus marks, feel free to animate the text layers. Rewind and preview the movie in a browser.

We don't know about you, but we have never seen a boat sit still in the water. It bobs up and down with the water, so let's fix that:

3. Move the Anchor element above the Boat element in the `Elements` panel. Hold down the Shift key and select both elements in the `Elements` panel.

4. Right-click (PC) or Command-click (Mac) the selected elements to open the `Context` menu. Select, as shown in Figure 4-19, Group `Elements` in `DIV` on the Context menu. This allows you to have both the boat and the anchor move up and down, in unison.

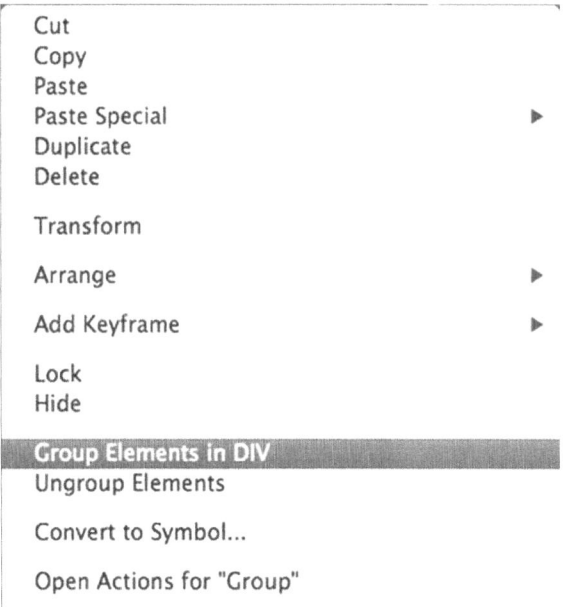

Figure 4-19. Grouping elements allows you to apply the same transition to all the elements in the group.

5. Select the `Group` element in the timeline and add a `Left` keyframe in the `Properties` panel at the 0 point.

6. Move the playhead to the 1.5-second mark and change the Top value in the timeline to 10 pixels.

7. Move the playhead to the 3-second mark and change the Top value back to 0.

8. Select the Transition strip and copy it. With the playhead still at the 3-second mark, paste the transition into the timeline. Your timeline should resemble that shown in Figure 4-20.

9. Rewind and test the movie.

**Figure 4-20.** A static Illustrator document comes to life in Animate.

# Fireworks and Adobe Edge Animate

If there is a tool in the Adobe line up that is the Rodney Dangerfield of the collection—*"I don't get no respect!"*—it would be Fireworks. Yet, if there were two tools that were made for each other, they would be Edge Animate and Fireworks.

Although Fireworks produces both vectors and bitmaps, where Fireworks fits into Edge Animate's imaging workflow is on the PNG, GIF, and JPG side of the process. The SVG feature is not available in Fireworks. A workaround would be to import Fireworks vectors into Illustrator and convert them there, but we agree with your initial reaction: "Why bother?"

The sweet spot for Fireworks lies in the fact that it is aimed directly at screen graphics. Unlike Photoshop and Illustrator, Fireworks was never intended to produce print material or to do any other graphics heavy lifting. The problem is, far too many graphics and web design pros are unaware of this due to Adobe's abysmal inability to counter this misperception. Yet, with the rise of mobile and multiscreen environments, more and more designers and developers are gravitating toward Fireworks for that very reason.

> *We will be using Fireworks CS6 for this section of the chapter. All of the techniques presented work in Fireworks CS5. If you have that version, feel free to follow along.*

The following exercises are not intended to turn you into a Fireworks power user. They simply walk your through some of the common tasks you will encounter using Adobe Edge Animate. All we ask is that by the time you complete them, you would come to realize that Fireworks just might become a valuable tool in your toolbox. Let's get started.

## Resizing and Optimizing Images

In the world of the web, small is beautiful because the smaller and more efficient an image is, the faster it loads into the browser. This is one of the strengths of Fireworks. It easily creates optimized GIF, JPG, and PNG images destined for Animate. To find out how, follow these steps:

1. Open the HouGou.png image in the Exercise folder in Adobe Fireworks. As shown in Figure 4-21, if you look at the Width and Height values of the image in the Properties panel, an image size of 2,896 by 1,944 simply isn't going to work. This image needs to be resized to 800 by 500.

**Figure 4-21.** The image is, physically, too large.

2. Press Command/Control-A to select all three layers in the image and open the Modify menu. When it opens, select Transform > Numeric Transform to open the Numeric Transform dialog box.

3. Select Scale from the pop-down menu and, as shown in Figure 4-22, change the scale amount to 30%. Notice how the dimensions of the image change in the dialog box. Click OK to accept the change.

**Figure 4-22.** Image resizing is a fairly quick process in Fireworks.

4.　When the dialog box closes, the image will shrink but the canvas doesn't. Click anywhere on the canvas—not the image—and click the Fit Canvas button (Figure 4-23), found in the Properties panel. The canvas shrinks to fit the contents of the image.

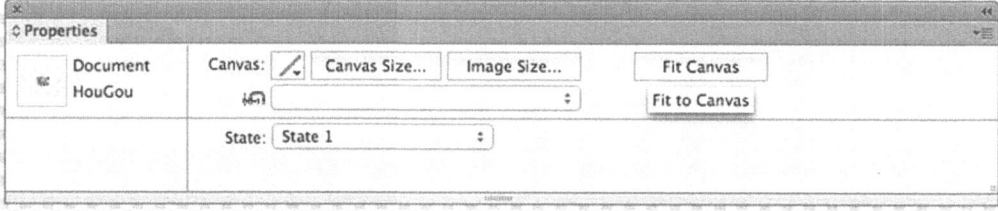

**Figure 4-23.** You can resize the canvas directly from the Fireworks Properties panel.

The image is still a little bit too large. Follow these steps to crop it to the proper size:

5. Select the Crop tool and drag out a crop area.

6. In the `Properties` panel, change the `Width` and `Height` values, as shown in Figure 4-24, to 800 × 500. Move the crop area around the image, and when you are satisfied, press the Return/Enter key to accept the crop.

**Figure 4-24.** Cropping by the numbers is a great feature of Fireworks.

# Preparing Fireworks Images for Export to Edge Animate

The plan for this image is to have Animate make the gentleman pop his head up to peer over the wall. What you don't do is simply export the image as a PNG image because all that would do is flatten it.

Animate can accept JPG, PNG, and transparent PNG images and, truth be told, the creation of these images is one of the little-known strengths of Fireworks. In fact, Fireworks can be used to design the interface used in an Edge Animate composition, and the files can then be output as individual files, with transparency, and assembled in Edge Animate.

> *Here's a fact that is not widely known. The entire interface for Adobe Edge Animate, from dialog boxes to panels, has been created in Fireworks.*

In this exercise we are going to create an Edge Animate project that contains three images, with transparency, created from a single Fireworks image. The process of getting a multilayer Fireworks image ready for animation in Adobe Edge Animate involves three steps:

- Create a layer for each image.

- Optimize the layers as PNG 32 images with Transparency.

- Output the layers.

This may seem like a lot of work, but in fact it requires you to type a name and click the mouse a couple times. To get started, follow these steps:

1. Add two new layers by clicking the New/Duplicate Layer button (the file folder with the + sign) at the bottom of the Layers palette. Name the layers Man and Wall. Rename Layer 1 to Background (Figure 4-25).

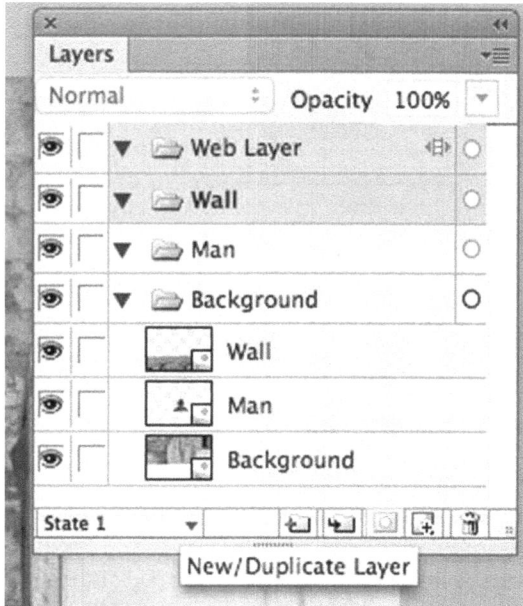

**Figure 4-25.** Items destined for motion in Adobe Edge Animate need to be placed in their own layers.

2. Select the Wall sublayer in the Background layer. Click the circle in the Wall layer and the image moves to the Wall layer. Repeat this with the Man sublayer. Had you not done this, the three sublayers would be flattened when they are exported.

Now that the images destined for Adobe Edge Animate are in their own layers, we can turn our attention to optimizing them as 32-bit PNG images. Here's how:

3. Open the Optimize panel—the icon looks like a TV set at the top of the Panels strip—or select Window > Optimize.

4. When the panel opens, select PNG32 from the preset pop-down, shown in Figure 4-26, and set the Matte color to None. This step just prepared all of the layers in the image for output to the PNG32 format. You can also optimize each layer, but that is a bit out of this book's scope.

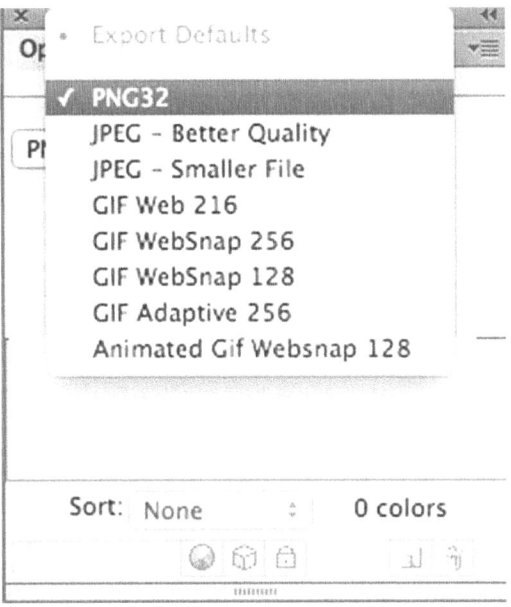

**Figure 4-26.** The Optimize panel prepares layers for output.

The final step in the process is to output the layers as individual images for use in Edge Animate. Here's how:

5.  Select File > Export to open the Export panel.

6.  Select Layers to Files from the Export pop-down, shown in Figure 4-27. Feel free to name the file, but be sure the files created are destined for the Animate PNG folder in your Exercise folder.

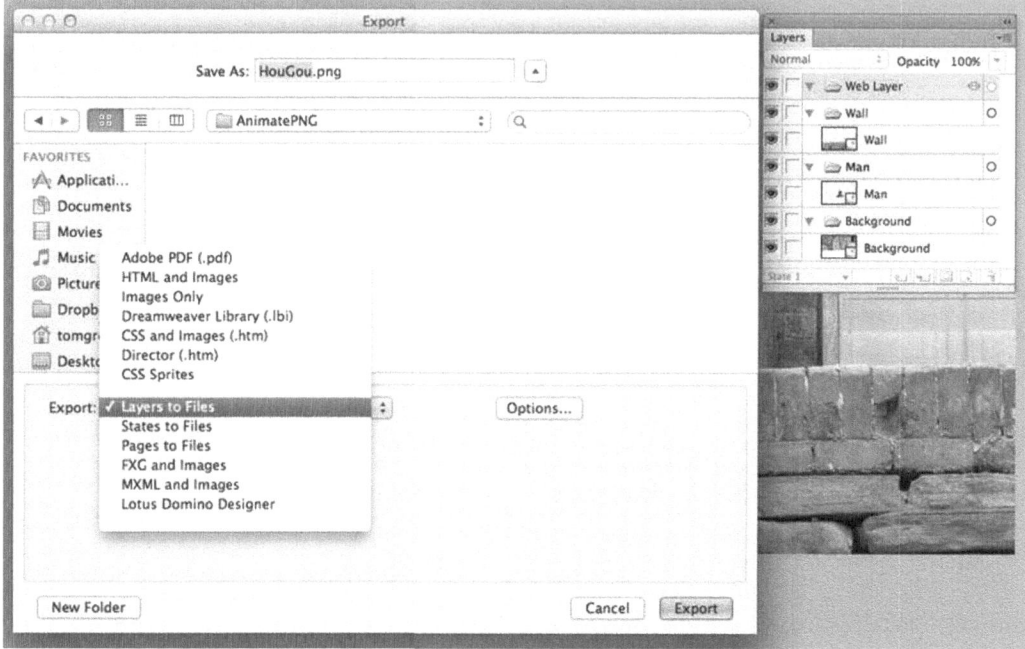

**Figure 4-27.** Use the Export menu to create the files used by Edge Animate.

7. Click OK. The files are exported and, if you check the Animate PNG folder, you will see three PNG images, with layer names, in that folder.

> *There is an even easier way of getting this file into Edge Animate without going to all of the trouble of putting the Fireworks layers into motion in Edge Animate. Fireworks allows developers to create extensions that . . . well . . . extend the capabilities of Fireworks. One of the most important Fireworks extension developers is John Dunning, who has developed an extension that exports a layered Fireworks file as a fully editable .an file for Edge Animate. If you find the developing Fireworks to Animate workflow to be intriguing, then you need this free extension, which is available at* http://johndunning.com/fireworks/about/EdgeAnimate.

8. Launch Edge Animate and create a new document that is 800 pixels wide by 500 pixels high. This matches the size of the HouGou image canvas.

9. Import the three files in the Animate PNG folder into Adobe Edge Animate. They will arrive in the Elements panel and all of them will be tucked up against the upper left corner of the Stage.

10. Select the Wall element on the Stage and move it to the bottom of the Stage. Rearrange the elements so that the Wall element is above the Man element, as shown in Figure 4-28.

**Figure 4-28.** The Fireworks layers are imported into Adobe Edge Animate.

11. Move the playhead to the 0 point, select the Man element, and move him down so he is hidden by the wall in front of him. Click the Pin to activate it.

12. Move the playhead to the 1.5-second mark and move the Man element back to his start position.

13. Click once on the Transition strip and apply the Ease Out > Cubic ease.

14. As shown in Figure 4-29, the man's head appears and slowly comes to rest.

**Figure 4-29.** Fireworks to motion in Animate in less than 2 minutes.

What you need to understand from this very simple exercise using the Export Layers feature of Fireworks is that it is a huge productivity booster. The ability to export layers as 32-bit PNG files with transparency means you can create rather complex interfaces and other objects in Fireworks and then use Edge Animate to reassemble them and put them into motion in very short order. Whether it is buttons, icons, images, or full-blown designs, we hope you are coming to the realization that Fireworks and Edge Animate make a pretty powerful team.

## Batch Processing Images for Adobe Edge Animate

This exercise is one that Fireworks users just adore. One of the more common uses for Adobe Edge Animate is to create slide shows that have multiple images that slide across the Stage. These images all need to be the same size and, in Photoshop, creating those actions can be a rather time-consuming process. Not in Fireworks. Fireworks has a batch processing command that makes this task a snap. Here's how:

1. Launch Fireworks and, as shown in Figure 4-30, when you come to the Welcome screen select File > Batch Process. The plan is to resize the four images in the Batch folder found in your Exercise folder to images that are each 400 pixels wide.

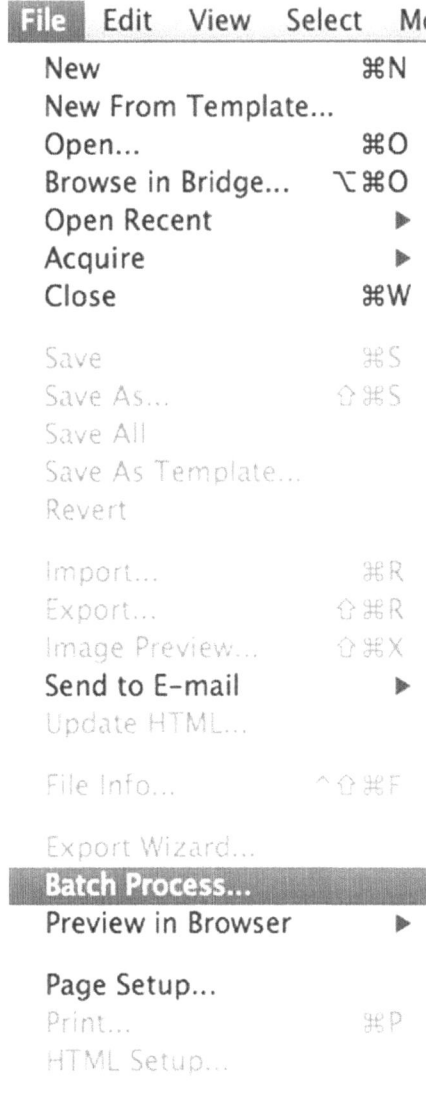

**Figure 4-30.** You start with the Batch Process command.

2.  Navigate to the Batch folder in your Exercise folder. The four images, as shown in Figure 4-31, are listed. Select the images and click the Add button to add the images to the queue. Keep in mind what you are about to do works just as well for 40 images as it does for the four in this exercise.

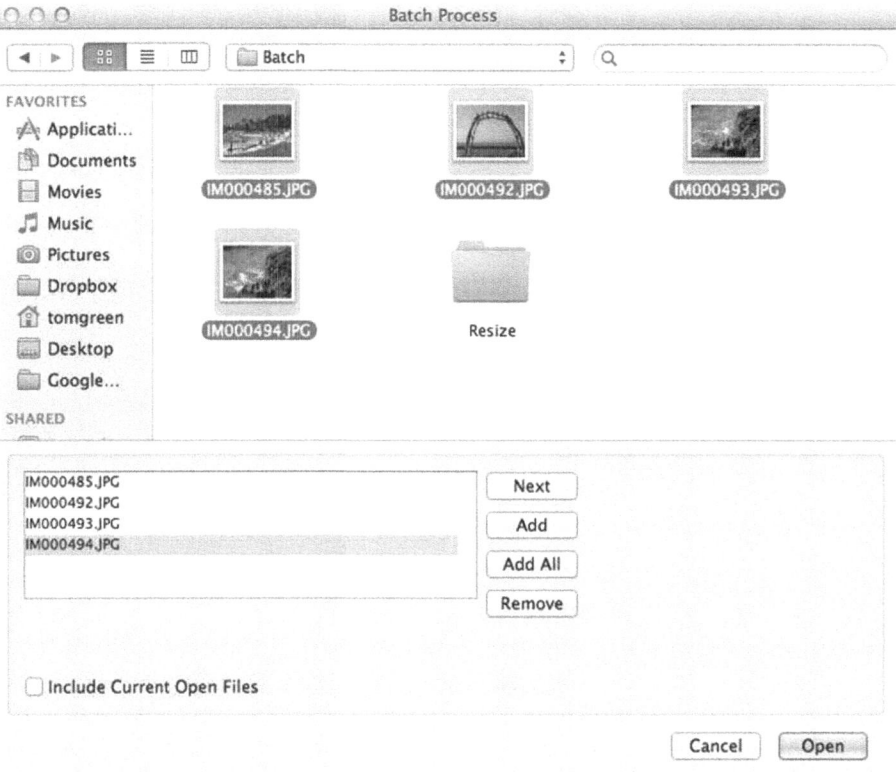

**Figure 4-31.** Identify the images to be resized.

> *Why is there a **Resize** folder in the **Batch** folder? One of the sacred rules of manipulating images is never work on the original. You will be saving the resized images to that folder in a minute, and you don't want to replace the original images.*

3.  Click the Next button to open the Batch Process dialog box.

This is where the magic happens. The images are going to be resized to 400 × 300, which is about 20% of the original size. To get that number, we simply opened one of the images in Fireworks and changed the width in the Properties panel to 400. The height value changed to 300. Armed with those numbers, we can quickly resize the images in the queue to those dimensions.

4. With the `Batch Process` dialog box open, click `Scale` in the `Batch Options` area and click the Add button to add `Scale` to the `Include in Batch` area. As you may suspect, you can add any of the Batch Options to the batch. For example you could scale and rename the images.

5. Open the `Scale` pop-down and select `Scale to Size`. Enter the width and height values as shown in Figure 4-32. Click the `Next` button.

**Figure 4-32.** The magic happens in the Batch Process dialog box.

6. When the `Saving files` screen appears, click the `Custom Location` radio button and browse to the `Resize` folder, as shown in Figure 4-33. Click the `Choose` button to be returned to the Batch Process dialog box.

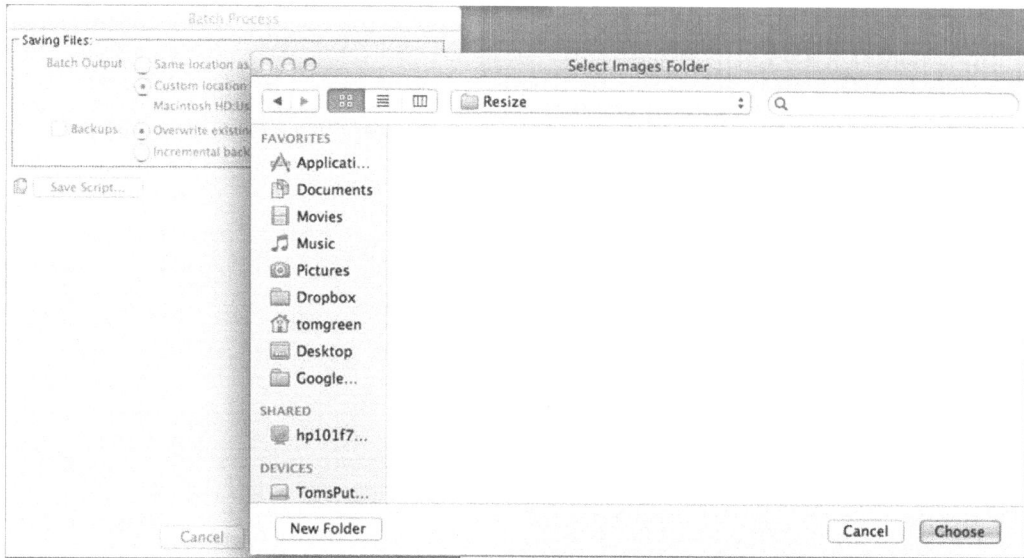

**Figure 4-33.** Identify the folder where the resized images will be placed.

7. Click the Batch button. The interface will close and a progress bar will show you the operation. When it finishes the Batch Progress dialog box (Figure 4-34) will notify you. Click OK and you will be returned to Fireworks. If you open the Resize folder, you will see all of the images have been resized and placed in this location.

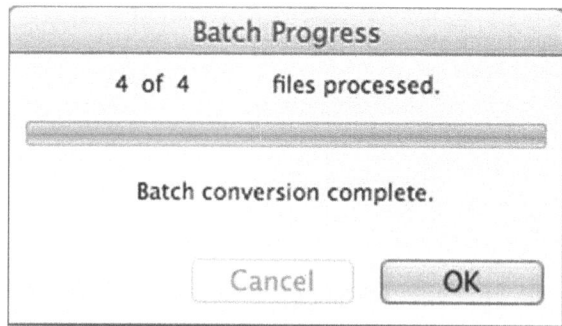

**Figure 4-34.** The image processing is complete.

## BONUS ROUND: CREATE A LOWLY ANIMATED GIF

As we pointed out in the previous chapter, playing video in Edge Animate is one of those items that are on the Edge Animate wish list. Still, there is a way of doing it, and it involves that staple of the web: the lowly animated GIF. It works surprisingly well.

During a visit to the Terracotta Warriors exhibit in China, one of the authors shot a video of dancers at the Chin Emperor's tomb. We are going to use this as the example, and this is what was done prior to creating the files used in this exercise:

- A short 1.5-second clip was pulled out of the footage in QuickTime and pasted into a new QuickTime document.

- The clip was then exported out of QuickTime as a JPEG image sequence. The neat thing about this is the images, 53 of them, are sequentially numbered.

- Each image is 1,280 by 720, which is where Fireworks steps in and comes to the rescue.

> If you don't have Fireworks, a copy of the final file—Chin.gif—can be found in the **Complete** folder.

Let's get started:

1. Open Fireworks and select File > Batch Process. Add all of the images in the VidSequence folder to the Batch, scale them to 25%, and save the scaled images to the Sequence folder found in the VidSequence folder.

2. When the batch process is finished, select File > Open and navigate to the Sequence folder. Select all of the images in the folder and, in the Open File dialog box, select Open as Animation (Figure 4-35). Click Open.

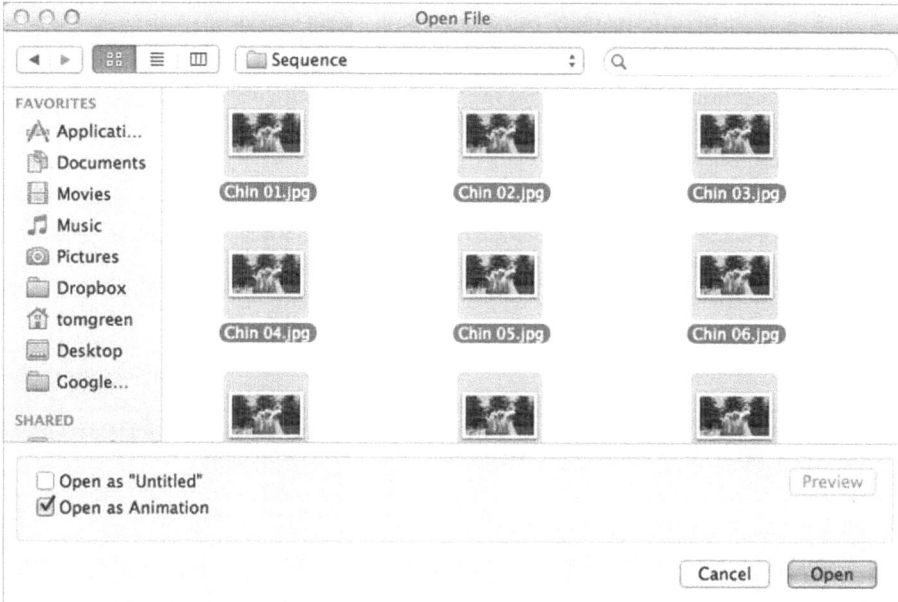

**Figure 4-35.** Image sequences can be opened as animations in Fireworks.

3. When the file opens, you will see the first image in the sequence just imported. Click the States tab and, as shown in Figure 4-36, you will see that each image in the batch has been brought in as a "frame" in the animation. If you click the Play button at the bottom of the canvas, you can watch the clip.

**Fig 4-36.** The 53 images are imported into the file, and clicking the Play button let's you watch the animation.

4. You may have noticed the animation plays a bit slowly. To fix that, select all of the states in the States panel and double-click the number 7 on the right side of the state to open the State Delay input box, as shown in Figure 4-37. This is the frame rate, and you are essentially being

told that each image in the sequence will appear on screen for about 7/100 of a second. Change the number to a 3 and press the Return/Enter key to accept the change.

**Figure 4-37.** Changing the frame rate of a GIF animation.

5.  At this point in the exercise, all you need to do is to save the file as a GIF file, quit Fireworks, and import the file into Adobe Edge Animate. When the file appears on the Stage, it will start to play and, as shown in Figure 4-38, the animation will play.

*In the spirit of complete disclosure, the Animated GIF file weighs in at a whopping 2.5MB. Most animated GIF files are significantly smaller than the 320-by-240 size we use in this example, which explains the "unusual" weight. If the dimensions were reduced to 64 by 48 and the GIF color palette was reduced to 128 colors, for example, there would be a corresponding massive decrease in file size. We chose this physical size simply to demonstrate how one creates an animated GIF in Fireworks.*

**Fig 4-38.** GIF animations can be added to Adobe Edge Animate projects.

> *What's with an Animated GIF? Aren't they throwbacks to a bygone era of the web? Not with Edge Animate. Edge Animate allows you to add a preloader to your composition and the format for an Edge Animate preloader is Animated GIF. This exercise, therefore, does double duty. It can be used as an Animated GIF in your Edge Animate composition or used as a preloader. In fact, we show you how to create and use a preloader in Chapter 8.*

# Preparing Flash Animations for Use in Edge Animate

There seems to be a perception in the market that somehow Edge Animate is a Flash replacement. Nothing could be further from the truth .In fact, Adobe's decision to pull Flash out of the mobile space was driven not by an admission of defeat for Apple's refusal to allow it on iOS devices, but by a market that is fragmented thanks to competing operating systems, feature sets, device capabilities, carriers, and even the networks the devices use. Trying to develop a Flash presentation that worked consistently across devices was futile.

As Flash was losing its predominance for the creation of mobile web-based motion graphics, the W3C was quietly working its way through the HTML 5 specifications, and web developers started to regard HTML 5 as their way out of the morass of competing standards and platforms. Even more important, they saw HTML 5 as one way to provide users with a consistent experience regardless of platform. Realizing this, Adobe shifted its focus to the HTML 5 space, and Edge Animate is one of many of the Edge Tools and Services products developed to fill the hole left by Flash.

So where does this leave Flash? To paraphrase Mark Twain: "The reports of Flash's death are greatly exaggerated." As the focus shifted to HTML 5, Adobe asked a simple question: Where does Flash fit? The answer, unsurprisingly, was in the gaming space. Flash CS6 also marks the next step in the evolution of Flash as a media delivery platform in the HTML 5 universe, thanks in part to the CreateJS Toolkit designed for Flash Professional CS6 and two other new features: the ability to output Sprite Sheets and PNG sequences.

# Creating a PNG Sequence in Flash Professional CS6

Although a discussion of the CreateJS Toolkit is out of the scope of this book, creating PNG sequences and Sprite Sheets for Edge Animate isn't. A PNG sequence essentially renders each frame of a Flash movie clip or graphic symbol as a separate PNG image. Sprite Sheets do essentially the same thing, but all of the images in each frame are rendered, in sequence, in one document. From there a web developer can write the CSS code that moves around a single document already loaded into the browser rather than loading individual images created by a PNG sequence. Let's start with a PNG sequence:

1.  Open the Ant.fla file located in your Exercise folder. When it opens, you will see an ant standing in front of some grass (Figure 4-39). If you test the movie, the ant's head moves, the antennae wiggle, and the arm moves. All of this motion is contained in the Ant movie clip in the Flash Library.

**Figure 4-39.** We start with a simple animated character.

2. The focus of our attention is the ant. Double-click the Ant movie clip in the Library to open it. As you can see, the motion is created through the use of a combination of motion and shape tweens across the 31 frames of the animation.

3. Right-click the Ant movie clip in the Library to open the Context menu, shown in Figure 4-40. Select Export PNG Sequence.... This feature is new to Flash CS6 and only works with movie clips.

> *Another way of accessing this menu item is to right-click the movie clip on the Flash Timeline panel.*

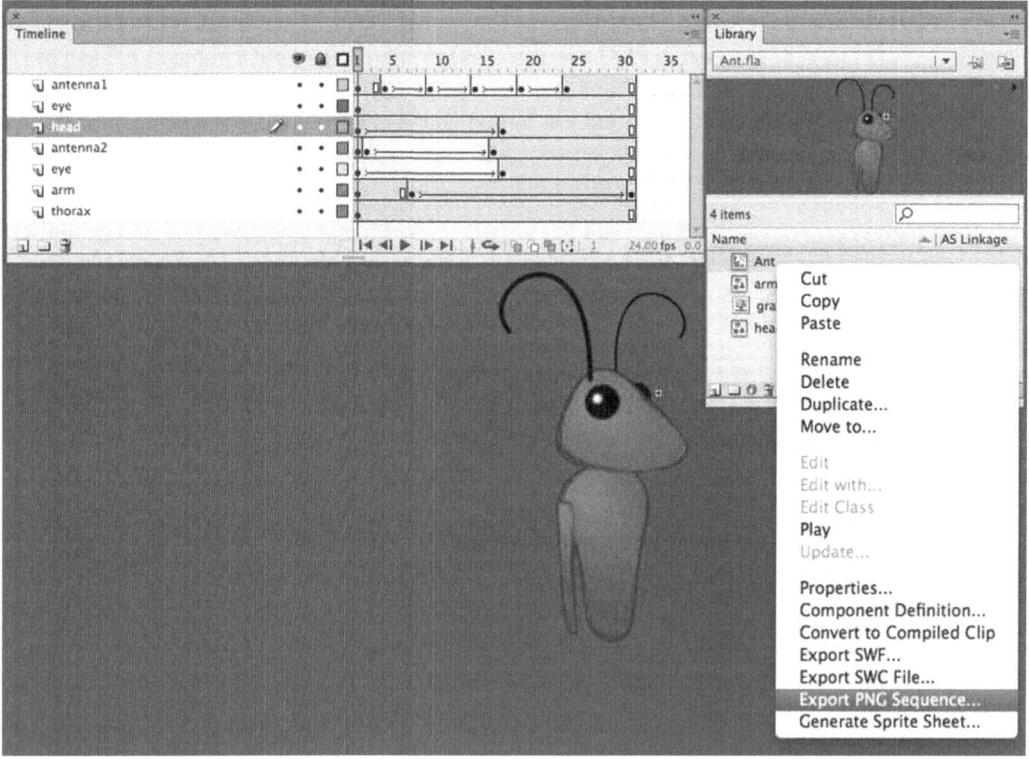

**Figure 4-40.** Export PNG Sequence... has been added to the Context menu in Flash Professional CS6.

4. When the Export PNG Sequence dialog box opens, navigate to the PNGSequence folder located in the same folder as this exercise. Click Save to target this folder.

5. The next dialog box you see, shown in Figure 4-41, is where you have to make some decisions:

- *Total*: The number of frames should not be confused with the number of images to be exported. This animation has a frame rate of 24 fps, so for 31 frames, this roughly translates to 1.5 seconds on the timeline, or 36 images.

- *Width and Height*: You can set the dimensions of each PNG image.

- *Resolution*: The default is the screen resolution of your computer. If you are targeting these images for a display with a higher resolution, this is the place to make the change.

- *Colors*: This area allows you to choose the bit depth for the PNG image, not the number of colors. Your choices are 8, 24, and 32 bit.

- *Smooth*: Select this check box to ensure the edges of the images blend into the background.

**Figure 4-41.** You control a lot of the properties for the images about to be exported.

6. Click the Export button and the sequence of images will be created and placed in the PNGSequence folder.

> *We showed you how to animate a PNG sequence in Edge Animate at the end of the previous chapter.*

# Creating a Sprite Sheet in Flash Professional CS6

The term *Sprite Sheet* might be a bit confusing, because sprites aren't the small, delicate graphics you may be imagining. A sprite is actually one very large image containing all of the images in the animation that is shifted around in a web page using the `background-position()` property of the CSS standard.

> One of the best descriptions of Sprite Sheets we have encountered comes from Chris Coyier at *http://css-tricks.com/css-sprites/*: "The origin of the term 'sprites' comes from old school computer graphics and the video game industry. The idea was that the computer could fetch a graphic into memory, and then only display parts of that image at a time, which was faster than having to continually fetch new images. The sprite was the big combined graphic. CSS Sprites is pretty much the exact same theory: get the image once, shift it around and only display parts of it, saves the overhead of having to fetch multiple images."

Follow *these steps to create a CSS Sprite Sheet in Flash Professional CS6:*

1. Open the `Ant.fla` image in your `Exercise` folder.

2. Open the Library and right-click the ant movie clip. Select Generate Sprite Sheet. . . from the Context menu to open the `Generate Sprite Sheet` dialog box, as shown in Figure 4-42.

> If you are creating a Sprite Sheet from Flash only, use the movie clip that has motion. Nested movie clips will not work.

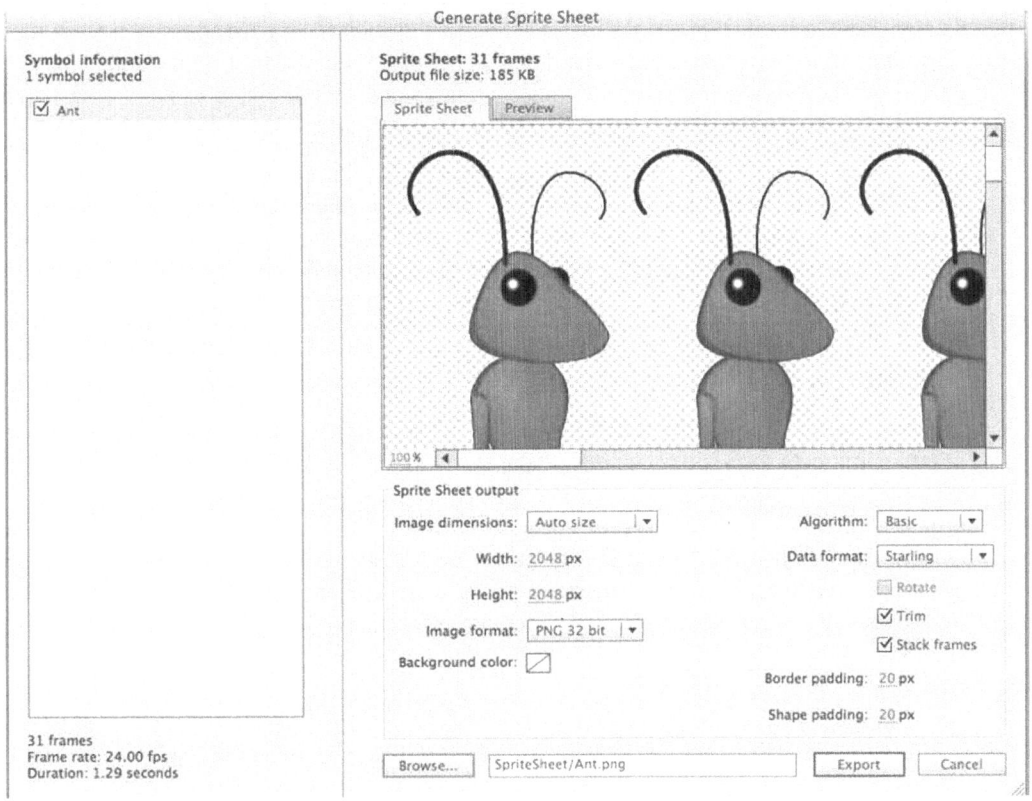

**Figure 4-42.** The Generate Sprite Sheet dialog box.

Let's look at what each area of this new dialog box does:

- *Symbol information*: All of the objects selected when the Generate Sprite Sheet... command is chosen will appear in this list. The check box let's you decide which instances of the objects will be placed in the Sprite Sheet.

- *Sprite Sheet*: Click this tab and you get a preview of the objects on the Sprite Sheet.

- *Preview*: Click this tab and you can play the animation.

- *Image dimensions*: The choices in this pop-down don't have anything to do with the contents of the Sprite Sheet. They set the dimensions of the Sprite Sheet. Leave it at the default Auto Size.

- *Width and Height*: These numbers allow you to manually set the dimension of the Sprite Sheet.

- *Image format*: You can choose between PNG and JPEG. If you need transparency, don't choose JPEG.

- *Background color*: This sets the background color for the Sprite Sheet.

- *Algorithm*: Your two choices are determined by the final destination for the Sprite Sheet. In the case of Adobe Edge Animate, you will have no problems with selecting Basic. If your target is a gaming engine, you would be wise to familiarize yourself with that engine's requirements.

- *Data format*: When a Sprite Sheet is created, two documents are created: the actual Sprite Sheet and a data document. Again the final use for the Sprite Sheet determines your choice of data format here. The default is Starling, which is targeted to the Flash Player's Stage 3D feature. Sparrow is aimed at iOS, and JSON is a good choice if you don't know the final use. Keep in mind, if all you need is the Sprite Sheet, the choice of data document format is irrelevant.

- *Border and Shape padding*: These numbers determine the spacing between the images in the Sprite Sheet .

- *Browse*: Use this to navigate to the folder that will contain the Sprite Sheet. In the case of this exercise, navigate to the SpriteSheet folder in the Exercise folder.

3. Click Export to create the Sprite Sheet.

4. Quit Flash and open the SpriteSheet folder. You will see, as shown in Figure 4-43, the Sprite Sheet and an XML document, which is the data document. We opened the Sprite Sheet in Fireworks to show you what the actual sheet looks like.

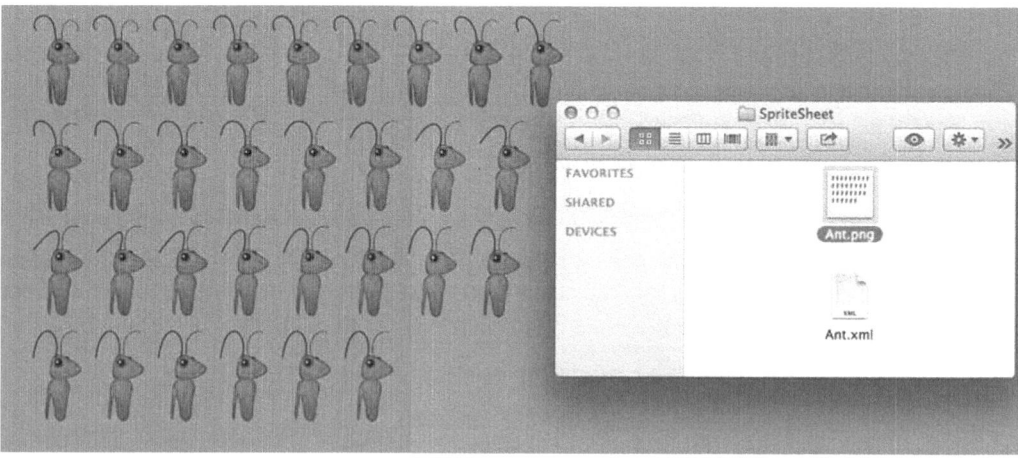

**Figure 4-43.** The files generated by Flash and the actual Sprite Sheet.

# Creating Sprite Animations in Edge Animate

With the Sprite Sheet created, we can now turn our attention to using it in Edge Animate. Before we do, it won't hurt to understand what it is we will be doing.

In Animate, everything on the Stage is contained in an element. This element can be thought of as a CSS div and, as such, several CSS properties can be manipulated in Edge Animate. In this case, the animation won't be created by moving the images around on the Stage. Instead the images will be moved around inside the element containing the Sprite Sheet. This is because the Sprite Sheet isn't seen by CSS as an image on the Stage but as a background image in the element or div containing it. This is a very fine distinction but is critical to your successfully using Sprite Sheets in Edge Animate. Let's get started.

1. Open the Ant.an file located in your Exercise folder. When it opens, you will see we have placed the Flash-generated Sprite Sheet on the Stage and used the grass background from the Flash file as well. As shown in Figure 4-44, we have added a vertical guide to help with the alignment of the ant as we move around inside the ant element.

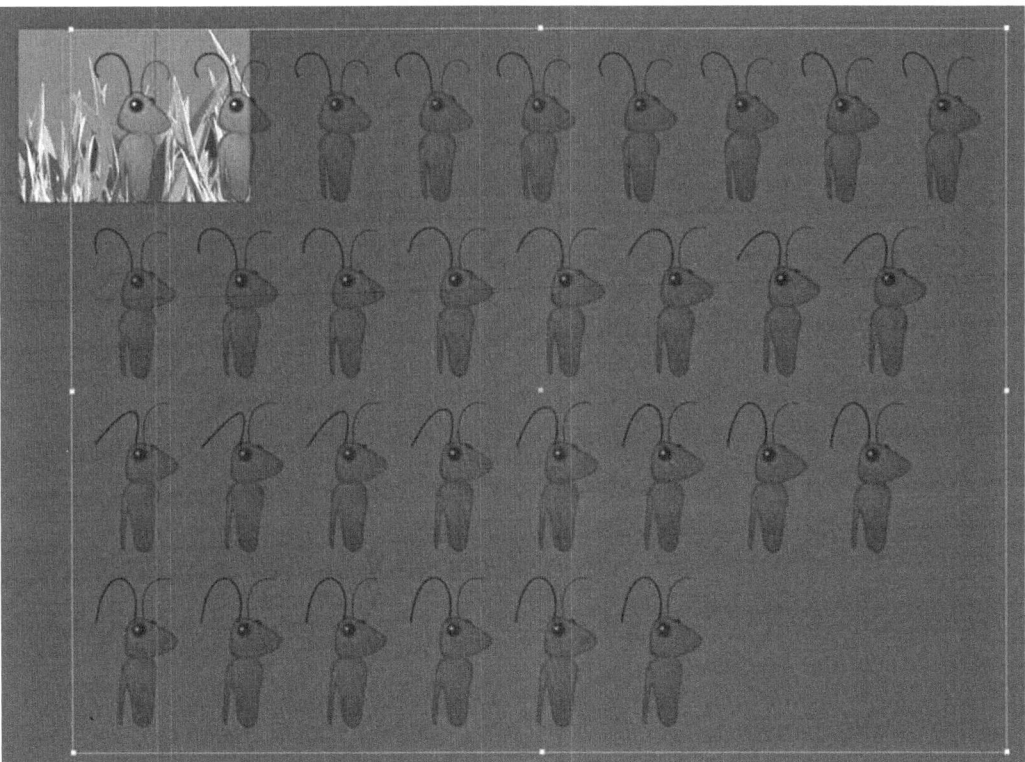

**Figure 4-44.** The Sprite Sheet from Flash is on the Edge Animate Stage.

*Here's a little teachers' trick. Before you output a Sprite Sheet for animation, preview it in Flash and look for edges that don't move. They will be where you will place the guides in Edge Animate. In this case, the ant's torso doesn't move, so we used a vertical guide to identify a static area in the image.*

2.  Select the Ant element on the Stage and turn on Clipping in the Properties panel. Change the right value to about 250 and the bottom value to about 366. What we have done is identify the area that will be shown on the Stage.

3.  With the Ant element still selected, turn off Autokeyframes and AutoTransitions. This will create the "flip book" effect as each image "appears" inside the element rather than moving within the element. Finally set the Grid Size to 24/sec and click the Show Grid button. This ensures the animation will run smoothly by giving us an accurate grid for the placement of keyframes.

4.  Twirl down the Image area of the Properties panel and, with the playhead at the 0 point of the timeline, add an XY keyframe (Figure 4-45). You will also notice a `Background Position` keyframe has been added to the timeline.

**Figure 4-45.** The motion is created by changing the X and Y position of the Background Image in the selected element.

5. Move the playhead to the next mark on the timeline. Add another XY keyframe in the Properties panel and scrub the X value, we used −216, to move the next ant into position. You should also note there is now a hollow keyframe on the timeline.

6. Repeat steps 4 and 5 for the rest of the ants in the Sprite Sheet. You will have to change the Y value only when you move to the next row of ants.

7. When you finish, you should have a regular row of hollow keyframes (Figure 4-46) and an ant in motion if you scrub the timeline or test the project in the browser.

**Figure 4-46.** The ant is in motion.

## You Have Learned

In this chapter, you have learned about the following:

- The various graphic formats used by Adobe Edge Animate
- How to create Adobe Edge Animate graphics in Photoshop

- How to create SVG graphics in Illustrator

- The emerging workflow between Fireworks and Adobe Edge Animate

- The emerging workflow between Flash Professional CS6 and Adobe Edge Animate

We covered a lot of ground here by showing how to use the various graphics applications provided by Adobe to create the graphics used by Adobe Edge Animate. We started by explaining the technology behind the formats and then dove into creating Adobe Edge Animate projects such as a banner ad for a cruise lines, floating hot air balloons, adding "video" clips using an animated GIF to Adobe Edge Animate, and exploring the creation of PNG sequences and Sprite Sheets in Flash Professional CS6.

So far, every Adobe Edge Animate project you have done is straight motion graphics. In the next chapter we dig into the fascinating world of typography and Adobe Edge Animate. We'll see you there.

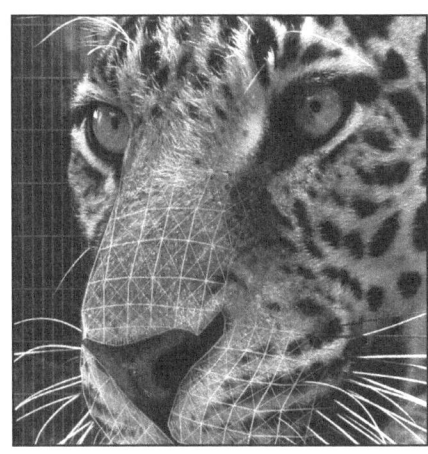

# Chapter 5

# Working with Type in Edge Animate

"Letterforms that honor and elucidate what humans see and say deserve to be honored in their turn. Well-chosen words deserve well-chosen letters; these in their turn deserve to be set with affection, intelligence, knowledge and skill. Typography is a link, and it ought, as a matter of honor, courtesy and pure delight, to be as strong as the others in the chain." Robert Bringhurst

This quote from Bringhurst's masterwork, *The Elements of Typographic Style* (second edition, Hartley and Marks, 2002), sums up the essence of type use in Adobe Edge Animate. The words we put on the Stage and subsequently put into motion are usually well chosen. They have to be, because they are the communication messengers, providing the user with access to understand the message you are trying to communicate. This chapter will focus on using type to do just that. The problem with type on the Web is that typography wasn't in the equation. Still, when it comes to using type on the Web, things are changing for the better.

Here is what we will cover in this chapter:

- A brief typography primer
- Adding text in Adobe Edge Animate
- Formatting text
- Adding and using drop shadows
- Clipping text
- Using web fonts in Adobe Edge Animate

If you haven't already downloaded the chapter files, they can be found at `http://www.apress.com/9781430243502`. In this chapter, we will be using these files:

- `Autumn.an`
- `Quote.rtf`
- `Shadow.an`
- `Clipping.an`
- `TypeKit.an`
- `GoogleFont.an`
- `AdobeWebFont.an`

# Fonts and Typefaces

Before we explain the difference between a font and a typeface, let's get really clear on one point: type is not that gray stuff that fits around your "whizzy" Adobe Edge Animate animations. It is your primary communications tool.

Reading is hard-wired into us. If it were not, you wouldn't be looking at this sentence and assimilating it in your brain. You have a need for information, and words are how you get it. The thing is, the choice of font and how you present the text not only affect the message, but they also affect the information presented. You can see this in Figure 5-1. The phrase "Edge is cool" takes on a different meaning in each instance of the phrase. Using the same Times New Roman typeface, but with the bold and italic variants, the message "changes," depending on the style applied.

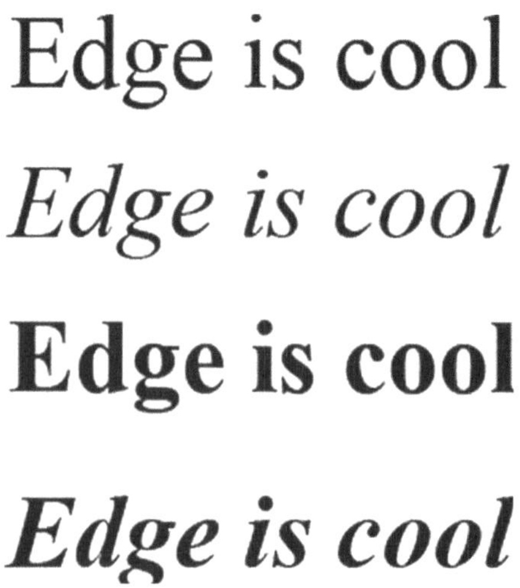

Edge is cool

*Edge is cool*

**Edge is cool**

***Edge is cool***

**Figure 5-1.** It is all about the message.

You can take this to the next level and see that not only variants but also the typeface itself have an effect on the message. Figure 5-2 shows five examples of the same information presented using different typefaces. You can see how the message changes even more dramatically.

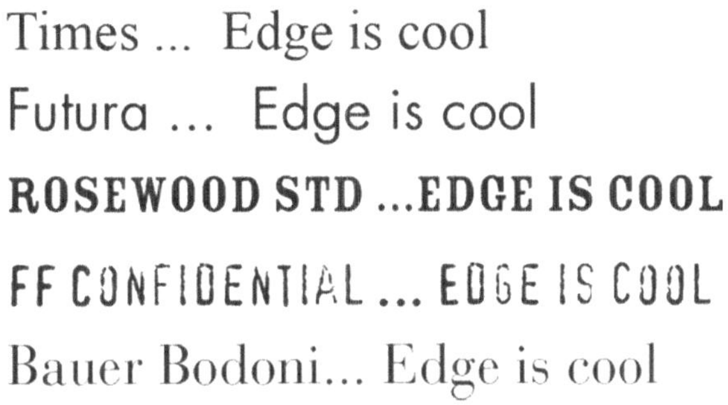

Times ... Edge is cool

Futura ... Edge is cool

ROSEWOOD STD ...EDGE IS COOL

FF CONFIDENTIAL ... EDGE IS COOL

Bauer Bodoni... Edge is cool

**Figure 5-2.** It is all about the message and the typeface chosen.

When choosing your fonts, you also have to be aware of their impact on readability and legibility. Both are achieved by an acute awareness of the qualities and attributes that make type readable. These attributes would include the typeface, the size, the color, and so on.

To illustrate this point, take a look at a small exercise one of the authors uses in his classes. What word is shown in Figure 5-3? Don't be too hasty to say "legibility." What are the sixth, seventh, eighth, and ninth characters? What letters are the first and second letters? Suddenly things become a bit disorienting.

ᴸᴸᶜᴳᴵᴠᴵᴵᴵᵛᵧ

**Figure 5-3.** What word is this?

This disorientation is important for you to understand. Our visual clue to legibility and readability, as shown in Figure 5-4, is the flow along the tops of the letters. This is why text that consists of all capital letters is usually so hard to read.

Legibility

**Figure 5-4.** We get our clues to letterforms from the tops of the letters.

We include this exercise because there is a huge temptation on the part of people new to Adobe Edge Animate to prove they're one of the "cool kids" and use font and color combinations that make otherwise legible text impossible to read. A good example of this is Figure 5-5. The word is set in a medium gray color on a dark gray background, and the size of the text is 10 pixels. The text is very difficult to read, and yet somehow the "cool kids" think this is some sweet action. Wrong! They just killed all access to the information contained in the text.

**Figure 5-5.** It is all about the message and the font chosen.

Figure 5-6 goes in the opposite direction. Type, even in signage, is used as a clear communication vehicle for the message.

Although paying attention to design is critical, from a type perspective, font-rendering technology in Edge Animate makes the use of a wide variety of fonts in your Animate projects a definite reality. In many respects, the ability to import fonts into Edge Animate gives you the opportunity to give those "well-chosen words" those "well-chosen letters" using the characters from a world of font choices rather than relying on the usual list of web-safe fonts. The ability to animate those well-chosen letters also gives you the ability to draw the viewer's attention to the message.

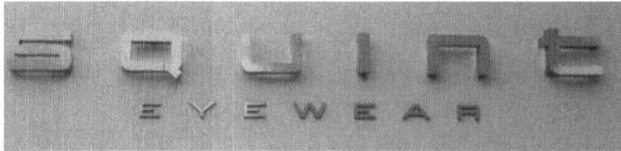

**Figure 5-6.** The message comes through loud and clear.

# Adding Text

In 2003, the noted Japanese designer Kenya Hara produced a series of stunning ads for his company, Muji. These ads contained nothing more than a photo of a horizon and the company name. In his 2007 book, *Designing Design* (Lars Muller Publishers), Kenya explains the concept: *"The 2003 campaign uses photographs of the horizon as an empty vessel of epic proportions."* Although we can't hope to even come close to Kenya's accomplishment, the following exercise uses his concept of "emptiness" and a single word to convey the message. Let's get started:

1. Open the Autumn.an file located in your Exercise folder. What you are looking at, as shown in Figure 5-7, is an autumn scene of the Niagara escarpment in southern Ontario.

**Figure 5-7.** We start with a simple horizon element.

2. Select the Text tool and click once on the Stage. Enter the word Autumn. You will notice that the text entry in Adobe Edge Animate is quite different from what you may be used to. The word, as shown in Figure 5-8, appears in a box and also on the Stage.

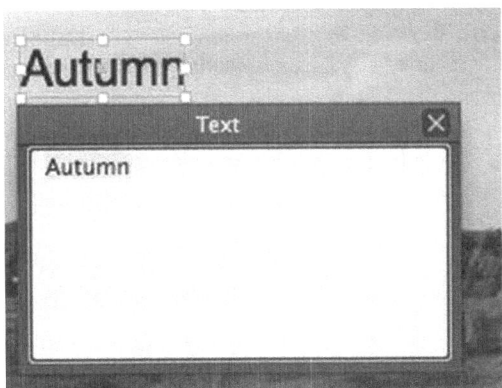

**Figure 5-8.** Adding text to an Edge Animate document

*One aspect of text you need to be aware of is how it is edited. If you need to fix a typo, add some text, or change a word, double-click the text to open the Text Input box.*

3. Having entered the text, the next step is to format it in the Properties panel shown in Figure 5-9. Click the double arrows at the bottom of the Text properties to reveal all of the choices available to you. Let's take a moment and review the various bits and pieces of this panel.

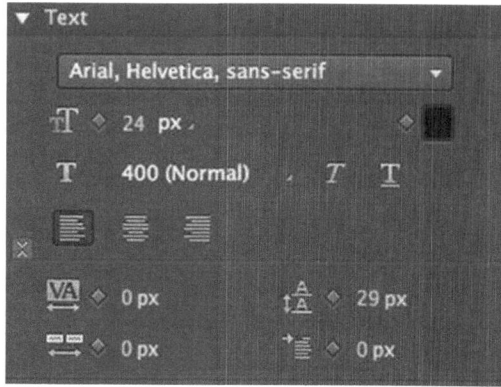

**Figure 5-9.** Your formatting options are found in the Properties panel.

- *Font*: This pop-down list lets you choose to apply the standard set of web fonts and their substitutes. These substitutes are referred to as the *fallbacks*. For example, If Arial is not installed on the viewer's device or computer, the browser will use Helvetica.

- *Size*: Scrub this value to increase or decrease the size of the text.

- *Color picker*: Click this to apply color to text.

- *Font weight*: You have to admit the font Times Roman Bold Oblique sounds rather neat. The problem is that CSS3 doesn't have a clue what the term *Bold* means. In Edge Animate, which uses CSS3, the weight of the fonts is expressed on a numerical basis. If you click the 400 (Normal) weight in the Properties panel, the pop-down shown in Figure 5-10 appears. The values 100 to 900 specify font weights where each number represents a weight darker than its predecessor. In all cases, 400 is generally considered the "normal" or Roman weight, and 700 is bold.

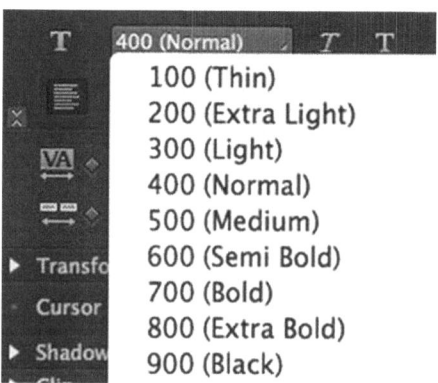

**Figure 5-10.** Font weights are expressed numerically.

Be careful with the font weights. When you add a font to an Edge Animate composition, it may or may not include all of the weights. The unavailable weights will not be grayed out in this menu. Choose a weight that is not available, Geneva 500 for example, and the weight will default to Geneva 700.

- *Alignment*: The choices are flush left, centered, or flush right.

- *Letter spacing*: Don't confuse this with kerning. Scrub this value and you increase the space between letters in the text block, not letter pairs. Negative values aren't allowed.

- *Line height*: Just like its "leading" counterpart, this choice adds space between lines of text.

- *Word spacing*: Increases the space between the words in the text block. Negative values aren't allowed.

- *Indent*: Scrub this value to indent a text block, not the first line. Negative values can't be applied.

There is one other aspect of using fonts in Edge Animate: contextual selectors. At the top of the Properties panel is the pop-down list, as shown in Figure 5-11. The list contains a number of element/tag selectors commonly used in CSS. This is deliberate. Remember, Adobe Edge Animate uses CSS to create motion, and the formatting you choose will be applied to the element/tag selectors in the CSS created by Adobe Edge Animate.

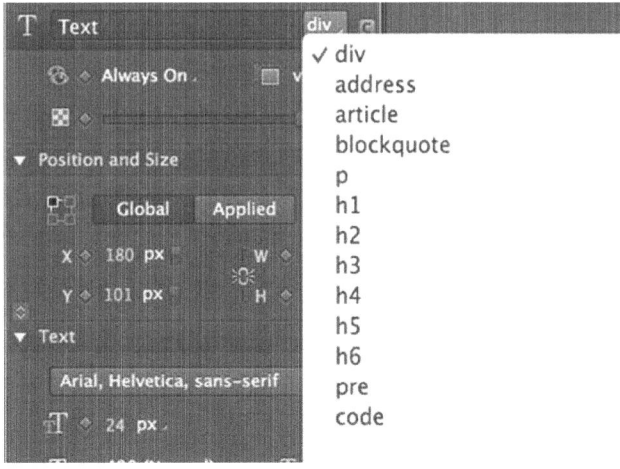

**Figure 5-11.** You can apply CSS formatting to your text in Adobe Edge Animate.

4.  With the text selected, use these values in the Properties panel:

    - Location: 342, 150

    - Font: Arial Black, Gadget, sans-serif

- Size: 40

- Color: #FFFFFF

- Alignment: Left

5. Deselect the text and, as shown in Figure 5-12, you get a real sense of how well-chosen words benefit from well-formatted letters. To understand how font choice affects the message, change the font to one of the others in the font pop-down.

**Figure 5-12.** A single word, if properly formatted, can speak volumes.

## Working with Text Blocks in Edge Animate

Edge Animate can also work with blocks of text, but there are a few things you need to be aware of. Let's find out:

1. Delete the text on the Stage.

2. Open Quote.rtf in a word processor and copy the paragraph—it is the quote that leads off this chapter—to the clipboard.

3. Quit the word processor and return to Edge Animate.

4. Select the Text tool, click once on the Stage, and paste the text on the clipboard into the text entry box. The text, as shown in Figure 5-13, is placed using the last style chosen in the Font menu.

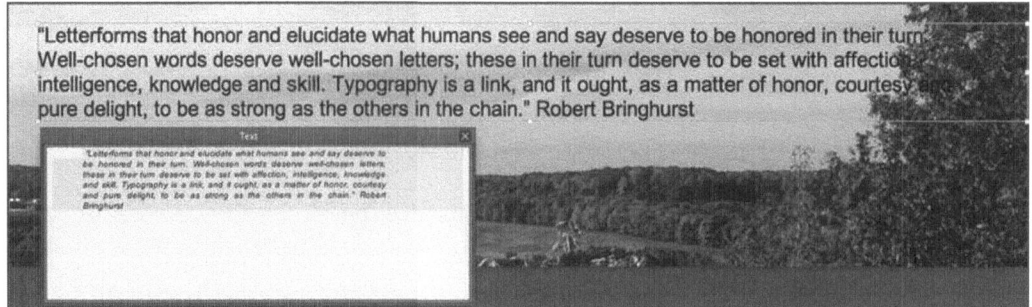

**Figure 5-13.** Blocks of text can be pasted into Animate or directly entered into the Text entry box.

5.  With the text box selected on the Stage, use these format settings:

    •   *Font*: Tahoma, Geneva, sans-serif

    •   *Size*: 18 pixels

    •   *Weight*: 500 Medium

    •   *Line height*: 28 pixels

6.  Obviously the line length for the text is not correct. Drag the right edge of the text box inward to between the words "say" and "deserve" in the first line of the text.

7.  You will notice the height of the text box doesn't change, although the text is all there. Pull the bottom of the box to the bottom of the text block. This behavior may be new to many of you used to text blocks that cut off the overflow text. In Edge Animate, the text is in an element and, in the case of text, the Overflow property is not set to Hidden.

8.  The next thing to do is to format the author's name to be under the quote. Double-click the text to open the Text dialog box, click once in front of the author's name and press the Return key. As shown in Figure 5-14, there is a lot of space added in the dialog box, but the name just shifts down a line in the text on the Stage. Just add another space to move the name down one more line.

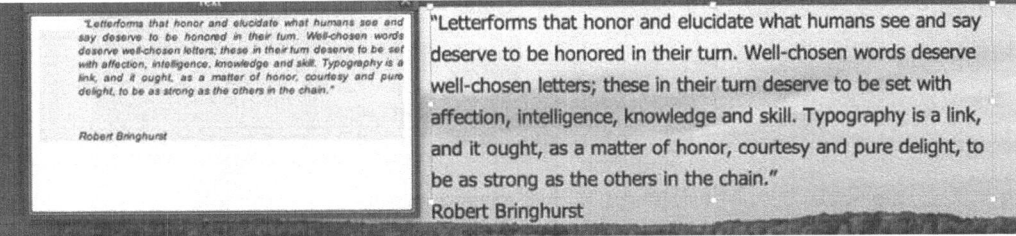

**Figure 5-14.** There is a difference between what you see in the text box and what you see on the Stage.

What you can gather from this is that all of the text in a text box is treated as a single entity. If you try, for example, to change the quote's color from black to white, this change will apply to all of the text in the text element on the Stage. When working with long blocks of text, this is something to keep in mind.

# Text Shadows

In Chapter 3 we showed you how shadows can be added to objects. The same techniques can be applied to text as well. When applying a drop shadow to objects and text, one aspect of a shadow—the light source—tends to get overlooked.

When objects are in motion and cast a shadow, the assumption is the light source is fixed into one position. This is not necessarily the case. Shadows can indicate depth—the farther away a shadow is from the object the fainter it becomes—and shadows can actually indicate a light source in motion. Let's explore these two concepts:

1. Open the Shadow.an file in your Exercise folder. When it opens, you will see a rusted steel door with the word Rust on the Stage.

2. Select the text and apply the following shadow settings:

   - *Color*: Black

   - *Horizontal*: 13 pixels

   - *Vertical*: 16 pixels

   - *Blur radius*: 13 pixels

As shown in Figure 5-15, a standard shadow appears under the text.

**Figure 5-15.** We start with a standard drop shadow.

3. Click once on the Pin and move the playhead to the 2-second mark of the timeline.

4. Change the Blur radius value to 30 and scrub the timeline. The shadow gets fainter, which indicates the text, as shown in Figure 5-16, has moved closer to the light source. What you can gather from this simple example is that shadow properties can be animated.

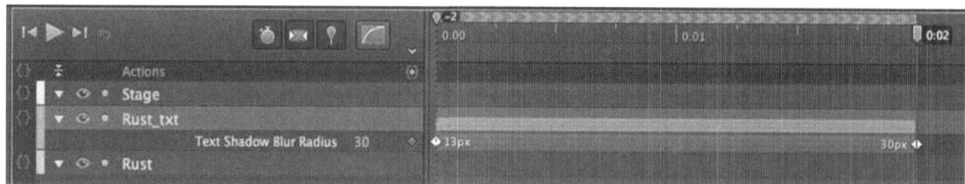

**Figure 5-16.** The Shadow Blur Radius can be tweened.

Knowing the Text Blur Radius can be tweened, it is logical to assume the Vertical and Horizontal Offset properties can also be tweened. Here's how:

5. Move the playhead—not the Pin—to the 0 point on the timeline and move the text to the upper left corner of the image. Change the Top value to –20 and the Left value to –33. The shadow is above and to the left of the text.

6. Move the playhead to the 2-second mark and move the text block to the bottom right of the image. Change the Top value to 32 and the Left value to 34.

7. Rewind the movie and press the spacebar to play the movie. The text position, the shadow blur, and the offset values (Figure 5-17) all change as the text moves down the Stage.

**Figure 5-17.** Shadows can be put in motion.

# Clipping Text

We have all seen those banner ads where a car or some other object zips across the ad and the text appears, letter by letter, as the object moves across the text block. This is not accomplished using fancy masking techniques or the use of a solid shape that is carefully scaled on the horizontal axis to reveal the text. It is done using the `clip:rect =()` property of the CSS specification.

The key to understanding how clipping works is the `rect` segment of the property. Remember, text sits in an element on the Edge Animate Stage, and each element is really nothing more than a box/rect with some content in it. The clipping property in Edge Animate allows you to animate the four sides of that box to create some rather interesting effects. In this example, we are going to "pull some words out of a hat" using the clipping property. Let's get started:

1. Open the `Clipping.an` file located in your `Exercise` folder. When it opens, as shown in Figure 5-18, you will see an extremely long arm has been animated to move over 2 seconds. The plan is to have the text under the arm appear as the arm move off the Stage.

**Figure 5-18.** For our next magic trick, we will pull some text out of a hat.

2. Move the playhead to the 0 point of the timeline and select the `Text` element.

3. With the text selected, click the Clipping switch in the Properties panel to turn on clipping.

4.  Change the `Right` value, as shown in Figure 5-19, to `0` and add a `Clip` keyframe The text box shrinks and the text disappears. The text really didn't disappear. The right edge of the element "clipped" off the contents.

**Figure 5-19.** Clipping text.

5.  Move the playhead to the 2-second mark of the timeline and scrub the right edge value in the Properties panel to reveal the text.

6.  Test the movie in a browser (Figure 5-20). It's not magic—it's clipping.

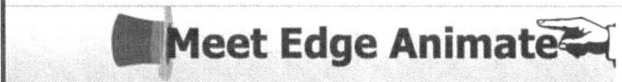

**Figure 5-20.** Clipping text is an effective technique to know.

# Meet Your New Best Friend: Web Fonts

It is important that we start this section by stating the obvious: Web typography, deservedly, has a really bad reputation.

In 1995, when Netscape added the `<font>` tag to HTML, it only took a short time for designers to realize just how limiting this tag was when it came to typography. This was especially true when they realized this lowly tag was controlling not only the content but also the style. One year later, the first CSS specification, separating presentation from structure, was published, and the standards movement really took hold shortly thereafter. Even then there was a serious issue, designers couldn't use fonts that were not installed on the user's computer.

Although a number of solutions—sIFR (Scalable Inman Flash Replacement) was one—appeared, they just didn't solve the font issue because they presented their own set of problems, ranging from a reliance on third-party software and text that couldn't be selected to increased load times. The crazy thing was the solution to the issues was actually contained in the CSS2 specification released in 1998. The solution? @ font-face. Why did it take so long for this rule to find its way to Adobe Edge Animate? A number of things derailed this rule, and it is a familiar tale.

First, the major browser manufacturers, Microsoft and Netscape, picked different methods of supporting web fonts in their browsers. Both ignored the most widely used font technology in the business: TrueType. Instead, Netscape went one way and supported TrueDoc, while Microsoft went in the opposite direction and developed its own format: Embedded Open Type (EOT) format. Although the two major type foundries at the time—Adobe and Monotype—supported the EOT format, market resistance to anything Microsoft hobbled EOT.

It took 10 years for this impasse to be resolved and, in 2007, Microsoft released the EOT specification and sent it to the W3C for approval. Naturally, this solution hit a roadblock. The other browser vendors refused to support it because of serious Digital Rights Management (DRM) concerns regarding legal liabilities. The design industry didn't exactly embrace it either. Microsoft's method of converting TTF (TrueType) fonts to EOT was seen as being confusing and difficult to use. What was needed was a solution that used OpenType, had no licensing issues, and was relatively code free.

That solution, which has finally received broad acceptance from all concerned, is the Web Open Font Format (WOFF). WOFF is essentially a compressed version of the file format used by the PostScript, TrueType, and OpenType fonts on your computer. What broke the logjam was WOFF's ability to include metadata allowing font vendors to "tag" their fonts along with private-use data, which is the reason WOFF has been embraced by the major foundries and the @font-face rule from the CSS2 specification is broadly used.

The upshot of all of this is web designers have a world of typography options available to them because fonts can now be "rented" by web sites by licensing a particular font to a URL or, if they are open source or royalty free, can be used in any web page. Not only that, but the text is fully searchable and, as time goes on, fonts used in other languages can be used on web sites. This also explains, to a great extent, why Adobe, in 2011, purchased Typekit, one of the first web font delivery and hosting services and, one year later, add the Webfonts app to the Edge Tools and Services, which offers a collection of Webkit, Google web fonts, and open source fonts that can be freely used in your Animate compositions. Naturally, this technology has been built into Edge Animate.

> *Before we start, it is important you understand that we will start by using a font from Typekit. If you don't have a Typekit account, you aren't out of the game. There are a number of other font delivery services out there—http://webfonts.fonts.com/en-US—that will supply you with a similar embed code to those used in this example. We also explain how to use the free Google fonts after this example. This is also one of the few exercises in this book where, for obvious copyright reasons, we won't be supplying a completed exercise file.*

# Adding Typekit Web Fonts to an Edge Animate Project

We still aren't happy using Arial Black in the Autumn project. It is a bit too heavy and the decision is to use a condensed font for the word. After hitting the typebooks, the team settles on Franklin Gothic Condensed from Typekit. Here's how to pick and add a Typekit web font to an Edge Animate composition:

> *Most vendors will allow you to try out their service on a limited basis, and one of the most important questions during the sign up process will be the URL of the site to which you are licensing the font. To see the fonts you will choose in your Edge Animate project, enter the following local IP address—127.0.0.1—when asked by a vendor. Remember, Edge Animate uses a Webkit browser to display stage content. This is the IP address used by the Edge Animate Stage.*

1. Log in to your Typekit account and you will see the Browse Fonts page shown in Figure 5-21.

**Figure 5-21.** There are quite a number of fonts to choose from.

2. On the left side of the page are the fonts available. The right side lets you narrow the selection. We want to use a Franklin Gothic Condensed font. We can use the filters on the right side to narrow the selection:

   • *Classification*: Sans Serif

   • *Properties*: Roman

   • *Width*: Narrow

   Notice, too, the Language Support list. By choosing a language, the glyphs and characters unique to that language will also be added to your font choices.

3. Locate the font named Franklin Gothic URW Condensed and click the +Add to Kit button. This adds the selected font to your lineup and takes you to the typekitEditor, shown in Figure 5-22.

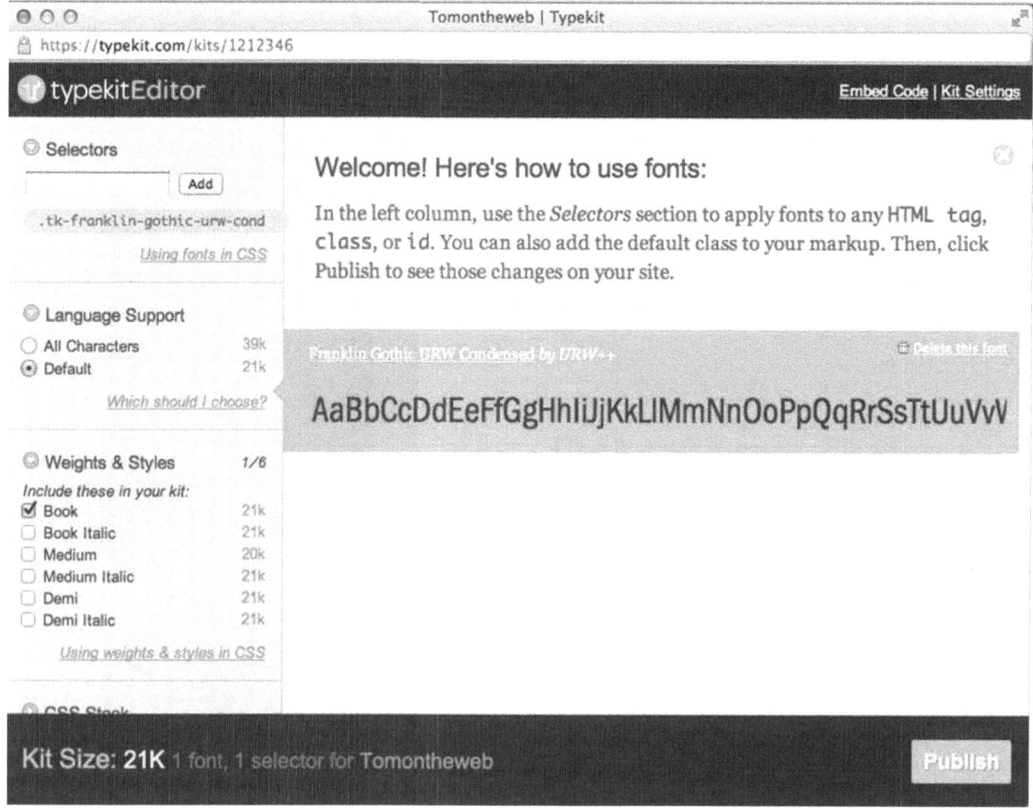

**Figure 5-22.** The typekitEditor is how the fonts are added to a project.

4. In the left column, select Book in the Weights & Styles section. This restricts the font to only that weight and keeps the file size to a manageable 21k.

5. Edge Animate needs to know what name to use for the font's selector and fallback font. Click the Using font family names in your CSS link to open the dialog box shown in Figure 5-23. Pull out a pen and write down, exactly including the quotation marks, the text selected in the top area of the dialog box.

## Using font family names in your CSS

In addition to using the Selectors setting to tell Typekit where to apply this font, you can use the font directly in your CSS rules with the following font-family value:

```
"franklin-gothic-urw-cond"
```

Here's an example:

```
h1 {
    font-family: "franklin-gothic-urw-cond";
}
```

You can also include a fallback font for older browsers by listing it after the Typekit font-family value. Here's an example of that:

```
h1 {
    font-family: "franklin-gothic-urw-cond",sans-serif;
}
```

Figure 5-23. Edge Animate needs to know what font family value to use when accessing the web font.

6. Click the Embed Code link. The dialog box shown in Figure 5-24 opens. Copy the code to the clipboard. You will need it in Edge Animate.

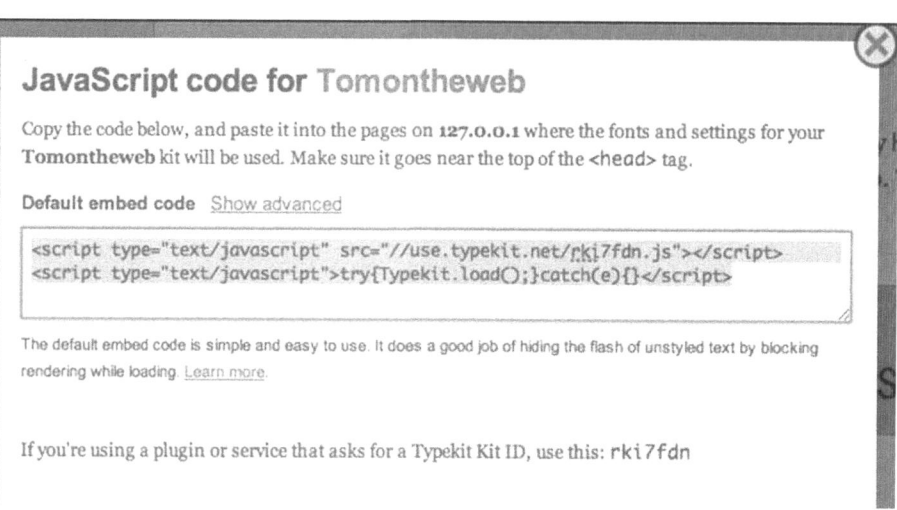

**Figure 5-24.** Copy the JavaScript embed code to the clipboard.

7.  Close the Embed code and click the Publish button. When the Updating Alert disappears, quit the browser.

## Adding a Web Font to Adobe Edge Animate

Having copied and pasted the JavaScript code to the clipboard, you will be using it in Adobe Edge Animate. Follow these steps:

1.  Open the TypeKit.an file found in your Exercise folder.

2.  If it isn't open, open the Library and click the + sign in the Fonts section to open the Edit Web Font dialog box shown in Figure 5-25.

3.  Paste the JavaScript on your clipboard into the Embed Code area.

4.  In the Font Fallback List area, enter the name of the font you earlier noted: "franklin-gothic-urw-cond", Arial, sans-serif.

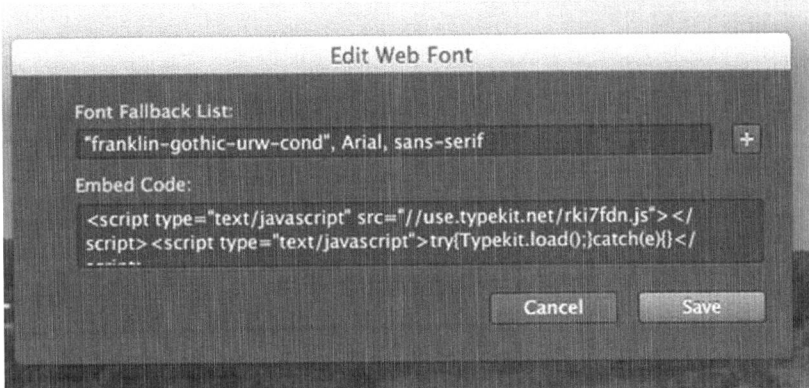

**Figure 5-25.** The web font and the fallback fonts are added to the Adobe Edge Animate project.

5. Click the Save button. The dialog box will close and you will see the font appear in the Library.

6. Select the text and, in the Properties panel, select your new font in the Font pop-down. When you release the mouse, the text, as show in Figure 5-26, is formatted using Franklin Gothic Condensed.

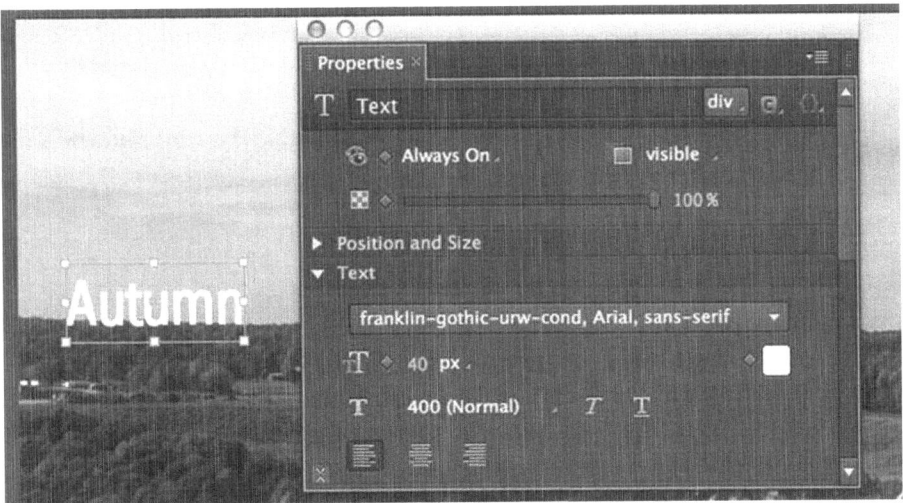

**Figure 5-26.** Web fonts can rapidly become your new best friend.

*The key to this exercise is not the Typekit font. It is the JavaScript code that you need and the web font vendors will supply the code. The only difference between this example and the other vendors is the route to the JavaScript. The other key point to keep in mind is the fallback font. You need it because there are still browsers out there that do not support the @ fontface tag.*

## Adding a Free Google Web Font to an Adobe Edge Animate Project

It comes as no surprise that Google is in the web fonts game. If you point your browser to http://www.google.com/webfonts, you have access to a rather extensive collection of fonts that can be used in your projects. In this exercise we are going to choose and use a free Google web font in an Adobe Edge Animate project. You will discover the process to be remarkable similar to using one from a commercial service such as Typekit. Let's get started:

1. Open the web page at http://www.google.com/webfonts as shown in Figure 5-27.

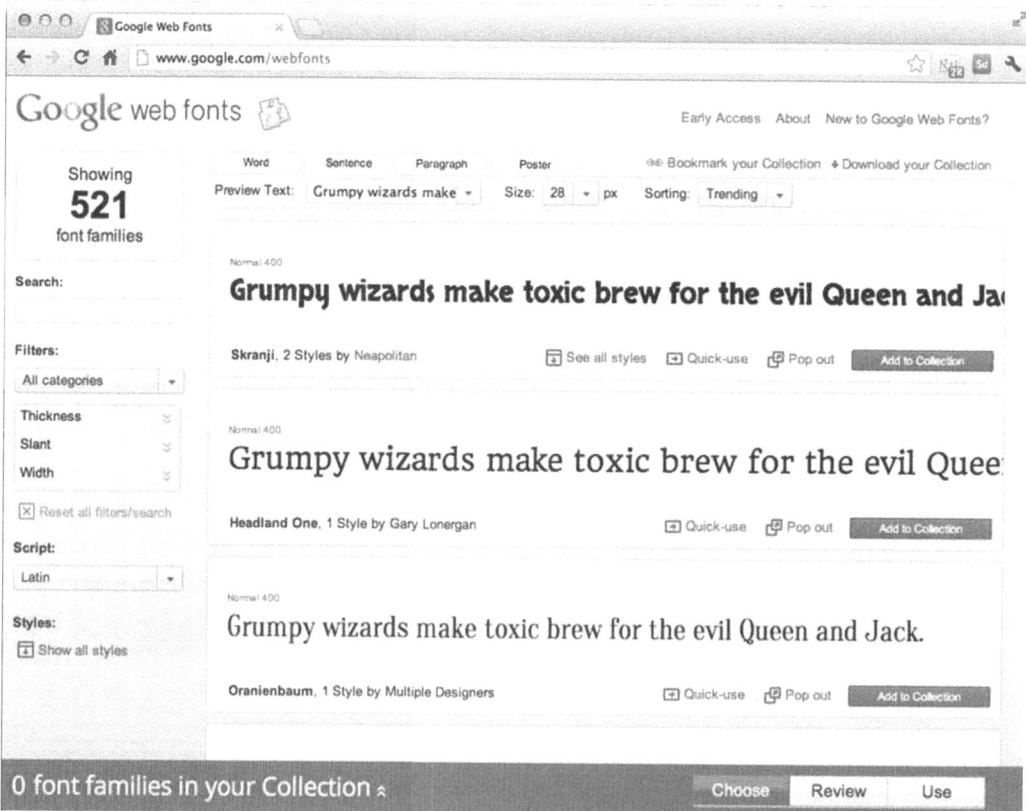

**Figure 5-27.** You start at Google's web fonts home page.

The plan is to use a relatively thin sans-serif as we did in the previous exercise.

2.  Select Sans Serif in the Filters pop-down. A list of suggestions, as shown in Figure 5-28, will appear to the right. At the top of this we chose 36 px as our starting point because we wanted to see a sample that was close to the 40 pixel size used in Adobe Edge Animate.

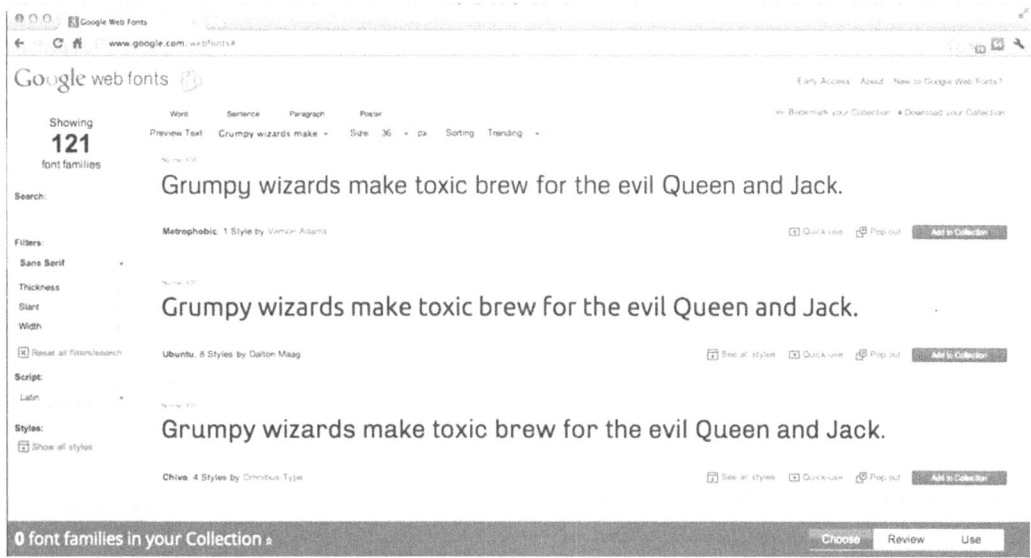

**Figure 5-28.** Picking a Google web font.

> *Unlike Typekit, you don't have access to the font weight variations used in Typekit. Google uses a slider-based approach for thickness, slant, and width to filter a font selection, which makes choosing an Ultra Bold Italic variation of the selected font extremely difficult.*

3.  Locate Ubuntu and click the Add to Collection button.

4.  Click the Quick-use button at the bottom of the interface to open the font page shown in Figure 5-29. At the top of the page are the various styles. We selected the Normal 400 variation. That little stopwatch on the right acts as a speedometer showing you what happens to page load speed as you add or subtract variations of the Ubuntu font.

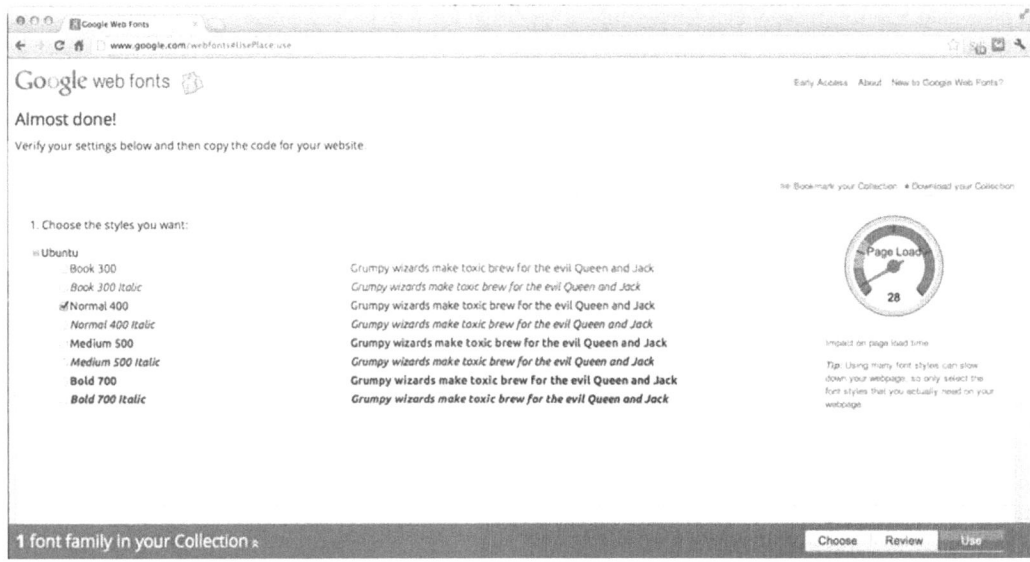

**Figure 5-29.** We settle on the Normal 400 variation of the Ubuntu font.

5. Scroll down the page. The next three areas, shown in Figure 5-30, allow you to choose the character sets and present you with the embed code and fallback fonts to use in Adobe Edge Animate.

**Figure 5-30.** The embed code and fallback path.

6. Copy the embed code to your clipboard and open the GoogleFont.an project in your Exercise folder.

7. When Adobe Edge Animate opens, click the + sign in the Fonts panel to open the Edit Web Font dialog box, shown in Figure 5-31. Enter a Font Fallback List and paste the Embed Code. The font will be added to the fonts panel.

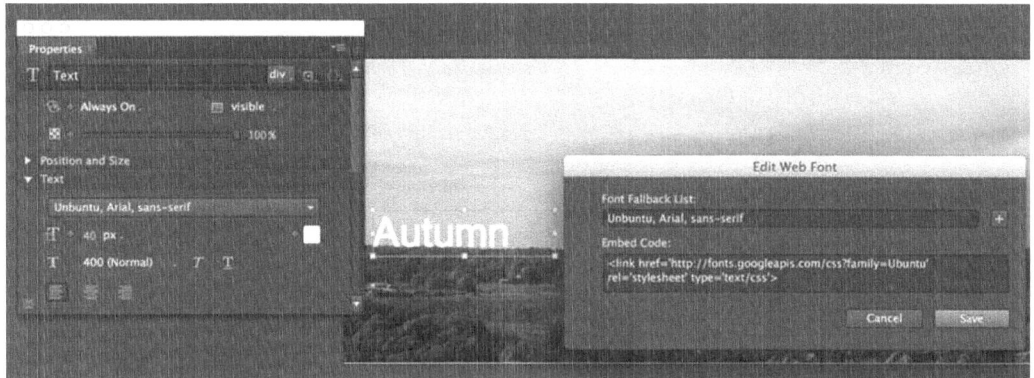

**Figure 5-31.** A Google web font is added for use in Adobe Edge Animate.

8. In the Properties panel, open the font pop-down and, as shown in Figure 5-32, your new font is in the list. Select the font and set the text to a size of 40 pixels and the color to white.

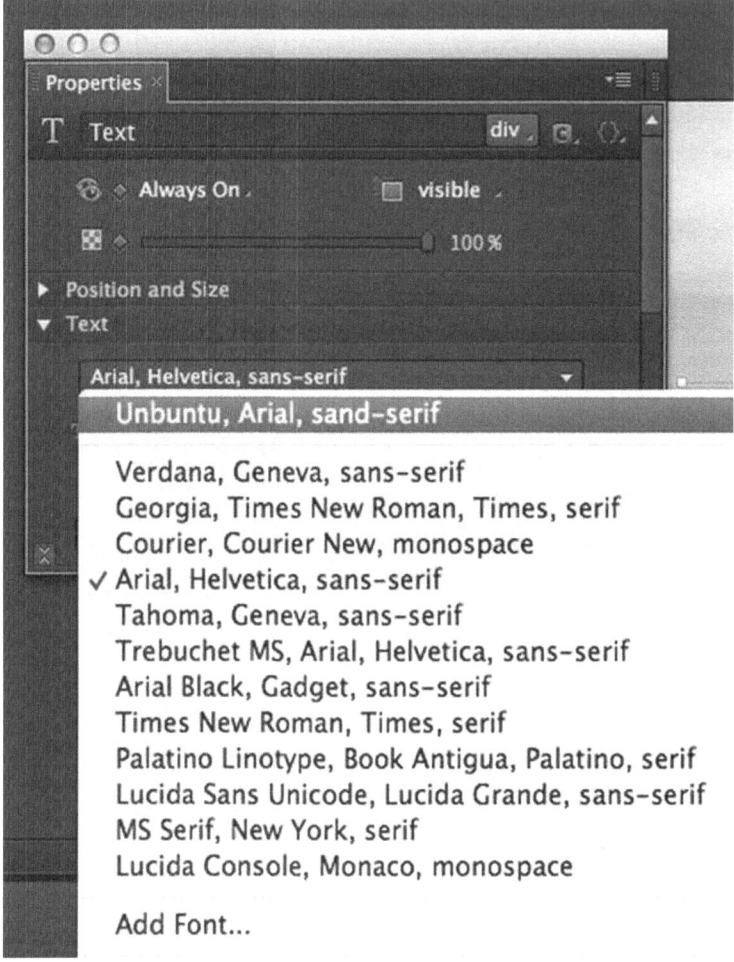

**Figure 5-32.** The Google web font has been added to the font list.

> *What if you change your mind and want to remove a font from the list? Simply click once on it in the Fonts area of the Library and press the Delete key.*

## Using Adobe Edge Web Fonts in Animate

In late September 2012, Adobe introduced a full range of HTML 5 tools and services under the Edge brand. Included in this offering was a font service called Web Fonts. This service, still in its infancy, is planned to become a rather extensive offering of free web fonts from a variety of vendors ranging from Typekit to Google web fonts and a number of open source font collections.

An obvious question is: "Can I use the Web Fonts in my Animate compositions?" The answer is yes but the workflow is a bit different from that used to add a web font to a composition. The reason is, Web Fonts was still in development when Animate was completed and, unlike Typekit and Google web fonts, there are no direct "hooks," like those from Google and Typekit, into Animate at the time of this writing. Even so, the workflow is not complicated. If you can copy and paste, you can use web fonts. Here's how:

1.  Open your browser and point it to `http://html.adobe.com/edge/webfonts/`. This will open the Adobe Web Fonts service page.

2.  Scroll down to the `Preview Edge Web Fonts` area, shown in Figure 5-33.

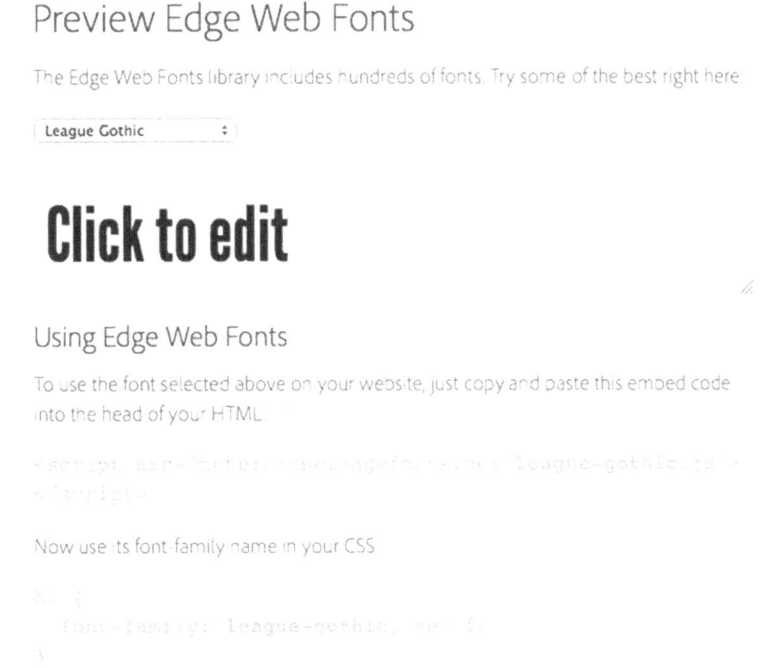

**Figure 5-33.** Fonts are chosen from the Preview Edge Web Fonts area of the page.

3.  Click the pop-down list to reveal the available fonts. Select `League Gothic`. A preview of the font will appear.

4.  Select the Embed code and copy it to your clipboard. Don't close the browser.

This is where the new workflow comes into play. You can't paste the Embed code on the clipboard into the Edge Animate Add Web Font dialog box. It needs to be added the to `<Head>` of the HTML document containing the Animate composition. In this case we will be using the HTML created by Animate. Here's how:

5. Open an HTML editor, we are using Dreamweaver CS6, and open the `AdobeWebFont.html` page. Switch to Code view.

6. Click once in `line` 7 of the code and paste the Embed code on the clipboard into the code between the `<head></head>` tags. (Figure 5-34). Save the file and quit your editor.

```
1    <!DOCTYPE html>
2    <html>
3    <head>
4      <meta http-equiv='Content-Type' content='text/html; charset=utf-8'>
5      <title>Untitled</title>
6
7 ▼  <script src="http://use.edgefonts.net/league-gothic.js"></script>
8
9    <!--Adobe Edge Runtime-->
10     <script type="text/javascript" charset="utf-8" src="AdobeWebFont_edgePreload.js"></script>
11     <style>
12       .edgeLoad-EDGE-670030010 { visibility:hidden; }
13     </style>
14   <!--Adobe Edge Runtime End-->
15
16   </head>
17   <body style="margin:0;padding:0;">
18     <div id="stage" class="EDGE-670030010">
19     </div>
20   </body>
21   </html>
```

**Figure 5-34.** The Web font embed code is pasted into the <head> of the HTML document.

7. Return to the web browser and, in the font family area, select just the words `league-gothic,serif` and copy it to the clipboard. Close the browser.

8. Open the `AdobeWebFonts.an` file located in your `Exercise` folder. When it opens, you will be informed that, as shown in Figure 5-35, the file has changed. This is to be expected because you added the embed code to the document's `<header>`. Click Yes.

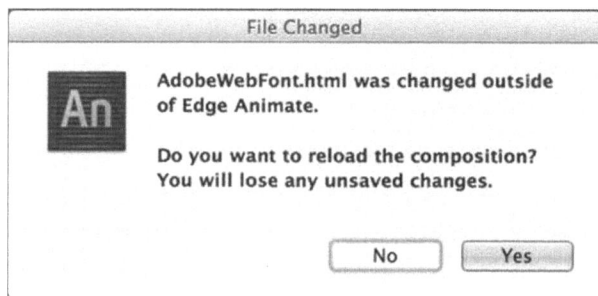

**Figure 5-35.** Notification that the file has been changed.

9.   Click the Add  Font icon and when the Add  Font dialog box opens, paste the contents of the clipboard into the Font Fallback List area. Click the Add Font button to accept the change.

10.  Select the text on the Stage and, in the Text area of the Properties panel, select league-gothic, serif. The text font changes to League-Gothic, serif (Figure 5-36).

**Figure 5-36.** The Adobe web font is added to Edge Animate.

# You Have Learned

In this chapter, we have covered the absolute basics of using type in an Adobe Edge Animate project. We covered:

- Typography fundamentals.
- Formatting text on the Adobe Edge Animate Stage
- The features of the text area in the Properties panel
- Adding shadows to text and putting them in motion
- Clipping text
- Adding a Typekit font to the Font panel
- Adding a Google web font to the Font panel
- Adding an Adobe Web Font to an Edge Animate composition

This also marks the midpoint of the book. So far we have covered the basics of using Adobe Edge Animate. From this point on, we will start looking at the really neat stuff you can do with the application, and it starts with interactivity. Turn the page and start learning how the code features of Adobe Edge Animate open an entire universe of possibility to your projects.

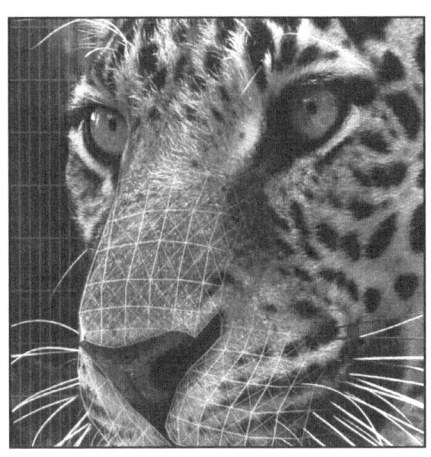

# Chapter 6

# Adding Interactivity in Edge Animate

Programming an Edge Animate composition, Flash movie, or mobile app is a complicated process requiring the ability to logically think through the minutia of what might, on the surface, seem to be a relatively insignificant task. This is the job of the coder or as he or she is more commonly known—the developer—and our goal is not to turn you into a programmer outright but to provide you with a basic understanding of the coding features built into Edge Animate.

Here's what we will cover in this chapter:

- Using the Code panel

- Understanding the fundamentals of events

- Using the code snippets bundled with Edge Animate

- How to add interactivity to an Edge Animate project

- The relation between labels and triggers on the timeline

- A method of adding nonlinear navigation to an Edge Animate project

If you haven't already downloaded the chapter files, they can be found at http://www.apress.com/9781430243502. In this chapter, we will be using these files:

- LabelsTriggers.an

- Symbols.an

- Button.an

- `SlideShow.an`

- `Tour.an`

Using the coding features in Edge Animate is, in many ways, like owning a car. Most of us, when shown the engine of a car in the showroom, immediately understand that maintaining it is beyond our ability and we resolve to leave the routine maintenance and repair to a qualified mechanic. Others, when the hood is opened, immediately dive into the intricacies of the engine and aren't happy until they understand how to replace the transmission. Whichever way you lean, it is hard to argue against at least acquiring the basic skills necessary to change the oil and maybe replace a flat tire.

To this point in the book, practically everything you have done has essentially moved stuff from "here" to "there." There has been no interactivity, and everything learned, as it moves from here to there, was linear. This is not a bad thing, but the very nature of the modern Web is this: *It is an interactive, nonlinear, environment.* It could be anything from a full-bore Flash application used in online banking to something as simple as a hyperlink in a web page, but what is common throughout is the use of code to enable that interactivity.

Thanks to the rise of HTML 5 and CSS3 and their ability to seemingly bring the Web to practically any device that has a browser, web connection, and a screen, there has been a corresponding increase in the usage of JavaScript and the jQuery library in the Web and mobile spaces. This is primarily in the areas of navigation within a document, creating animations, and handling events resulting from user or timeline interaction.

Before we start looking at how you can use code in Animate, we think it is important to stop and make a few very important points:

- Our assumption with this chapter is that you have a familiarity with the basics of coding. We will briefly touch on the important concepts of the JavaScript language and the jQuery library in order to you help you understand much of the code you will see in Edge Animate. We won't be going deepy into the subject, and we won't be providing comprehensive explanations of such terms as *functions*, *variable creation*, and so on.

- The process of adding complex interactivity to an Edge Animate composition involves the services of both a designer and a developer. The designer will add the "light" interactivity to show how he or she sees the project's functionality. It will be the developer's job to write or rewrite the code to make it much more efficient. If you are a designer with little coding experience, we are going to show you how to add that light code and give you an insight into the developer's tasks when it comes to Edge Animate.

- The word *foundation* in the title of this book is there for a very good reason. Our intent is not to turn you into a "power coder." We just want you to start working with the code features of Edge Animate.

- This is not a JavaScript lesson. It is not an HTML 5 lesson, nor is it a CSS3 lesson. There are books, several times larger, more in depth, and longer than this one, devoted to the subject. In fact one of the better books for learning JavaScript is Terry McNavage's *JavaScript for Absolute Beginners* (Apress, 2010).

- If you are unfamiliar with JavaScript, have little coding experience, or are thinking, "Uh, not me," don't skip this section. We are going to do some very simple stuff here, but it is the fundamental stuff you need to know and is designed to make you comfortable with the code features of Edge Animate.

We are going to start our foray into coding with a very simple overview of the language used by Edge Animate—JavaScript—and its jQuery library.

# Edge Animate and Code

Interactivity in Edge Animate can only be accomplished through the use of code. To do this, Edge Animate uses JavaScript as its base coding language and the jQuery library, which is a commonly used library of extremely useful predefined functions and objects.

Flash users will find JavaScript to be oddly familiar. This is because Flash's coding language—ActionScript—and Edge Animate's coding language—JavaScript—are both based on the ECMA-262 specification. ECMA International (formerly the European Computer Manufacturer's Association) is the governing body for a number of data storage specifications, character sets, and programming languages including those for C++ and C#.

Where does jQuery fit? According to the w3schools (the educational arm of the W3C), "jQuery is a lightweight, 'write less, do more,' JavaScript library." What that means is the whole purpose of this library is to make it much easier for you to use JavaScript in your Edge Animate compositions by reducing common tasks requiring a lot of JavaScript code to, in many cases, a single line of code.

Finally, you can approach coding in Edge Animate from two starting points.

If you are new to both JavaScript and jQuery, Edge Animate contains a comprehensive collection of prerolled scripts called *snippets* that can be used at the click of a mouse to perform button rollovers, launch URLs, and even change objects in the Elements panel. Although these snippets should be used for the absolute basics of interactivity, they are a great way of getting you started.

The second starting point is aimed at developers who are comfortable writing custom JavaScript and using jQuery. Edge Animate contains a code editor that allows you to write your own code or to edit the code produced by Edge Animate. Also, you can open the Edge Animate JS files in your code editor of choice and make your changes there.

# The Fundamentals of JavaScript

If you have any programming experience with ActionScript, you are familiar with the concepts of JavaScript. This section presents some of the absolute basics that will help you work with Edge Animate. Let's start with data types.

191

A *data type* simply describes, you guessed it, the type of some data. For example, if I had a data type of "fruit," then apples and oranges would be of the fruit data type, but cars and monkeys would not be. The data type is useful because it means we can test to make sure something is what we expect it to be.

When it comes to the data types you can use, JavaScript provides the usual list:

- *Numbers* can be whole numbers like 950 or decimals like .950. Numbers are expressed without any particular punctuation. For example, you might have a statement such as:

```
var myNumber = 25 + 15;
```

The 25 and 15 are added together, and the result—40—will be stored in a variable named `myNumber`.

- *Strings* are groups of characters, like your name or the words "Foundation Edge Animate." Strings must appear inside quotes, either single or double. Statements with valid strings might look like this:

```
var author ="Tom Green";
var bookTitle = "Foundation Edge Animate.";
```

You can combine two strings using the + operator. For example:

```
var author ="Tom" + "Green";
```

This line stores a single string `"Tom Green"` in the `author` variable. Many of the Edge Animate snippets will require you to enter text strings. To make it easier for you, these snippets will have dummy text between the quotation marks.

- *Booleans* are really neat because they can only have two values: *true* or *false*. They're often used to determine if a certain condition exists and do something if it does. Here's a typical statement that checks to see if the object is indeed `Circle1` and if it is, to do something:

```
Circle1 = true;
if (Circle1 == true) {
  doSomething();
};
```

The first line assigns the value `true` to the variable `Circle1`. If it's true that it is indeed Circle1, then the `doSomething()` function is performed. The `doSomething()` function is usually defined elsewhere in the code. It's important to remember that the operator compares equal values is `==`, not a single `=`. If you want strict equality—both the value and data type are equal—then you would use `===`.

- *Arrays* are nothing more than lists of things. For example, an array of groceries might look like this:

```
var groceries = ['milk','bread','soup','pasta'];
```

You would grab the milk from the array with a statement like this:

```
myMilk = groceries[0];
```

Just keep in mind that the numbering order for arrays always begins with a 0, so in this example `groceries[3]` will return "pasta."

- *Functions* are reusable custom code blocks that tell Edge Animate what to do. What you may not know is, in JavaScript, functions are considered a data type. As a result, functions have some interesting capabilities. For example, they can be stored in variables or arrays. A function might be declared like this:

```
function productName(first, last) { return first + ' ' + last; }
```

The key word `function` tells Edge Animate the code that follows is a function. The name of the function is `productName`, and it has two arguments: `first` and `last`. These arguments need to be provided when the function is called. What the function does appears between curly braces { }. In this example, the function joins three strings to create one string. The arguments `first` and `last` are strings, presumably the first and last names of the product. In between, a *string literal*—the two single quotes—is used to insert a space between the words. The code would look something like this:

```
var first = "Edge";
var last = "Animate";
function productName(first, last) { return first + ' ' + last; }
```

In this case, the variables `first` and `last` are presumed to be strings that have already been defined to represent a product's name. So if the variable `first` was given the value `Edge` and `last` was given the value `Animate`, then this statement would return the string `Edge Animate` when the `productName` function is called. If the space within the single quotes weren't there, the result would be `EdgeAnimate`

Here are some other aspects of the language you should keep in mind when you work in JavaScript:

- *JavaScript is loosely typed.* Unlike many other languages such as ActionScript, variables do not have a specific data type when they are created. This means a variable could be assigned a number value and then later a string value. For example `var myNumber = 25 +15;` could be used in one place as a number but in another as a string.

- *JavaScript is case sensitive.* Capitalization matters in JavaScript. That means edgeanimate, EdgeAnimate, and edgeAnimate could be used to name three separate variables. This is important because one of the most common coding errors is spelling. In the example above, using `mynumber` instead of `myNumber` will result in an error message if you haven't defined `mynumber`.

- *Variable names must be specific characters.* Variables must begin with a letter, $, or _. They cannot begin with a number. The rest of the characters in a variable must be letters, numbers, $, or _. Variables can't contain any other characters or punctuation.

- *JavaScript has reserved words.* Like most programming languages, JavaScript has a number of words that have special meanings. These are usually called *reserved words* or *keywords*. The following are examples of reserved words in the JavaScript language:

- var: Used to create variables

- if: Used to begin if . . . else conditional statements

- new: Creates a new instance of an object

- function: Used to define a function

- *JavaScript uses semicolons (;) to end statements.* To properly interpret JavaScript code, browsers need to know where one statement ends and the next begins. JavaScript uses semicolons to separate statements. If there's only one statement on a line, many browsers will let you get away with not putting a semicolon at the end, but it's considered a best practice to always put a semicolon at the end of a statement.

# Understanding the Document Object Model

The document object model, affectionately known as the DOM, is the skeleton of any web page and is a core concept of working with code in Edge Animate. A DOM is a conceptual definition of a web page that describes the elements that make up the Edge Animate composition and what they do.

Before you can make changes to an element in an HTML document, you need to identify or *select* that element. There are three common ways to identify the elements in a web page: by tag, by ID, or by class.

- Tags are HTML's basic method for identifying things like headings <h1> or paragraphs <p>. Tags always use angle brackets: < >.

- IDs are used to identify one unique item on a page. This is an extremely important concept to understand in Edge Animate. When you change the name of an element, you are, in fact, changing the name of the ID, and the ID, not the symbol name, for example, is how Edge Animate finds stuff on the timeline.

- Classes are used to identify similar elements on a page. To identify a photo as part of the "gallery" class, you could write:

```
<img class="gallery" src="images/Burnfileld.jpg">
```

Edge Animate makes all of this a bit easier for you. When you select an object on the Stage, the HTML tags for the selection, as shown in Figure 6-1, can be assigned to the selection in the Properties panel or if you click the Classes button—it looks like a C—beside the Tag pop-down, you can enter your own custom class name.

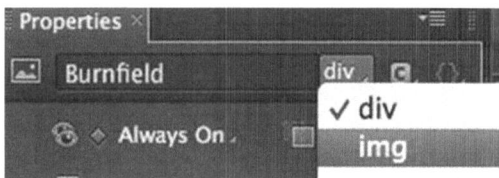

**Figure 6-1.** HTML tags and classes can be assigned in the Properties panel.

# Making Selections Through jQuery

JavaScript has several—some would say confusing—methods for getting an element by ID to move around the DOM to select different elements. This can be quite a problem for those not familiar with JavaScript. However, Edge Animate, through the use of the jQuery library, provides a rather simple way of selecting elements.

In Edge Animate, when you name an element, you are giving that element an ID. Let's assume you have placed a photo in an element and you change the element's name to Burnfield in the Elements panel. This is the same as writing `id="Burnfield"` in the `<img>` tag. Edge Animate also uses CSS and, as we know, CSS references IDs by placing a # (pound sign) in front of the name. jQuery uses the same system. If you want to reference `Burnfield` using jQuery, you'd write:

```
$('#Burnfield')
```

CSS also references classes by placing a period in front of the name. jQuery uses the same syntax. If you want to select all the elements in the `galleryRotate` class, it would look like this:

```
$('.galleryRotate')
```

Finally, if you want to select all the elements with `<img>` tags, you don't need any special character at the front. That would look like this:

```
$(img)
```

> The $ sign you see in the above examples is also used by the Edge Animate snippets. All it does is simply tell Edge Animate to use the jQuery library to find stuff. In fact, using jQuery(`img`) instead of $(`img`) is another way of doing things.

## The Word Sym Is Important

When you start working with the snippets or adding code in Edge Animate, you are going to see and use the reserved word `sym` a lot.

For example, here's a typical line of code used in Edge Animate:

```
sym.$("txt").hide();
```

In this case, `sym` stands for symbol and the term refers to an element on the main timeline. The dollar sign is the jQuery selector that looks up the element by its name (The ID is "txt".) The `.hide()` function hides the element. You can add this statement using the Script panel and then edit it for your own purposes. You could even copy and paste it into the code block and change `txt` to another element you want to identify rather than retype the code. In the pasted copy, you could even change the function `hide()` to another one that you want to use.

Here's another, more complex, example:

```
sym.getSymbol("Buttons").getSymbol("Team_btn").$("txt").html("The Project Team");
```

In this instance, the `getSymbol()` method finds the `Buttons` layer on the main timeline, which contains a symbol from the Library. The second `getSymbol()` instance tells Edge Animate to look in that Library symbol's timeline for an element named "Team_btn", use jQuery to find the `txt` element, and to change the text in that element to "The Project Team".

So much for theory. Let's put this knowledge to work by getting familiar with the place where the actual coding is done: the Script panel.

## Edge Animate Is Driven by Events

One of the core coding concepts in Edge Animate is that you have to tell Edge Animate what to do when something happens—this is known as an *event*. It could be something as simple as telling Edge Animate: "When this button is clicked, open this web page." This concept of "what to do when something happens" is the absolute core of the coding features of Edge Animate. The "what to do" when the mouse is clicked, for example, can range from the very simple—open a web page—to the extremely complex—do some banking, book a plane ticket—and the developer skills' spectrum between those two extremes gives you an idea of the breadth of this topic in Edge Animate. We'll start with "when something happens."

This is an important concept because events are things an element or object reacts to: Yell at Tom and he will look in your direction; Push Mike and he will lurch in the opposite direction. It is no different with Edge Animate. Events are occurrences triggered—timeline events in Edge Animate are called *triggers*—by user input, such as the mouse and touch events associated with an element or the `play` and `stop` events, which are tied to the timeline. For example, if you were to add a `stop` event to the timeline, you could reasonably expect the playhead to stop dead when it hits the point—the event trigger—where the `stop` event is placed. Add a `click` event to an element and something will happen when the user clicks—the event trigger—that element at runtime.

To start understanding this concept, we will create a new Edge Animate document and when it opens we will look for the `Open Actions` button—it looks like curly braces { }—as shown in Figure 6-2. This icon is found in three places: the `Document` name in the `Properties` panel, beside an `Element` in the `Elements` and `Timeline` panels, and beside the word `Actions` on the timeline. Clicking an `Open Actions` button opens the `Script` panel and a `Context` menu with a series of events that strictly applies to the nature of the element selected.

**Figure 6-2.** Clicking a Open Actions button opens the Script panel.

If you click the brackets beside the Stage element in the Elements panel, you will be presented with the list of events shown in Figure 6-3.

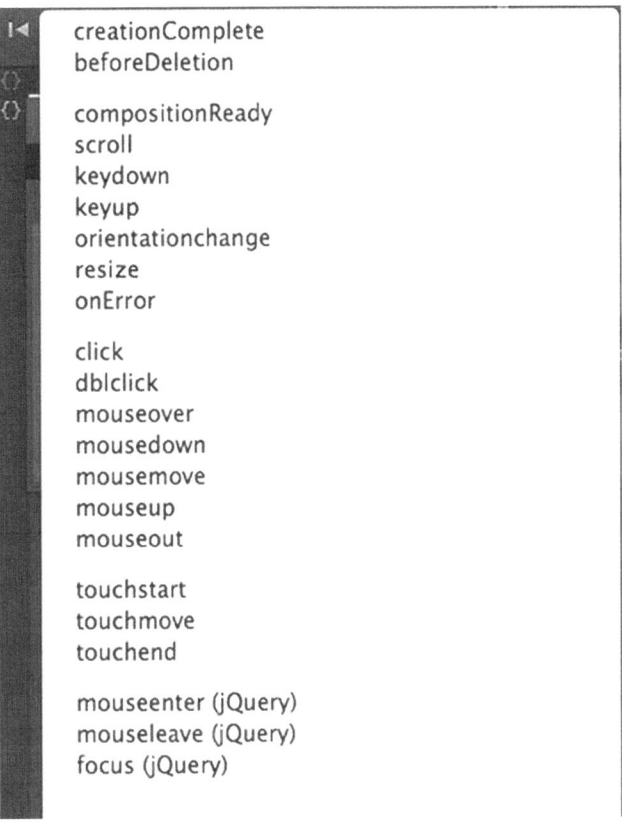

**Figure 6-3.** Clicking an element's Open Actions button opens a list of events. In this case, the events related to the Stage."

With Edge Animate, these events apply to where the script is inserted. If you click the { } beside the word Actions on the timeline, you will see a completely different set of events, as shown in Figure 6-4.

The key here is that you understanding that none of this can happen without using the Code and Actions panels.

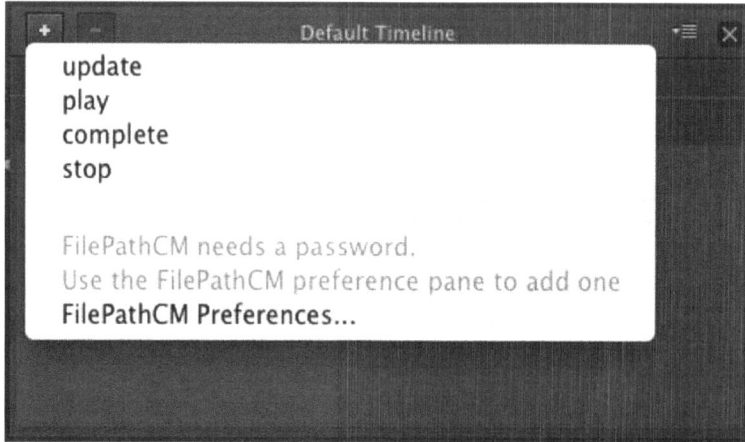

**Figure 6-4.** The Timeline panel has only four events available for it.

## The Code Panel

If you are working with a developer, he or she will inevitably want to open Animate's "hood" and dive into the code to either see how it is structured, to edit it, or to even add to the code. This is the function of the Code panel in Edge Animate—to provide you or your developer with a broad overview of all of the code contained in the project. Here's how to do this:

1.  Open a new, empty Edge Animate document and, when it opens, select Window > Code to open the Code panel. You aren't going to see much because there is no preloader and there is nothing on the Stage. Still, there is the DOM, and to see it, click the Full Code button and the basic code driving the project appears.

2.  Click the Display Snippets button beside the Full Code button and a panel, as shown in Figure 6-5, containing all of the snippets available in Edge Animate appears.

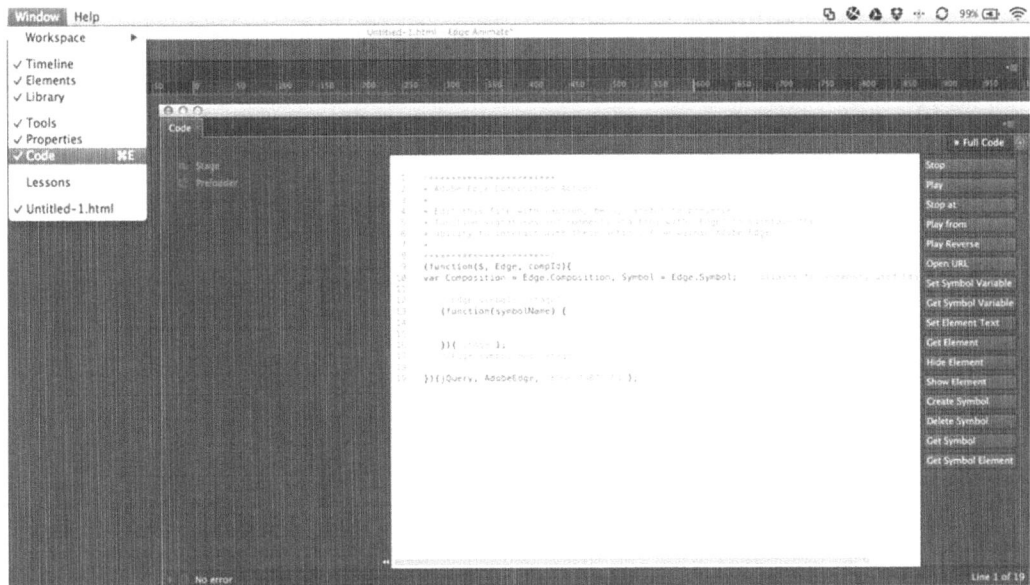

**Figure 6-5.** The Code panel is opened through the Windows menu.

Here's a quick overview of the features of the Code panel:

- The list down the left side of the panel shows you all of the elements in the project, including preloaders, to which you have attached scripts. Select one and the code will appear in the Script pane. This is a handy way, especially in complex projects, of isolating elements and working with their code because you don't need to search them out on the timeline or in the Symbols panel to access any code that may be attached to them.

- The Script pane is where the magic happens. If you are comfortable writing your own code, you can simply click inside this area and start coding. For the rest of us, a good place to start entering code is by clicking one of the code snippet buttons on the right.

- The code snippets are listed down the right side of the panel. In many respects code snippets are a "point-and-click way of adding code to a project. Click one of the snippets and the code is added to the Script pane.

- The Full Code button at the top of the panel gives you a macro view of all the code in the project. This code is also fully editable but *pay attention to the first sentence of the comment in the code. If you are even the tiniest bit unsure of what you are doing, stay out of this area and don't change a thing.*

3. Click the two arrows in the bottom left corner of the Script pane. The pane will expand to give you more working room in the Script pane.

4. Click once on the Toggle Code snippets button beside the Full Code button. The snippets disappear and you have even more room in the Script pane.

5. Another way of "buying space" in the Script pane is to change the size of the text in the pane. Click the Code Panel menu button and the Context menu pop-down shown in Figure 6-6 appears.

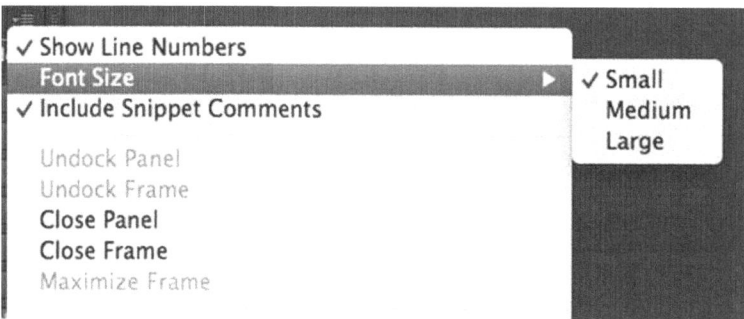

**Figure 6-6.** You can change the size of the font displayed in the Script pane.

Here's what the three choices in the Script pane's context menu do:

- **Show Line Numbers**: Depending on how you work, you can turn off line numbers in the Script pane. If you are new to scripting, our advice is to leave them on.

- **Font Size**: Choosing one of the three choices makes the font used for the code larger or smaller. Again, this is a personal preference, but if you are ever in a situation where you are presenting Edge Animate online or elsewhere, having a large font makes things easier for the audience or viewer to see.

- **Include Snippet Comments:** All of the code snippets that come packaged with Edge Animate are fully commented. These are green colored lines of text in the code preceded by //. Comments give you hints and suggestions as to what the code does and how to change it. Comments are ignored by Edge Animate when the project is running in the browser.

If you make a coding error, there is a basic error-trapping feature in Edge Animate's Code panel. Let's make a mistake and see how Edge Animate notifies us:

1. Open the Code panel in a blank document. In the Code panel select the Stage .

2. In Line 1 of the Code pane, enter var #Tom;. This is an obvious error because the pound sign is not allowed in variable names.

Edge Animate catches this error and, as shown in Figure 6-7, notifies you in a couple of places. Your first clue is the red dot that appears in front of the var. You are also notified of the Code Error at the bottom of the Code panel and you are told, below that notification, where the error is located and the nature of the error.

The other place where you are notified of coding errors is on the Stage. A red box with an x appears in the bottom right corner of the Stage. Click that button and the Code panel will open.

3.  Close the document and don't save the changes.

> *If you don't understand the error message or have only basic coding knowledge, then seriously consider having your developer deal with these issues.*

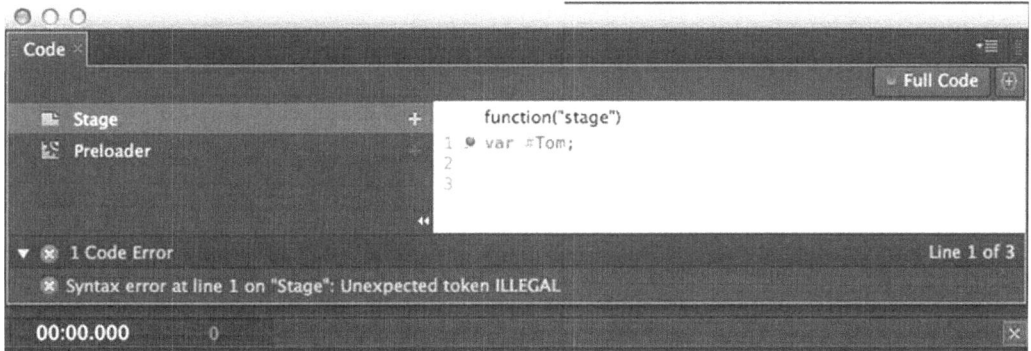

**Figure 6-7.** Coding errors are highlighted in a number of areas.

> *You may have noticed the Code panel is one of the few floating panels in Edge Animate. If you plan to make extensive use of this panel, it can be docked in whatever interface location works best for you.*

## The Actions Panel

The Actions panel is where you can add snippets—prerolled code—to your Edge Animate project. Let's see how this panel works by first opening the Stage element's Events and adding a `click` event. The really neat thing about this panel is the events listed are context sensitive. That means they will change depending on the element or object to which they are attached. Follow these steps to add a `click` event to the Stage:

1.  Open a new blank Edge Animate document. When it opens, select the Stage element on the timeline and click the Events button—it looks like a pair of curly braces—beside the selection. Select the `click` event from the list shown in Figure 6-8. The Actions panel will open.

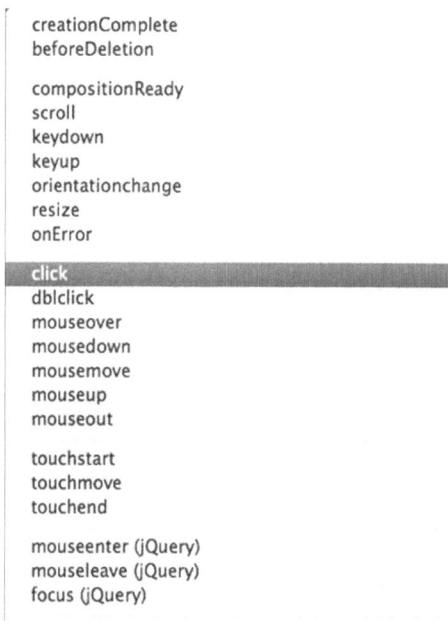

**Figure 6-8.** Adding a click event to the Stage element.

2.   The list of snippets that can be applied will appear on the right side of the Actions panel. Click once in Line 1 and click the Stop button. The code shown in Figure 6-9 will appear in the Script pane. What you have just done is, in plain English, to tell Edge: "Anytime you detect a mouse click on the Stage, stop the playhead."

**Figure 6-9.** Adding a code snippet to the Stage.

3.  Click the + sign at the top of the Actions panel. This button allows you to add other actions to the Stage or selected element. The list you see has the same actions presented when you clicked the Actions button beside the Stage element on the timeline.

> It isn't only mouse, key, and document events that can be added to your Animate movies. Your work is not limited to desktop screens. It can also show up on devices and tablets. This explains why there are three touch events—touchstart, touchmove, and touchend —in the list as well as jQuery events and even orientation and resize events.

4.  If you look at the Stage element on the timeline and in the Elements panel, you will notice there is a dot between the brackets. This is a visual indicator that there is code attached to this element. If you roll the mouse over the bracket, the dot will change color.

5.  Close the Actions panel. Click the Open Actions button for the Stage and the panel opens along with the code.

6.  Click the – sign in the Actions panel and all of the actions associated with the click event are removed and the dot disappears in the Actions button.

## Using Labels and Triggers

For any Edge Animate project to be made truly interactive, we need to control the playhead by stopping it where the user needs to make a decision. Once that decision is made, we need to scoot the playhead to where the user wishes to go and keep it there while the user interacts with the content. This is all accomplished by using labels and triggers.

*Labels* simply give you a commonsense way of managing navigation through the timeline. It is easier to use words that mean something rather than a time code. Also, labels can be shifted around on the timeline, meaning you don't waste time changing code.

A *trigger* is nothing more than the code that is executed—triggered—when the playhead moves into a particular frame on the timeline.

The common factor between triggers and labels is the fact they are only found on the timeline and, as such, can control the movement of the playhead on the timeline and that includes symbols, which also have their own timelines.

Let's see how this works. In this very simple exercise, you are going to learn the fundamentals of using triggers and labels. You will create a small Edge Animate movie that, when the user rolls over a button on the Stage, will show the user the photograph from which the button was created. In this case the photographs are the Pantheon in Paris and wine bottles in a Parisian street market. Let's get started:

1.  Open the LabelsTriggers.an file in your Exercise folder. When it opens, you will see, as shown in Figure 6-10, two buttons on the Stage. If you scrub the playhead to the half-second mark in the timeline, you will see a picture of the Pantheon. Scrub to the 1-second mark and you will see the wine bottles.

**Figure 6-10.** We start with two buttons on the Stage.

It is quite obvious how this project is going to function: Roll over the PantheonButton element and the playhead scoots to the one-half second mark of the timeline and stays there. For the other button, the playhead is sent to the 1-second mark of the timeline. To accomplish this we are going to need to identify three points of interaction on the timeline: the buttons, the Pantheon, and the wine bottles. Although we could simply note the times where the playhead stops and enter it into the code, this is an inefficient workflow. Things change, and if you change your mind about the timeline order or duration for those points, you will have to manually open the code at each point and change the time value. The easier way of doing it is to add a label to the timeline to give you a visual clue as to where those points are located. This way, if things change, you simply move the label to its new location. Follow these steps to add the labels.

2. Move the playhead to the one-quarter-second mark (0.00.250) point of the timeline.

3. Select Timeline > Insert Label or click the Insert Label button in the Timeline panel (Figure 6-11) to add a label. You will see a label named Label 1 on the timeline. Double-click the name to select it and change the text to Buttons.

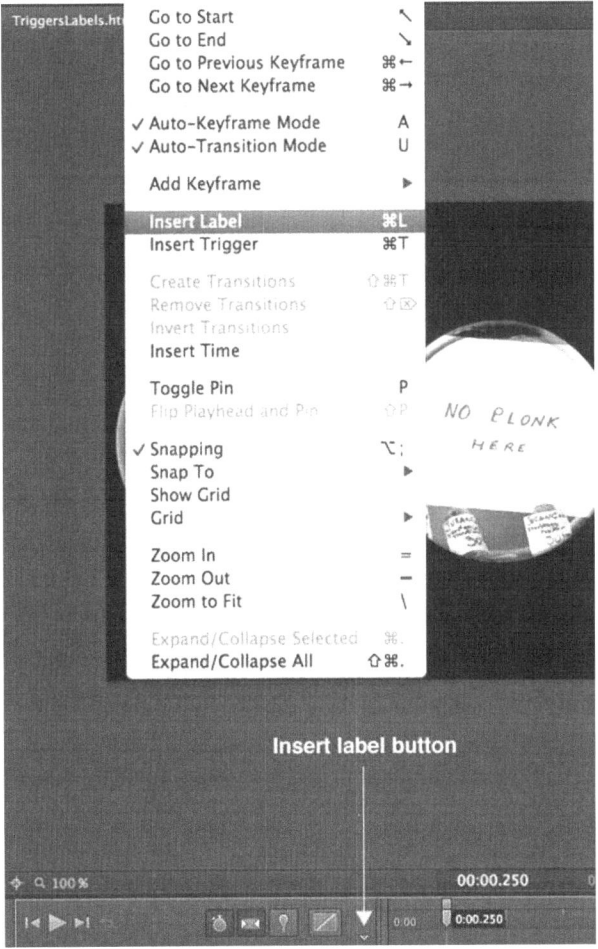

Figure 6-11. Adding a label to the timeline.

4. Add the labels named Pantheon and Wine to the timeline at the 0:00.750 and 0:01 marks of the timeline, as shown in Figure 6-12.

Figure 6-12. Labels on the timeline are navigation aids.

With the labels in place, we can now add the timeline triggers. Here's how:

5.  Drag the playhead over the Buttons label and select Timeline > Insert Trigger. When you release the mouse, the Actions panel will open. Alternatively you can click the Insert Trigger in the Timeline menu (Figure 6-13) to add the trigger.

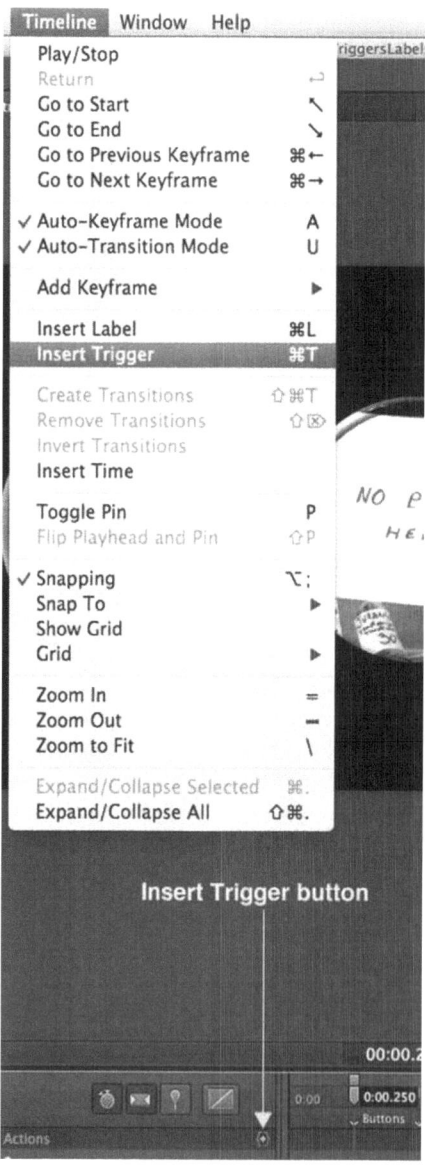

**Figure 6-13.** Triggers can be added using the menu or the timeline.

6. When the Actions panel opens, add a Stop action and close the Actions panel.

7. Repeat steps 5 and 6—try clicking the Insert Trigger button—for the other two labels. As you can see in Figure 6-14, each label now has a corresponding trigger associated with it.

> Don't forget you can press Ctrl+L or Command+L (Mac) to add a label. For triggers, the keyboard command is Ctrl+T or Command+T (Mac).

**Figure 6-14.** Labels and triggers work together.

If you test the movie, you can see how triggers and labels work together—sort of. The movie will stop dead over the Buttons label, and you can go no farther. Let's fix that:

1. Move the playhead over the Buttons label, select the Pantheon button, and click the Open Actions button for the element.

2. Select Click from the events and click the Play button when the Actions panel opens.

3. Add "Pantheon" as the parameter in the Script pane (Figure 6-15) and close the Actions panel.

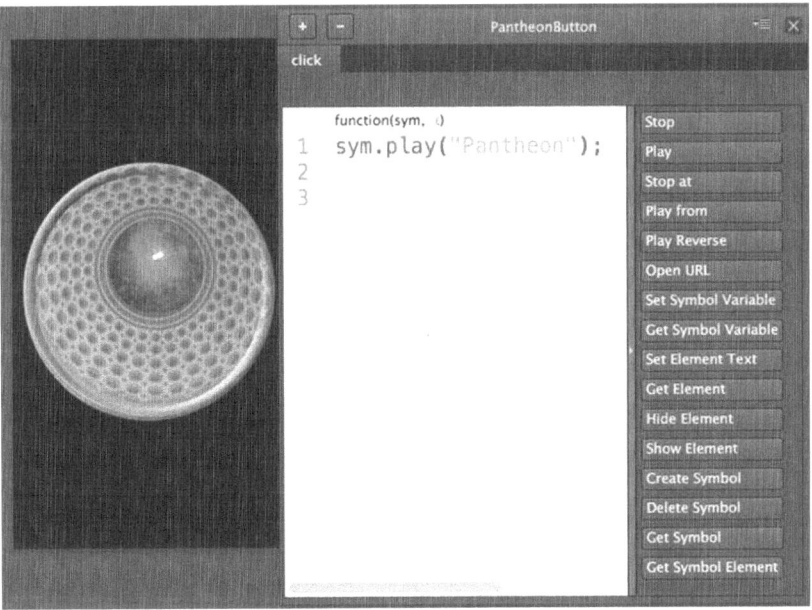

**Figure 6-15.** Click the button and go to the "Pantheon" label on the timeline.

We have no way of getting from the photo back to the buttons. To fix that, move the playhead to the Pantheon label and add a Play action to the photo that, when the user clicks the photo, the playhead returns to the Buttons label.

Repeat these steps with the WineButton element and the Wine label on the timeline. Test the movie and you should be able to click a button and see the image.

## Using Snippets to Manage Symbol Playback

Now that you have a basic understanding of the scripting features of Edge Animate, let's put that knowledge to work. In this exercise we are going to use the snippets to "wire up" a small project.

This project solves a common problem. A race car, using two symbols, when tested in the browser, zips across the screen but the wheels stop rotating about halfway across the stage. The problem is the animation of the car symbol has a duration of 2 seconds on the main timeline but the wheels only spin for 1 second. The solution to this issue lies in code. What we need to do is tell Edge Animate to keep the wheels spinning until we tell them to stop. Here's how:

1. Open the Symbols.an file in your Exercise folder.

2. Double-click the Wheel symbol in the Symbols panel to open the symbol.

If you press the spacebar, the wheel will spin until the playhead reaches the end of the animation. What you can correctly assume from this is we need to tell Edge Animate to return to the first frame of the Wheel symbol's timeline each time it hits the last frame of the animation. Here's how:

1. Drag the playhead to the end of the Transition strip.

2. Click the Insert Trigger icon in the Actions area at the top of the timeline. When you do this, the Actions panel appears. The key feature to note here is that the panel is named Trigger @1000 ms. What you are about to do is to use code to tell Edge Animate to "trigger" an action when the playhead reaches this keyframe, which is located at the 1-second mark (1,000 milliseconds) of the Wheel symbol's timeline.

3. Click the Play button in the snippets.

4. Click once between the brackets in the play() method and enter 0. The code, as shown in Figure 6-16, should now be:

```
sym.play(0);
```

What you have just done is tell Animate: "When you encounter this keyframe in the Wheel symbol, go back to time 0 of the Wheel timeline and keep playing." Code that plays over and over is called a *loop*.

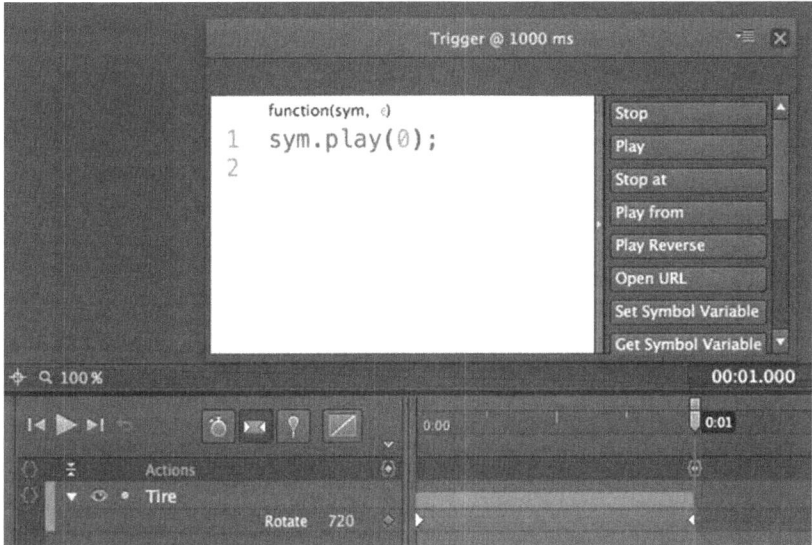

**Figure 6-16.** For simple loops, use timecode rather than labels.

5. Close the Script panel to accept the change and click the Stage link in the breadcrumb trail to return to the main timeline.

6. Test the movie in the browser.

Houston, we have a problem! Our script works because the wheels are spinning. The problem is they keep spinning when the car stops.

## Controlling Symbol Playback from the Main Timeline

One of the great strengths of code is the ability to control the action on the timeline. In this case we are going to control the playback of the Wheel symbol from the main timeline. To do this, you need two critical bits of information:

- Where the symbol is located

- The name of the element that holds the symbol to be controlled

Your first inclination is to think, "Well, shucks, all that stuff is in the Wheel symbol." No it isn't.

1. Double-click the Car symbol on the Stage to open it. The Wheel symbol contains the wheel animation and, as shown in Figure 6-17, the Wheel symbol instance is found in the elements, named Front and Rear. Symbols located inside other symbols are said to be *nested*.

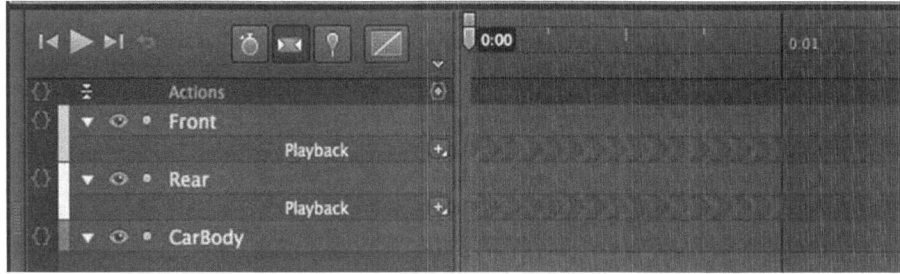

**Figure 6-17.** The Wheel symbol is nested within the Car symbol, and each instance of the Wheel symbol has a unique element name.

2. Return to the main timeline and add a trigger at the end of the animation.

3. When the Script panel opens, enter the following code:

```
sym.getSymbol("Racer").getSymbol("Front").stop();
sym.getSymbol("Racer").getSymbol("Rear").stop();
```

Let's go through that first line. To add an action to a symbol nested in another symbol you need to identify the parent element—Racer—and then identify the element nested within the parent containing the symbol to be controlled—Front. Having done that, you add the method to be applied to the element—stop();. In plain English, you are telling the main timeline: "When the playhead hits this trigger go into the Racer element containing the Car symbol and stop the Front element in that symbol from playing."

> *The buttons along the side of the Script panel are great for simple stuff, but when you need to get a bit more complex, like this example, you need to manually enter the code.*

4. Close the Script panel to return to the main timeline.

5. Select the Transition strip and add an EaseOutSine ease to the animation.

6. Save and test the movie. The car comes to a gentle stop and the wheels stop spinning.

## Creating Buttons

Now that you know how to control the main timeline and a symbol's timeline with code, let's add to that knowledge by creating a simple three-state—Up, Over, Down—button in Animate. As you saw from the previous exercise, you can scoot the playhead to various points on the timeline by entering the time or a label as a parameter. In this exercise we go a little bit farther.

In this exercise you will be coding up a button symbol that has "Up," "Over," and "Down" states. Showing these states based on mouse interaction is not terribly difficult to accomplish using triggers, labels, and snippets. The twist is adding the ability to go to a URL when the button is clicked. Let's get started by preparing the button symbol for interactivity:

1. Open the Button.edge file located in your Exercise folder. As shown in Figure 6-18, you start with a symbol—Google_btn—on the Stage and three graphics—Up.png, Over.png, and Down.png—in the Assets panel.

**Figure 6-18.** We start with a symbol on the Stage.

2. Double-click the symbol on the Stage to open the Google_btn timeline.

3. Add the following labels at the times indicated:

   • Up: 0:00:000

   • Over: 0:00:250

   • Down: 0:00:500

4. Move the playhead back to the 0 point of the timeline, select the Up graphic on the Stage, and, in the Properties panel, set the Display property to On. A Display keyframe will be added to the timeline.

5. Move the playhead to the 0:00:250 point and change the selection's Display property to Off.

6. Drag the playhead to the 0 point of the timeline and drag the Over.png graphic from the Assets panel to the Stage and set its X and Y positions to 0,0. Set the Over graphic's Display property to Off.

7. Move the playhead to the Over label and set the Over graphic's Display value to On. Set the Display property to Off at the Down label.

8. Drag the playhead back to the 0 point. Drag the Down graphic to the Stage and make sure it is positioned at 0,0. Set the Display property to Off.

9. Move the playhead to the Down label and change the Display property for the Down graphic to On.

10. To finish, add a stop() trigger under each of the labels. When you finish, your symbol's timeline should resemble that shown in Figure 6-19. If it does, return to the main timeline.

**Figure 6-19.** The symbol's timeline is prepared.

## "Wiring Up" the Button

With the symbol's timeline prepared, we need to give Edge Animate an idea of what to do when three events occur:

- When the mouse is over the button on the main timeline, show the Over graphic.

- When the mouse rolls off the button, show the Up graphic.

- When the mouse is clicked, show the Down button and go to the Google home page.

Follow these steps to add the code that makes this possible:

1. At the 0 point of the timeline add a stop() trigger. This will hold the playhead to the first frame of the movie.

2. Click the GoogleBtn element in the time and click the Open Actions button on the timeline. This is where the magic happens. We are going to attach three events to this element that tell Edge Animate what to do when the mouse is over the element, off of the element, or when the element is clicked.

> You may have noticed the timeline element is named **GoogleBtn** and the symbol is named **Google_btn**. When you move from Flash to Edge Animate, some naming habits don't disappear. It is a common best practice in Flash to name symbols and tack on what they do. This way we can look at a crowded symbol library and instantly find the Google button. We can think of no compelling reason to not continue this naming convention.

3.  Select the mouseover event and, when the Actions panel opens, enter the following code:

    ```
    sym.getSymbol("GoogleBtn").play("Over");
    ```

    In plain English, when the mouse is over the GoogleBtn element (mouseover), go to the label named "Over" in the Google_btn symbol.

4.  Click the + sign in the Actions panel and select the mouseout event, and when the Actions panel opens, enter the following code:

    ```
    sym.getSymbol("GoogleBtn").play("Up");
    ```

5.  Click the + sign in the Actions panel and add a click event. Enter the following:

    ```
    sym.getSymbol("GoogleBtn").play("Down");
    ```

6.  Press the Return/Enter key and click the Open URL button to add the code needed to go to the Google home page.

7.  Change the URL, as shown in Figure 6-20, from the default adobe.com to http://www.google.com.

**Figure 6-20.** Adding an external link to an element in Edge Animate.

8.  Close the Actions panel and test the project in a browser.

# Making Text Interactive

In this exercise we are going to create a very simple slide show. What happens is the user will click a text "button" and the image associated with the button fades in on the stage. As in the previous exercise, this is accomplished through the use of a combination of labels and stop actions on the timeline. The buttons will be "wired up" to tell Edge Animate where to send the playhead when a button is clicked. Follow these steps to pull a simple slideshow together:

1.  Open the SlideShow.edge file located in your Exercise folder. When it opens, as shown in Figure 6-21, you will see we have added the images and, when you scrub the timeline, we have added a fade in and fade out for each image. As well, we have added Display keyframes to turn the images off when they aren't being viewed. Finally, make sure that Auto keyframes is turned on in the timeline.

**Figure 6-21.** We start with the assets and image effects in place.

2.  Insert labels named Falls, Paddle, and Sign at the start of each image's Transition strip. These are the locations, shown in Figure 6-22, we will be using in the code to go to an image when the text is clicked.

**Figure 6-22.** The navigation labels are added to the project.

3. With the labels in place, we need to stop the playhead over the keyframe where the image comes into focus. Drag the playhead until it is over the middle keyframe of the Falls layer.

4. Add a Trigger and, when the script panel opens, select the Stop snippet. Repeat this step for the Paddle and Stop layers.

5. Right-click (PC) or Ctrl-click (Mac) on the High Falls text element on the Stage and select Open Actions for FallsTxt from the Context menu.

6. Select the click event from the list.

7. When the Script panel opens, click the Play button to add a Play snippet.

8. When the snippet appears in the code, click once between the brackets and enter "Falls" as the parameter for the play method.

9. Close the Script panel.

10. Repeat steps 6 to 10 for the other two text elements. Enter "Paddle" and "Sign" as the parameters for the play methods.

## Finishing the Slideshow

If you test the movie, the navigation works as expected. Even so there is a bit of improvement that can be done to make this a better experience. In this case we need to:

- Add a Play button at the start of the slide show
- Fade out the buttons that don't relate to the image

Let's get started.

1. Making sure the playhead is at the 0 mark of the timeline, drag the play.png image from the Assets panel to the Stage.

2. Add a trigger, and when the Script panel opens, add a stop action to the timeline.

3. Double-click the Play image's name in the Elements panel and rename the element PlayBtn (Figure 6-23). This way you know exactly what is contained in this element.

**Figure 6-23.** The play.png image's element name is changed to PlayBtn.

4. Click the Actions beside the PlayBtn element in the Elements panel. Select the click event from the list and, when the Script panel opens, click the Play snippet. This will add the following snippet:

sym.play();

By not adding a parameter to the play method, you are essentially sending the playhead off to the next frame in the movie and letting it play from there.

5. Close the Script panel.

6. Click once on the Play button and, in the Properties panel, change the Element Display value to On.

7. Move the playhead a couple of frames forward on the timeline and change the Element Display value to Off. The button disappears. We can now deal with the three text blocks.

8. With the playhead at the 0 mark on the timeline, add an Opacity keyframe for each of the text elements.

9. Move the playhead to the start of the Falls image and reduce the Opacity of the PaddleTxt and StopTxt elements to 50% and add an Opacity keyframe to the FallsTxt element under the trigger.

10. Move the playhead to the end of the Falls Transition strip and reduce the FallsTxt Opacity value to 50%.

11. Move the playhead to the start of the Paddle image and add an Opacity keyframe to the PaddleTxt element.

12. Move the playhead to the next keyframe in the Paddle element and change the `PaddleTxt` element's `Opacity` value to 100%.

13. **Move the playhead to the end of the** Paddle **layer's Transition strip and reduce the** PaddleTxt **element's** Opacity **to 50%.**

14. Move the playhead to the start of the Stop image and add an `Opacity` keyframe to the `StopTxt` element.

15. Move the playhead to the next keyframe in the `Stop` element and change the `StopTxt` element's `Opacity` value to 100%. **Move the playhead to the end of the** Stop **transition strip and reduce the** StopTxt **element's opacity value to** 50%.

16. Save and test the movie. As you can see in Figure 6-24, changing opacity values bring the image and the relevant text into sharper focus.

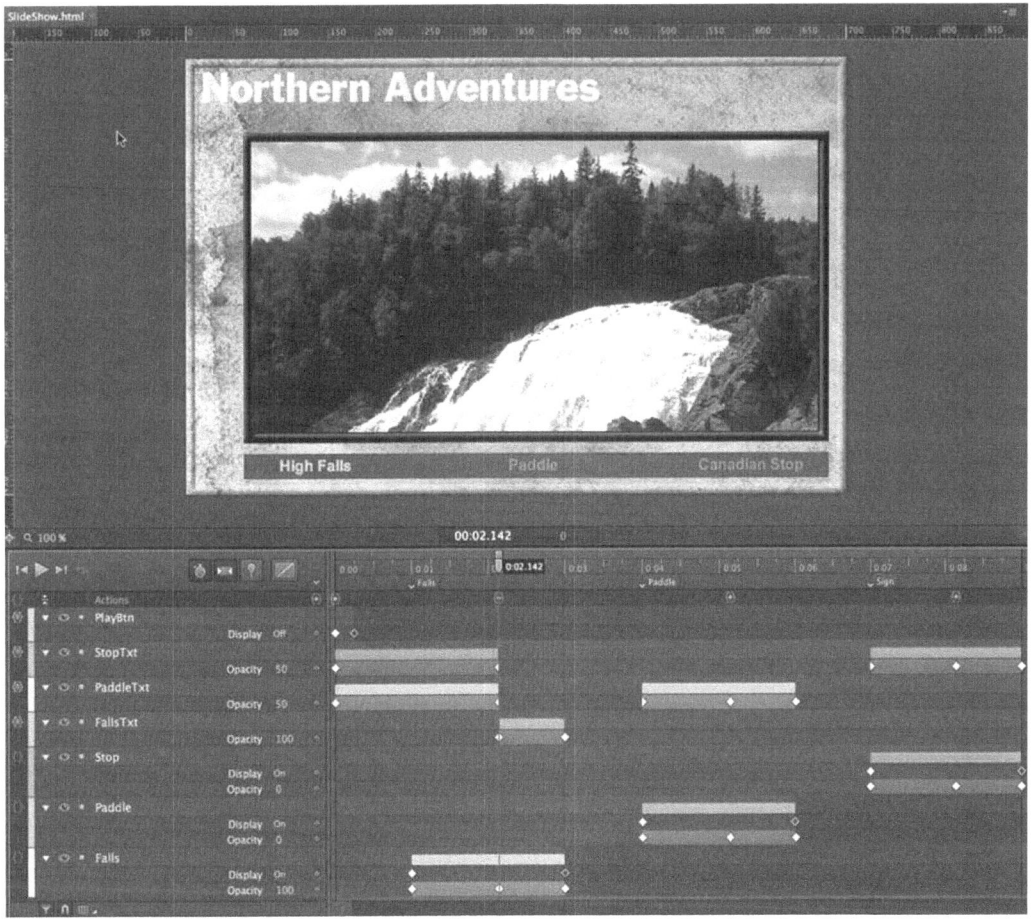

**Figure 6-24.** Actions, triggers, and timeline changes all contribute to making this project stand out.

217

Did you happen to notice anything that was missing when you tested the movie in the browser? When you rolled over the buttons, there was no cursor change to indicate the text and the Start buttons were "hot." Let's fix that:

1. Pull the playhead back to the 0 point and, with the Shift key held down, select the Stop button and the three text blocks.

2. Click the Auto button in the Cursor area of the Properties panel and, as shown in Figure 6-25, select the Pointer cursor.

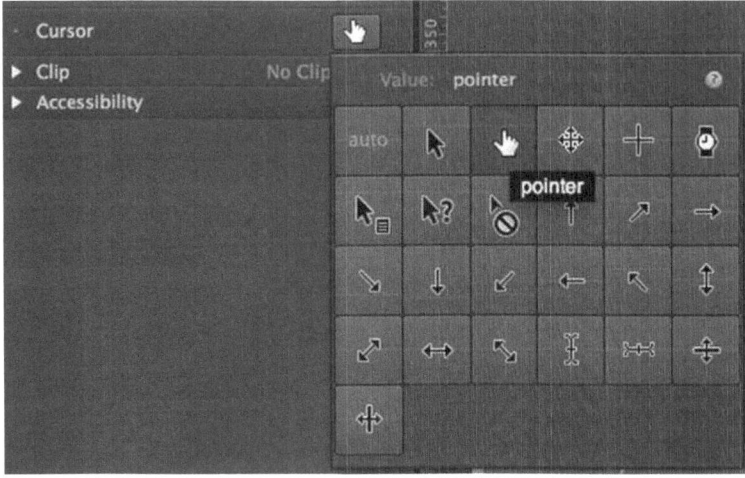

**Figure 6-25.** Adding a cursor change to a button.

3. Save and test the movie in a browser. The user, as shown in Figure 6-26, now knows where to click the mouse.

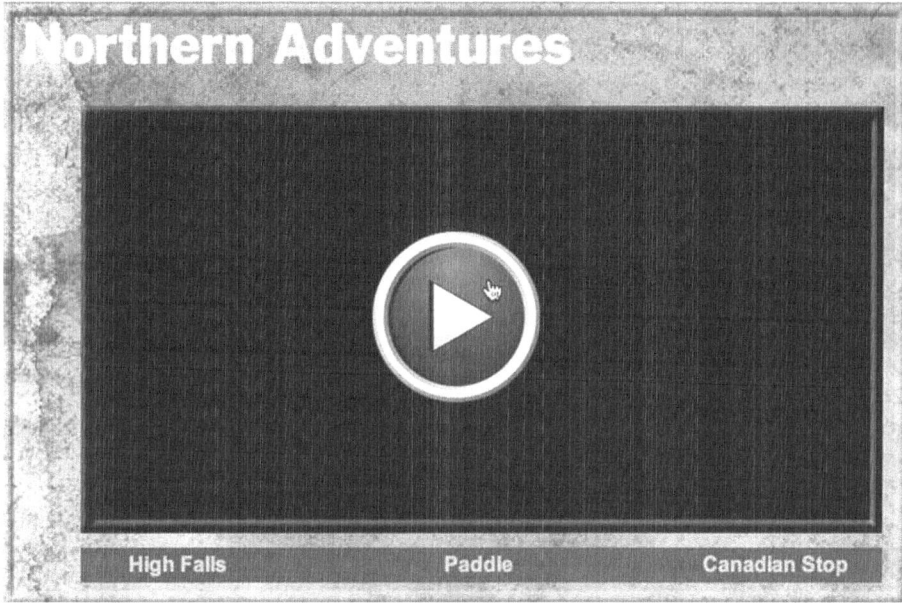

**Figure 6-26.** It is the attention to detail that determines success"

# Your Turn: Pulling It Together

In this final exercise we are going to create a project that pulls together much of the material covered in this and the previous chapters. We are going to create a page that encourages visitors to consider visiting Switzerland. Don't focus on that because many of the techniques we will cover can be used in portfolios, product pages, or any other situation where you need an eye-catching design that encourages the user to explore further.

In this exercise we will:

- Review the concept and wireframing process for the project
- Use code to change the cursor
- Create an interactive rollover symbol
- Use a preloader
- Create a Down-level stage

## The Planning Process

It has been decided that we will be preparing a Swiss tourism page, and the client is pretty clear that imaging will be the key. We understood this page was to be "image heavy" and that the images were going to be the interactive elements on the page. After poring through a few dozen photos that we were handed, we settled on six images. One was so striking we decided it would be the page background rather than a separate image. The question was: How to place them on the page?

Rather than waste time designing a bunch of composites, we decided to simply create our initial wireframe designs in Adobe Proto. This gave us the freedom to experiment with placement of the images. After a number of concepts ranging from filmstrips and sliders, we settled on the arrangement shown in Figure 6-27. It was fairly striking, nicely balanced, and gave us the "space" to add a brief on the "back" of the image along with a button directing the viewer to "Learn more."

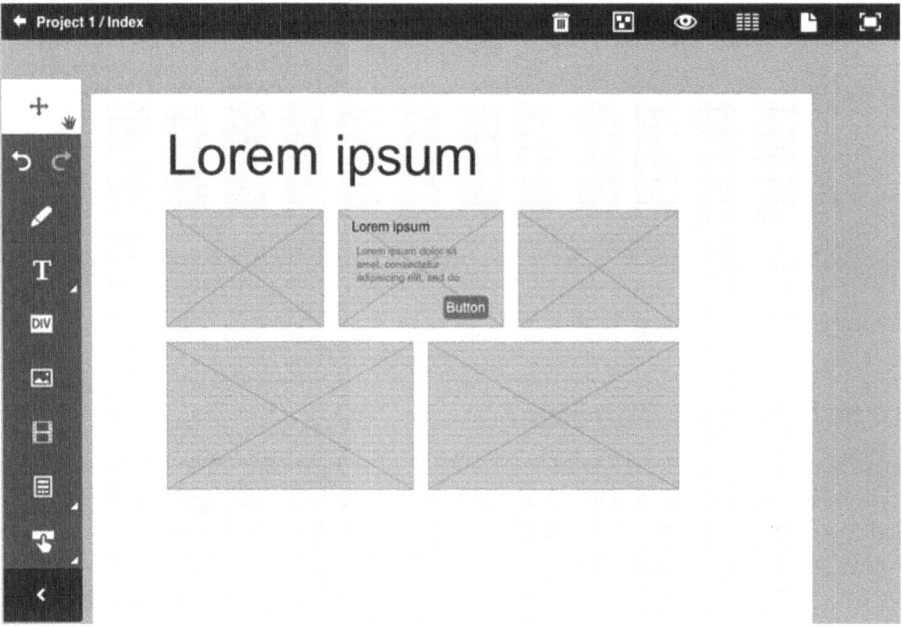

**Figure 6-27.** The initial sketches were done in Adobe Proto.

> *Adobe Proto is a touch app for Android and iOS devices that lets you create quick wireframe sketches on a variety of layout grids. These sketches can then be uploaded to the Creative Cloud and imported into Adobe Dreamweaver or you can take a screenshot and build the project over the screenshot in another application.*

Once we had the basic layout in place, we moved into the next phase—tweaking the wireframe in Fireworks and slipping in the content. This gave us the opportunity to change the page size to 1,200 by 800 and to "fiddle" with various image sizes to accommodate the placement determined in Proto. Using a simple colored box, we finally settled on an image size of 300 by 225 for the images in the upper row and a size of 460 by 395 for the images in the bottom row. The images being placed into each position were cropped, resized, and put into position. The background image turned out to be too strong, but we liked the colors in the image. Rather than choose a different image, we opened the image in Fireworks, applied a 20-pixel Gaussian blur to the image, and, as shown in Figure 6-28, dropped it into place.

**Figure 6-28.** The comp is assembled in Fireworks.

> *Yes, this step can be done in Photoshop or, in a pinch, in Illustrator. We use Fireworks simply because it is designed for screen-based work. Remember, nobody cares how you did it. They care that you did it.*

After turning off the guides, we looked at the images and realized they sort of just "laid" over the background image. After discussing a number of solutions, ranging from putting each one in a frame to applying a bevel, we dialed back our thinking and decided the simplest way of providing the "separation" was to simply add a 1-pixel horizontal light gray hairline along the top of the image.

With the design and imaging out of the way, we can now move to the assembly phase of the project in Edge Animate.

> *This is a common issue and it can even be dealt with in Edge Animate. If you are in Edge Animate and need to edit an image simply right-click (PC) or Ctrl-click (Mac) on the image in the **images** folder in the Edge Animate Library and select **Reveal in Finder** from the **Context** menu. When the folder containing the image opens, simply double-click the image to open it in your editing software, make the change, and save the image. When you return to Edge Animate, you will be informed the image has been changed and prompted to update the Edge Animate project.*

## Creating the Image Rollovers

We'll start by creating an image rollover for each of the images on the Stage. This tells you a couple of things:

- Each image should be converted to a symbol

- Each symbol on the Stage needs to accommodate mouseover, mouseout, and click events

- Each symbol needs some text and a Learn more button that, when clicked, opens a web page

Let's get started:

1. Open the Tour.edge file located in your Exercise folder. When the file opens, you will see we have placed the images on the Stage.

2. Select View > Guides and you can see, as shown in Figure 6-29, that we have re-created the grid from the Fireworks comp. This is especially helpful should we need to replace images or even expand the number of images used.

**Figure 6-29.** The grid is re-created in Edge Animate.

3.   With the playhead at the 0 point of the main stage, add a `stop();` trigger to the timeline. We only need the one frame.

4.   Select the `Cathedral` image on the Stage and convert it to a symbol named `Cathedral`.

5.   Double-click the `Cathedral` symbol in the `Symbols` panel to open its timeline.

6.   When the Cathedral symbol opens, add a label named "`Start`" at the 0 point and another named "`Flip`" at the half-second point.

7.   Add `stop();` triggers under each label.

8.   Select the `Church` element in the timeline and set its `Display` property to On at the 0 point of the timeline. Set it to Off at the half-second mark.

9.   We next need to create the "back" of the interactive images. Select the rectangle tool and draw a rectangle with the following properties:

   •   `Stroke: None`

   •   `Color: Black`

   •   `Width: 300`

   •   `Height: 245`

   •   `Left: 0`

223

- Top: 0

- Element name: Box

10. Set the rectangle's Display property to Off at the 0 point and to On at the half-second mark.

11. Select the Text tool, click on the black box, and enter the following text: Bern Cathedral

12. Use the following properties for the text:

   - Font: Arial, Helvetica, sans-serf

   - Size: 30 px

   - Color: White

   - Font weight: 700 (Bold)

   - Left: 27 px

   - Top: 17 px

   - Element Name: Cathedral Head

13. Add another text area and enter the following text: Construction of this gothic style cathedral started in 1421 and was completed in 1893. It is the tallest cathedral in Switzerland.

14. Use the following properties for the text:

   - Font: Arial, Helvetica, sans-serf

   - Size: 16 px

   - Color: White

   - Font weight: 500 (medium)

   - Left: 27 px

   - Top: 63 px

   - Element name: Cathedral Text

15. Drag the Learn.jpg image from the Images folder to the Stage, resize it, and place it below the Cathedral Text on the Stage, as shown in Figure 6-30. Don't forget to set its Display property to Off at the 0 point.

16. Return to the main Stage.

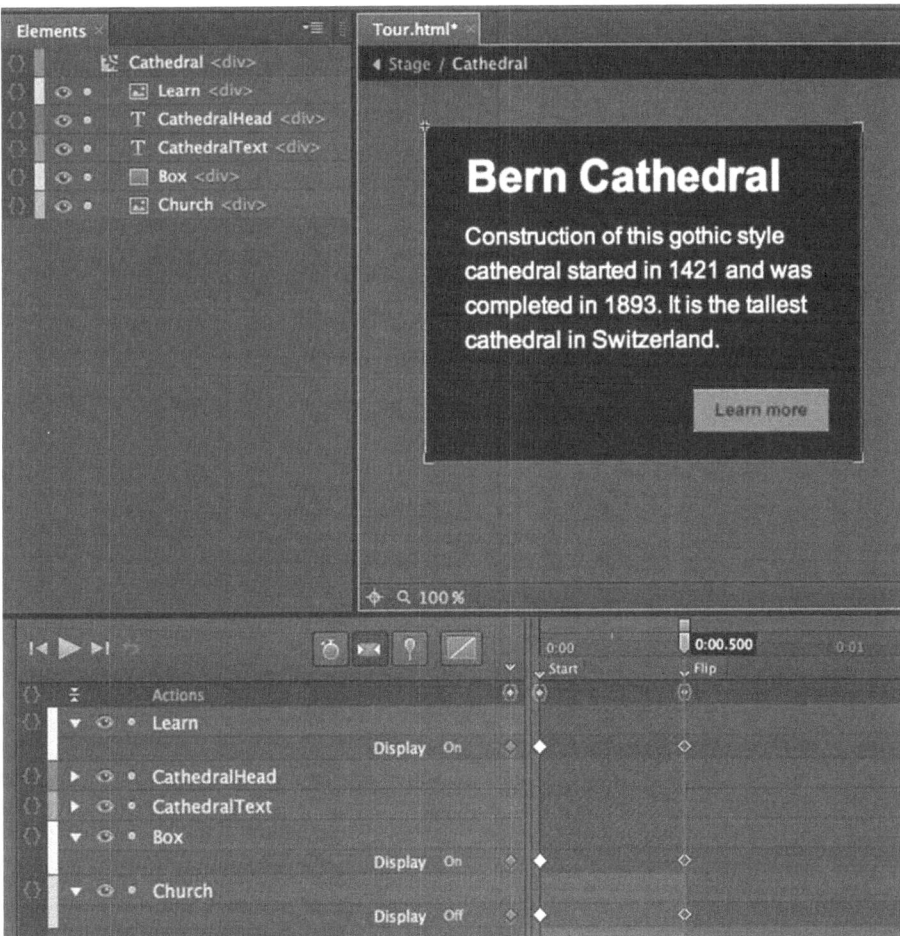

**Figure 6-30.** The Cathedral symbol is ready to go.

## Wiring Up the Cathedral Symbol

Now that we are on the main stage, we can concentrate our efforts on adding interactivity to the symbol.

1.  Click the Open Actions button for the Cathedral element on the timeline and select a mouseover event.

2.  Click once in the Script pane and enter the following code:

    ```
    sym.getSymbol("Cathedral").play("Flip");
    ```

    What you are telling Edge Animate to do is to go to the Cathedral symbol and shoot the playhead in the symbol to the marker named Flip.

3. In the Actions panel, click the + button and add a mouseout event. Add the following code to the Script pane:

```
sym.getSymbol("Cathedral").play("Start");
```

4. In the Actions panel, click the + sign and add a click event. When the Actions panel opens, select Open URL and replace the URL in the code pane with http://www.bern.com/en/city-of-bern/highlights/cathedral-of-bern.

5. Close the Actions panel and test the project in a browser. As shown in Figure 6-31, everything works as it should—sort of.

6. Quit the browser to return to Edge Animate.

**Figure 6-31.** Testing in a browser.

We added the "sort of" qualifier in step 5 because, when you test in the browser, the user doesn't have a clue the image is hot. There is no cursor change to indicate the image can be clicked. We could use the Cursor property in Edge Animate, but there is also a code-based approach to this problem that we think is rather neat.

1. Open the `Cathedral` element's Actions and click the `mouseover` tab.

2. Click once at the end of the first line of code, press the Return/Enter key, and add the following line of code:

```
$(this.lookupSelector("Cathedral")).css('cursor','pointer');
```

In plain English, when the mouse is over this object and its element name is Cathedral, it should change this object's cursor property in the CSS to the pointer.

3. Close the Actions panel and test in a browser. As shown in Figure 6-32, the cursor changes when the mouse rolls over the symbol. When it rolls off, it switches back to the arrow.

**Figure 6-32.** A code-based cursor change.

*We are going to stop wiring up the images at this point because, as we like to say: "If you can do 1, you can do 100." Each of the remaining images has exactly the same Edge Animate workflow as that used in the Cathedral symbol. If you want to finish them up, feel free to add your own text to the images.*

## Dealing with the Web

The crazy thing about the Web is we have no control over how people view our pages, the browser they use, or the computer they use to view our content. We always have to keep this in the back of our minds and accommodate those who, shall we say, aren't as well "teched up" as we are. As well, we tend to get bored with the "usual" web fonts, so let's say we have decided to use a Google web font—Open Sans—for the headline. In this concluding part of the exercise, we'll switch up the font and accommodate users with slow connections or browsers that can't handle HTML 5. Let's start with the web font:

1. Point your browser to `http://www.google.com/webfonts` and locate the `Open Sans` font.

2. Open the `Embed` code and copy it to the clipboard.

3. Return to Edge Animate and click the `Add Web Font` button in the `Fonts` area of the Library.

4. Paste the embed code into the `Embed Code` area of the dialog box.

5. Enter 'Open Sans', `sans-serif` into the fallback list, and click OK to accept the change.

6. Select the text on the Stage and apply your new font. The font, as shown in Figure 6-33, is now applied to the headline.

**Figure 6-33.** The headline uses a web font.

Keep in mind those single quotes around *'Open Sans'* are important. If you have a Typekit account, you need to put the name between double quotes—*"futura-pt"*—as shown in Figure 6-34. If you don't include the quotes the supplier uses, the font won't render. This is, to be honest, quite frustrating because the suppliers all have their own way of doing things. There is no standard. Typekit uses double quotes, Google uses single quotes, and the Edge Webfont service doesn't use quotes at all.

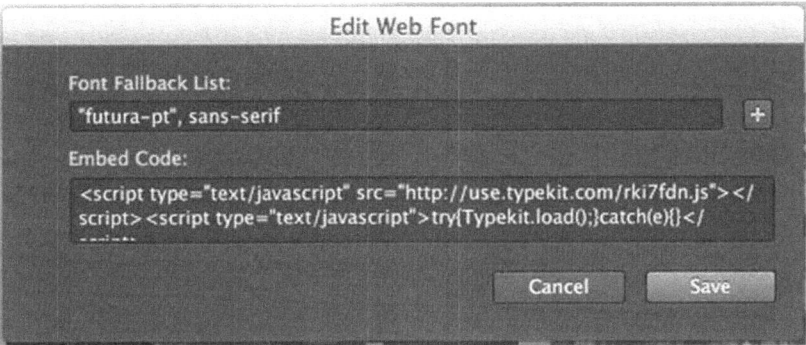

**Figure 6-34.** Typekit fonts use double quotes around the font name.

Next up is the preloader. Although preloaders got a really bad reputation during the early days of Flash, they have their uses in the HTML universe. The last thing you need is for a user to sit looking at a blank screen as the content loads into the browser. In Edge Animate, preloaders are GIF animations that load super fast and play. Let's get this in place:

1. Click once on the `Stage` element and, in the `Properties` panel, twirl down the `Preloader` area.

2. Click the `Edit` button and the Stage changes. In fact the alert box actually tells you, "*You haven't set up a preloader yet.*"

3. If you look at the breadcrumb trail, you will see the Preloader is actually treated much like a symbol with its own independent timeline. Drag the `preloader.gif` file from the Library to the Stage. When you release the mouse, the animated GIF, as shown in Figure 6-35, plays in a continuous loop. Return to the main Stage.

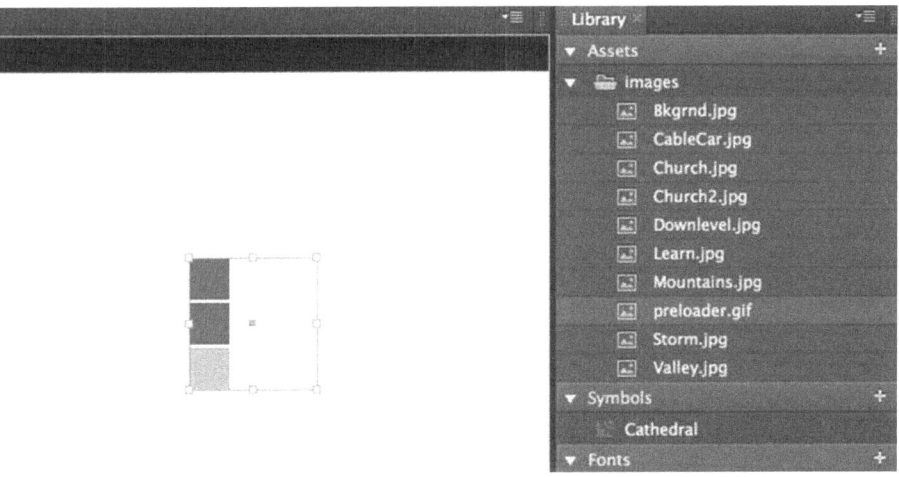

**Figure 6-35.** An animated GIF preloader is added to the Stage.

*Asking you to browser test the movie is a bit of a waste of your time. At best, you may see a brief flash of the preloader. This is because you are testing locally and that connection is about as fast as it gets.*

*For those of you wondering, the preloader is nothing more than a series of 28 by 28 pixel squares on an 88 by 88 pixel canvas in Fireworks CS6. The colors chosen were sampled from the images in the project. The preloader was then turned into an eight-frame animation using the States panel, as shown in Figure 6-36. The file was then saved as a GIF animation. Total production time? Under 10 minutes.*

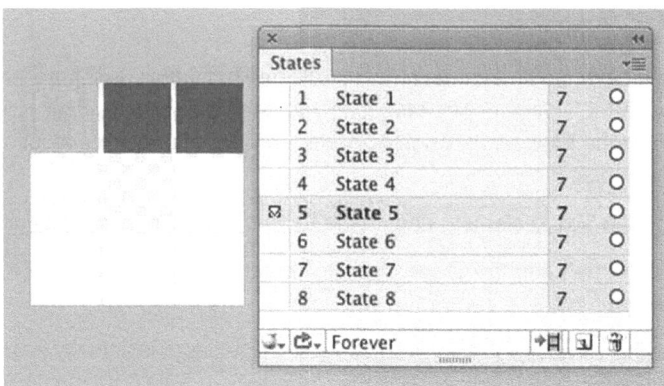

**Figure 6-36.** The GIF animation used in the preloader is created in Fireworks CS6.

It is a simple fact of Internet life that we are in a transition period from HTML 4 to HTML 5. This means there are a lot of browsers still in use that can't display HTML 5 content. Let's not only tell viewers they can't experience our page, but also suggest they might consider upgrading to a more "modern" browser such as Google Chrome:

1. In the `Properties` panel, click on the `Edit` button for the `Down-level stage`. Again a blank stage will open prompting you to add some content.

2. Drag the `Downlevel.jpg` image from the Library to the Stage and, using the Smart Guides, make sure it is centered on the Stage.

3. With the image still selected, click once in the `Link URL` area and enter: `https://www.google.com/intl/en/chrome/browser/`. What you have done, as shown in Figure 6-37, is provide a link to the Google Chrome installer. You don't need to use Chrome. If you prefer to use another modern browser, simply add its link instead.

4. Click `Stage` in the breadcrumb trail to return to the main Stage.

5. Save the project.

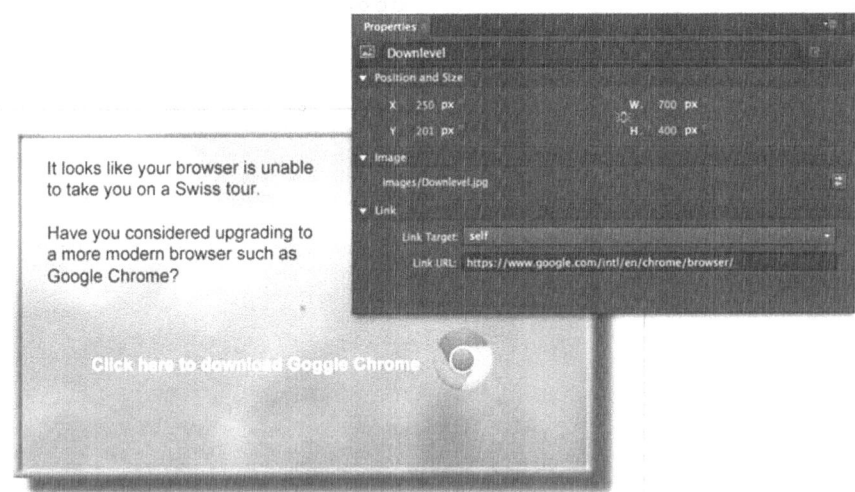

**Figure 6-37.** We complete the project by adding a Down-level stage to accommodate "non modern " browsers.

# You Have Learned

In this chapter, you have learned the following:

- The many code features of Edge Animate

- How to add actions to symbols

- One method of controlling a symbol on the timeline

- How to create an interactive button

- The relation between labels and triggers on the timeline

- A method of adding nonlinear navigation to an edge project

- How to use code to change a cursor

There was a lot of ground covered in a very short time, but we hope you have learned how to code or "wire up" an Edge Animate project using the snippets that come "packaged" with Edge Animate and how to add your own custom code to the Script panel.

Now that you have had a bit of experience using scripts in Edge Animate, our plan from this point on in the book is to include code that will make your life easier. Speaking of code, that is sort of what drives the Web, and in the next chapter we explore how your Edge Animate projects live in an HTML universe.

Turn the page and we'll see you there.

# Chapter 7

# Edge Animate and the Web

Today's modern Web is vastly different from the Web we grew up with. In many respects, this change came about as the Web became "untethered." The ubiquitous ethernet cable plugged into the computer processing unit or a laptop is rapidly disappearing. Surveys are showing that the monitor on your desk is no longer the primary web-viewing medium. Tablets, smartphones, "phablets"—hybrids of tablets and phones—are now the devices of choice in an increasingly mobile web universe. Even the way web pages are designed has undergone a profound change. No longer does the metaphor of a paper page apply as web pages shrink, expand, and shift their design in response to the screen real estate available on the device displaying the content.

Even content, as we know it, has undergone a profound change. As the demand for print publications diminishes, many prominent magazines and newspapers are turning out fully interactive digital versions of their print publications that can be delivered wirelessly and then viewed or "read" on smartphones and tablets.

In the midst of all of this change, the technology driving the creation and delivery of web content has changed. Plug-ins used to display content are a thing of the past. HTML 5 is establishing itself at a rather astonishing rapid pace. CSS3 is used to add special effects to CSS elements. jQuery is used to adapt content to displays. JavaScript has once again become a workhorse animation coding tool.

Within all of this change is Edge Animate, a visual editor in this HTML universe and a tool for creating consistent interactive and motion graphics experiences in the modern web universe.

Your first clue that Edge Animate is a web application is the name of the file that appears in the tab of the Stage panel. It contains the name of the file but, instead of using the .an extension, it uses the .html extension. That's your first clue, but there is a lot going on behind the scenes that you don't see. For example, test a composition and it opens in a browser. Add a web font and the font chosen appears in Edge Animate thanks to the Webkit browser built in to Edge Animate. Content is placed into divs or elements on the Edge Animate Stage. When you change the properties for a selection, the appropriate CSS3 or HTML 5 code is shown to you, and Responsive Design is built into the application because properties can be expressed as either pixel or percentage values.

This chapter will look not at the design aspects of using Edge Animate, but where it fits into the HTML universe. As such we will be covering:

- Preparing content for older browsers
- Adding preloaders to Edge Animate compositions
- Creating poster frames
- Examining the web publishing options available to you
- The purpose of the files created by Edge Animate
- Adding Edge Animate compositions to Dreamweaver CS6
- Adding Edge Animate compositions to Adobe Muse
- How to work with HTML and CSS inside Edge Animate

If you haven't already downloaded the chapter files, they can be found at http://www.apress.com/9781430243502. In this chapter we will be using these files:

- Mishipeshu.an
- Flowers.jpg
- Plant.jpg
- Tags.an
- External.an

> This chapter focuses on the end game of the Edge Animate process: How to get your Edge Animate file "web ready" and some of the browser issues you need to consider. With this in mind, we will be briefly touching on publishing for Adobe Digital Publishing Suite (DPS) and iBooks. We delve deeper into this subject in Chapter 9.

# Edge Animate's Web Publishing Options

Once an Edge Animate composition is finished and approved, you don't simply save the file, merrily pop open a web editor, and go to work. Your first step in the process is to "publish" the file.

As we explained earlier, Edge Animate's native formats are HTML, JavaScript, and CSS. There is no native file format that needs to be converted to work on the Web. Given this fact, you may wonder why there is even a publishing option at all since the code could easily be modified and integrated into a web site using standard HTML tools like Dreamweaver. Although this is certainly true, there are several viable reasons to utilize the publishing options in Animate. With publishing, your project's code is minified, which increases the speed of JavaScript load times. Furthermore, your projects are compatible with non-HTML browsers and can be imported into DPS folios and e-publications. Let's examine the publishing options within Edge Animate. These options are divided into targets, which can be found under the Publish Settings under the File menu.

## Choosing a Target

Open the Publishing Settings tab in the File menu. Edge Animate provides three specific delivery targets, as shown in Figure 7-1, for exporting your compositions:

- Web (.html)

- Animate Deployment Package (.oam)

- iBook/OS X (.widget)

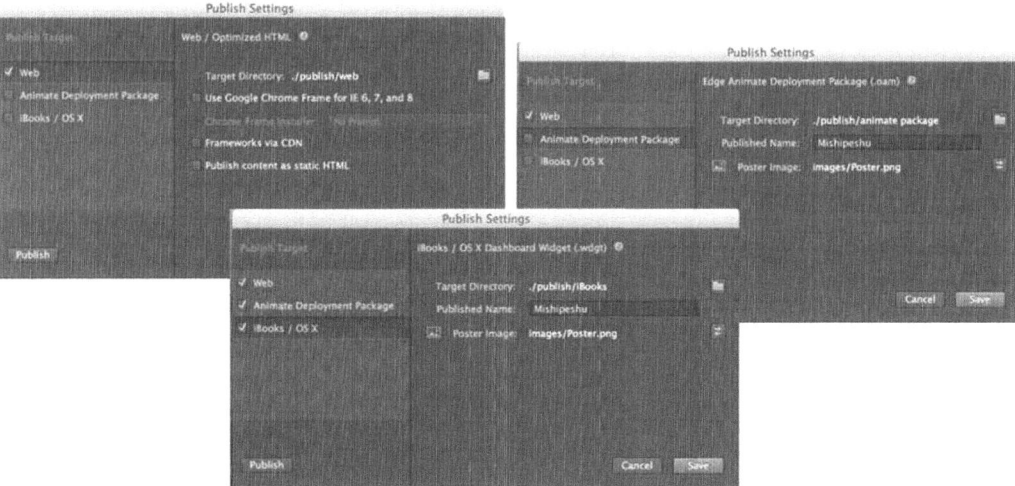

**Figure 7-1.** The publishing targets in Edge Animate.

In any given scenario, there is the possibility that you'll need to publish your Edge Animate project to multiple platforms. Edge Animate's publishing settings make this task very easy to accomplish in a few easy steps.

# Web Publishing

The web publishing option allows you to export your Animate composition in a format that is compatible with the Web. There are various options that can be selected, including support for older Internet Explorer browsers, code caching and "minifying," and search engine optimization (SEO). Follow these steps to configure the Web publishing target:

1. In your Exercise folder, open the folder named 01_Publishing and then open the Mishipeshu.an file.

2. Choose File > Publishing Settings to open the Publish Settings dialog box.

3. Select the Web tab to open the Web/Optimized HTML.

4. If you leave the target directory blank, your web content will be copied inside the default Publish folder in the same directory as your Edge Animate file. This is acceptable, but a more efficient way of doing things is to set your target directory to your content's final destination. For example, you can set your target directory to a content folder inside the root folder of the locally stored web site. Furthermore, under each publishing option, you can set a different target directory. In this case, let's accept the default location.

5. At this point, you can set other web compatibility options such as enabling Google Chrome Frame, which provides HTML 5 compatibility for older versions of Internet Explorer; enabling Frameworks via CDN (content delivery network), which allows your Edge Animate runtime to look for a cached version of the jQuery and Edge Animate runtimes in the browser cache first, increasing overall download speeds; or, Static HTML, which allows you to publish your web content as optimized content that search engines can read. Let's enable all three options (Figure 7-2).

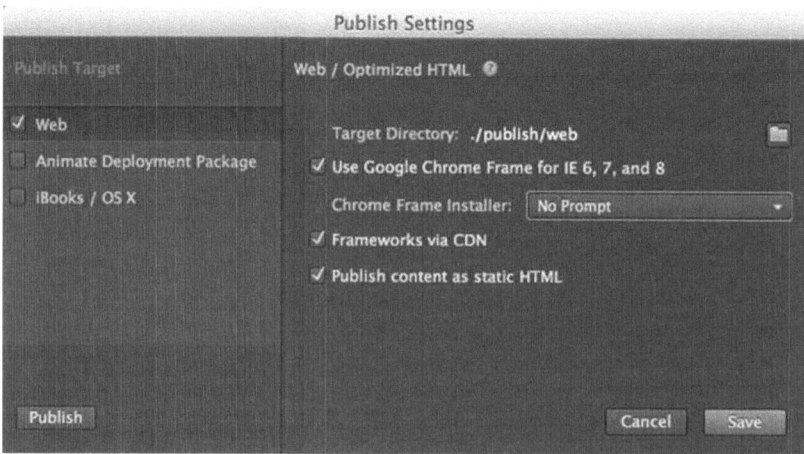

**Figure 7-2.** Configuring the Web/Optimized HTML publishing options.

# Edge Animate Deployment Package

Similar to publishing for the Web, the Edge Animate Deployment Package essentially collects all the necessary HTML, CSS, and JavaScript files into a single OAM file that can easily be imported into Dreamweaver CS6, Muse web sites, or InDesign Folios. Follow these steps to configure an Animate Deployment Package:

1.  Click the Edge Animate Deployment Package tab.

2.  Again, you could select a different target, but in this case, we will use the default location, which is inside the Animate Package folder inside our Publish folder.

3.  We can keep the published name as Mishipeshu or change it to a different name. In this case, we will keep the same name.

4.  We can keep the Poster Image defined earlier, or choose a new poster image from the Animate Library by clicking the double arrow icon. In this case, let's keep the original image (Figure 7-3).

5.  Click the Save button.

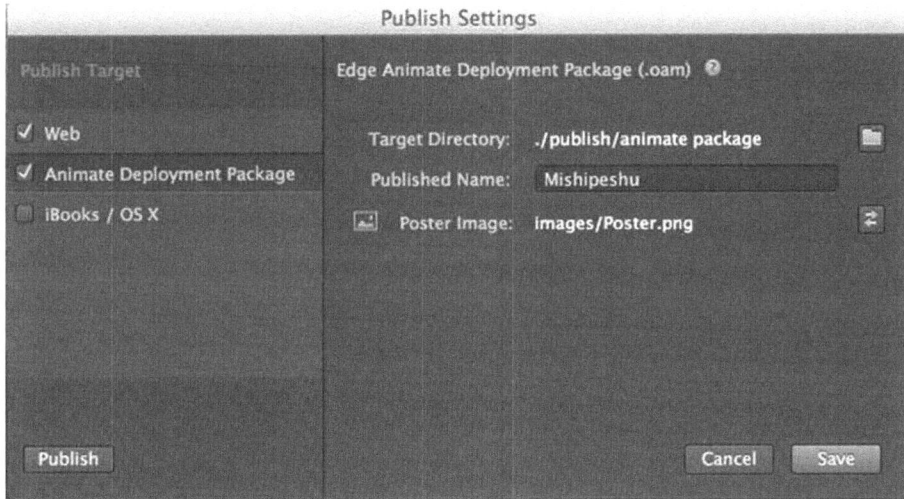

Figure 7-3. Configuring the Animate Deployment Package publishing options.

# iBooks/OS X Publishing

Publishing to the iBooks/OS X format exports a single OS X dashboard widget file—with the .wdgt extension—that can be imported into iBooks documents created by Apple's iBooks author or installed as dashboard widgets in OS X. Let's configure the iBooks/OS X tab:

1.  Click on the iBooks/OS X tab.

2. We could select a different target, but in this case, we will use the default location, which is inside the iBooks folder inside our Publish folder.

3. We can keep the published name Mishipeshu, or if we want, we can change it to a different name. In this case, we will keep the same name.

4. We can keep the Poster Image we defined earlier or choose a new poster image from our library by clicking the double arrow icon. In this case, we will keep the original image.

5. Click the Save button (Figure 7-4).

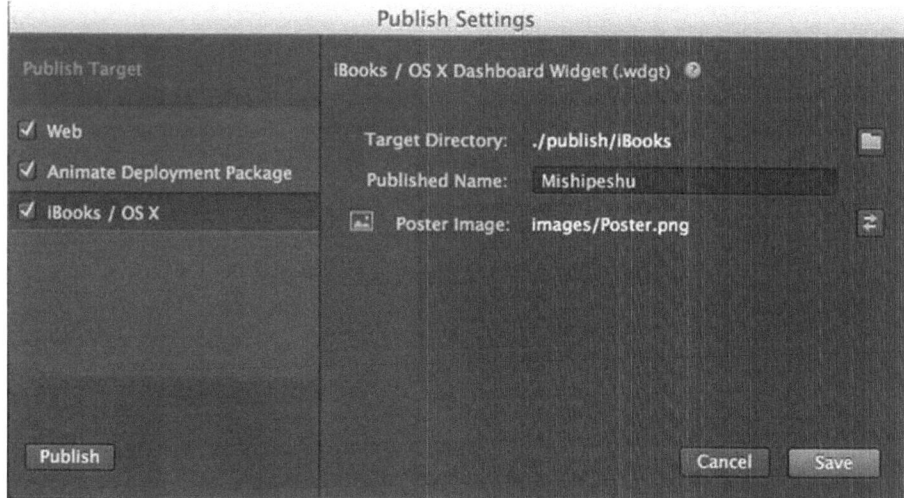

**Figure 7-4.** Configuring the iBooks/OS X dashboard widget publishing options.

# Publishing Our Edge Animate Content

Now that we have configured our publishing options, we are ready to publish our Edge Animate composition.

1. In the File menu, click Publish.

Houston, we have a problem? Although Edge Animate has successfully exported our web and .oam package content to our designated publish folder, we learn we have encountered an error publishing our iBooks content (Figure 7-5).

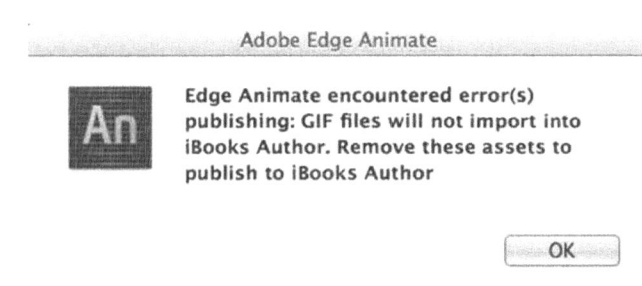

**Figure 7-5.** Publishing GIF files to iBooks Author is not supported.

Why the error message? Apple's iBook format does not support GIF files, which we have utilized for animations in our down-level and preloader stages. This is a common problem and, unfortunately, fixing it is not as easy as changing a few settings. We have to remove our preloader and down-level stages, but more importantly, we need to remove any GIF files from our images library. Here's how to do that:

2. Click the View menu and select the Preloader Stage.

3. Choose Edit, Select All, and delete the contents on the Stage.

4. Click the View menu and select the Down-level Stage.

5. Choose Edit, Select All, and delete the contents on the Stage.

6. Now, we need to delete the GIF files from our library. Click the MishipeshuIcon.gif and preloader.gif files in the Library panel.

7. Ctrl-click (Mac) or right-click and choose Reveal in Finder. In Windows, right-click and choose Reveal in Explorer.

8. Remove the two GIF files from the image directory by either deleting them or dragging them to the desktop.

9. When you return to Edge Animate, you will get another error indicating that files were changed or deleted outside of Edge Animate, to which you will be asked if you want to reload the lost images. Click No (Figure 7-6).

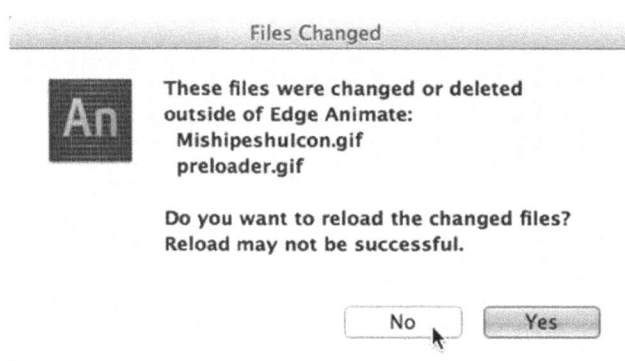

**Figure 7-6.** Removing files from our images folder results in this warning message.

1. In the File menu, choose Publishing Settings.

2. Make sure that Web and Animate Deployment Package options are unchecked.

3. Make sure the iBooks/OS X option is checked and click the Publish button on the bottom right.

> *Although we can configure multiple targets in our publishing setup, it's important to note that when we target for digital publication like InDesign Folios or iBooks, in all likelihood we would not include a down-level or preloader stage, which often uses GIF files. As a result, the previous publishing workaround would not be required. In Chapter 9, we'll delve into creating and exporting content for digital publications.*

# The Purpose of the Files Edge Animate Creates

You may have noticed early on that Edge Animate creates certain files along with its native file (.an extension) once you save your composition. The reality is, Edge Animate really doesn't have a native file format other than HTML itself. In fact, the .an file is merely a JSON file, which simply points to the HTML file of the same name. Let's further explore the files Edge Animate creates (Figure 7-7).

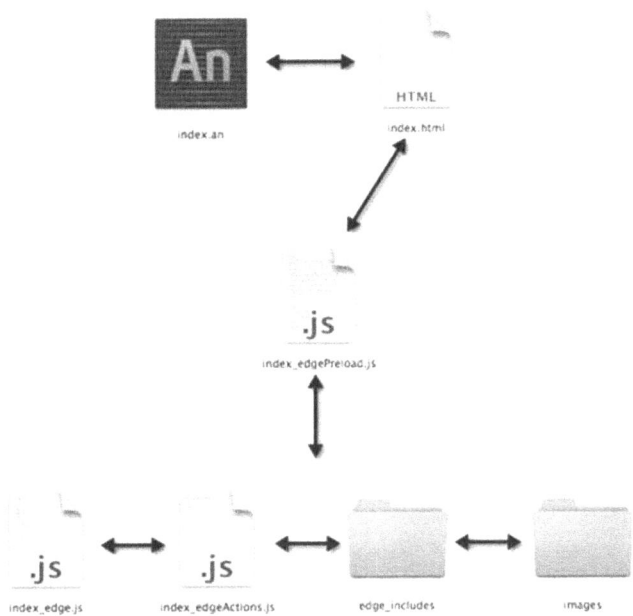

**Figure 7-7.** Edge Animate's file structure.

# The .an File

As we explained earlier, the .an file (Figure 7-8) is really a JSON file that points to the HTML file created by Edge Animate. As a derivative of JavaScript, JSON (JavaScript Object Notation) is a very readable language that defines simple data structures. Information about the main stage, symbols, and the preloader and the down-level stages are some examples of the data stored within the .an file. The key thing to keep in mind here is the .an file is just a pointer to the actual HTML file that Animate creates. It is also the file that, when double-clicked, opens Animate.

**Figure 7-8.** Just some of the JSON code inside the .an file.

# The HTML File

The HTML file (Figure 7-9) created by Edge Animate is the starting point for your composition. As a standard web file, it is the key to what happens next regarding your Edge Animate content. Inside the HTML file is the Stage div, which is the wrapper for your presentation. The Stage div is initially hidden unless you publish your content as static, which, as we've mentioned earlier, creates SEO friendly code inside the stage div. Also included in the HTML file is the edgePreload.js script.

**Figure 7-9.** An example of the code inside the HTML file created by Edge Animate.

# The .edgePreload.js File

The .edgePreload.js file (Figure 7-10) is a yepnope.js file. As explained by the yepnope project page (yepnopejs.com), yepnope is an asynchronous conditional resource loader that loads only the scripts your users need. It is similar to Modernizr but much faster. What is the purpose of a yepnope.js file? The .edgePreload.js tests for conditions that exist for your end user, such as the capability to run HTML5 content. Depending on the testing condition's results, the .edgePreload.js determines which resources your Edge Animate project loads. The .edgePreload.js file is created dynamically as you work within your Edge Animate project. It is extremely important that this file not be edited.

**Figure 7-10.** An example .edgePreload.js file created by Edge Animate.

# The .edge.js File

The .edge.js file (Figure 7-11) defines the content of your Animate presentation. Content such as symbols, states, assets, and font resources are organized and detailed within this file.

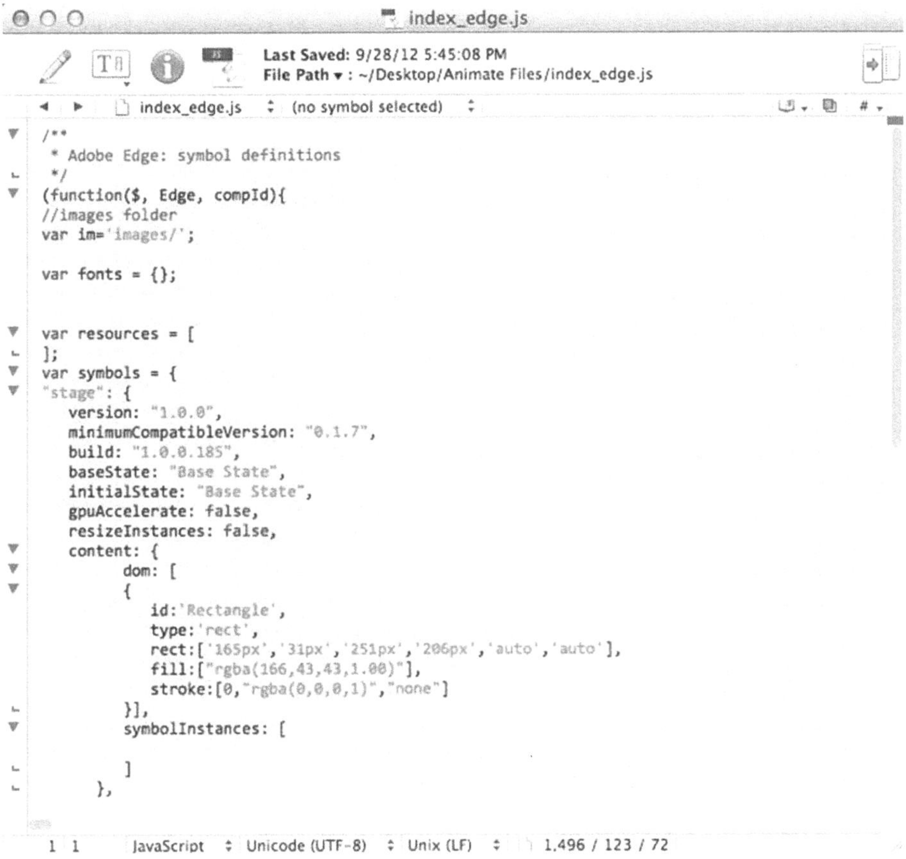

Figure 7-11. An example .edge.js file created by Animate.

# The .edgeActions.js File

The `.edgeActions.js` file (Figure 7-12) is where all your custom JavaScript code is stored. When you create mouse or touch events or timeline triggers, for example, the code is added to the `.edgeActions.js` file. Although it is possible to edit the file externally, it is important that you do so with a bit of caution, making sure you keep references starting with "'Edge" consistent so you are able to work with the actions once they are reloaded within Edge Animate.

```
000                          index_edgeActions.js
    ◇    [TB]   ⓘ         Last Saved: 9/28/12 5:45:08 PM
                          File Path ▾ : ~/Desktop/Animate Files/index_edgeActions.js    ⬚⬚
    ◀ ▶ ◇ ⬚ index_edgeActions.js  ⬍ (no symbol selected)  ⬍                    ⬚ ▾  ⬚  # ▾
▼   |/***********************
    * Adobe Edge Animate Composition Actions
    *
    * Edit this file with caution, being careful to preserve
    * function signatures and comments starting with 'Edge' to maintain the
    * ability to interact with these actions from within Adobe Edge Animate
    *
L   ************************/
▼   (function($, Edge, compId){
    var Composition = Edge.Composition, Symbol = Edge.Symbol; // aliases for commonly used Edge classes

        //Edge symbol: 'stage'
▼       (function(symbolName) {

L       })("stage");
        //Edge symbol end:'stage'

L   })(jQuery, AdobeEdge, "EDGE-251700571");



    1 | 1      JavaScript  ⬍ Unicode (UTF-8)  ⬍ Unix (LF)  ⬍  ⬚ 580 / 63 / 19                  //
```

**Figure 7-12.** A .edgeActions.js file created by Edge Animate.

# The .edge_includes Folder

The .edge_includes folder (Figure 7-13) is a repository for all required libraries. The libraries include:

- edge.js: A library that defines the object and classes used in your presentation.

- jQuery.js: A multibrowser library that simplifies HTML scripting.

- jQuery.easing.js: A library that stores the easing functions within the jQuery user interface.

- json.js: A library that stores information on how to work with the JSON JavaScript subset language.

| .js | .js | .js | .js |
| edge.1.0.0.min.js | jquery-1.7.1.min.js | jquery.easing.1.3.js | json2_min.js |

**Figure 7-13.** The .edge_includes files that Edge Animate creates.

## The Images Folder

The Images folder stores all your image assets in your Edge Animate library. Anything that is added to the Images folder is added to the Edge Animate project's library.

# Edge Animate Compositions and Dreamweaver CS6

Now that you understand the nitty-gritty of how Edge Animate integrates with the Web, including the files it creates, we can turn our attention to incorporating an Edge Animate composition within Adobe Dreamweaver CS6. Of course one of the cool things about Dreamweaver CS6 Creative Cloud subscription is the built-in support for adding Edge Animate content media to an existing web page. This was included in a major Dreamweaver update released in September 2012. This new feature makes it dead simple to add Edge Animate content to your Dreamweaver projects. Here's how:

The first thing we need to do is set up our Dreamweaver site. This creates our link structure so we can add our Edge Animate content.

1. Locate and open the folder named `Dreamweaver` in your `Exercise` folder.

2. Copy the folder name `Mishipeshu` to your documents folder on your hard drive.

3. Launch Dreamweaver and select Site: Manage Sites.

4. Click the New Site button.

5. In the Site Name field enter Mishipeshu.

6. In the Local Site Folder field, click the folder icon and locate the `Mishipeshu` folder that you copied to your documents folder.

7. Click the Save button.

8. Click the Done button.

## Inserting the Edge Animate Composition into Dreamweaver

Now that we have the site set up in Dreamweaver, we are ready to import the Edge Animate content into a Dreamweaver page. The new Insert Edge Animate feature in Dreamweaver CS6 lets you insert an `Animate Deployment Package` (OAM formatted file) with ease. For this next exercise, we will be using the OAM file we exported in the previous publishing exercise, which we have included in our Dreamweaver site inside the folder named `animate`.

1. Launch Dreamweaver and open the `index.html` file in the Mishipeshu site defined in the previous section.

2. Click on the Split button to open the Code and Design view panels.

3. Locate the `comment in` line 83 of the Code window.

4. Click once in line 84 of the Code window. The Animate project is going to be inserted here.

5. Select Insert > Media > Insert Edge Animate Composition. The Select Edge Animate dialog box will open.

6. In the dialog box, locate the `animate` folder and insert the `Mishipeshu.oam` file.

7. You will get a dialog warning that informs you that the composition name already exists. Click OK.

8. In Design view, you will see the An icon, which indicates you have included an Edge Animate presentation and, as shown in Figure 7-14, the code from the OAM file is added.

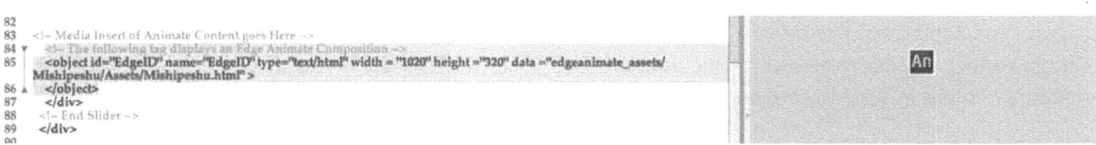

**Figure 7-14.** Dreamweaver adds the code and places an icon on the page when an OAM file is inserted into the page.

9. Click the Design view button, then click the Live view button to view the page with the Animate presentation.

# Inserting Edge Animate Content Using an iFrame

At this point, we are done and could publish our Dreamweaver web site to the Web. But what if we are using an older version of Dreamweaver or another web authoring application? The good news is the method is almost as easy. We could meticulously copy the header references and stage div code from our generated Edge Animate HTML file, but this starts to get ugly if we want to work with multiple Edge Animate compositions on the same page. Instead, we'll just define and create an inline frame (iFrame) to handle our Edge Animate content. We will be using the web publishing output files we generated in the previous publishing exercise, which we have included in our Dreamweaver site inside the folder named `iframe`. Here's how we do that:

1. In Dreamweaver, open your Mishipeshu web site, locate the `index.html` file in the root folder, and open it.

2. Click on the Split button to bring up the code and design view.

3. Locate the `animate-wrapper` div in the `code view` window.

4. Select and delete the Edge Animate code between the `animate-wrapper` div contents. This is the code that was automatically inserted when we imported our composition using the Insert Edge Animate feature in Dreamweaver CS6 in the previous exercise.

5. As shown in Figure 7-15, enter the following code:

```
<iframe src="iframe/Mishipeshu.html" width="1000" height="300" frameborder="0"
scrolling="no"></iframe>
```

6. Click the Refresh button in the Properties panel to accept the code change.

7. Save your file and click the Preview/Debug in Browse button and select a browser from the list to preview the page.

> To test your results, preview the index.html file locally on your computer system or upload the contents of the **Mishipeshu** folder to the Web. By inserting your Edge Animate compositions with this technique, you should be able to incorporate your animations on any web platform such as WordPress, Drupal, or Joomla.

```
82
83    <iframe src="iframe/Mishipeshu.html" width="1000" height="300" frameborder="0" scrolling="no"></iframe>
84
85        </div>
86        <!-- End Slider -->
87    </div>
88
89
```

**Figure 7-15.** Use an iFrame for other web platforms.

# Adding Edge Animate Compositions to Adobe Muse

One of the cool things evolving on the modern Web are the tools we now have at our disposal. Apart from Edge Animate, another new tool that Adobe has introduced is Muse.

Muse is targeted at designers who don't want to learn code but still desire to create web sites. Muse is quite easy to use and operates much the same way as Adobe InDesign. Certainly we could go in depth with our explanation and discovery of Adobe Muse, but the point here is how to incorporate an Edge Animate composition in an Adobe Muse web site. Once again, Adobe has made the workflow between Edge Animate and Muse stunningly easy in their most recent version (2.0) of Muse by including the ability to place Edge Animate compositions within Muse page layouts. Here's how easy it is to include Edge Animate content within Muse:

1. In your Exercise folder, open the folder named Muse and then open the Mishipeshu.muse file to launch Muse.

2. In Plan Mode, double-click the Home page.

3. Select File > Place.

4. In the Muse folder, locate the file named Mishipeshu.oam. This is the file we created from our publishing exercise earlier, the same file we used in our Dreamweaver CS6 example. Select the file and click Open.

5. Your cursor will display a small preview of the Animate composition and a corner alignment guide. Click just below the top guide and right below the gray transparent header bar to place the Edge Animate content on the page.

6. With the Edge Animate content placed on the page, move it until it is in position below the black header bar. In this case, we aligned it to X = 0 and Y = 0 using the Timeline tab of Transform panel shown in Figure 7-16.

7. Save your file and preview in a browser.

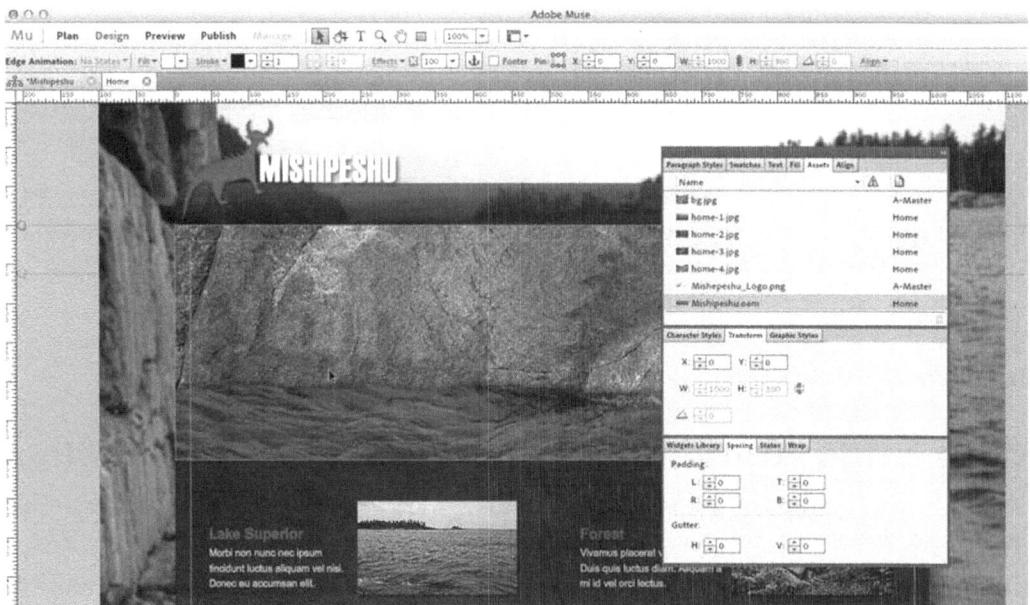

**Figure 7-16.** Placing an Edge Animate composition in Adobe Muse.

# Preparing Content for Older Browsers

With all the glitz and glamour of CSS effects, responsive imagery, web fonts, and animation that are integral features of the modern Web, the spotlight on older browsers has shown their inability to render HTML5 and CSS3. The days of the desktop computer's majority are dwindling, but the fact remains that older desktop computers with older browsers installed still represent a large group of systems incapable of viewing advanced content. Should we shut this older community out of our Edge Animate creations? Of course not! A better goal is to politely nudge them into upgrading their systems by providing viewable content that their old browsers can handle. This is the purpose of the down-level stage.

The down-level stage is a separate stage from the main Edge Animate Stage. It can be accessed from the View menu. The down-level stage is designed to house graphics and text compatible with older browsers. You won't be animating or adding transparencies or other effects when you create a down-level stage. In fact, all of the fancy stuff is disabled in the down-level stage. And that's exactly the point. Your job is to provide a simple screen for older browsers to deal with your advanced Edge Animate content. Let's build a simple down-level stage:

1. Navigate to the `Down-Level Stage` folder in this chapter's exercise. Double-click the `Mishipeshu. an` file to launch the composition.

The plan for any down-level stage is to identify a screen or point in the composition that conveys the message behind the composition. Let's find that point:

2. Move the playhead to the 1.00-second point in the timeline. The screen shown in Figure 7-17 is ideal for our needs.

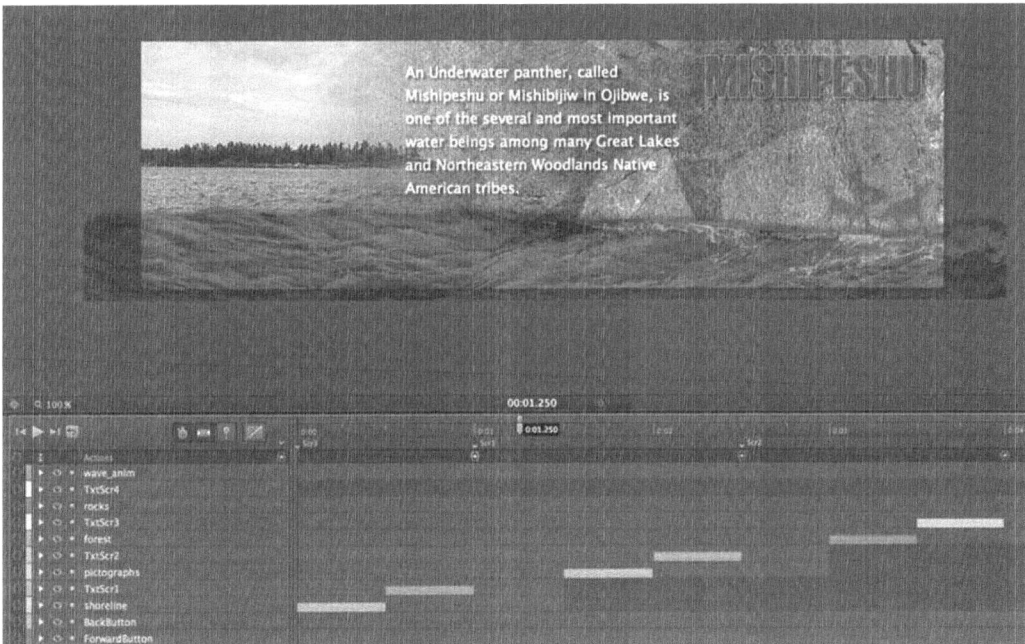

**Figure 7-17.** The first step is to identify a point in the composition to be used as the down-level stage.

Having identified the content to be used in the down-level stage, the next step is to create the stage. A down-level stage is nothing more than content—an image and some text—that can be rendered by older browsers.

3. The image portion of a down-level stage is nothing more than a simple screen capture. This capability is built in to Edge Animate. In the `Properties` panel under `Poster`, click the `Camera` icon to open the `Capture a Poster Image` dialog box.

4. As you can see in Figure 7-18, you are presented with two options: Create a new poster image or, if one already exists, replace it with a new one. Click the `Capture` button. A new image—`Poster. png`—will be placed in the Images folder.

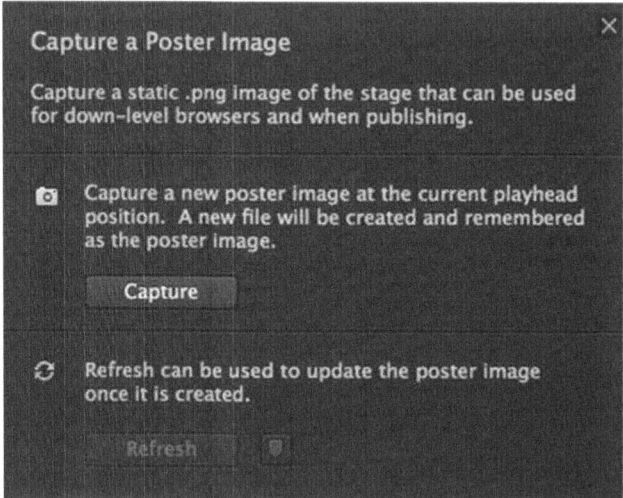

**Figure 7-18.** Poster Image capture options.

> *The Poster Image is a special image that is stored in the Edge Animate library. You can capture a Poster Image anywhere on the timeline by placing the playhead at a specific point on the timeline and selecting the Poster Image camera icon. Edge Animate keeps track of where you captured the last Poster Image (by a Pin) and allows you to update the current poster frame based on your last frame point or the new point you specify. The Poster Image can also be used when publishing to different formats, which we will cover later.*

With our Poster Image stored in the library, we move next to creating our simple down-level stage. Here's how:

5.  There are two ways to create a down-level stage. The first is to select Down-level Stage from the View menu. The second, as shown in Figure 7-19, is to click the Edit button in the Down-level Stage area of the Properties panel. Regardless of the method used, they both result in a dialog box telling you there is currently no down-level stage.

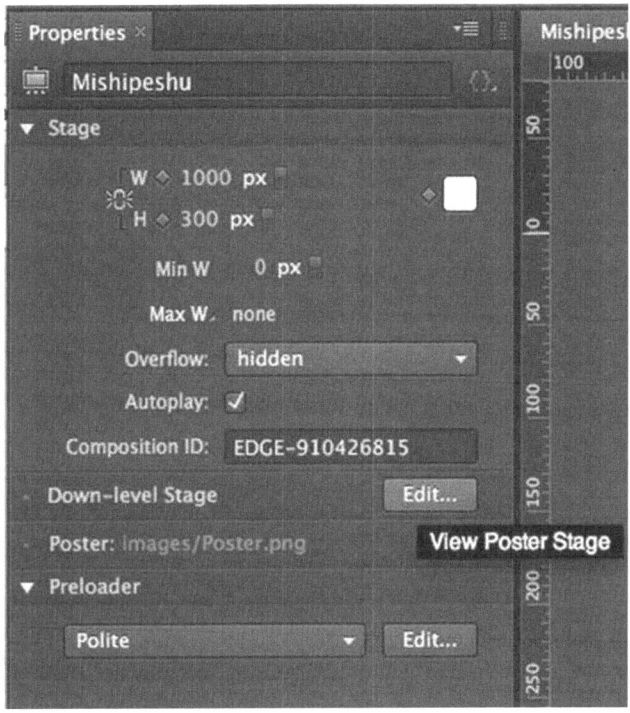

**Figure 7-19.** Creating a down-level stage in the Properties panel.

If you look closely at the Stage, you will notice, as shown in Figure 7-20, a breadcrumb trail, a changed `Properties` panel, and the `Alert` box. What you can gather from this is your down-level stage is really nothing more than a child of the main Stage that will only come into play when a nonmodern browser is detected.

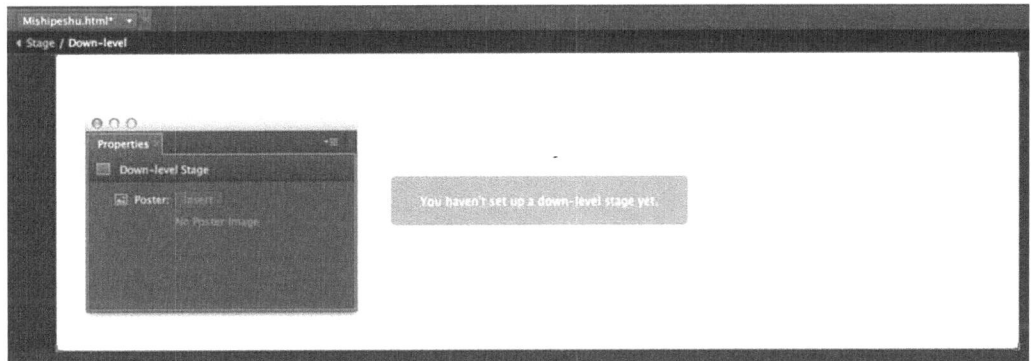

**Figure 7-20.** The down-level stage is ready to be created.

6. In the `Properties` panel, click Poster: Insert. This places the `Poster.png` image on the Stage.

7. From the library images, drag the `MishipeshuIcon.gif` to the upper left corner of the Stage.

8. Click the Text tool and enter the following text: `'This content requires a modern browser that supports HTML5 and CSS3. Please upgrade your browser.'` Drag the text block to the bottom of the screen.

9. In the Properties panel, format the text using these settings:

   • *Font*: Verdana, Geneva, sans-serif

   • *Size*: 16 pixels

   • *Alignment*: Centered

   • *Color*: Use these RGB values: 243,160,15 (dark orange)

10. With the Text box still selected, enter the following address in the Link-URL field: `http://google.com/chrome`

11. We can set our link target to open in the same window or a new window in the `Link Target` box. Accept the default `self`. As shown in Figure 7-21, the down-level stage has been created.

**Figure 7-21.** A typical down-level stage.

# Testing a Down-Level Stage

Now that our down-level stage has been created, how do we know it works? One cool trick is to employ the power of Adobe Browser Lab (`https://browserlab.adobe.com/en-us/index.html`).

Adobe Browser Lab (Figure 7-22) is a complimentary online service that you can use if you have a free Adobe ID. When you specify a URL in the link field, Browser Lab will render it in a series of screen shots showing how it would appear in various browsers. In other words, you don't need to keep an old copy of Internet Explorer 7 on your computer just for testing. There are several ways you can test your down-level stage:

*FTP*: Upload your Edge Animate file using an FTP program to a web site, then copy and paste the Absolute Link from the web site into Browser Lab.

*Dreamweaver*: You can open your Edge Animate file and send it to Browser Lab for testing using Dreamweaver. You will need to copy your Edge Animate files into the root folder of an existing Dreamweaver site before locally testing it in Dreamweaver.

*Firebug*: If you are running Firefox and have installed the Firebug plug-in, you can install the Adobe Browser Lab Firebug Plug-in (`https://addons.mozilla.org/en-US/firefox/addon/adobe-browserlab-for-firebug/`) and test your file locally in Browser Lab.

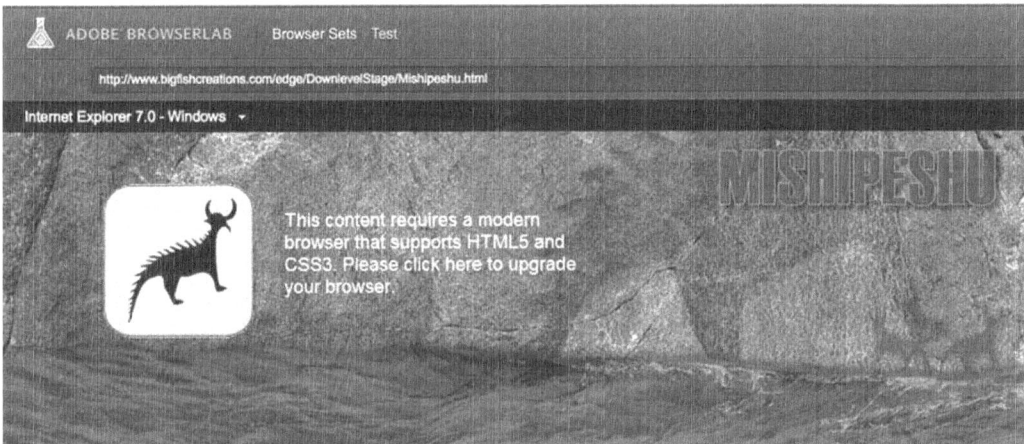

**Figure 7-22.** Testing our down-level stage in Adobe Browser Lab.

# Adding Preloaders to Edge Animate Compositions

A practical goal in web design is to keep your file size down to a minimum while maintaining an overall decent quality. However, in situations where our Edge Animate compositions include rather large files, we want to provide a way for our users to be alerted to the fact our composition needs some time to download our assets before it displays our presentation. We accomplish this task by including a preloader stage in our Edge Animate composition. The preloader stage is a separate stage within our Edge Animate presentation where we can load small graphics and text that informs our web user that our Edge Animate file is downloading before it plays. We want our preloader stage to be small and load fast, yet provide enough visual feedback to the user as to what is going on behind the scenes. In fact, Edge Animate has a few default preloader animations built in, which makes our job in creating one a bit easier. Let's explore this further:

1.  In your Exercise folder, open the Preloader folder, then open the Mishipeshu Preloader folder, and then open the Mishipeshu.an file.

2.  In the View menu, select Preloader Stage.

3.  You will see a blank stage and Edge Animate will display a message that says "You haven't set up a preloader yet."

4.  In the Properties panel, click the Insert Preloader Clip-Art button.

5.  Double-click a Clip-Art option to insert it on the Stage. In this case, we chose the Loading Bar.

6.  In the top bar, set the css-background color to transparent (Figure 7-23). That completes the preloader. You won't be able to see it when you test the file locally because it will load too quickly. To see the preloader, you will need to publish the Edge Animate file to the Web and view it there.

**Figure 7-23.** Selecting our factory preset Preloader Clip-Art loading animation.

# Designing Our Own Preloader

The default preloaders within Edge Animate are quite usable out of the box. However, we may want to build our own custom preloader for our project. This is a fairly easy task to accomplish, but we want to keep in mind a few things. First, we want to keep our preloader files rather small so they load quickly while our large graphics continue to load in the background. Second, we want to provide some kind of animated feedback to our users that something is actually happening, in this case, our large graphics are downloading. We can achieve both these goals by employing the old-school power of the animated GIF. By creating an animated GIF for our preloader, we can give our user a visual signal that things are happening all within a quick, highly compressed graphic file. Adobe Fireworks is a fantastic tool to employ when we want to create a simple animated GIF file. Let's give it a try:

1. Open Fireworks and create a new document 125 pixels by 25 pixels.

2. Select the Type tool and choose the font Arial Black (or similar) and set the point size to about 15 points. Type the word LOADING in all caps.

3. Rename the Firework's layer to text.

4. Right-click or (option-click Mac) and select Share Layer to States. This will share the layer to the animation states that you will be creating in the next step.

5. Create a new layer and rename it anim.

6. Select the anim layer and draw a box 25 pixels by 25 pixels.

7. Select a dark orange fill color. In this case we chose #B25900.

8. In the Properties panel, position the square at X = 0, Y = 0 on the Stage.

9. Click the States panel and then right-click or (option-click Mac) and add a new state after the current state.

10. Move the orange square to X = 25, Y = 0.

11. Repeat steps 9 and 10 and move the orange square 25 pixels to the right on the X axis until you have five states.

12. Select all the states and right-click (or option-click on Mac) to open the properties for the Frame Rate. Set it to 15.

13. Under the Optimize panel, set the Export File Format to Animated GIF.

14. Click the Preview tab in the top of the window and click the Play/Stop button in the bottom right of the Stage to preview the animation.

15. Now, choose File > Image Preview to bring up the export preview window.

16. Click Export and save the file as preloader.gif in the Mishipeshu preloader images folder.

In Edge Animate, the exported file should appear in the images folder in the library. Let's complete the custom preloader:

17. In the preloader stage, click on the Loader-Bar and delete it.

18. In the library under images select your custom preloder.gif image and drag it to the center of the Stage. We centered ours at X = 424 and Y = 195.

19. Drag the Mishupeshuicon.gif file on to the Stage just above your preloader. We placed ours at X = 412 and Y = 27.

20. Save your file.

In order to preview your preloader, you want to upload it to the Web. That way, your high-resolution files will be able to slowly download in the background while your custom preload stage displays the loading status.

# Edge Animate and HTML/CSS Overflow

One of the key things to understand about Edge Animate is the fact that it utilizes HTML/CSS and JavaScript/ jQuery to perform its magic. By default, elements in Edge Animate are placed inside an HTML div tag. Some Edge Animate div elements can be nested inside other elements simply by dragging them on top of the other in the Elements panel. Furthermore, every single element in Edge Animate is nested inside the Stage div element. In fact, as we mentioned in Chapter 1, Edge Animate is quite different from other Adobe design tools like Flash, Photoshop, Fireworks, and Illustrator because it uses a div as the canvas and therefore utilizes Overflow to determine how to display elements in the gray area that are not visible on the Stage. Let's do a quick experiment.

1. Open Edge Animate and create a new document with the default stage size of 550 pixels by 450 pixels.

2. Select the Rectangle tool and draw a gray rectangle that stretches across the Stage, roughly 766 pixels wide.

3. Draw another rectangle above the gray one and change the color to red. Make sure the rectangle is 550 pixels wide and center it on the Stage (Figure 7-24).

4. Select the Stage div and, in the `Properties` panel, click the actions button and select `compositionReady` from the pop-down list. The compositionReady area is where you can insert code to run after the composition has fully loaded. In this case, we want to center our composition when we choose preview in browser.

5. Enter the following code:

```
$("#Stage").css("margin","auto")
```

This will center our Stage when we view it in the browser.

6. Preview your composition in the browser. Notice how the rectangles are the exact same width when we preview our composition in the browser, even though our rectangles were drawn in different sizes on the Stage.

7. Go back to your Edge Animate file and click the `Stage` div in the Elements panel. When you look under the `Properties` panel, you'll notice that `Overflow` is set to `hidden`. This is the default setting for the Stage. Therefore, when you view your Edge Animate composition in a browser, the div that contains your composition, the Stage, will function like a mask and crop away everything that flows outside the boundaries.

8. Change the Overflow to `visible` in the pop-down menu and preview in the browser.

9. Notice how the bottom gray rectangle is now longer than the red rectangle.

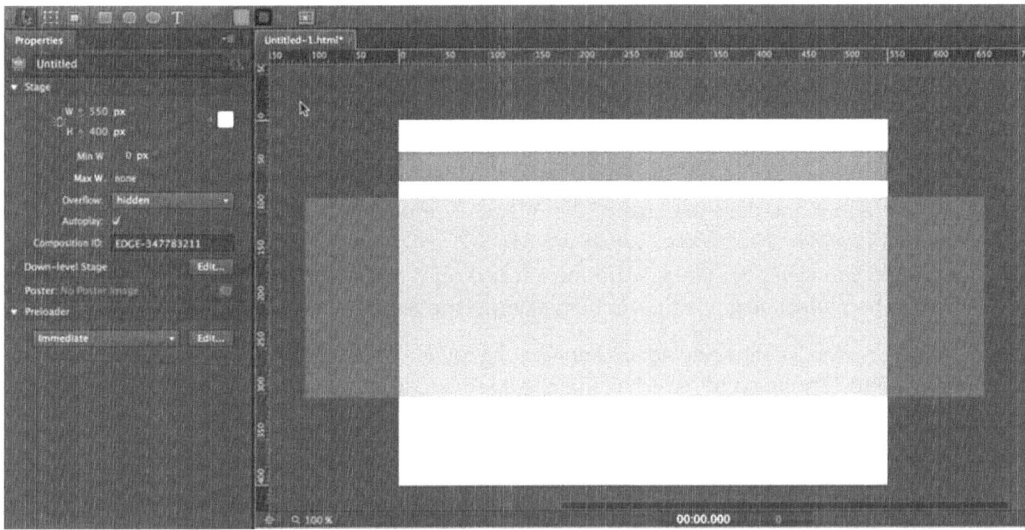

**Figure 7-24.** The rectangle experiment.

> *Edge Animate can read and open HTML documents. In fact, as we explained earlier, Edge Animate uses HTML as its default format. When you create and save a new document in Edge Animate, an .html extension is added to the document title and Edge Animate saves an .an file in the same directory. When you open the .an file, Edge Animate appends the .html extension next to the document title. The .an file is really a JSON file, which is a derivative of JavaScript. The only purpose for the .an file is that it defines the structure of the Edge Animate project, such as the symbols, preloader stage, down-level stage. The key thing to remember is Edge Animate's native file format is HTML.*

# Further Exploration of Overflow

Our experiment from the previous exercise yielded some keen insights about the Edge Animate Stage. But, as we explained, Edge Animate's content largely exists inside divs and is controlled by the CSS "Box Model" and HTML. The CSS Box Model is a method that displays elements enclosed within its defined box via criteria such as margins, padding, borders, and position. Overflow, which plays a large part in how each Edge Animate element interacts with the others on the Stage, is an important concept to grasp when designing your content. Let's try another experiment:

1.  Open Edge Animate and create a new document 900 pixels by 266 pixels. Save the document and name it `overflow`.

2. Choose File > Import and find your chapter `Exercise` folder, open the `Overflow` folder and import `flowers.jpg` and `plant.jpg` to the Edge Animate Stage. Edge Animate will add the images as elements in the Elements panel.

3. Move the `flowers` element to the far right of the Stage.

4. In the Tools bar, select the `Rectangle` tool, then draw and center a rectangle over the `plant` element about one-third the size of the image. The goal here is to cover about one-third of the plant image with a rectangle, which we will use as a mask. The top and bottom edges of the rectangle can cover the plant, while the left and right sides of the rectangle should not. It doesn't have to be perfect, just don't cover both sides of the plant with the rectangle.

5. With the rectangle still selected, click the `background-color` chip in the Properties panel and set the color to `transparent`, which is the checkerboard icon.

6. In the `Elements` panel, drag the `plant` element over the top of the `Rectangle` element you just created. This will create a parent–child relationship between the `Rectangle` (parent) and `plant` (child) element.

7. In the `Elements` panel, click the `flowers` element.

8. Select the `Rectangle` tool and draw and center another rectangle over the `flowers` element, but this time make sure it is exactly the same size as the `flowers` element. Set its color to `transparent`.

9. Drag the `flowers` element in the `Elements` panel over the top of the rectangle you just created `Rectangle2` to create another parent–child relationship (Figure 7.25).

10. Select `Rectangle` and `Rectangle2` in the Elements panel and under `Overflow` in the Properties panel choose `hidden`.

11. In the `Elements` panel, click `plant` to select the plant element on the Stage. Hold the Shift key down (to constrain the vertical position) and move the `plant` to the left on the Stage until it disappears off the Stage. Then, add a keyframe.

12. Move the playhead to the .2-second mark and, while holding the Shift key down, move the `plant` to the right until it disappears on the right side.

13. Move the playhead to the 00 mark.

14. In the Elements panel, click `flowers` and under `Transform`, add a scale keyframe.

15. Move the playhead to the 2- second mark and adjust the scale to 300%.

16. Test your creation in a browser.

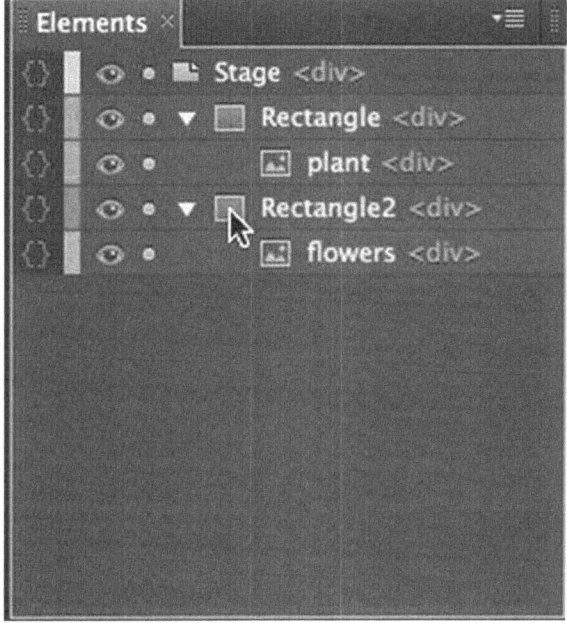

**Figure 7-25.** Creating our parent–child relationships by dragging one div element over the other. The indented elements indicates a child.

What you should notice that is the two rectangles you created and set to "hidden" have constrained (cropped) the elements to the box size. The plant element moves from left to right and within the Rectangle div and the flowers element scales up to 300% inside the Rectangle2 div.

Change the overflow value on the Rectangle2 Element div to Visible. Now preview your composition in a browser. The flower element scales up to 300% but is still cropped by the Stage div.

Now, click the Stage div in the Elements panel and change the Overflow to visible and preview in the browser. Notice, in Figure 7-26, how the flowers in the third example now stretch (overflow) beyond the Stage div. It is important to understand that just by changing the overflow options on our stage elements, we can create a different presentation of our elements.

**Figure 7-26.** Manage the Overflow property to control stage elements.

This demonstrates that Edge Animate utilizes the CSS Box Model to organize and display elements on the screen. This is very convenient, especially when the goal is to move our Edge Animate content to the Web.

# Beyond the DIV Tag

As we discussed earlier, Edge Animate's default setting is to enclose all stage elements inside an HTML div tag. However, Edge Animate can also assign different tags to stage elements. You might be asking yourself, why would I want to do that? The answer is accessibility. Within Edge Animate, you can change the tag type of your stage elements, therefore allowing you to specify HTML tags like the paragraph tag <p> or the heading 1 tag <h1> as well as accessibility via the title tag (tooltips) and tab order. Let's explore this further.

1. In your Exercise folder, open the tags.an file found inside the Tags folder.

2. Click the triangle next to the Content <div> to reveal the other elements in the document. Notice that they are all div elements (Figure 7-27).

**Figure 7-27.** When we open our tags.an file for the first time, we see all our elements are div elements.

3. Click on the SoupTitle element and in the Properties panel, click the tag menu button and switch from <div> to <h1>.

4. Select Ingredients inside the IngredientBox and switch from <div> to <h2>.

5. Click the IngredientsTxt and change the tag to <p>.

6. Click the Description element and change the tag to <blockquote>.

7. Finally, click the logo and soup elements and change their tags to <img>.

Having changed the tags on our elements, we can add further accessibility options based on the tag we have defined. For example, if we click our <img> tags, notice that we now have new options in the Properties panel to describe our images further, such as the Alt and Title. This further allows us to add HTML accessibility to our project, ensuring compatibility with the widest possible audience and devices. Feel free to enter an Alt description and a Title description in the fields for each of the images as follows:

8. For the Soup image: Alt = Chicken Noodle Soup  and Title = Soup

9. For the Logo image: Alt = Food A Logo and  Title = Logo

We can add Titles to the remainder of our non- `<img>` elements along with a Tab index number. This allows navigation via the Tab key without using a mouse. To do this, we click each element and assign an incremental number in the Tab index option along with our Title in the title field. We want to do this in a logical order, for example, in a clockwise direction starting from the top left. Click each element, starting from the top left, and assign the following titles and tab numbers:

10. For the SoupTitle element: Title = Chicken Soup   Tab = 1

11. For the Ingredients element: Title = Ingredients Tab = 2

12. For the IngredientsTxt element: Title = List of Ingredients Tab = 3

13. For the Description element: Title = Brief description of chicken noodle soup Tab = 4

14. For the Logo element: Title = Logo Tab = 5

15. For the Soup element: Title = Soup Tab = 6

16. Test the project in a browser. Press the Tab key and tab around each section on the screen. Hover the mouse over the objects to view your Titles as tooltips.

> *When you publish your Edge Animate project, you can enable in the settings to publish your project as a static HTML page, which writes the tags as static tags in the HTML file rather than inside the Edge Animate JS file. By exporting your project as static HTML, it becomes more SEO friendly.*

## Your Turn: Loading External Content into Edge Animate

Many years ago we received an extremely wise bit of advice from a developer: "Code is code." Whether it be HTML, CSS, JavaScript, or jQuery, the underlying concept is always code. The difficulty lies in writing it, but thanks to the extensive use of jQuery in Edge Animate, the content from many of the most popular services out there—in this section Google Maps and YouTube—is available to you through built-in APIs (application programming interfaces). Similar to how Typekit provided the embedding code for us to work with type in the previous chapter, Google's services provide the code that can easily bring their content into Edge Animate. All you need to do is simply copy and paste it into your composition. Let's get started:

1. Open the External.an file located in your Exercise folder. When it opens, you will see, as shown in Figure 7-28, that we have created a simple interface containing two buttons on the left and a background for the content on the right. You can assume from this that clicking either button loads a Google map or a YouTube video into the project.

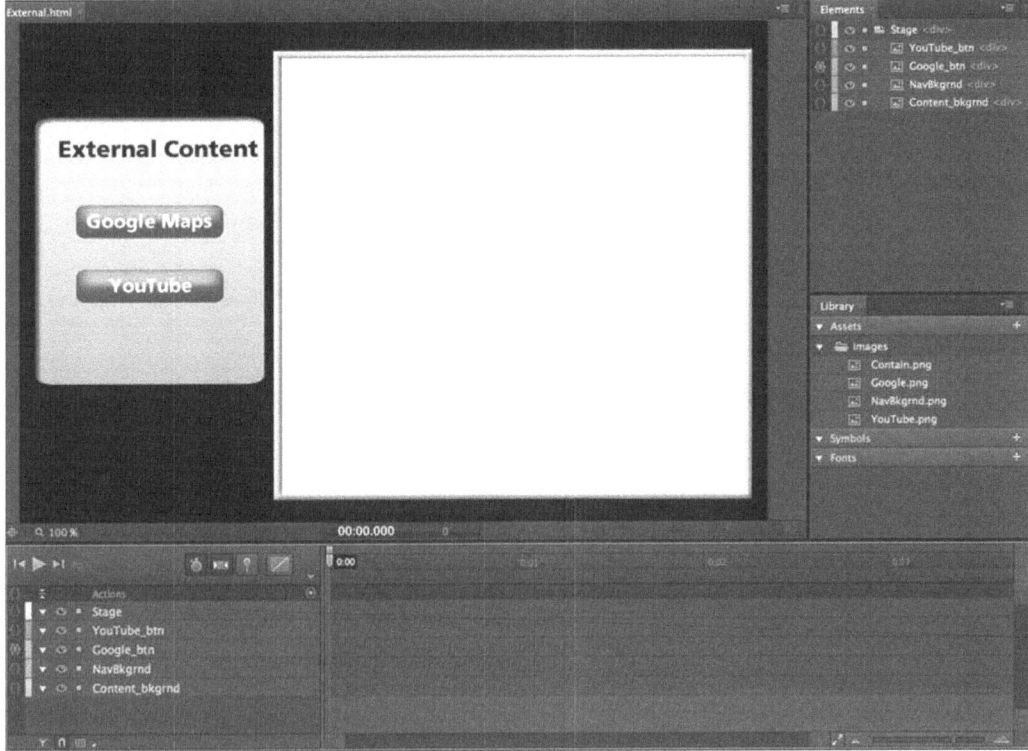

**Figure 7-28.** We start with a very basic interface.

2.  With the playhead at the 0 point of the timeline add a stop() action to the timeline. This will stop the playhead and give the user the opportunity to click either button.

3.  Move the playhead to the 1-second mark of the timeline and add a label named Google and a stop() action trigger.

4.  Move the playhead to the 2-second mark and add a label named YouTube and a stop() action trigger.

With the main timeline set up, we can now concentrate on "wiring up" the project to display the content from Google Maps and YouTube. The first step is creating the "container" for the content.

5.  Select the Rectangle tool and draw out a rectangle that fills the white area of the Content_bkgrnd element. Set the fill color to None and add a 1 or 2 pixel dashed stroke around the box. The stroke is just to give you a visual reference. It can be removed before you publish the project.

6.  Rename this element "container" and convert it to a symbol named "Google."

7. Double-click the Google symbol to open the symbol and edit it in place. We are now ready to wire up the project.

## Adding a Google Map to Edge Animate

A very common feature of web pages is a Google map showing the location of a business or local point of interest. In this case, one of the authors lives in Oakville, Ontario, and one of his favorite places is the trail alongside Lake Ontario that starts at Lakeside Park. Let's add that location to Edge Animate.

> *You don't need to use this location. Feel free to use any location that interests you. The key here is not the map. It is the code.*

1. Open Google Maps and enter Lakeside Park, Oakville, ON. You should see the park and harbor as shown in Figure 7-29.

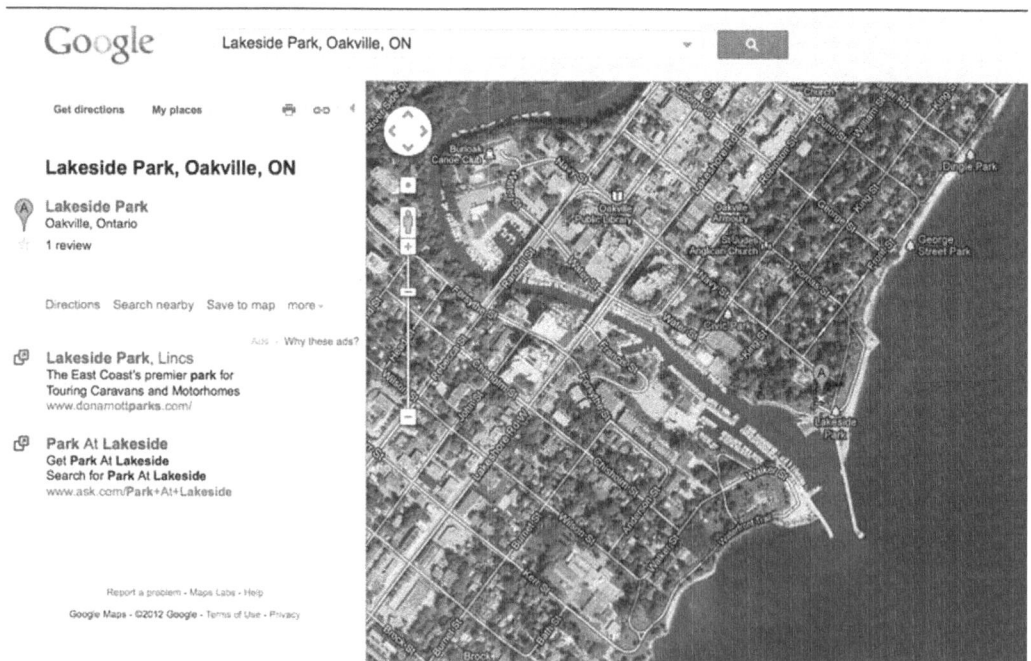

**Figure 7-29.** Open the location in Google Maps.

2. Click the link icon at the top-right of the left-hand panel to open the Link dialog box shown in Figure 7-30. Click once in the Paste HTML area to select the iFrame code. Copy it to the clipboard. Quit Google Maps to return to Edge Animate.

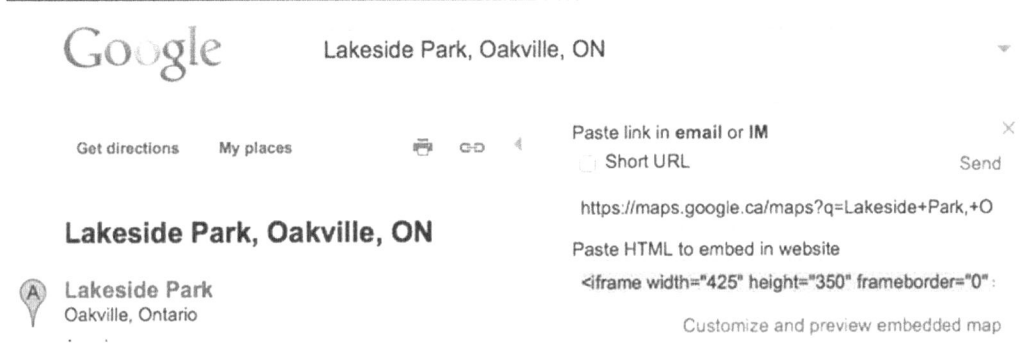

**Figure 7-30.** Copy the iFrame code to the clipboard.

> *When you click in the box below "Paste HTML to embed in website," you automatically select all the code, although it may look like you did not. You can also click the "customize and preview embedded map" link to open up a window to further customize the code and select it and then copy it to the clipboard.*

3. Click once on the Stage to deselect the container. Since we are editing the symbol itself, the symbol name, which in this case is Google, should now appear in the Properties panel.

4. In the Properties panel click the `Open Actions` button beside the symbol. When the Actions menu appears select the `creationComplete` action (Figure 7-31). We need to do this because, according to the Edge Animate API documents: "creationComplete **fires immediately after a symbol is created and initialized but before** autoPlay occurs." In short, it buys the time to load the map into the Google symbol before it appears in the browser.

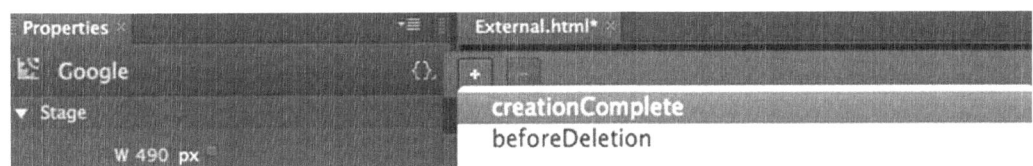

**Figure 7-31.** Everything starts with a `creationComplete` event attached to the symbol.

5. When the code editor opens, enter the following code:

```
var container = sym.$("container");
```

We start by simply giving the box that we just created the variable name of `container`.

6. Press the Return/Enter key once and enter:

```
var map = ' ';
```

The plan here is to create a variable, named "map," for our Google code that we copied from the clipboard in the previous exercise then paste that code in between our single quotes.

7.  Click once between the single quotes in line 2 and paste the iFrame code on the clipboard between them. You may notice the width and height values, shown in Figure 7-32, are "hard wired" into the iFrame. Let's change them so the values reflect the size of the box holding the map.

```
creationComplete

     function(sym, e)
  1  var container = sym.$("container");
  2  var map = ' <iframe width="425" height="350" frameborder="0"
```

**Figure 7-32.** The width and height values should reflect those of the container element in the Edge Animate composition.

8.  Although you could simply note the values in Edge Animate's Properties panel and enter them, you really should let the software handle this duty. Select the width value between the double parentheses and enter:

```
'+container.width ()+'
```

This sets the width of the container to the current width of the Google symbol without you having to worry about a number. The height needs the same change. Select the value and replace it with:

```
'+container.height()+'
```

Your additions should resemble those shown in Figure 7-33.

```
var map = ' <iframe width="'+container.width()+'" height="'+container.height()+'"
```

**Figure 7-33.** Setting the width and height values of the iFrame code to match the dimensions of any symbol.

9.  The last step is to add the iFrame to the target container. Click once in line 3 of the Code panel and enter:

```
container.html(map);
```

10. Return to the main timeline and select the Google element.

11. In the Properties panel set the Google element's Display property to Off. Move the playhead to the Google marker and change the Display property to On.

12. Save and test the movie. Click the button and (Figure 7-34) the map appears.

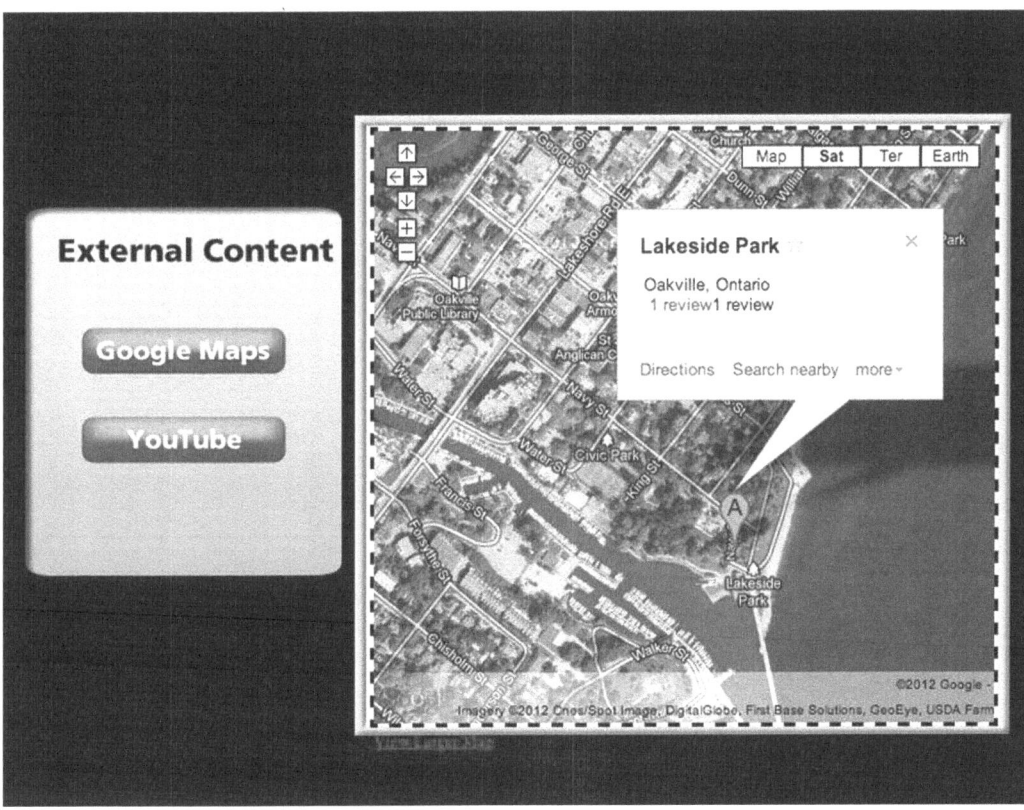

**Figure 7-34.** That's exactly where we want to go.

## Adding a YouTube Video

Adding a YouTube video uses the same steps as adding a Google map but there are a couple of things you should be aware of before adding YouTube content to you compositions.

If you open the Extend.an file in this chapter's Complete folder, you will see we have added a YouTube video. If you test it in the browser and click the YouTube button you will see, as shown in Figure 7-35, a couple of children tubing through the winter snow outside the home of one of the authors.

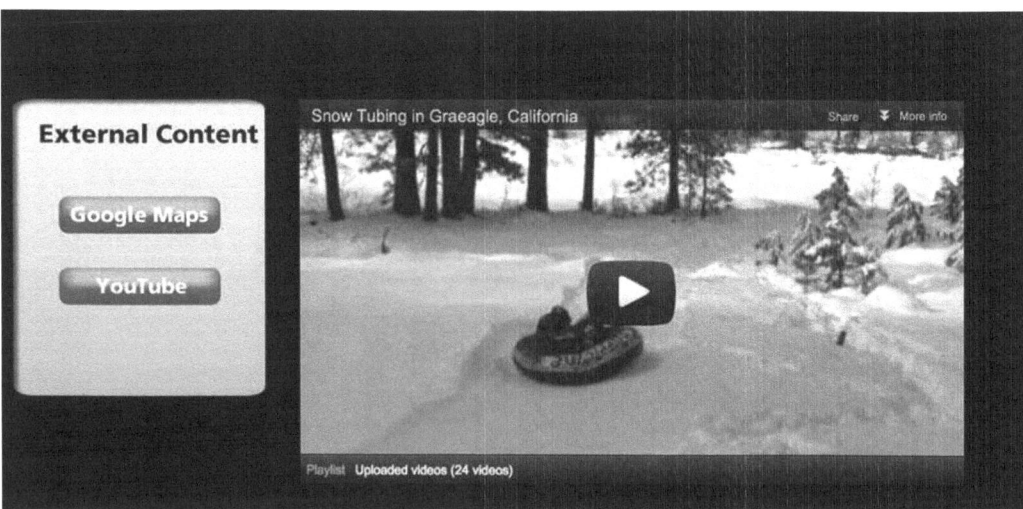

**Figure 7-35.** The YouTube video is in place.

If you open the code for the YouTube symbol, you will see the `creationComplete` code is not terribly different from the Google code other than the fact that we have used numbers for the width and height values. There is a reason for this.

If you point your browser to the video on YouTube—`http://www.youtube.com/watch?v=tjXcL2mhsOM&featu re=share&list=UU4Ns36PLecNVFaOoeLDLdwg`—and open the Embed code, by clicking the `Share` button, you will see the dialog box displayed in Figure 7-36.

**Figure 7-36.** The YouTube embed options.

If you select one of the sizes, the width and height values in the code will also change. You are also given the opportunity to choose a custom width. This is where problems can arise if you pick the wrong size. The default sizes all use an HD 16:9 ratio. If your custom width and height values don't have the same ratio, there is a pretty good chance the video will distort.

For example, a common non-HD video size is 640 pixels wide and 480 pixels high. That is an aspect ratio of 4:3, and HD video resized to those dimensions will either distort or sprout black bars at the top and bottom of the video. This technique is called *letterboxing* and it is how a 16:9 aspect ratio video gets shoehorned into a 4:3 aspect ratio.

If you are at all unsure as to whether the video will fit into a "container" element in Edge without distortion or letterboxing, our advice is to use one of the measurements from YouTube shown in Figure 7-36.

# You Have Learned

This chapter has covered the following:

- How to publish an Edge Animate composition

- A thorough review of all of the files created by Edge Animate when a composition is published

- Dealing with iBooks and its hostile relationship with GIF images

- Adding Edge Animate compositions to Dreamweaver CS6 and Adobe Muse

- Creating a down-level stage

- Using Browser Lab to test a down-level stage

- Creating a preloader stage

- Adding accessibility to an Edge Animate composition

- How Overflow works in Edge Animate

- How to add a Google map or YouTube video to an Edge Animate composition

As we have pointed out throughout this book, Edge Animate lives in a web universe. We started by reviewing the various publishing options available to you, thoroughly reviewed the purpose of each file created when an Edge Animate project is published, created a down-level stage to adapt to older browsers, explored how to change Element tags to deal with accessibility, and finished up by adding a Google map and a YouTube video to an Edge Animate composition.

Now that you have the basics of using Edge Animate under your belt, let's take your skills for a ride and add a little wow to your work. That's the subject of the next chapter. We'll see you there.

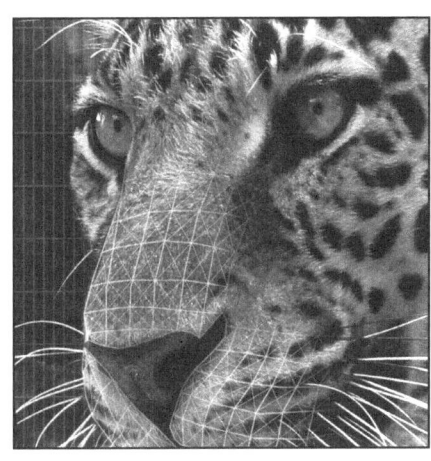

# Chapter 8

# Adding a Bit of "Wow"

Practically everything you have learned so far falls within the realm of "safe." We have spent a lot of time demonstrating and reinforcing the fundamentals of using Edge Animate. This chapter will take your shiny new Edge Animate skills out for a joy ride and show you how to drive a truck through them.

In this chapter we are going to create a series of projects. The difference is that many will be start-to-finish projects: They start with an idea, move through asset creation, and finish up in Edge Animate. It will also give you a great idea of how some of the tools—common and not so common—in the toolbox can be used to create the assets that are subsequently used in Edge Animate.

Here is what we will cover in this chapter:

- *Project 1*: A deep dive into the emerging Fireworks/Edge Animate workflow

- *Project 2*: Complex timeline animations

- *Project 3*: One symbol and a little code goes a long way

- *Project 4*: Create an Edge Animate preloader in Flash

- *Project 5*: Create a code-based pop-down menu

If you haven't already downloaded the chapter files, they can be found at http://www.apress.com/9781430243502. In this chapter, we will be using these files:

- Background.jpg

- Shadow.ai

- Starfield.an

- WallArt.an

# Project 1: Falling Letters

A common Edge Animate technique is to have a word or phrase animate from above the Stage into its final position. To add a little "jazz" to the animation, one might choose to tween the opacity from 0% to 100% as the text moves into its final position. This is fine, but it is "safe." The letters or words are a solid block of text with a color. In this exercise, let's move out of that comfort zone.

As one of the authors is fond of saying, "the art of motion graphics is the art of illusion." The plan here is to have the letters of the word EDGE fall into place in the Edge Animate composition, but the letters will look as if they were part of the background image. The background image, shown in Figure 8-1, is a cement texture that looks like a spotlight is shining on it, but, as you can see, the light falls off at the edges. The plan is to have the letters of the word pick up the texture of the background and fade out depending on their proximity to the edge of the light.

The key to this technique is in the asset preparation phase of the project. Although there are a number of ways to prepare this file, we are going to use Fireworks because it is a lot more efficient. Let's get started:

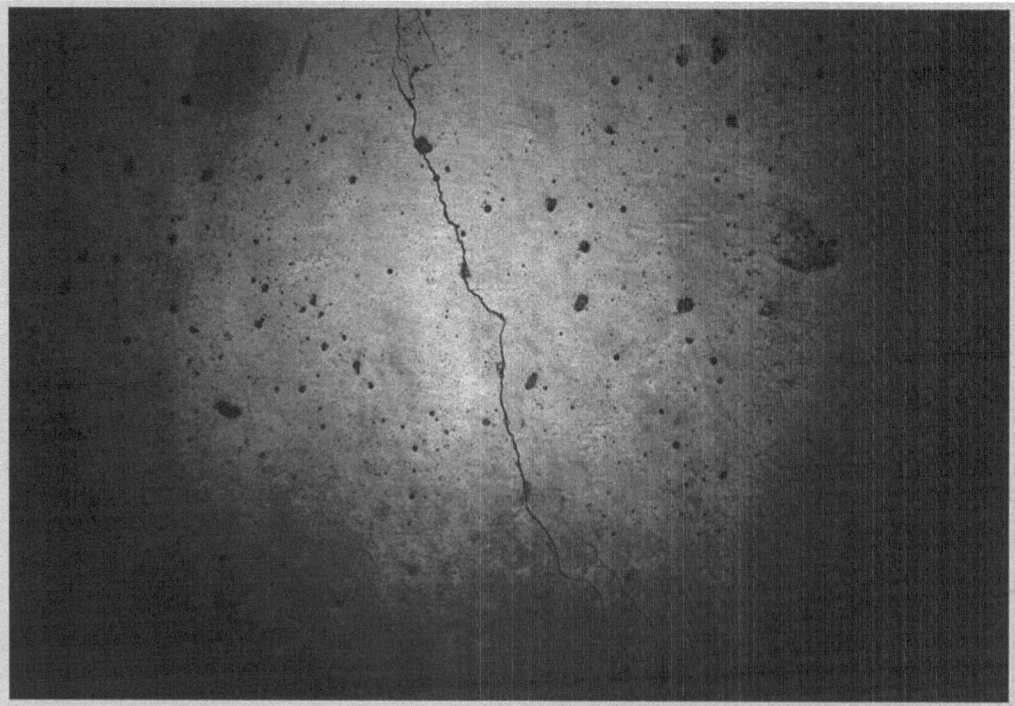

**Figure 8-1.** The trick is getting the letters to interact with the background image.

## The Fireworks Approach

As we pointed out in Chapter 4, Fireworks really streamlines this process thanks to its ability to export layers as individual PNG 32 images that contain transparency.

1. Open the Background.jpg image in Fireworks. When the image opens, lock the Background layer.

> *What's the difference between a PNG 32 image from Fireworks CS6 and a PNG image with transparency from Photoshop CS6? Not much really. The real difference is Fireworks' ability to optimize and render semitransparent pixels. In several side-by-side comparisons, the PNG 32 image created by Fireworks is significantly smaller, in file size, than the one produced by Photoshop.*

2. Select the Text tool, click once on the image, and enter the word EDGE.

3. Select the text on the canvas and, as shown in Figure 8-2, use these settings:

   - *Font*: Arial Black or other very bold sans-serif font. We used David Carson's BigEd Sr.

   - *Size*: 250 pixels

   - *Color*: White

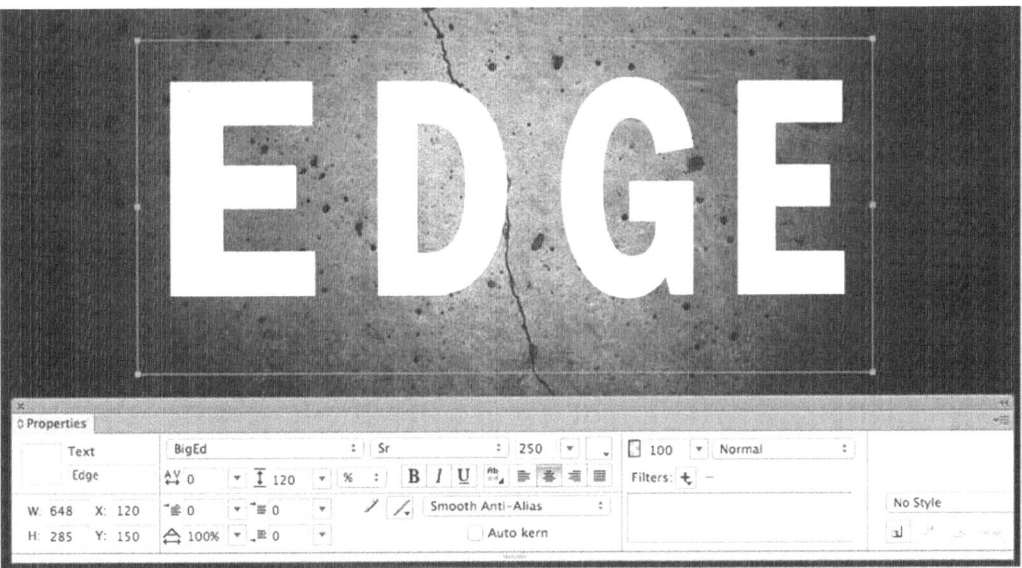

**Figure 8-2.** The text is added to the canvas.

With the text in place, we can now concentrate on preparing it for the effect. The first thing we need to do is create a shadow on the wall for the text.

4.  Duplicate Layer 1 by dragging it over the New Layer icon in the Layers panel. This will give you a new layer named Layer 2. Select Layer 1 and rename it Shadow.

5.  Turn off the visibility of Layer 2 in order to concentrate on the task at hand.

6.  Select the text block on the canvas and select Text > Convert To Path. This converts each character in the text block to a vector outline.

7.  With the text block still selected, select Modify > Ungroup to change the text from a block of text to individual pieces of line art in the Shadow layer.

8.  Select the first letter E and, in the Properties panel, select Effects > Shadow and Glow > Drop Shadow to open the Drop Shadow dialog box.

9.  In the dialog box, shown in Figure 8-3, set the Distance to 25, the Opacity to 50%, and the Softness value to 8. Click the Knock Out checkbox to turn off the fill. The letter outline, with shadow, appears on the background image.

**Figure 8-3.** The drop shadow with knock out is applied to the letter E.

10. Repeat steps 8 and 9 for the remaining three letters.

11. Open the Shadow folder in the Layers panel and rename each of the images to ShadE, ShadD, ShadG, and ShadE2. One of the keys to working with Edge Animate and Fireworks is to make sure everything has a unique name that makes sense. Lock the Shadow layer.

### Creating the "Falling" Letters

It is time to turn our attention to the letters that will be put in motion in Edge Animate:

1. Turn on the visibility of Layer 2, select the text in the layer, and convert the selection to outlines and ungroup the letters.

2. Add three more layers to the Layers panel and, starting with Layer 2, rename them E, D, G, and E2.

3. With the new layers created, you need to move the content for each one into its respective layer. To move the images to the new layers, select the D in the layers panel and click the dot (as shown in Figure 8-4) on the right side of the D layer. The artwork moves to that layer. Repeat this step for the other two letters.

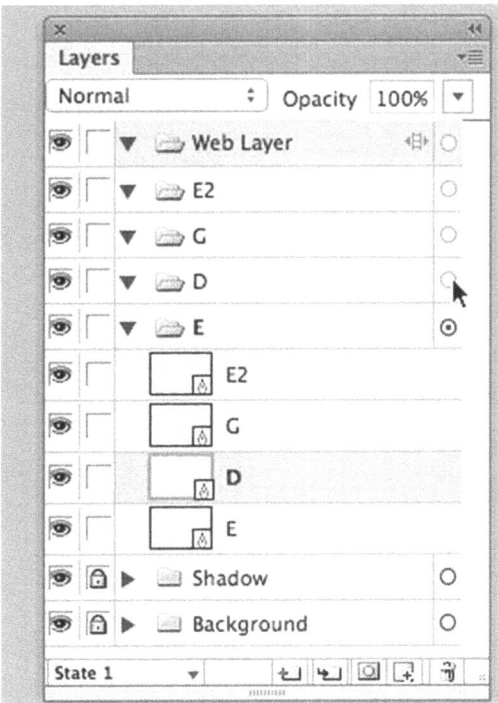

**Figure 8-4.** Each letter needs to be moved to an independent layer.

*Why a separate layer for each letter? Remember, we are going to be exporting each layer out of Fireworks as a separate PNG image. If these images were all in the same layer, that layer would be flattened to a single text block.*

A problem becomes immediately apparent. The plan is to have each letter look as if it were a part of the background. Changing opacity really doesn't work because all that does is uniformly fade the image and not take the fading light in the background image into account. It's time for an illusion.

4.  With the E layer selected, select the Rectangle tool and draw a rectangle that fits the dimensions of the canvas.

5.  In the Fill area of the Properties panel, click the Gradient button and, when the Gradient dialog box opens, as shown in Figure 8-5, change the colors to Black and White, and set the Gradient to Radial.

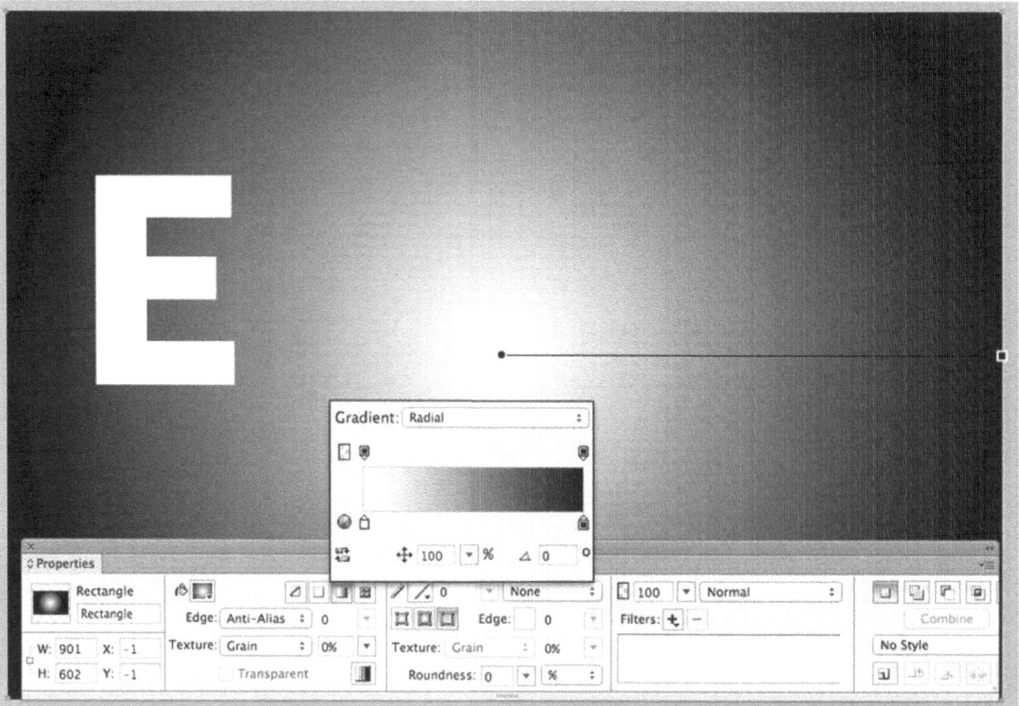

**Figure 8-5.** The illusion starts with the creation of a radial gradient in a rectangle.

6.  To make sure the radial size closely matches that of the light in the background image, reduce the opacity of the gradient layer, click once on the gradient on the canvas, and, when the gradient handle appears, move it in or out to change the radial dimensions. When you finish, raise the Opacity of the gradient back to 100%.

7.  Copy the gradient rectangle and paste it into the remaining layers. The rectangle layer should be above the letter in each of the layers.

8. In the E layer, select both the Gradient and the letter. Select Modify > Mask > Group As Mask. The letter now fades off to match the gradient.

9. With the E layer still selected, at the top of the Layers panel, reduce the Opacity value to about 20%. Use your judgment here. If this opacity value doesn't work for you, play with the value. Repeat these two steps for the remaining layers, being sure to adjust the opacity for each layer. Each of the letters now has a distinct edge and fade, as shown in Figure 8-6.

**Figure 8-6.** The magic lies in the mask.

With the effect created, you need to slip each letter's shadow under the letter to ensure it travels properly into Edge Animate. We will also need to turn each letter and its mask into a separate bitmap. To do that, follow these steps:

10. In the E layer, right-click the contents and select Flatten Selection from the Context menu. This turns the vector and the mask into a single object with gradient opacity.

11. Unlock the Shadow layer and move the ShadE item to the E layer. Make sure that ShadE is under the E layer.

12. Repeat these two steps for the remaining three layers.

13. Delete the Shadow layer. It has no content, so it makes sense to get rid of it.

14. Save the file as a PNG file just in case you need to change something.

### Exporting the Files

Exporting the files for use in Edge Animate is the last part of the process. Follow these steps:

1. Unlock and delete the Background layer. This is a JPG file, and converting it to a 32-bit PNG format with transparency is going to add nothing to the project but some extra "weight."

2. Open the Optimize panel, as shown in Figure 8-7, and select PNG 32 as the format and set the matte color to None. What this does is tell Fireworks that each layer in your Fireworks image is to be treated as a PNG 32 image when the file is exported.

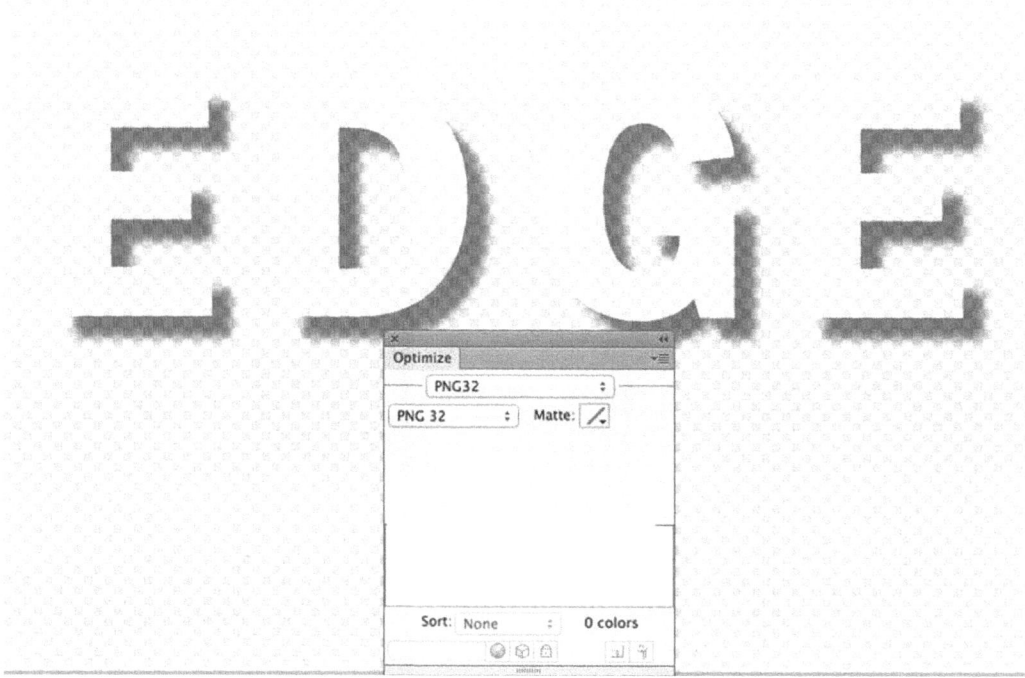

**Figure 8-7.** The settings in the Optimize panel apply to all layers in the Fireworks file.

3. Select File > Export to open the Export dialog box, as shown in Figure 8-8.

4. Select Layers to Files from the Export pop-up menu and navigate to the folder where you will be saving the files. Name the file, select Trim Images, and click the Export button. You may briefly see an export progress bar.

5. Save the file and quit Fireworks.

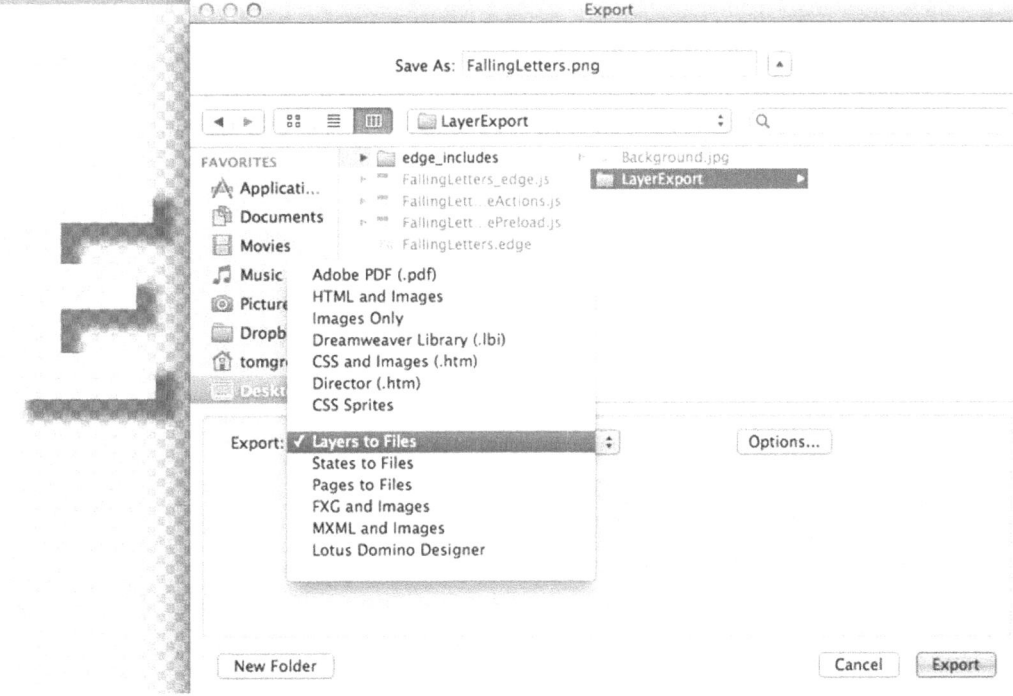

**Figure 8-8.** The layers will export to separate PNG images using the Layer name from Fireworks.

> *Yes, this whole imaging project can be created in Photoshop. In fact, the steps are remarkably similar.*

### Creating the Edge Animate File

Now that we have created our assets, we move over to Edge Animate and prepare the animation.

1. Launch Edge Animate and create a new document that is 900 pixels wide and 600 pixels high.

2. Import the Fireworks images you just created along with the Background.jpg image into Edge Animate.

> *If you don't have Fireworks, the files can be found in the **FireworksImages** folder.*
>
> *Also, don't forget: You can drag and drop your files directly from the file system into Edge Animate without using File > Import.*

3. Move the Background element into position at the 0,0 point.

4. Change the layer order of the letter elements to spell the word EDGE (with E2 as the final E in EDGE).

5. Move the letters onto the Stage, as shown in Figure 8-9, to their final position in the animation.

**Figure 8-9.** We are ready to start animating.

6. Making sure Autokeyframes is active, select the first letter E on the Stage, click the Pin, and move it to the 1-second mark of the timeline.

7. Drag the selection upward until it is just off the top of the Stage. If you scrub the playhead, the letter will fall from the top of the Stage to its final position.

8. Pull the playhead back to the 0 point and, with the letter E still selected and the Pin still at the 1-second mark, reduce the Opacity to 0 in the Properties panel. If you scrub the playhead, the letter will fade in as it moves down the Stage.

9. Click once on the Transition strip to select it. Click the Eases button and select EaseOut > Bounce. If you press the spacebar, you'll see the letter, as shown in Figure 8-10, fades in as it moves down the Stage and bounces before it comes to rest.

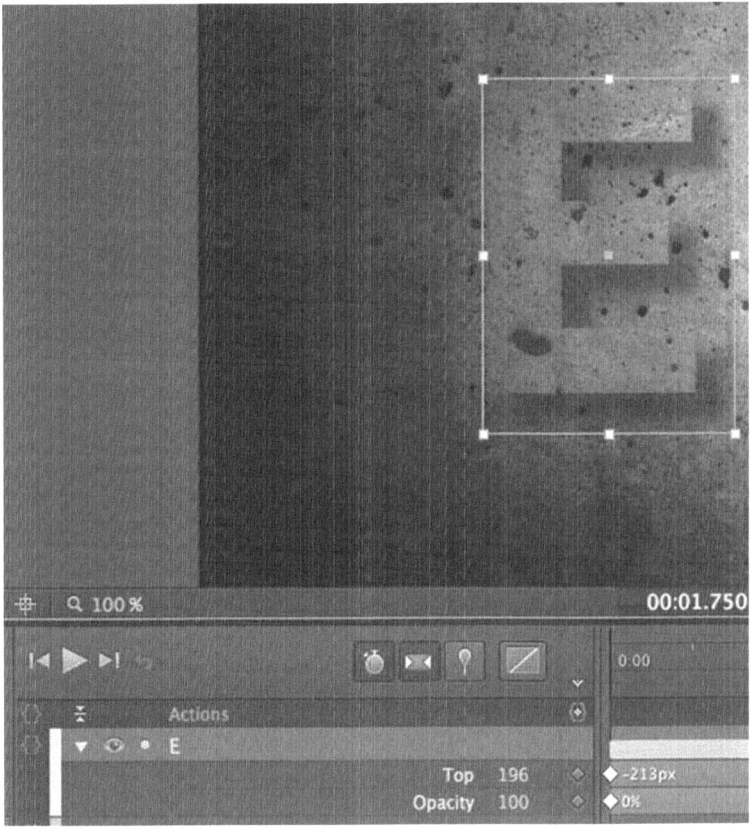

**Figure 8-10.** The first letter is animated.

At this point you could note all of the values for the transitions and apply them to the other letters. But that would be a waste of time because there is a much faster way of animating a series of elements. Here's how:

10. Click once on the Transition strip for the letter E and copy the strip to the clipboard.

11. Select all of the remaining letters.

12. Select Edit > Paste Special > Paste Transitions To Location (Figure 8-11). This rather nice feature will apply all of the transitions in the E element to the other selections. By selecting Paste Transitions To Location, you will see all of the letters mimic the motion of the E element. If you were to select Paste Transitions From Location, the E would move down the Stage while the other letters faded in as they moved up the Stage.

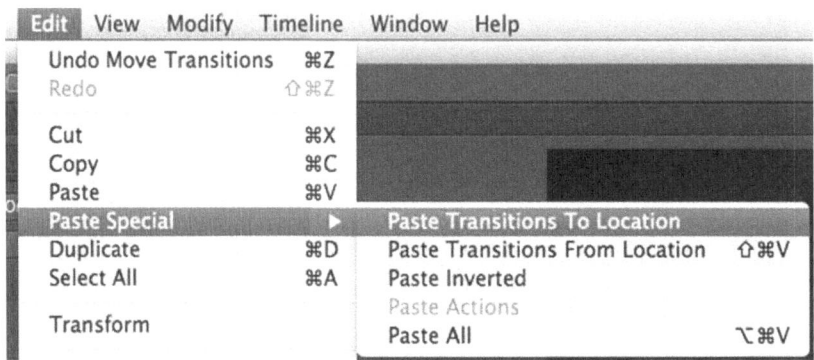

**Figure 8-11.** Sometimes one transition does indeed fit them all.

13. Having all of the letters appear at once is okay, but we can do better. Stagger the start of the Transition strips, as shown in Figure 8-12, in half-second increments. If you test the movie now, the letters gently fall into place.

**Figure 8-12.** Stagger the transitions to change the timing of each layer.

# Project 2: Attracted to Detail

The key to the successful completion of a motion graphics project is attention to detail.

In this exercise, a magnet will travel across the Edge Animate Stage, and when it stops above a letter on the Stage, the letter gets attracted up to the magnet. The details are in the motion of the letters and what happens to the drop shadow under each letter when the letters get pulled up to the magnet. Let's get started:

## Create the Assets in Illustrator

The plan is rather simple, the word EDGE is sitting on the Stage, and the letters in the word fly up to the heads of a magnet when it passes over the letters. The letters are sitting over a white to dark gray gradient, and there is a small shadow under each letter. It sounds simple, but this one can get a little tricky. Here is how we constructed the assets. You can either open the Shadow.ai document in your Exercise folder or create your own:

1. Create a new Illustrator document that is 720 pixels wide by 480 pixels high. We named it Shadow.

2. Create a rectangle that matches the Stage dimensions of the Edge Animate project and fill the rectangle with a Linear gradient (Figure 8-13) that uses black, white, and a dark gray to achieve the effect of depth that we were looking for. The dark to light gray gradient at the bottom gives us a sort of stage to work with.

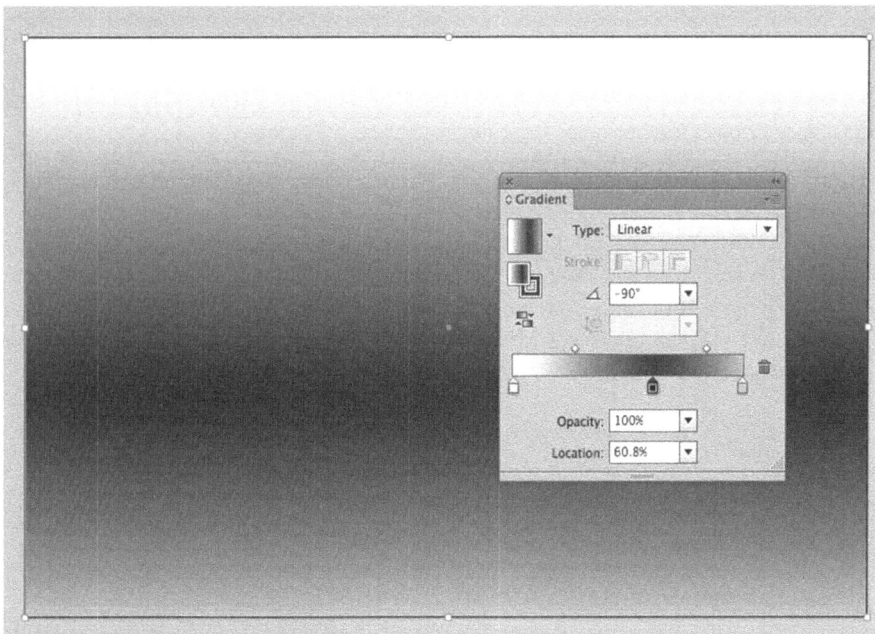

**Figure 8-13.** The settings for the background gradient.

3.  The next step is to add the text. We chose to use the Blackoak Std font for our lettering. If you don't have this font, feel free to use one of your own. What appealed to us about this choice was that it is a rather striking woodcut that looks stretched. It is great for display purposes and fits the specifications rather nicely.

4.  We added the letters E, G, and D, setting them in a 72 point size, as shown in Figure 8-14. Why only three letters? Edge Animate allows us to reuse graphics in the Assets panel, making the second E redundant.

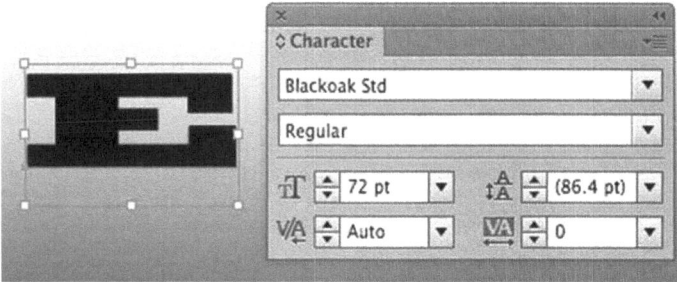

**Figure 8-14.** The letters are formatted.

5.  The magnet was based on a photograph of a horseshoe magnet. We drew a stylized version of the magnet in a separate Illustrator document and imported it into our project document where it was resized to fit the document.

6.  The shadow was created by drawing a small oval under a letter, filling it with black, and then applying a 10-pixel feather selecting Effect > Stylize > Feather.

7.  The text would present an issue if it is going to be used in Edge Animate. It is a nonstandard font and will not appear in the Font pop-down in the Edge Animate Properties panel. This means there is a very real risk that the font used in Illustrator will be substituted with something else in Edge Animate. The solution is to select each letter and select Text > Create Outlines. This converts each letter to a vector shape. To add a bit of contrast between the letter and the background gradient, we added a 2-pixel white stroke to each letter. The project assets, shown in Figure 8-15, were almost ready to send to Edge Animate.

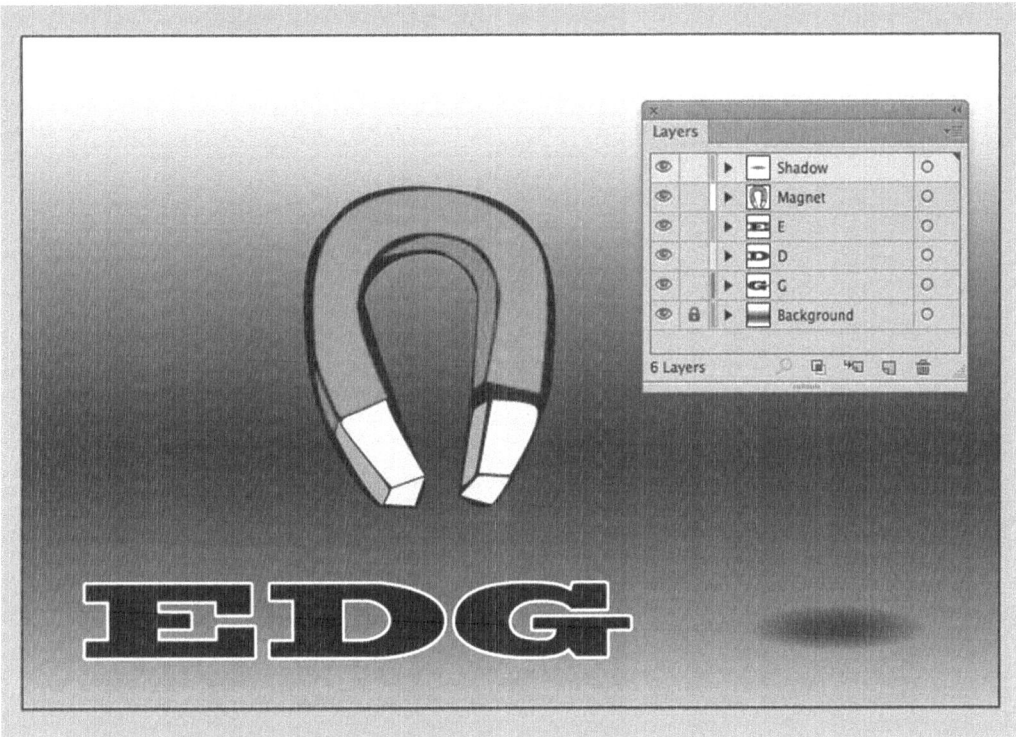

**Figure 8-15.** The assets are assembled in Illustrator.

8. This project can't simply be sent to Edge Animate and put into motion. As you discovered in Chapter 4, Edge Animate can't read an AI file. This means the vector images—the Magnet, E, D, and G—need to be converted to SVG images. Also, the background, being a rather simple gray scale gradient, was exported out of Illustrator as a JPG image.

9. The shadow was a little trickier. The SVG format has a bit of difficulty rendering feathered shapes containing opacity. Instead, the shadow was exported out of Illustrator as a PNG image and, when the dialog box shown in Figure 8-16 appeared, we selected Transparent from the Background Color options.

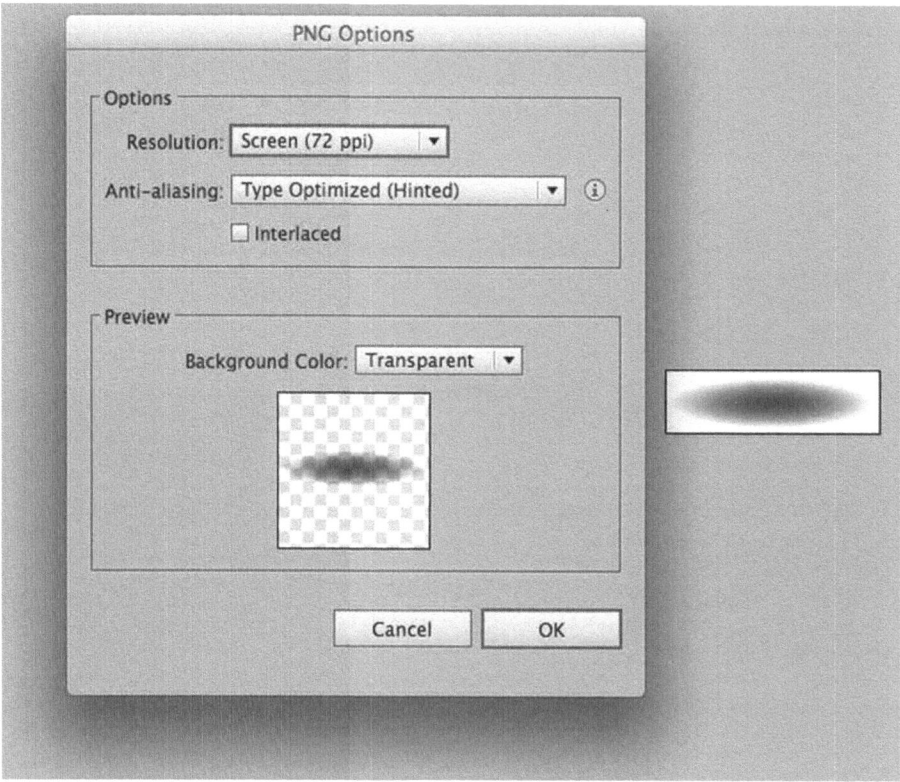

**Figure 8-16.** Exporting a PNG with transparency out of Illustrator.

## Assembling the Project in Edge Animate

Rather than create a long, repetitious assembly exercise, we'll walk you through the steps to have the magnet pick up the first letter. It will be the same process for the remaining letters. Let's get started:

1. Open a new Edge Animate document and set the Stage size to 720 by 480 pixels. This matches the size of the background gradient image.

2. Import the images located from the Exported_Illustrator folder in the Exercise folder into the Edge Animate document.

3. Select the D and G elements on the Stage and delete them. This will remove them from the Stage, not the library.

4. Drag the magnet to a point just off of the left edge of the Stage and position the remaining letters and shadows as shown in Figure 8-17. The E used for the balance of this exercise assumes the letter is placed at 51, 347. You are ready to animate.

Add extra instances of the Shadow.png and the E.svg images in the Library panel to create the letters and shadows.

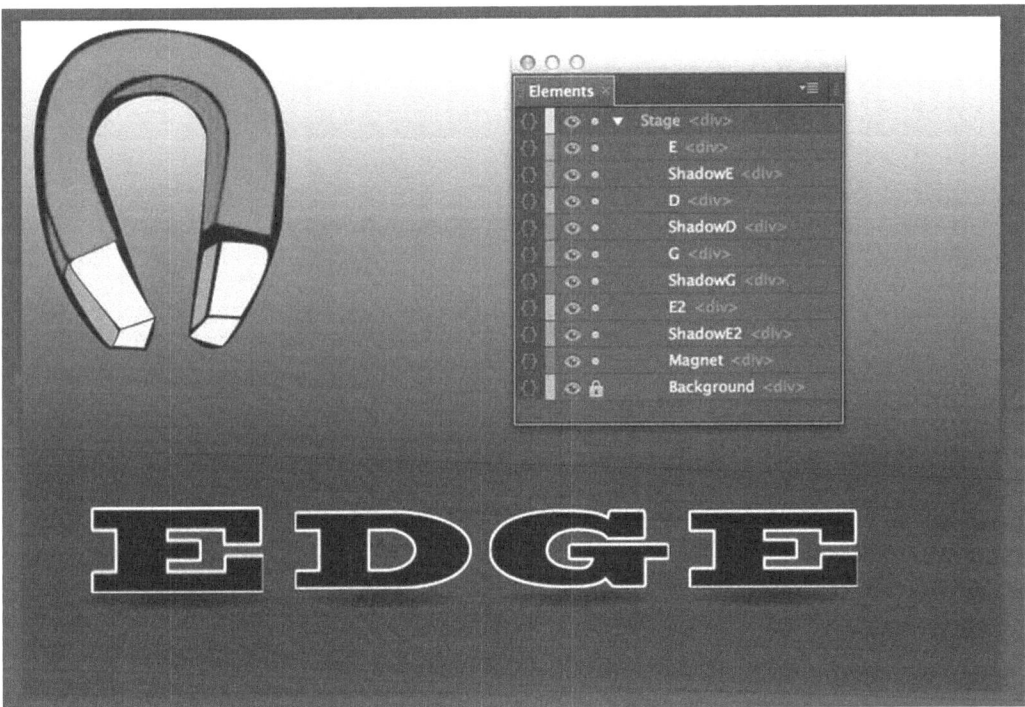

**Figure 8-17.** The assets are in Edge Animate and ready to be put in motion.

5. To ensure the shadows are below the letters, move the Shadow elements in the Elements panel below their letters. Also, move the Magnet element to the layer directly above the Background element. Lock the Background element.

The plan is to have the magnet move across the Stage and stop above a letter. The letter will then rise to the tips of the magnet and, as the letter moves upward, the shadow shrinks. One way of accomplishing that task is to add a Location keyframe to the magnet and move it along the left axis. This results in an extra, unused transition—Top—on the timeline. Here's a way of reducing this clutter:

6. Right-click the Magnet element in the Timeline. This will open the context menu shown in Figure 8-18. When the menu opens, select Left and a keyframe will be added to the timeline.

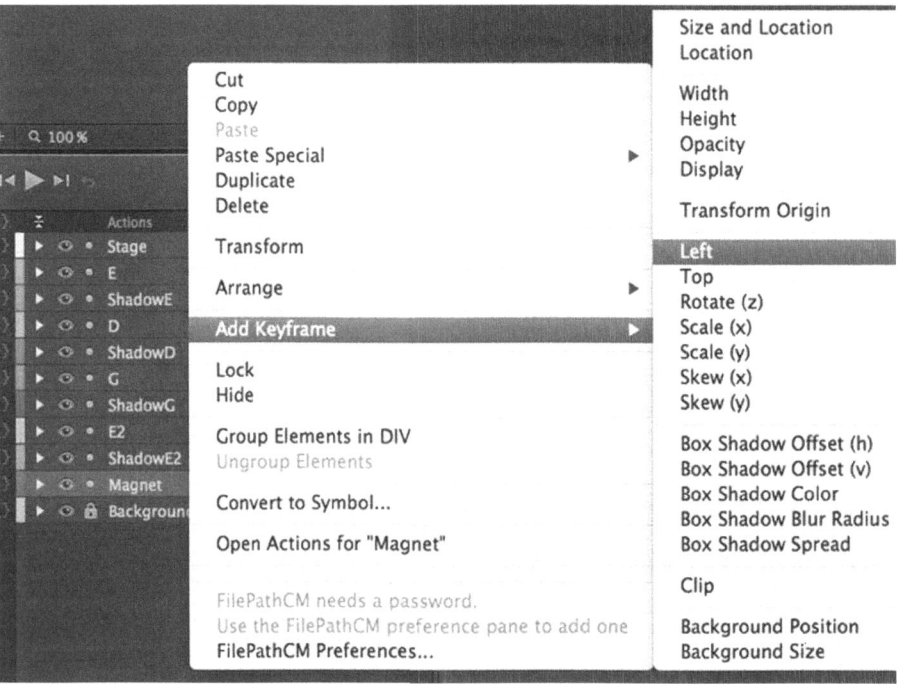

**Figure 8-18.** Use the Add Keyframe menu to add single transitions to the timeline.

7. Move the playhead to the 3/4-second mark of the timeline and scrub the magnet's Left value on the timeline to move it to a position above the letter E.

8. With the playhead still at the 3/4-second mark, select the letter E on the Stage and add a Rotate keyframe.

9. Move the playhead to 1-second and change the Rotate value to –8.

10. Move the playhead to the 0:01.250 mark of the timeline and add Scale(x), Scale(y), Skew(x), and Skew(y) keyframes. These properties are about to change.

11. Still at 0:01.25, change the Rotate value to 8.

12. Move the playhead to the 0:01.700 mark of the timeline and change the following values:

   • Scale(x): 72

   • Scale(y): 98

   • Rotate: 3

   • Skew(x): -52

   • Skew(y): -6

13. Move the playhead to 0:01.750 and change the Left value to 204. If you scrub the timeline, the letter will rock and, as shown in Figure 8-19, tumble up to the magnet. To "smooth out" the motion, apply an EaseOutSine ease to the transition. One finishing touch is required: the shadow.

**Figure 8-19.** The letter is "attracted" to the magnet.

The difference between an okay motion graphics project and a great one is attention to detail. One detail that is commonly overlooked is the shadow beneath each letter. As the letter rises and skews, the shadow should get fainter and also change shape. It also makes sense to turn its Element Display property off when the shadow disappears. Let's get that done:

1. Select the shadow on the Stage, move the playhead to the start of the timeline, and, in the Timeline, set the Display value to On.

2. Move the playhead to the 0:00.750 mark of the timeline and add a Scale and Display keyframes to the Shadow layer on the timeline.

3. Move the playhead to the 1 second mark of the timeline and change the Scale(x) value to 110%. The shadow gets wider when the letter rocks.

4. Move the playhead to 0:01.250 and make the following changes:

    • Scale(x): 132

    • Scale(y): 130

5. Move the playhead to 0:01.500 and make the following changes:

    • Scale(x): 108%

    • Scale(y): 212%

6. Move the playhead to the 00:01.700 point and add an Opacity keyframe.

7. Move the playhead to 00:01.750 and set the Opacity to 0 and the Display value to Off.

8. Add Left keyframes to the E and Magnet layers. Move the magnet on the X axis to a position just over the letter D. Move the E along with the magnet.

9. Scrub the timeline. As the playhead moves across the shadow, it reacts to the motion of the letter E (Figure 8-20). To see the full effect, test the animation in a browser.

10. All you have to do now is complete the animation by essentially repeating the Letter and Shadow steps for the remaining elements on the Stage.

> Don't forget, to hide the magnet when it moves off the Stage and in the Properties panel set the stage's Overflow property to Hidden.

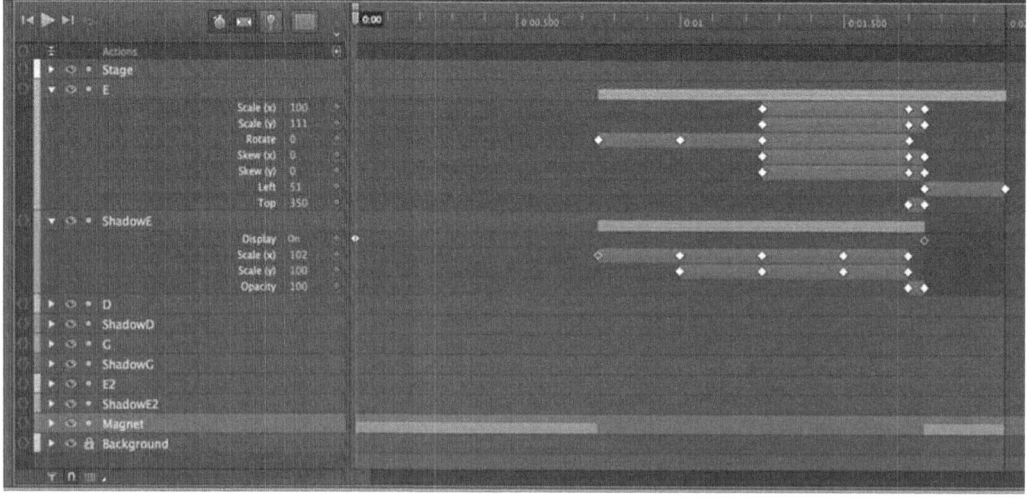

**Figure 8-20.** The timeline looks complex but it really isn't.

# Project 3: Create a Starfield

If there is one thing we enjoy most, it is sitting at the side of a lake at dusk and watching the stars appear in the night sky. We are going to reproduce this effect and along the way discover a great use for the playback feature for symbols in the timeline.

The first thing you need is a star. This graphic can be created in Illustrator, Photoshop, or Fireworks by simply drawing a small shape—10 pixels maximum—and then applying a blur of some sort to the star. Save the image out as a PNG or SVG image with opacity and import it into Edge Animate. Now that we have a star, let's head for the lake:

1. Open the Starfield.an file located in your Exercise folder. When it opens, you will see, as shown in Figure 8-21, a calm lake at dusk. We have also included a star graphic, but feel free to delete it and add your own.

**Figure 8-21.** We start with a lake at dusk.

2. Drag the star image from the Library to the Stage and convert it to a Symbol named Star.

3. Double-click the Star symbol on the Stage to edit it in place.

4. When the Symbol timeline opens, add Opacity and Rotation keyframes at the 0 point. Reduce the Opacity to 10% or a value you choose.

5. Drag the playhead to the 00:00.750 point of the timeline and change the Opacity to 100%.

6. Drag the playhead to 00:01.500 and reduce the Opacity back to 10% and set the Rotation value to 360.

7. This animation has to loop or we won't have twinkling stars. Move the playhead back to the 0 point and add a label named Start.

8. Drag the playhead to 00:01.500 and add a Play trigger that goes to the Start label. The code should be sym.play("Start");.

9. If your Star symbol timeline resembles Figure 8-22, return to the main timeline.

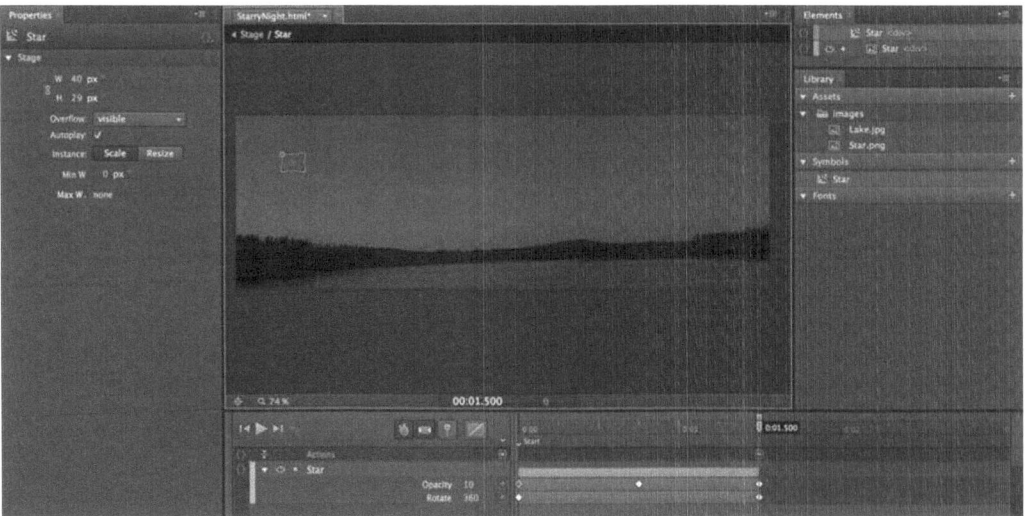

**Figure 8-22.** The Star symbol is ready to be turned into a starfield.

## Creating the Starfield

Obviously there should be more than one star in the sky, and they should twinkle randomly. Here's how to accomplish this task:

1. Select your symbol on the Stage and, if it is still a bit large, making sure Autokeyframes is turned off, scale it down using the Properties panel.

2. With your star selected, create six or seven copies of the star symbol. Do this by copying, pasting, and dragging the copy to a random position in the sky. If you scrub the timeline, you will have a bunch of stars that twinkle in unison. Let's fix that.

3. Select the first star in your timeline and click the Add Playback Command button in the timeline. The Playback command pop-down menu, shown in Figure 8-23, appears. Select the Play From … command.

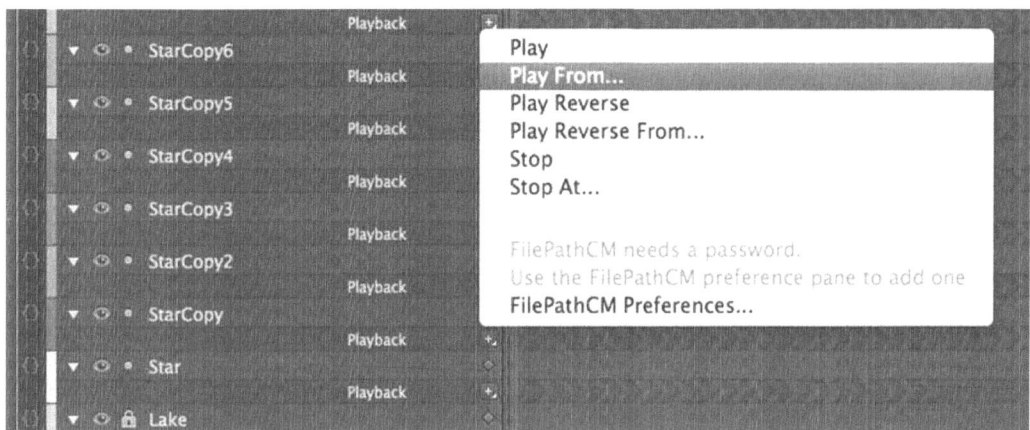

**Figure 8-23.** The Playback commands.

When you select the Play From ... command, the dialog box shown in Figure 8-24 appears. Scrubbing across the numbers changes the start position of the playhead in the symbol, not on the main timeline. The pop-down under the numbers—Start—sets the marker in the symbol where you may wish to start playback. In this case, we need to change the time because there is only one marker. Just keep in mind the duration of this symbol is 00:01.500, so a value greater than that defeats the purpose.

**Figure 8-24.** Use the Playback commands to move the playback point inside a symbol.

4. Select each star on the Stage and randomly change the playback point. Also move the Playback icon on the timeline for each instance of the symbol, as shown in Figure 8-25, to add a bit more randomness.

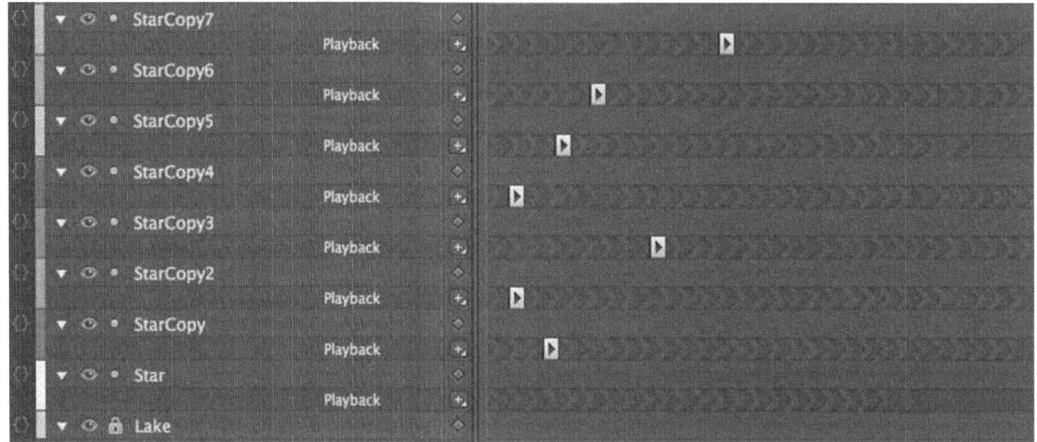

**Figure 8-25.** Add even more randomness by moving the Playback to different points on the timeline.

5. There are a lot of layers on the timeline. Let's make it a bit more manageable. Select all of the stars on the Stage and convert them to a single symbol named Starfield.

**Look, Up in the Sky . . .**

It's not exactly Superman, but there is a way to create a rather interesting shooting star effect and actually make it follow a curved path across the sky. Here's how:

1. Drag the Star.png image or your star from the Library to a point just off the upper left corner of the Stage.

2. With the star selected, add Translate(x), Translate(y), Scale(x), Scale(y), and Opacity keyframes to the timeline.

3. Change the Scale(x) and Scale(y) values to change the size of the star. Smaller values will make it look like it is higher in the sky.

4. Move the playhead to 00:00.750 and move the star to a point just above the trees at the back of the lake and reduce the Opacity to about 60%. If you scrub the timeline, the star moves across the sky and gets fainter as it moves farther from the viewer.

We have a small problem. The problem here is the motion of the star, which reinforces something we have constantly reinforced throughout this book: *Watch the world around you*. When a star moves toward the horizon, it moves in an arc. Let's fix that now:

5. Move the playhead to 00:00.300 and add a Top keyframe.

6. Drag the playhead to the 00:00.600, add a Left keyframe, and move the star downward about 1 or 2 pixels.

7. Drag the playhead to the end of the animation and move the star a couple of pixels downward using the Top value, as shown in Figure 8-26.

**Figure 8-26.** Arcs are created using subtle changes on the Top axis.

8. The final step is to set the star's Display property to Off. If you test the movie in the browser, you now have a more "realistic" shooting star.

# Project 4: Create a Flash Preloader

Somewhere along the line, Flash suddenly lost its luster as an animation application. Although Adobe has pulled Flash Player development out of the mobile space, there seems to be this preconception that Flash is somehow dead. Not quite. In fact it has a number of important uses when it comes to Edge Animate. In this example, we are going to look at one that is generally not known but has been a feature of Flash since its inception: the ability to output a Flash animation as an animated GIF.

What's the big deal with that, you may ask? The big deal is that Edge Animate only uses the animated GIF format for its preloaders. This means you can create timeline-based Flash animations and use them as preloaders for your Edge Animate projects. Let's see how all of this works:

1. Open Flash Professional CS6, or any other version of Flash for that matter, and create a new ActionScript 3.0 document.

2. Select Modify > Document and, when the Document Settings dialog box opens, change the Stage size to 88 pixels wide and 88 pixels high. Change the Stage color to a dark gray—Figure 8-27—and change the Frame rate to 30 fps. Click OK. We chose the height and width values to match those of the preloaders included with Edge Animate.

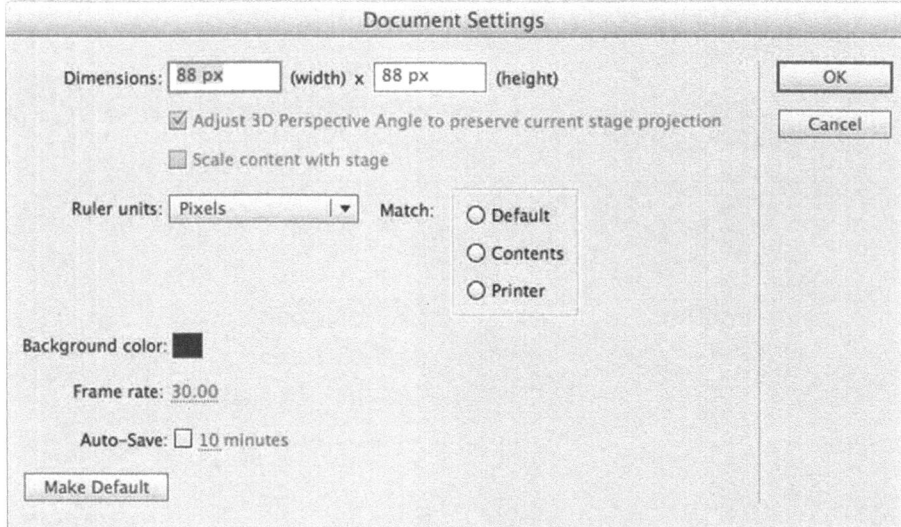

**Figure 8-27.** Set up the Flash stage to match the dimensions of an Animate preloader animation.

3. When the document opens, set the Stroke Color to White and the Fill Color to Black in the Tools panel.

4. Select the Oval tool and draw a circle on the Stage. We created one that is 70 by 70 pixels.

5. Select the stroke and fill of the object and, using the Align panel, align the circle to the center of the Stage. Deselect.

6. Select the Stroke and, in the Properties panel, as shown in Figure 8-28, set the Stroke width to 10.00 pixels.

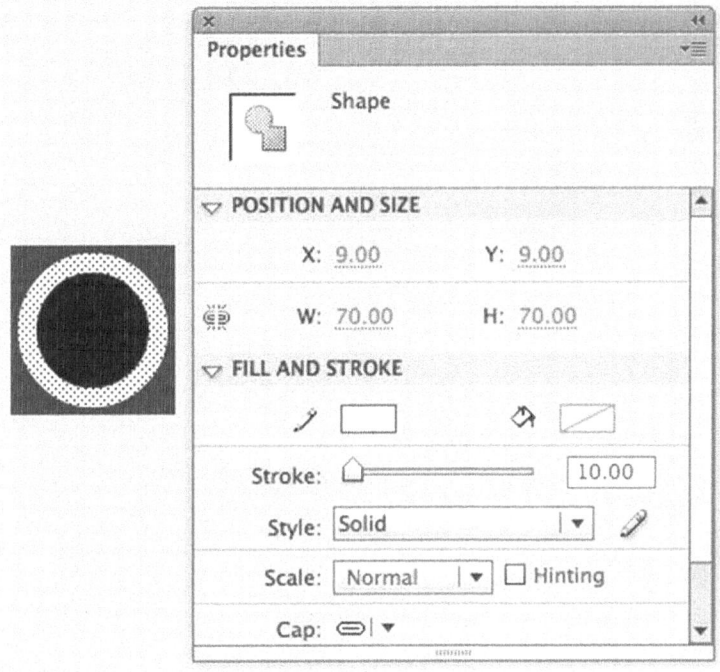

**Figure 8-28.** The circle is prepared.

7. Select Frame 30 of the timeline and add a keyframe.

8. Select the circle and change the fill color to #990000 (Burgundy) and the Stroke color to #666666 (Dark gray).

9. Right-click between the two keyframes on the timeline and select `Create Shape Tween`. The tween area turns green, indicating a Shape Tween, and an arrow between the two keyframes will appear. If you scrub the timeline, you will see the stoke and fill colors change.

10. Save the file and select `File > Export Movie` to open the `Export Movie` dialog box.

11. Click the `Format` pop-down and, as shown in Figure 8-29, select `Animated GIF`.

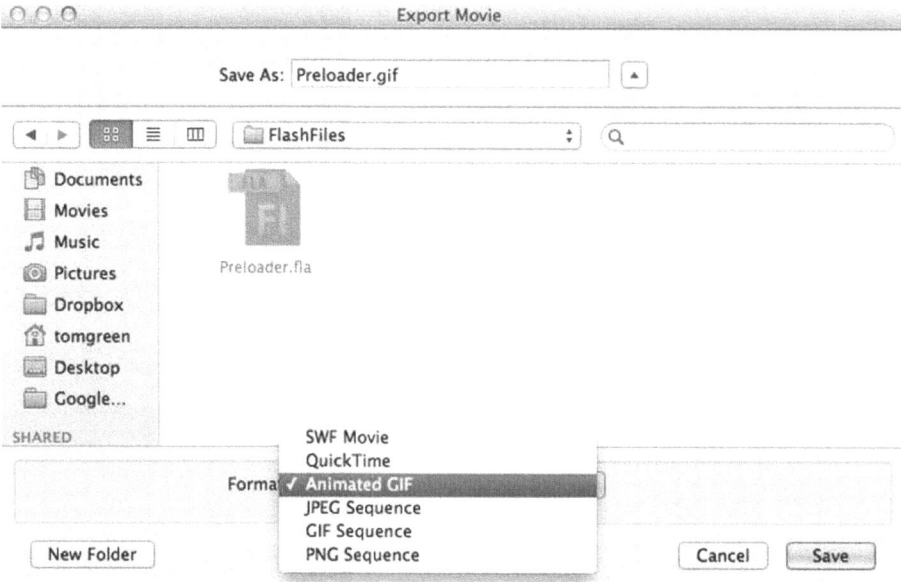

**Figure 8-29.** Exporting a Flash document as an animated GIF file.

**12.** Click Save to save the file and open the Export GIF dialog box, shown in Figure 8-30. These choices primarily handle the resolution, color handling, and other options. Click OK to accept these settings and, when you are returned to the main Flash timeline, quit Flash.

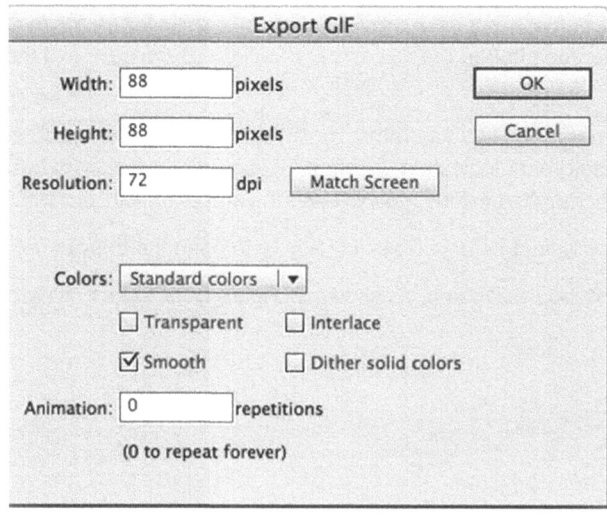

**Figure 8-30.** The Export GIF dialog box in Flash.

> *Although we are showing you an extremely simple example of using Flash with Edge Animate, practically any animation you can create on the Flash timeline, including some of the animations in the Flash templates, can either be converted to an Animated GIF file and used as a preloader in Edge Animate or exported as a Sprite Sheet (Chapter 4) and used as an animated sequence in Edge Animate. As you may have suspected, the rumors around the impending death of Flash have been greatly exaggerated.*

With our preloader created, let's take it for a spin in Edge Animate:

1.  Open a new Edge Animate document.

2.  Click the `Edit` button in the `Preloader` area of the Properties panel. This will open the `Preloader` stage.

3.  Select `File > Import` and navigate to your Flash preloader. If you don't have Flash, we have included the preloader in the `Exercise` folder.

4.  When the file is imported, the animation plays and, as shown in Figure 8-31, a copy of the preloader is added to the Edge Animate Library.

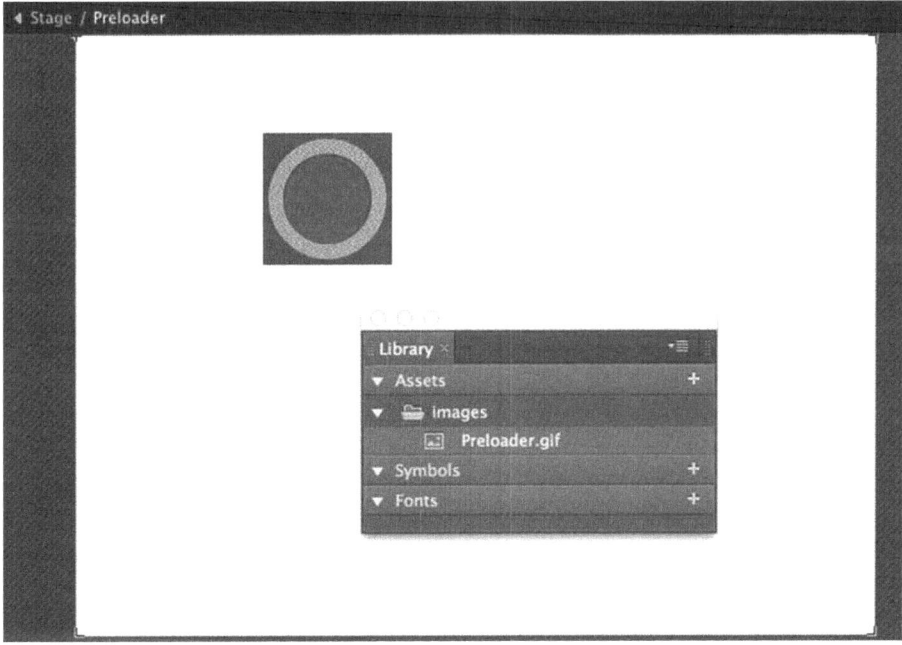

**Figure 8-31.** The Flash GIF animation is added to Edge Animate as a preloader.

# Project 5: Creating a Pop-Down Menu in Edge Animate

One of the most common techniques in the HTML universe is the creation of pop-down menus. In Edge Animate, the creation of a pop-down menu gives you the ability to add some interactivity to the pop-down menu. Still, the technique, when you first undertake the task, may seem to be a bit overly complicated. In actual fact, it isn't. The complication has its root in the technique being a "different way of doing it."

In this exercise, the designers and developers of a site dedicated to graffiti wall art have decided one of the features on the page will be the appearance of a pop-down navigation menu. When the user rolls over a certain area of the page, the menu appears. The menu is to contain four strips:

- A strip that will navigate to a page that explains the scope of the wall art project

- A strip introducing the team members involved in the project

- A strip that will navigate to a page encouraging viewers to submit their photos

- A strip that will lead to a Contact page

That sounds like a tall order for Edge Animate. Not really. Let's get started:

1.  Open the WallArt.an located in your Exercise folder. When it opens, you will see, as shown in Figure 8-32, the project's home page. The plan is simple, when the user rolls over the Who We Are text, the menu appears. It also disappears when the user rolls off the text.

**Figure 8-32.** We start with the design of the Wall Art Project's home page.

One of the maxims of web design is simple: Let the software do the work. Keeping that maxim in mind, it becomes rather apparent that you only need to create a "dummy" menu strip and then wire up the project to build the menu using code. The code will be used to:

- Show the menu on rollover

- Hide it when the mouse rolls out of the menu

- Add the appropriate text to each strip

- Change the text's color when the mouse is over a menu strip item

What it comes down to is a rather uncomplicated task: create a menu strip and let the code features of Edge Animate handle the rest. Let's build the strip:

2.  Select the Rectangle tool and draw a rectangle that is 165 pixels wide, 22 pixels high, filled with white, with a black solid stroke that is 1-pixel wide.

3.  With the shape selected, convert it to a symbol named MenuStrip.

4.  Open your symbol, select the Text tool, and enter xx. Set the text as Verdana with a size of 14 pixels. Name this element txt. As shown in Figure 8-33, we have a menu strip.

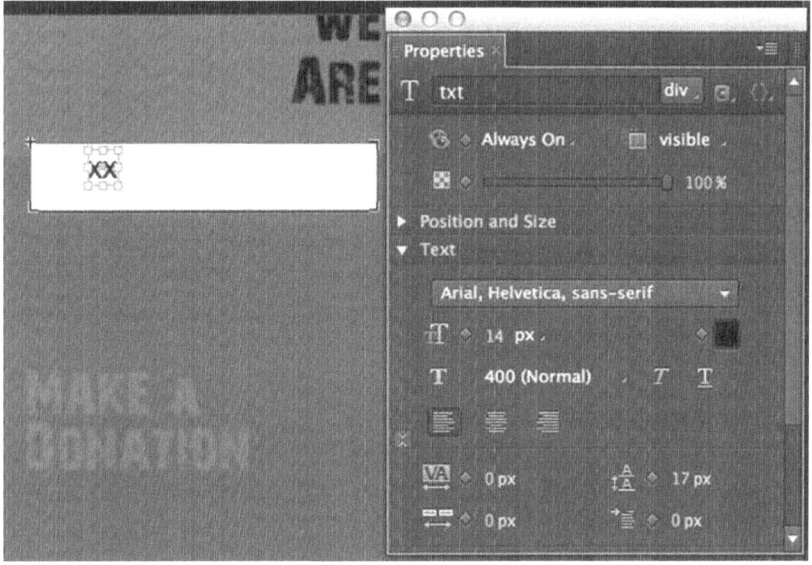

**Figure 8-33.** The menu strip is nothing more than a small rectangle with some dummy text.

The next step is to create the text color change and prepare the strip for interactivity.

5. With Autokeyframes turned on, add a Text Color keyframe and move the playhead to the 00:00.333 mark of the timeline.

6. Select the text and change the text color to blue (#1720E7).

7. Add a Frame Label named Off.

8. Move the playhead to the 0 point of the symbol's timeline and add a Frame Label named Over.

9. With the playhead still at the 0 point of the timeline, add a Stop action trigger.

10. The final step is to create another rectangle that is 167 pixels wide by 24 pixels high. Set both the Fill and the Stroke to None, and make sure the box is at 0,0 and covers the menu box. Name this Element HotSpot.

11. With the HotSpot element selected, click the Open Actions button and add a mouseover action. When the Script panel opens, click the Play button and enter "Over" between the brackets. Your script should be:

    ```
    sym.play("Over");
    ```

12. Click the + sign and add a mouseleave action. Again, click the Play button and enter "Off" as the parameter. Close the Script pane, and the MenuStrip's timeline should resemble that shown in Figure 8-34.

**Figure 8-34.** The MenuStrip symbol's timeline.

Let's take a second to clearly understand what you just did. When the symbol appears on the main timeline, the text will be black due to the stop action in the Trigger. The HotSpot element is important because it identifies the boundaries of the symbol for the mouse. By making the HotSpot slightly larger than the box, there is a bit of extra "mouse room." When the mouse is over the HotSpot, the playhead scoots over to the Off marker and the text turns blue. When the mouse rolls off of the element, the playhead is shot back to the Over marker.

> The use of the word HotSpot is deliberate. If you are a Flash user, you identify this area as the "Hit" area in a button symbol. Unfortunately, Edge Animate doesn't have a formal Button symbol, so you have to create your own Hit area.

**Create the Pop-Down Menu**

Next up: creating the menu. Here's how:

1. Return to the main timeline and drag an instance of the MenuStrip symbol to the Stage. Convert it to a symbol named Menu. This new symbol is now nested in the MenuStrip symbol. Double-click this new symbol to edit it in place.

2. Add three more instances of the MenuStrip symbol and align them to the left.

3. Starting from the top of the timeline, as shown in Figure 8-35, name each of the four elements:

   • Contact_btn

   • Send_btn

   • Scope_btn

   • Team_btn

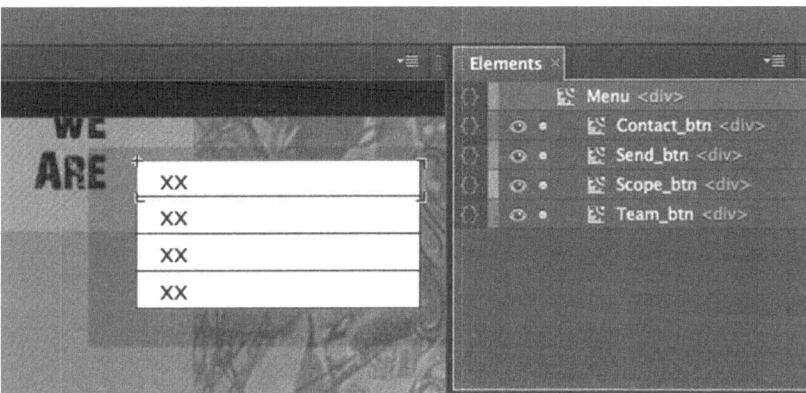

**Figure 8-35.** The pop-down menu is created and the elements named.

4. Return to the main timeline and move the symbol into position close to the Who We Are text. We used an x value of 655 and a y value of 142 for the Menu symbol.

5. To have this menu function properly, it, too, needs to be enclosed within an invisible box. Select the Rectangle tool, set the stroke, and fill to None and draw a rectangle that will define where the mouse has to be for the menu to appear. Name this element Container and name the element containing the Menu symbol Buttons.

> *You might want to consider adding a stroke to this box as you determine the best placement for the HotSpot. Once you are satisfied, you can set the stroke back to None.*

**6.** In the Elements panel, nest the Buttons element in the Container element.

### Wiring Up the Menu

The design aspect of the project is complete. It is time to let the software do the work by writing the code. Let's start:

**1.** Click once on the Open Actions button for the Stage element and select compositionReady from the menu.

**2.** When the script panel opens, enter the following code:

```
sym.$("Buttons").hide();

sym.getSymbol("Buttons").getSymbol("Team_btn").$("txt").html("The Project Team");
sym.getSymbol("Buttons").getSymbol("Scope_btn").$("txt").html("The Project Scope");
sym.getSymbol("Buttons").getSymbol("Send_btn").$("txt").html("Send us art");
sym.getSymbol("Buttons").getSymbol("Contact_btn").$("txt").html("Contact Us");
```

Understanding this code is fairly easy. It is executed when the project has loaded into the browser—compositionReady.

The first thing to happen is the Buttons symbol, nested inside the Container element, is hidden. At the same time, Edge Animate initializes the menu items by going into the Buttons element on the main timeline. As you may recall, this element contains the symbol named Menu. The reason you don't use the symbol name is because you gave it the name Buttons on the main timeline.

Once the symbol is located, Edge examines the layers of the symbol looking for the element—Team_btn—named in the code. Each one of those is an instance of the MenuStrip symbol, and Edge starts looking for the txt element in that symbol.

Once that element is located, Edge changes the "xx" to the text indicated.

What you can gather from this is the use of getSymbol() is a great way of working with the timelines of symbols on the main timeline or even symbols nested inside each other. This exercise is a very handy method of changing the text in a symbol that is reused on the timeline, and it reduces the amount of design work you may otherwise undertake.

**3.** Close the Script panel and click the Open Actions button for the Container element.

**4.** Select mouseenter from the menu and, when the Script panel opens, enter the following code:

```
sym.$("buttons").show();
```

When the mouse enters the boundary of the Container element, the Menu symbol appears.

**5.** Click the + sign in the Script panel and select mouseleave. Enter the following code into the script panel:

```
sym.$("buttons").hide();
```

When the mouse leaves the boundary of the Container element, the Menu symbol disappears.

6. Test the project in a browser. When you roll over the button, the menu, as shown in Figure 8-36, appears.

**Figure 8-36.** The menu works.

# You Have Learned

In this chapter, you created some pretty complex Animate projects that built on the skills you have learned to this point in the book. Among them:

- A deep dive into the emerging Fireworks/Animate workflow

- A rather complex timeline animation technique

- How the creation of one symbol can be the basis of many symbols

- How to use a little-known feature of Flash CS6 to create an Edge Animate preloader

- A code-based rollover menu

We covered a lot of ground here, and we hope you are feeling pretty good about what you have learned so far. You should have also discovered there is a lot you can do once you understand the fundamentals of using Edge Animate.

To this point, we have concentrated on using Edge Animate in a web-based environment. One of the newer aspects of Edge is that it can also be used in digital publishing. In fact, many digital magazines are now using Edge Animate animations in their pages. Intrigued? Turn the page and let's find out.

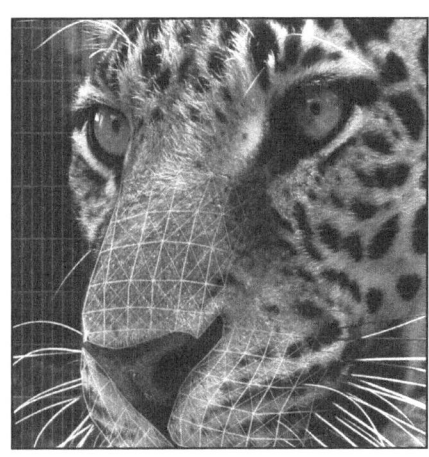

# Chapter 9

# Edge Animate and Digital Publications

Information exchange prior to the 15th century was by word of mouth. That changed when Johannes Gutenberg invented movable type and revolutionized the distribution of information. With a printing press, anyone could share and distribute knowledge, wisdom, religious ideology, or literary works. The control of information was no longer in the hands of the political or religious elite as movable type printing became the first mass broadcast medium. Fast forward to the late 20th century when the personal computer was invented and later embraced in the home and office. Soon, connectivity evolved through Internet technology, later expanding via mobile and Cloud technologies. With all these modern advancements, one thing is absolute—our society is deep within the digital revolution.

One of the current driving forces behind this revolution is digital publishing. Although similar to web publishing, digital publishing differs largely in its workflow. Whereas web publishing involves programming, coding, and graphic design using web-specific tools, digital publishing uses tools and workflows already established in traditional print publishing. So, is it fair to say digital publishing is closer to traditional print publishing? Maybe. But the key differences are important to understand, namely, interactivity, distribution method, and final output. With traditional print publishing, the final output is a tangible item that is produced on printing devices and then distributed through publishing channels such as bookstores and newspaper publishers. It is a copy of the original work. With digital publishing, there is no printing process involved, and the final output is a perfect copy of the original. This digital copy is then distributed using an on-demand model through larger channels, such as the World Wide Web, or smaller channels, such as subscriber networks. With digital publishing, nothing tangible is produced other than the ones and zeros that make up the content displayed on a digital device. Furthermore, users can interact with digital published content in much the same way they interact with web content, which includes clicking buttons, tapping icons that animate or reveal pop-up information, listening to audio, viewing video or animations, or even opening a web page within the digital publication itself. This is why Edge Animate is perfect for creating content for digital publications.

This chapter will show how to integrate our Edge Animate compositions into digital publications. We will be covering the following topics:

- Understanding print vs. screen models and resolution

- Digital publishing formats

- Adding Edge Animate content with iBooks Author

- Adding Edge Animate content with Adobe InDesign

- Using Folio Builder to create a simple folio

If you haven't already downloaded the chapter files, they can be found at http://www.apress.com/9781430243502. In this chapter we will be using these files:

- Yosemite.iba

- Yosemite.indd

- Yosemite.wdgt

- Yosemite.oam

# Understanding Print vs. Screen Models and Resolution

As we explained earlier, digital publishing follows a very similar workflow to traditional print publishing. However, since the output is digital and largely intended for screen presentation, traditional principles of print output and design differ. To better understand this, let's briefly go over the different print and screen color models and compare resolutions.

## CMYK Subtractive Color Model

Traditional printing utilizes color spaces referred to as CMYK, a subtractive color model. This is the process of combining inks, paints, or dyes together to produce a full range of colors in printed output. This color spectrum is based on three main colors: cyan, magenta, yellow (Figure 9-1). Black is added as an undertoning, hence the acronym CMYK. It might seem a bit confusing that this is called the subtractive color model because the colors are added together to create a full spectrum of color output. But the name does not refer to what is printed on a tangible item, such as a piece of paper. Subtractive color refers to how our eyes view the colors based on how the colors are absorbed (subtracted) or reflected on the final output target, such as the printed page.

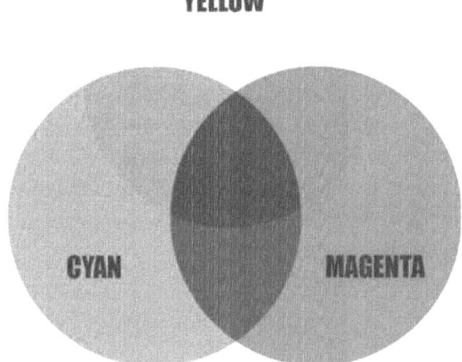

**Figure 9-1.** The subtractive color model.

# RGB Additive Color Model

Digital or screen presentation utilizes the color space of RGB, an additive color model. In this model, light (instead of ink or paint) is added and mixed from different color sources to produce the full spectrum of color. The model is created by combining light that is projected from three main colors—red, green, and blue—hence the acronym RGB. Unlike the subtractive color model, which starts with white, the additive color model starts with black, and color is created by combinations of light projected on black (Figure 9-2). This is the color space that we work with in most web design tools, and it is the color space for Edge Animate. It is a good idea to start in this color space when designing for a digital publication.

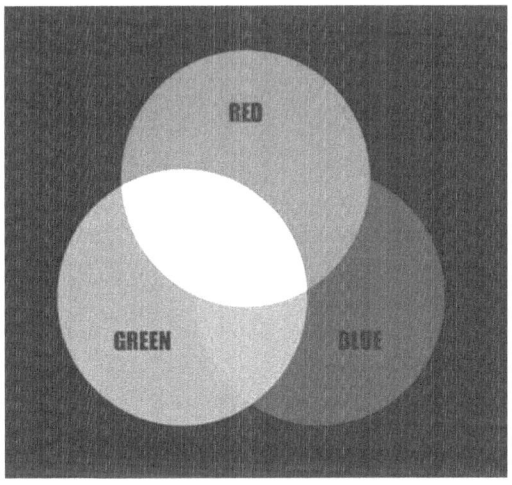

**Figure 9-2.** The additive color model.

# Resolution

The second difference between traditional publishing and digital publishing is resolution. In simple terms, resolution is the number of pixels (dots) it takes to create a raster graphic image. Traditional printing typically uses a much larger pixel density image to reproduce accurate and sharp images on the printed page. This can be a resolution anywhere between 150 and 300 dpi (dots per inch). Digital publishing typically requires a much lower resolution, normally between 72 and 96 dpi. We talked about the image formats that Edge Animate supports in Chapter 4, most of which are raster graphic formats. Some digital publishing programs will resample higher resolution raster files and even convert vector-based files to lower resolution screen formats when they export content to a final delivery format. However, it's a good practice to start in a screen-based resolution when designing for digital publications.

# Digital Publication Formats

Anything that can be printed can be converted to a digital publication: from brochures, to executive summaries, corporate reports, school reports, publications, and books, just to name a few. In fact, you might be reading this book in a digital format. Standard digital publishing formats allow for compatibility between devices and systems to accurately display content on multiple devices. Let's take a look at three of the main publishing formats available.

## The EPUB Format

The electronic publication format, EPUB, is the most common file format used for digital publishing today, largely because it was adopted as a standard in 2007 by the International Digital Publishing Forum and thus has been widely used by publishers to produce electronic publications. The format allows for content to be reflowed and thus easily adapted to different devices and screens. In addition, EPUB supports inline raster and vector images, CSS styling, digital rights management, and metadata. Although EPUB is a common format, it does have its design limitations because the current format lacks the ability to precisely fix content on the page or include specialized formatting.

## The iBooks Format

Apple's iBooks format is a proprietary format based on the EPUB format. Files created using this format are only compatible with the iBooks Reader application. Currently, the only application that supports the export of this format is Apple's iBook Author, which unfortunately, is only available on Mac computers running Lion or greater.

## The Folio Format

Although the EPUB format is widely used and supported, its limitations were understood early on by Adobe, who had pioneered digital publication with their application-independent Portable Document Format (PDF) in early 1990. It is clear that from this understanding, they developed the Folio format, a proprietary format that Adobe InDesign utilizes, along with other tools and online-hosted services that allow for the production of rich interactive digital publications that preserve much of the original design integrity of the publication.

# Edge Animate's Formats for Digital Publishing

As you learned in Chapter 7, you can prepare your Edge Animate content for delivery in other formats, namely, formats compatible with digital publishing applications like Apple iBooks Author or Adobe InDesign. The two main formats that Edge Animate supports are iBooks / OS X Dashboard Widget format—with the .wdgt extension—which is supported by Apple's iBooks Author, and the Animate Deployment Package—with the .oam extension—which is supported by Adobe's InDesign. To create these formats, you first need to define your publishing output options (as we learned in Chapter 7), and then Edge Animate gathers all of your project files (such as your HTML, CSS, and JavaScript files) along with any of your assets and packages them, when you select publish, into a single WDGT or OAM file. These separate published formats can be imported into their targeted digital publishing application. Because the .wdgt and .oam extensions are the two main digital publishing formats Animate supports, we will concentrate our attention on how to incorporate our Edge Animate content in publications created with iBooks Author and InDesign.

## Adding Animate Content with iBooks Author

Apple's iBooks Author is a free program that allows you to create iBooks publications. Getting Edge Animate content into an iBooks Author document is literally drag-and-drop simple because iBooks Author does the under-the-hood work for us. The first step to get content out of Edge Animate is to publish it to Apple's iBooks / OS X Dashboard Widget format. If you remember our Chapter 7 exercise, anything we create in Edge Animate can be exported to the WDGT format except for GIF files. Let's take a look at the steps:

> If you have an Apple desktop or laptop computer running Mac OS Lion and above, you can download the free iBooks Author application from the App Store and follow along with the next section. Unfortunately, there is no Microsoft Windows version available.

1. Launch Apple iBooks Author.

2. In the File menu, locate your **Exercise** folder and open the **iBooks Author** folder, then open the Yosemite.iba document (Figure 9-3).

**Figure 9-3.** Opening our iBooks Author document.

3.  In the **View** menu, make sure **Page Thumbnails** is selected.

4.  Select page 3. This is where we will be dragging and dropping our Edge Animate widget.

5.  If you want to preview the Edge Animate content first in your web browser, click to open the Yosemite.html file inside the **Yosemite** folder, which is inside your **Exercise** folder. We are going to import an Edge Animate composition we have prebuilt, which is located in the **publish** folder inside the **Yosemite** folder.

6.  Switch to the **Finder** and locate the **publish** folder in your **Exercise** folder. Inside the **publish** folder you'll see a file named Yosemite.wdgt.

7.  Drag and drop the Yosemite.wdgt file on page 3 of your iBooks Author document (Figure 9-4).

**Figure 9-4.** Dragging and dropping our WDGT file into iBooks Author.

8.  Once we have released the mouse, iBooks Author automatically creates an Interactive element on the page and embeds our WDGT file. We can reposition the WDGT file if we so choose or update the default title text as well, and that's how easy it is to place an Animate composition into iBooks Author (Figure 9-5).

Lorem ipsum dolor sit amet, consectetuer adipiscing elit, sed diam nonummy nibh euismod tincidunt ut laoreet dolore magna aliquam erat volutpat. Ut wisi enim ad minim veniam, quis nostrud exerci tation ullamcorper suscipit lobortis nisl ut aliquip ex ea commodo consequat. Duis autem vel eum iriure dolor in hendrerit in vulputate velit esse molestie consequat, vel illum dolore eu feugiat nulla facilisis at vero eros et accumsan et iusto odio dignissim qui blandit praesent luptatum zzril delenit augue duis dolore te feugait nulla facilisi. Lorem ipsum dolor sit amet, consectetuer adipiscing elit, sed diam nonummy nibh euismod tincidunt ut laoreet dolore magna aliquam erat volutpat. Ut wisi enim ad minim veniam, quis nostrud exerci tation ullamcorper suscipit lobortis nisl ut aliquip ex ea commodo consequat.

Duis autem vel eum iriure dolor in hendrerit in vulputate velit esse molestie consequat, vel illum dolore eu feugiat nulla facilisis at vero eros et accumsan et iusto odio dignissim qui blandit praesent luptatum zzril delenit augue duis dolore te feugait nulla facilisi. Nam liber tempor cum soluta n eleifend option congue nihil imperdiet doming id quod mazim placerat facer possim assum. Lorem ipsum dolor sit amet, consectetuer adipiscing elit, sed diam nonummy nibh euismod tincidunt ut laoreet dolore magna aliquam erat volutpat. Ut wisi enim ad minim veniam, quis nostrud exerci tation ullamcorper suscipit lobortis nisl ut aliquip ex ea commodo consequat. Duis autem vel eum iriure dolor in hendre-

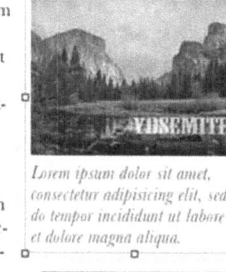

*Interactive 1.1 Lorem Ipsum dolor amet, consectetur*

*Lorem ipsum dolor sit amet, consectetur adipisicing elit, sed do tempor incididunt ut labore et dolore magna aliqua.*

Edit HTML

rit in vulputate velit esse molestie consequat, vel illum dolore eu feugiat nulla facilisis at vero eros et accumsan et iusto odio dignissim qui blandit praesent luptatum zzril delenit augue duis dolore te feugait nulla facilisi. Lorem ipsum dolor sit amet, consectetuer adipiscing elit, sed diam nonummy nibh euismod tincidunt ut laoreet dolore magna aliquam erat volutpat. Lorem ipsum dolor sit amet, consectetuer adipiscing elit, sed diam nonummy nibh euismod tincidunt ut laoreet dolore magna aliquam erat volutpat. Duis autem vel eum iriure dolor in hendrerit in vulputate velit esse molestie consequat, vel illum dolore eu feugiat nulla facilisis at vero eros et accumsan et iusto odio dignissim qui blandit praesent luptatum zzril delenit augue duis dolore te feugait nulla facilisi. Ut wisi enim ad minim veniam, quis nostrud exerci tation ullamcorper suscipit lobortis nisl ut aliquip ex ea commodo consequat wisi enim ad minim veniam, quis nostrud exerci tation ullamcorper suscipit lobortis nisl ut aliquip ex ea commodo consequat. Duis autem vel eum iriure dolrerit in vulputate velit esse molestie consequat, vel illum dolore eu feugiat nulla facilisis at vero eros et accumsan et iusto odio dignissim qui blandit praesent luptatum zzril delenit augue duis dolore te feugait nulla facilisi.

Autem vel eum iriure dolor in hendrerit in vulputate velit esse molestie consequat, vel illum dolore eu feugiat nulla facilisis at vero eros et accumsan et iusto odio dignissim qui blandit praesent luptatum zzril delenit augue duis dolore te feu-

**Figure 9-5.** Repositioning our Animate element in iBooks Author.

# Previewing Our iBooks Author Document

Now that we have added our Edge Animate content to our document, we need to preview and test our publication to make sure it behaves as expected. The only way to do that is by using an iPad. In iBooks Author, the Preview menu function automatically opens our publication in the iBooks app. In order to do that, we need to make sure our iPad is connected to our Apple desktop or laptop computer via the USB cable. Let's test our document:

1. Connect your iPad to your Apple desktop or laptop computer.

2. Open the iBooks reader app on your iPad. If you don't have it installed, you can download it for free from the App Store.

3. Under the File menu in iBooks Author, select Preview.

4. The iBooks app will automatically open our document.

5. Navigate to page 3 and pinch or tap with your fingers on the Edge Animate content to begin testing.

6. Our Edge Animate content opens in a window. Tap on the mountains to activate the interactive elements in our original Edge Animate file (Figure 9-6).

**Figure 9-6.** Our zoomed in Edge Animate content as it looks on our iPad screen.

This exercise demonstrates how you can easily import Edge Animate content into iBooks Author. What you want to take away here is that anything you can create in Adobe Edge Animate—animated bar graphs, interactive pie charts, games, spinning logos, and so forth—can be published to the WDGT format and imported into Apple iBooks Author. Once inside the iBooks document, the WDGT file is a self-contained media element like an image, or QuickTime movie, or an audio file that a user can interact with. The icon that represents the imported Edge Animate WDGT file is a placeholder that will autoflow with other elements inside the iBooks document, such as text and graphics, as the user changes the orientation of the device or enlarges the text display, for example. When the Edge Animate WDGT placeholder is clicked, the Edge Animate content is scaled and autoadjusted to fit the current orientation of the device screen (i.e., portrait or landscape).

# Adding *Edge Animate Content with Adobe InDesign*

As one of Adobe's flagship design applications, InDesign provides several ways to get Edge Animate content into publications. There are two digital publishing formats InDesign creates: EPUB and Folio. As we explained earlier, the EPUB format uses an open standard that allows content to reflow. In our previous exercise, you may have noticed your content flowing differently as you rotated your iPad screen. As you recall, the iBook format is similar to the EPUB format, but it is modified to handle advanced media integration, such as movies and audio. And this is the rub: the more common EPUB 2.1 format utilized by a large majority of EPUB readers does not support advanced media integration (i.e., Adobe Edge Animate content). Although the recently approved EPUB 3.0 format supports HTML 5, CSS3, video, and audio, there are few readers capable of handling the EPUB 3.0 format. Certainly, this will change in the future as more and more publications go digital and the format becomes readily supported.

The limitations of EPUB change when we switch to using the Adobe Folio format, which is an integrated digital publishing format based on Adobe's PDF format. The Folio format supports advanced media integration within the Adobe InDesign environment. That means we can utilize all of InDesign's creative toolset for our publications, and with the OAM publishing workflow built in to Edge Animate, we can place our Edge Animate content within InDesign and publish our final document to the Folio format for viewing on a range of tablet devices from Apple to Android.

---

*If you don't have a copy of InDesign CS6, you can download a trial version from Adobe's Creative Cloud. Adobe recently added the Digital Publishing Suite Single Addition to InDesign. This edition allows you to submit an unlimited number of iPad apps to the Apple App Store as well as publish and test your Folio files locally and manage them online using the Adobe Digital Publishing online resources.*

---

Let's *get started.*

1. Locate the **InDesign Folio** folder inside your **Exercise** folder and open the Yosemite.indd file.

2. Under the **Window** menu, choose **Workspace** > **Digital Publishing**.

3. Click **Pages** under the **Window** menu to see the document overview. Notice we have two design layouts: one for iPad H (horizontal) and one for iPad V (vertical) display (Figure 9-7).

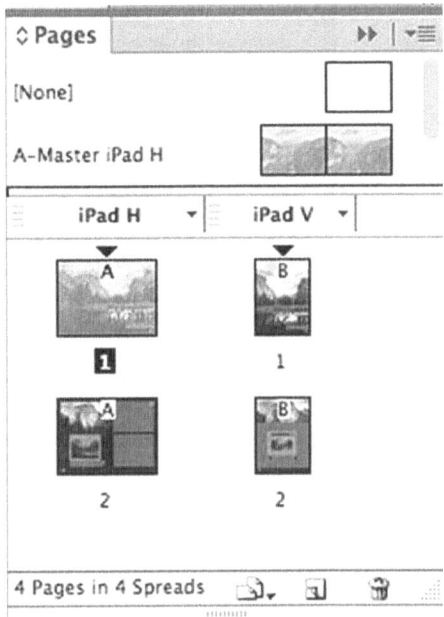

**Figure 9-7.** An overview of our design layouts in Adobe InDesign pages view.

4. Double-click page 2 in the **iPad H** column. This will zoom the display to page 2.

5. We want to create a button below the El Capitan image that, when clicked, opens our Edge Animate content. First, we need to place our button graphic. Click under the **File** menu and choose **Place**.

6. Navigate to the **Links** folder and choose the file named Button_Img.jpg and click Open.

7. The cursor will display a small preview of the image. Click just below the El Capitan image to place the Button_Img.jpg file in the document.

8. With the Button_Img.jpg still selected, click on **Window** > **Styles** > **Object Styles**.

9. Select **Animate Content** (Figure 9-8). You can also apply your own effects here if you so choose.

10. Choose **Edit** > **Copy**.

11. In the **Pages** panel, double-click the page 2 of **iPad V**.

12. Choose **Edit** > **Paste**.

13. Position the Button_Img.jpg file in the open space between the body text.

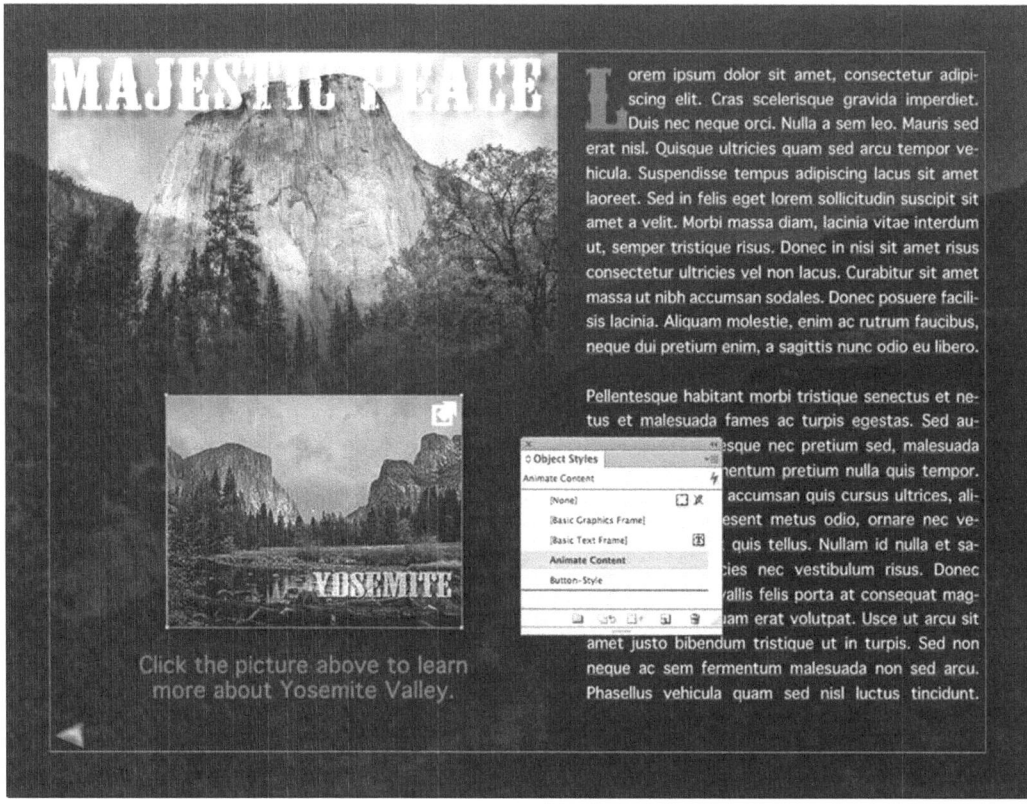

**Figure 9-8.** Our button image placed and styled on page 2 of our iPad H layout.

# Creating Multistate Objects

Now that we have our button images placed in our document, we need to create the states necessary to add interactivity to our folio. If you have worked with programs such as Adobe Flash, Fireworks, or Muse, you may have worked with states before. Essentially, a state is like a moment in time for a particular object. In that moment, whether it is when the mouse rolls over the object or something is clicked, whatever appearance or navigation that is associated with that state is displayed and then acted upon. The plan here is to create a two-state object that when clicked or tapped displays the Edge Animate content in an overlay window above the current page. We also want to add a close button to hide that state after our user has had a chance to interact with our Edge Animate content. To insert a multistate object, follow these steps:

1.  Double-click page 2 on the `iPad H` layout.

2.  Choose **File** > **Place** and drop the `openBtn.png` file on the page.

3.  Position the `openBtn.png` file on the top right corner of the `Button_Img.jpg`.

4. Select openBtn.png and Button_Img.jpg and choose **Object > Group**.

5. Make sure the Show Guides option is enabled under **View** > **Grids & Guides**.

6. In the **Tools** palette, choose the Rectangle tool (or type M on your keyboard).

7. Draw a rectangle to cover the contents on the page within the guidelines.

8. Choose **Window** > **Color** > **Swatches** and select White (paper).

9. Choose **Object** > **Arrange** > **Send Backward**.

10. With the white rectangle still selected, choose **File** > **Place** and click closeBtn.png to place it on the inside of the **rectangle** and on the top left corner.

11. Shift-click the rectangle and the Button_img.jpg and select **Window** > **Interactive** > **Object States**.

12. In the **Object States** panel, click **convert selection to multi-state object** (Figure 9-9).

13. In the **Object Name** field, enter **iPadH_MultiStates**.

14. Repeat steps 2 through 12 for page 2 in the **iPad V** layout, but enter the Object Name **iPadV_MultiStates**.

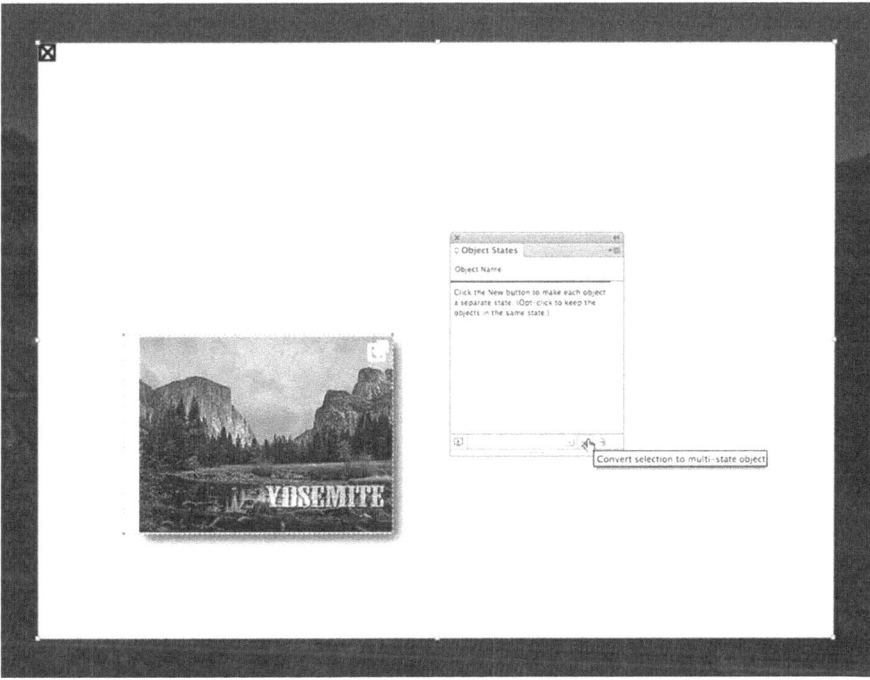

**Figure 9-9.** Converting our selected objects into a multistate object.

# Wiring Up Our Multistate Objects

We need to add interactivity to our multistate objects. We do this by creating an invisible hotspot and then converting that hotspot into a button that switches to a different state upon a mouse click or a finger tap.

First, we wire up the button click that will switch to our State 2 rectangle where we will be placing our Edge Animate content later:

1.  Double-click page 2 of the **iPad H** layout.

2.  Select the Rectangle tool and draw a box over the Button_img.jpg.

3.  Choose **Window** > **Interactive** > **Buttons and Forms**.

4.  Click the **Convert to Button** icon, which is next to the Trash can icon.

5.  Name the button **iPadH_Btn**.

6.  Make sure the **Event** is set to **On Release or Tap**.

7.  Under **Actions**, click the + icon and select **Go to State**.

8.  In the **State** drop-down, choose **State 2**.

Next we wire up our close button that will switch back to State 1 when our user clicks or taps it:

9.  Choose **Window** > **Layers** to open up the **Layers** panel.

10. Click the triangle next to **Layer 1** to open the sublayers within.

11. Click the small outlined square on the right side of the **iPadH_MultiStates** sublayer to select that sublayer. It will turn blue when selected (Figure 9-10).

**Figure 9-10.** Selecting our iPadH_MultiStates sublayer.

12. In the **Object States** panel, select **State 2**.

13. Select the Rectangle tool and draw a small rectangle over the closeBtn.png image on the top left corner of the white rectangle.

14. In the **Buttons and Forms** panel, click the **Convert to Button** icon.

15. Name the button **iPadH_CloseBtn**.

16. Make sure the **Event** is set to **On Release or Tap**.

17. Under **Actions**, click the **+** icon and select **Go to State**.

18. In the **State** drop-down, choose **State 1** (Figure 9-11).

19. Save your file.

**Figure 9-11.** Wiring up our close button state.

> *We want to repeat the previous procedures and wire up our iPad V buttons, making sure we name them accordingly. You can reference the finished project in the complete folder of your chapter exercise files.*

# Placing an Edge Animate OAM File in InDesign

With our buttons and states set, we are now ready to place our Edge Animate content in our InDesign file. Again, as you recall from Chapter 7, we learned how to publish to an Animate Deployment Package or OAM file. This is the easiest way to import Edge Animate content into InDesign and is the method we will be using for the next exercise.

If you remember from the previous exercise, we added a second state to our buttons that contained a white rectangle. This is where we will be placing our Edge Animate OAM file. The trick here is to first place the Edge Animate content, position it, cut it from our layout, and then paste our copied file into a selected state. Why do we have to do it this way? The answer is that we really don't have to do it this exact way. We could, for example, place all the state's elements on the layout at the same time in layer form (one on top of the other) and then select the whole lot and convert them to a multistate object. The reason we are doing it this way is because we have to add an object to our multistate object, which in this case is our Edge Animate file, and we want the position of that object to match the position of our white rectangle, which we are using as an alignment guide. Here's the procedure for the iPad H page:

1. Open the Pages panel and double-click page 2 in the **iPad H** layout side.

2. Choose **Window** > **Layers** and make sure the sublayers are showing by clicking the triangle toggle button next to **Layer 1**.

3. Click the small outlined square on the right side of the **iPadH_MultiStates** sublayer to select that sublayer. It will turn blue when selected.

4. If the **Object States** panel is hidden, bring it up by choosing **Window** > **Interactive** > **Object States**.

5. In the **Object States** panel, make sure **State 2** is selected. This is the state where our white rectangle resides.

6. Choose **Edit** > **Deselect All**.

7. Under the **File** menu, choose **Place**.

8. In the **Links** folder, locate and select the Yosemite.oam file and click Open.

9. Click anywhere on the pasteboard (this is the white area surrounding the page).

10. Our Edge Animate OAM file is now inside a frame. Drag it over the top of the white rectangle and center it.

11. With the Edge Animate content still selected, click **Window** > **Folio Overlays**.

12. Make sure **Allow User Interaction** is checked.

13. Check **Auto Play** and set the delay to 0.125 seconds (Figure 9-12).

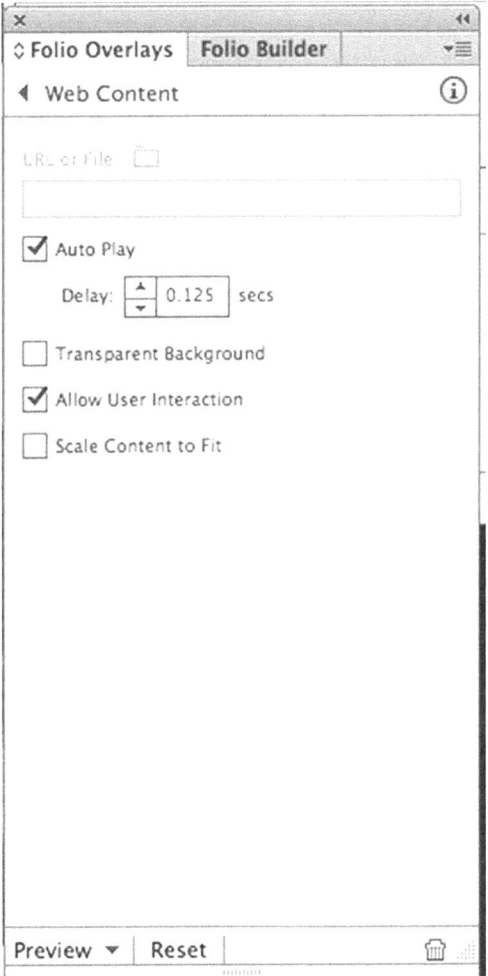

**Figure 9-12.** Wiring up our close button state.

14. Now, choose **Edit > Cut**. This removes our content and copies it to the clipboard.

15. In the **Object States** panel, click **State 2**.

16. On the bottom of the **Object States** panel, click the **Star** icon to "paste copied objects into selected state" (Figure 9-13).

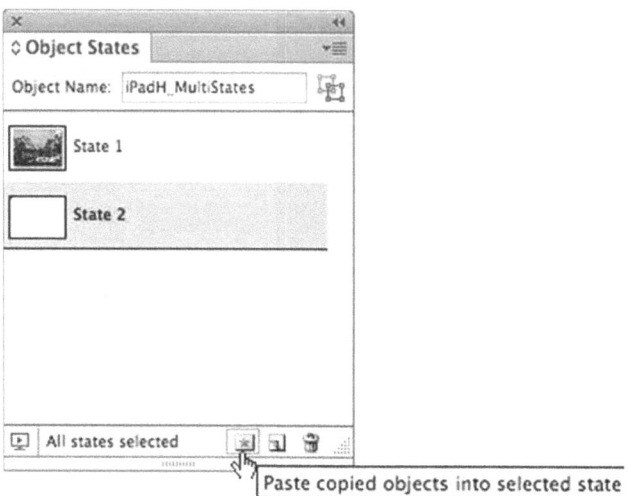

**Figure 9-13.** Adding additional objects to a multiobject state.

Here's the procedure for the iPad V page:

1.  Open the **Pages** panel and double-click page 2 in the **iPad V** layout side.

2.  Choose **Window** > **Layers** and make sure the sublayers are showing by clicking the triangle toggle button next to **Layer 1**.

3.  Click the small outlined square on the right side of the **iPadV_MultiStates** sublayer to select that sublayer. It will turn blue when selected.

4.  If the **Object States** panel is hidden, bring it up by choosing **Window** > **Interactive** > **Object States**.

5.  In the **Object States** panel, make sure **State 2** is selected.

6.  Choose **Edit** > **Deselect All**.

7.  Under **View** > **Guides and Grids**, make sure **Smart Guides** is checked.

8.  In the **Tools Palette**, select the Rectangle Frame tool (or type F on the keyboard).

9.  Draw a frame that is 640 pixels wide by 480 pixels high, and with the Selection tool, move and center the frame over the white rectangle.

10.  With the new frame still selected, click **File** > **Place**, then select the Yosemite.oam file in the **Links** folder and click Open to place it inside the new frame.

11.  Bring up the **Folio Overlays** panel as before and make sure **Allow User Interaction** is checked along with **Auto Play** and set the delay to 0.125 seconds (Figure 9-12).

12. Now, choose **Edit > Cut**. This removes the Edge Animate content and copies it to the clipboard.

13. In the **Object States** panel, click **State 2**.

14. On the bottom of the **Object States** panel, click the **Star** icon to "paste copied objects into selected state" (Figure 9-13).

15. Save your file.

## Previewing Our Folio with InDesign

Now that we have added our multistate objects, buttons, and Edge Animate content, we are ready to preview our folio before we convert it for viewing on the iPad. We can do that right within InDesign using the Adobe Content Viewer.

1. Under the **File** menu choose **Folio Preview** (Figure 9-14). This will launch the Adobe Content Viewer installed with InDesign.

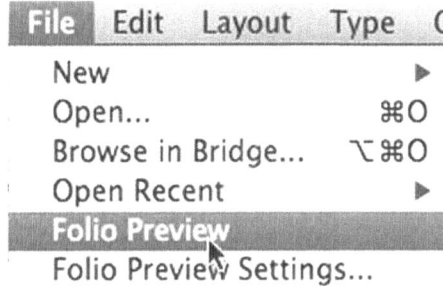

**Figure 9-14.** Previewing our folio in InDesign.

2. Test your folio by clicking on the buttons to open the Animate content.

3. Interact with the Animate content.

4. When you are finished, click the Close icon to return to the button page.

5. Save your InDesign file.

# Using Folio Builder to Create a Simple Folio

So far you have learned how to build a basic folio file in InDesign, add Edge Animate content, and preview it in the Adobe Content Viewer. Included in the Digital Publishing Suite are several tools you can use to publish your folios so they can be viewed on digital devices such as Apple's iPad.

A folio holds content referred to as articles. Articles can be created from pages in an existing InDesign document or created from separate InDesign documents. Rather than diving deep into the ins and outs of creating folios, which is really beyond the scope of this book, what we want to focus on is converting our existing InDesign document into a simple folio that we can share and preview on a tablet device such as the iPad.

## Creating Articles

We first need to convert our pages into articles so they can be added to a folio. Here is how we would do that:

1. If you closed the **InDesign** document from the last exercise, locate it in your **Exercise** folder and open it.

2. In the **Layers** panel, make sure the **Background** layer is unlocked.

3. In the **Pages** panel, double-click page 1 in the **iPad H** layout side.

4. Under the **Edit** menu, choose **Select All** (Command+A [Mac] or Ctrl+A).

5. Under the **Window** menu, choose **Articles**.

6. Click the **Create New Article button** (next to the Trash can icon) to create a new article (Figure 9-15).

7. Name the article **Cover_H** and make sure **Include When Exporting** is checked.

8. Repeat steps 2 through 6 for page 2 in the **iPad H** layout, and name it **Page2_H**.

9. Repeat steps 2 through 6 for page 1 in the **iPad V** layout, and name it **Cover_V**.

10. Repeat steps 2 through 6 for page 2 in the **iPad V** layout, and name it **Page2_V**.

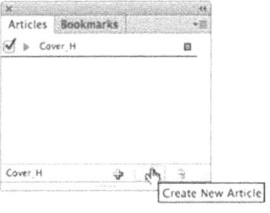

**Figure 9-15.** Creating a new article for our folio by selecting the entire contents from the page.

## Creating a Folio and Adding Articles

Now that we have created our folio articles, we need to create the actual folios where they'll reside. We do that with the Folio Builder inside InDesign. Although we could connect our iPad to the USB port of our computer, launch the Adobe Content Viewer App on our iPad, and then click the preview button in the bottom of the Folio Builder panel to bring up our folio preview in the iPad, the plan here is to log in to the Adobe Digital Publishing Service with our Adobe ID and then upload and share our folios for viewing on our Apple iPad (Figure 9-16). This is a more practical way to preview our folios, since it also allows us to share them with other people.

> *If you don't have an Adobe ID, you can get one for free at* http://www.adobe.com. *With an Adobe ID, you have access to numerous FREE Adobe services, one of which is the Digital Publishing Suite Single Edition, which is included with a Creative Cloud license.*

**Figure 9-16.** Logging into Adobe's Digital Publishing Suite is a great way to view our folios as they will appear on a tablet device.

Let's get started:

1.  Under the **Window** menu, choose **Folio Builder**.

2.  Click **Sign In** and enter your Adobe ID (Figure 9-16).

3.  Once you are signed in, click the **Create new folio** button on the bottom of the **Folio Builder** panel.

4.  Name the Folio **Yosemite – Valley of Beauty**.

5.  Make sure your target is **Apple iPad** and your orientation is set to both **Landscape and Portrait Folio**.

6.  Leave the **Right Edge Binding** unchecked and make sure the **Default Format** is PDF.

7.  In the **Cover Preview** box, click the folder icon under **Vertical** and choose Yosemite_ Cover_V_Prv.jpg in your **Links** folder.

8.  In the **Cover Preview** box, click the folder icon under **Horizontal** and choose Yosemite_ Cover_H_Prv.jpg in your **Links** folder.

9.  If you want to edit your folio offline, check the **Create Offline Folio** option.

10. Click OK. Folio Builder uploads the basic structure of your folio with the parameters you just set.

11. At the bottom of the **Folio Builder** panel, click the **Add Articles** icon. This will add all the open articles that we just created in the **Articles** panel. Enable the **Horizontal Swipe Only** option, which limits the swiping of pages only from left to right (Figure 9-17).

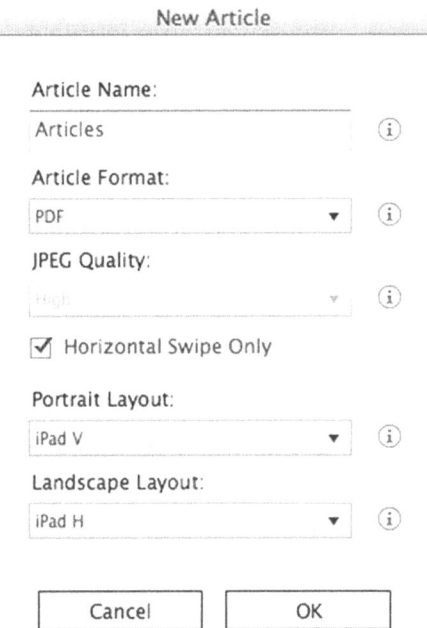

**Figure 9-17.** Adding our open articles to our folio.

12. Select **Articles** in the **Folio Builder** window and open the pop-down menu in the top right corner and choose **Update** (Figure 9-18). This will upload an updated version of your folio to your Adobe account.

13. To view your folio, download the free Adobe Content Viewer App for iPad from the App Store and then log in to your Adobe Account.

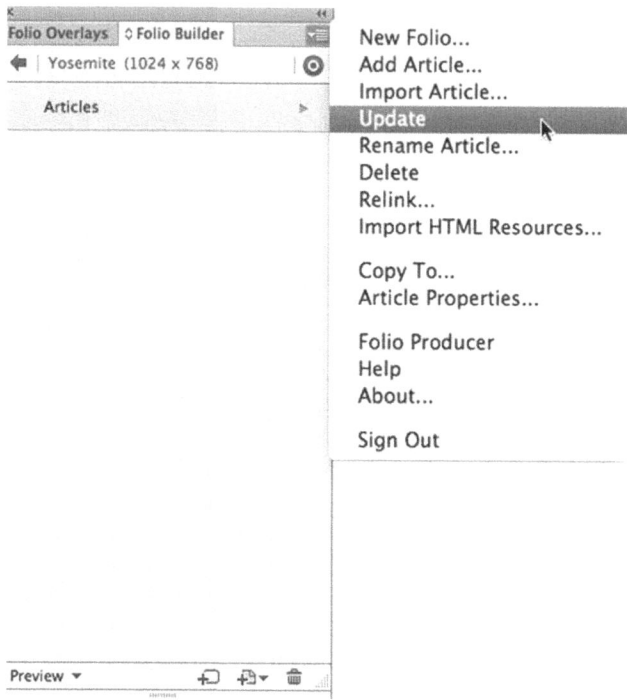

**Figure 9-18.** Uploading our folio to the Cloud using the Update option in the Folio Builder panel.

# You Have Learned

In this chapter, we learned how to add Edge Animate content to digital publications. We learned some practical knowledge and skills including:

- Print and digital publishing workflows

- Various digital publishing formats

- Working with Animate content in iBooks Author

- Working with Animate content in Adobe InDesign

- The basics behind Folio Builder and uploading and sharing folios

The end result we gained here is the knowledge of just how easy it is to bring Edge Animate content into digital publications. And that's the point. Dragging and dropping or placing Edge Animate content into a publication is dead simple thanks to the streamlined publishing options included in Edge Animate. Can you imagine keeping track of image assets, JavaScript files, HTML files, and the likes when working with larger iBook or InDesign folio projects? Indeed, it would certainly be a nightmare.

Now that you have a taste of just how easy it is to work with Edge Animate content in your digital publications, we hope you will explore it further. But, before you do, we've got one more chapter for you that will set you on the path to the future, because mobile computing is growing in leaps and bounds and overtaking desktop computing. Of course, Edge Animate is a perfect tool for the mobile world that will provide you with great flexibility and cutting-edge features for years to come. If this is something you find exciting, turn the page to learn how to take your Edge Animate compositions mobile.

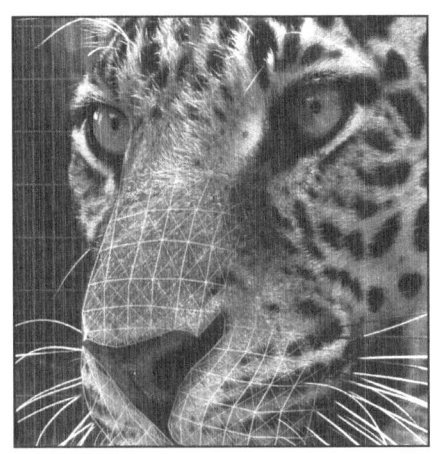

# Chapter 10

# Edge Animate Goes Mobile

A few years ago, one of the authors had an interesting and, perhaps, eye-opening experience. While spending some time in the local mall, he noticed members of a family casually strolling through the main shopping center who were obviously window shopping. "Here was a happy family sharing some time together in the local mall while planning their holiday purchases," he thought. What struck the author was that each family member had a mobile phone and was happily texting or chatting away to his or her intended party while slowly walking through the mall. The seamless integration of these devices into this family's life was apparent, and certainly it is no mere coincidence.

Mobile phones and similar devices have changed our lives. We rely on their technology on a regular basis because they are small, powerful, and portable enough to be with us practically everywhere we travel. We have access to our information or can obtain new information in just a few taps or with the swipe of a finger. We make buying decisions with our devices, we document our lives via the photo or movie capabilities of our devices, or we use them to share data and communicate with others. Our mobile devices are shaping the way we communicate, understand, and interact with our world.

How does Edge Animate fit into this ever-growing mobile world? That is exactly what we will cover in this chapter as we explore new methods of taking your Edge Animate compositions beyond the desktop and into the mobile world. This chapter will cover:

- An introduction to the modern mobile Web

- Phones, tablets, and phablets

- Creating a mobile app with Edge Animate and PhoneGap Build

- Using Edge Inspect with Edge Animate

- Responsive design with Edge Animate

If you haven't already downloaded the chapter files, they can be found at: `http://www.apress.com/9781430243502`. In this chapter we will be using these files:

- `Stonehenge/index.an`

- `Inspect/index.an`

- `Responsive/index.an`

- `appicon.png`

# The Modern Mobile Web

To understand where we are with the modern mobile Web, we first have to understand where we have been. Toward the end of the 1990s, as cell phones became more commonplace, the need to connect to larger networks and utilize Internet features like messaging and content browsing began to grow. Though Apple's Newton can be credited with having the first mobile browser, it wasn't until technologies such as WAP, NTTDocomo's i-mode platform, and Openwave's HDML platform were introduced that mobile data services grew in demand and expanded as the technology improved. When cellular phones advanced from first generation (1G) to second generation (2G) capabilities, connectivity speeds increased, which resulted in expanded features and capabilities of mobile data services. In fact, one feature that is still in use today, Short Message Service (SMS), grew as 2G technologies took hold. Of course, it was logical that technology would move forward, thus, the introduction of 3G and later 4G speeds further solidified the mobile Web.

As native mobile apps began to proliferate, the mobile web browser advanced as well. Devices became smaller and more powerful, and the ability to literally run a desktop-like web browser in a mobile setting was slowly becoming a reality. But there was a problem: battery life. It was evident that mobile devices needed to conserve processing power, which would result in power conservation and lead to higher battery life. Although native mobile apps addressed many of these power issues, the ability to experience the "full Web" was the holy grail for the mobile industry. The problem was desktop browser plug-ins like Adobe Flash, which supported advanced animation, audio, video, and interaction in a desktop browser, were unfortunately some of the worst power hogs when tested in a mobile browser. This lead to Apple banning the Flash plug-in from their devices and setting the course toward advancements in HTML 5, CSS3, JQuery, and JavaScript as the new standard of web content. This is where the power of Edge Animate resides today.

# Phones, Tablets, and Phablets

With the advancements achieved in today's modern mobile Web, it is no surprise the mobile market is bulging at the seams as new devices appear on what seems to be a monthly basis. As we mentioned earlier, there is no real "standard" in the device industry other than modern mobile web browsers capable of viewing advanced HTML and CSS content. Although this is a great benefit for us when we design in Edge Animate, we need to understand that the device market can be a minefield in terms of screen real estate and device features. Fortunately, Edge Animate has tools that help us deal with that, which we will get to later in the chapter. First, let's talk briefly about the different types of mobile devices available in today's market.

## Smartphones

A smartphone is a mobile phone that has the ability to run an advanced mobile operating system. Two of the most dominant mobile operating systems today are Google Android and Apple iOS, which, as of the publication date of this book, power 85% of the world's smartphones.

Some of the key features in smartphones include:

1. Ability to utilize a mobile operating system to run mobile apps

2. Web access

3. Advanced messaging

4. Camera and video capabilities

5. Advanced sensors like accelerometers, gyroscopes, and compasses

6. Ability to change view orientation when rotated (i.e., portrait to landscape mode)

Although smartphones offer numerous advanced features, one thing to keep in mind when developing Edge Animate content for them is screen size, which should not be confused with screen resolution. The average smartphone screen size is about 4 inches across the diagonal. When you are targeting your design for a screen of that size, make sure you scale your content accordingly (i.e., smaller and simpler animations, larger buttons, and readable text). Keep in mind that users interact with your design using their fingers, so make sure your design has room to accommodate larger fingers.

## Tablets

True touch screen tablet computers have only been around for a few years but have grown to a huge installed device base largely due to the introduction of Apple's iPad, which currently dominates in user installed base by a whopping 69% as of third-quarter stats for 2012. Tablets are essentially large smartphones minus the phone feature, in most cases.

Although tablets share many features with smartphones, they differ in three key areas:

1. Larger screen size and higher resolutions

2. Longer battery life

3. Ability to use a stylus or pen device

When targeting your Edge Animate content for tablet devices, you have a bit more flexibility in your design since you are dealing with larger screen real estate. However, screen orientation is often adjusted to the user's preference. If you remember in Chapter 9, we designed two versions of our Yosemite presentation, one that accommodated portrait viewing and one that accommodated landscape viewing. Later in this chapter we will delve into how easy it is to make these types of adjustments right within Edge Animate.

## Phablets

Right between a smartphone and a tablet is the aptly named phablet, which is essentially a device with a screen larger than 5 inches but smaller than 7 inches. Not to be confused with e-book readers, although they may resemble them in size, phablets possess similar features and technology found in smartphones and tablet devices. Samsung's Galaxy Note devices are examples of phablets currently on the market. Although the recently introduced Apple iPad Mini is not technically in this class due to its 7.9-inch screen size, it could certainly fit here given its overall size and feature set. The so-called phablet is a sort of in between device that is not quite a tablet and not quite a smartphone (Figure 10-1).

Although phablets share many features with smartphones and tablets, they differ in a few key areas:

1. Larger screen resolution than a smartphone

2. A near full-size Web experience in a compact and "pocketable" design

**Figure 10-1.** A mobile device size comparison.

# Creating a Mobile App with Edge Animate and PhoneGap

We have covered some ground here learning about the history of mobile computing, including where mobile technology is today. And, with each chapter of our book, you've learned a little bit more about the power of Edge Animate. Here is the kicker to this whole story: You now have the power to create a mobile application without even having to learn a new programming language like Java (which Android requires) or Objective-C (which iOS requires). You can thank HTML 5, CSS3, JavaScript, Edge Animate, and Adobe Edge PhoneGap Build for changing all of that!

You might be wondering, what is PhoneGap Build? In simple terms, PhoneGap Build is a modified version of the original open source PhoneGap mobile development framework originally developed by Nitobi. Nitobi contributed the code to the Apache Foundation, which support the Apache community, a group of developers and users who support open source software projects. After Nitobi contributed the PhoneGap framework to Apache, it was renamed Apache Cordova. Then, Adobe acquired Nitobi and modified the framework to what is now PhoneGap Build. The difference between Apache Cordova and Adobe PhoneGap Build is in its ease of use. Adobe has included all the major software developer kits (SDKs, or, devkit for short) in their online service. Prior to PhoneGap Build, you would have had to obtain and install SDKs for the specific mobile devices you were targeting. With PhoneGap Build, all of the SDKs are in the Cloud; you simply upload a zipped copy of your HTML 5 content, which, as we have learned, can be created completely within Adobe Edge Animate.

Of course, there are some limitations when designing a mobile application using only Edge Animate and PhoneGap Build, and we are by no means suggesting you quit your daytime job and become a mobile app developer. The point here is Edge Animate paired with PhoneGap Build makes for a solid team that you can utilize to build a seriously decent mobile application and rapidly deliver it to multiple mobile device platforms. The take away here is: Design once. Distribute to multiple platforms.

Let's get started.

> *For this exercise, we have predesigned an Edge Animate mobile application so we can focus on the steps needed for uploading it to the Adobe PhoneGap Build service. PhoneGap Build is included with a membership to Adobe Creative Cloud. You'll find PhoneGap Build within Edge Tools & Services. Of course, you could build your own Edge Animate mobile presentation and just follow along with the steps to upload it to PhoneGap Build. For our design, we set our stage width to 320 by 480 pixels since we are initially targeting the standard iPhone. Currently, PhoneGap Build does not support tablet resolutions. We can actually work around that by using percentage values for our elements, which you will see in a later exercise. In addition, if you want to create an iOS app, you will need an Apple computer and an Apple iOS developer certificate, which includes a provisioning profile key for the iOS build. More on that later.*

1. Launch Edge Animate.

2. In the File menu, locate your Exercise folder and open the Stonehenge Mobile folder, then open the index.an document.

3. Let's take a look at our presentation first. In the File menu, choose Preview in Browser. (Figure 10-2).

**Figure 10-2.** Previewing our Edge Animate designed mobile app in the browser.

4. With your mouse, click the animated birds and the other buttons to see the interactive content behind them. Notice we have used things we have learned from previous lessons, such as symbols, animation, interactivity, and external content. And, as you can see, we've kept the content within the constraints of the iPhone's screen size of 320 by 480 pixels and provided reasonably sized buttons and text. Remember what we mentioned earlier about making our presentation as device friendly as possible.

The other thing to pay attention to here is the fact that we have named our file index.html. Why did we do that? PhoneGap looks for an index file to use as a starting point when building a mobile application. If we don't include a file named index, we will get an error after we attempt to generate our device builds in PhoneGap.

5. Select File and choose Publish Settings.

6. For the Publishing Target, choose Web. This will export and minify our Edge Animate presentation, which is best when uploading to PhoneGap.

7. Close the index Edge Animate file and open the Stonehenge Mobile folder in your Exercises folder and locate and open the publish folder. Then locate and open the web folder.

8. The goal here is to create a ZIP archive of the contents inside our folder so PhoneGap is able to easily locate our index.html file after we upload our ZIP file to the service. Select all of the files and folders within the web folder.

9. Right-click one of the selected icons and choose Compress 6 Items from the menu (Figure 10-3), or Send to > Compressed (zipped) folder on a PC. You can also find this command under the File menu.

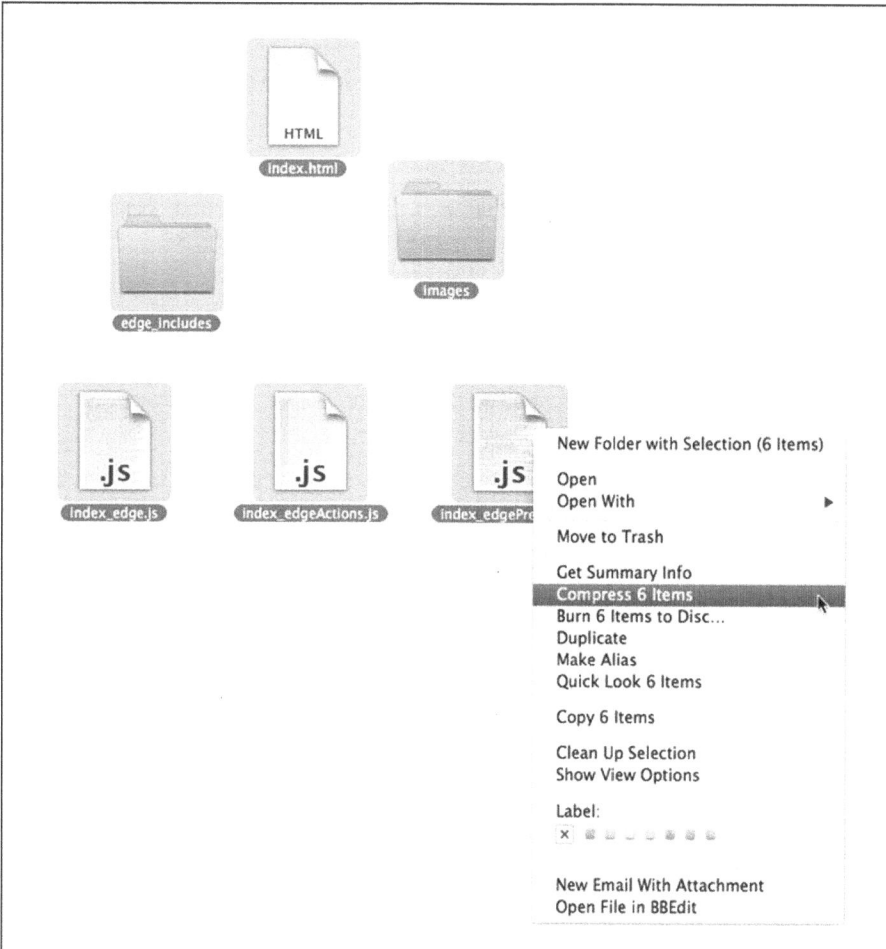

**Figure 10-3.** Compressing our published and minified Stonehenge Animate composition in the Mac OS X Finder using the Compress option.

1. We now end up with a file named `Archive.zip` inside our web folder (give the new archive an appropriate name when you create it on the PC). This is the file we will be uploading to the Adobe PhoneGap Build service.

> If you are using Windows, there are ways to create a compressed ZIP file using a similar method to the one listed above. You could also use a program like WinZip to create a ZIP file. Consult your help menu or user's manual for more information on how to create a ZIP file with your particular version of Windows, since it can vary.

# Logging In and Setting Up PhoneGap Build

Now that we have our zipped file containing the contents of our Edge Animate mobile application, we need to send it to the PhoneGap Build service. We start that process by first logging in to the Adobe Creative Cloud service. As you remember from our previous chapters, the Creative Cloud is a monthly subscription service that gives you access to all of the Adobe Applications, like Edge Animate, in the Cloud. With our Creative Cloud membership, we get access to the Adobe PhoneGap Build service.

1. In your web browser, log in to the Adobe Creative Cloud at `http://creative.adobe.com` using your Adobe ID.

2. Once you are logged in, click Apps in the top black bar.

3. Under `Edge Tools & Services`, click `Package apps` next to the `PhoneGap Build` icon (Figure 10-4).

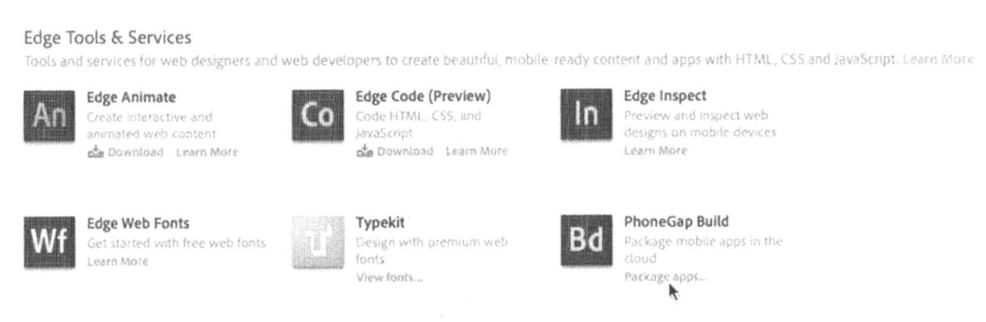

**Figure 10-4.** Opening PhoneGap Build in Adobe Creative Cloud.

4. When you open PhoneGap Build for the first time, you'll see a window with a welcome message from Adobe, a `Your apps` tab, which lists apps you have previously created, and two other tabs labeled `open-source` and `private` (Figure 10-5).

> *Since we entered Adobe PhoneGap Build from the Creative Cloud, our default choice is set to a private app. For the purposes of this exercise, we will be concentrating on using PhoneGap Build with Creative Cloud and not GitHub, which is an open-source online repository for software development. If you find yourself wanting to delve deeper into software development, you might consider signing up for a GitHub account. It is free if your project is open source, or, if you plan to offer a public repository and manage your sharing permissions such as allowing specific employees to have access to your repository, you will need to sign up for a monthly plan. More information about plans can be found on the GitHub web site at `https://github. com/`.*

**Figure 10-5.** The Adobe PhoneGap Build welcome screen.

5. Click the Upload a .zip file button and select the Archive.zip file that you created earlier in the web folder inside the publish folder of our Stonehenge Mobile project folder.

6. Click Open. A dialog box will display indicating that your ZIP file is being uploaded.

7. Once your ZIP file has been uploaded, PhoneGap will assign it the default name of PG Build App.

8. Rename the app Stonehenge and add a description in the app description field. In this case, we entered "A short presentation about the mystery of Stonehenge" (Figure 10-6).

9. Select enable debugging. This will help you if there are errors during the build.

10. Select enable hydration to decrease the time it takes to compile the app and automatically push updates directly to your app in installed devices.

11. Click the Ready to build button to start the build process.

**Figure 10-6.** Configuring the options for our PhoneGap application.

# More Configuration and Customization

When you click the `Ready to build` button, PhoneGap begins building the various device applications. When the builds are complete, notice that the icons related to the specific devices turn blue, except iOS, which is red because we did not enter an iOS developer certificate and provisioning key (Figure 10-7).

*Why is the iOS icon red? In order for you to create a build for Apple's iOS, you need to add a developer certificate and a provisioning profile key to the iOS build. To obtain these, you will need to register as an Apple iOS Developer for $99 per year. Why does Apple require you to register as a developer? There is no real official Apple answer for this other than the fact that when you sign up as an iOS developer, it allows you to upload an unlimited amount of apps and you can tap into the App Store marketing since Apple gives you a free web page for each app you upload, which includes an app review section. It is also certain that Apple invests those yearly fees into maintaining, updating, and supporting the iOS SDKs for app development. In addition, a developer certificate allows you to register your iOS devices so you are able to copy and test your apps in the native iOS environment before they are published.*

**Figure 10-7.** Upon completion of various app builds, PhoneGap will indicate success via a blue icon and create a QR code for your application.

At this point we could stop and deliver our application for testing on our mobile device. Keep in mind that we designed our app with a resolution based on the standard iPhone, but we told PhoneGap to create builds for other devices. In theory, we should be able to install those builds on the corresponding device without a problem other than screen size. PhoneGap makes it very easy to distribute it by providing download links to the various builds and also includes a QR (quick response) code for easy application delivery via the QR reader applications that are available for most devices.

Let's add some finishing touches:

1. Click on the app title Stonehenge to open the details of the App.

2. Click the Collaborators tab and then click the add a collaborator button. You can add collaborators as testers or developers. Testers have read-only access while developers have read and write access. It is important to make sure your collaborators have an existing Creative Cloud membership and then use their e-mail addresses associated with that membership when you invite them.

3. Add a tester, and to test it, add your e-mail address that you used to log in to the Creative Cloud. The reason we are doing this is so you can see the messages generated when you add a collaborator.

4. If you followed step 3, you now should have a message in your e-mail inbox that notifies you that you've been added to the PhoneGap app you just created. This is an example of how your collaborators will be notified.

5. Now click the Settings tab. We are going to update our app's icon.

6. Scroll down to Configuration and click the Choose File button under the generic Icon File image.

7. Navigate to your Exercise folder and find the Stonehenge Mobile folder and select the appicon. png file. This is an image file that we have already created in Adobe Fireworks. We plan to use this image as our application icon. You can create an app icon in any graphics program, not just Fireworks.

> The appicon.png file is 114 by 114 pixels, which is standard size for an iPhone icon. Although it is beyond the scope of this chapter, we could add various sized icons to a config.xml file to be included in the published web files to support the various-sized device icons for specific mobile devices. The goal here is to keep it simple. The fact is, the icon size that we chose is a decent compromise for most smartphone devices, except for the Blackberry, which requires a smaller icon. On most devices, the icon will be scaled up or down depending on the particular resolution of the host device.

8. Next, specify a package, which is the unique identifier for your application. The format that is typically preferred is a reverse domain look-up style. So, for example, if you own a domain, you could use com.mydomain.stonehenge.

9. Under version, specify a version number, which typically uses a major, minor, patch style format with three numbers, such as 0.0.1. If you modify your application, you would update the version number in this box, which would then be automatically pushed to your end user if you have enabled hydration. In this case, we will enter 0.0.1 in the version field.

10. Click the Save button on the bottom right of the Configuration tab (Figure 10-8).

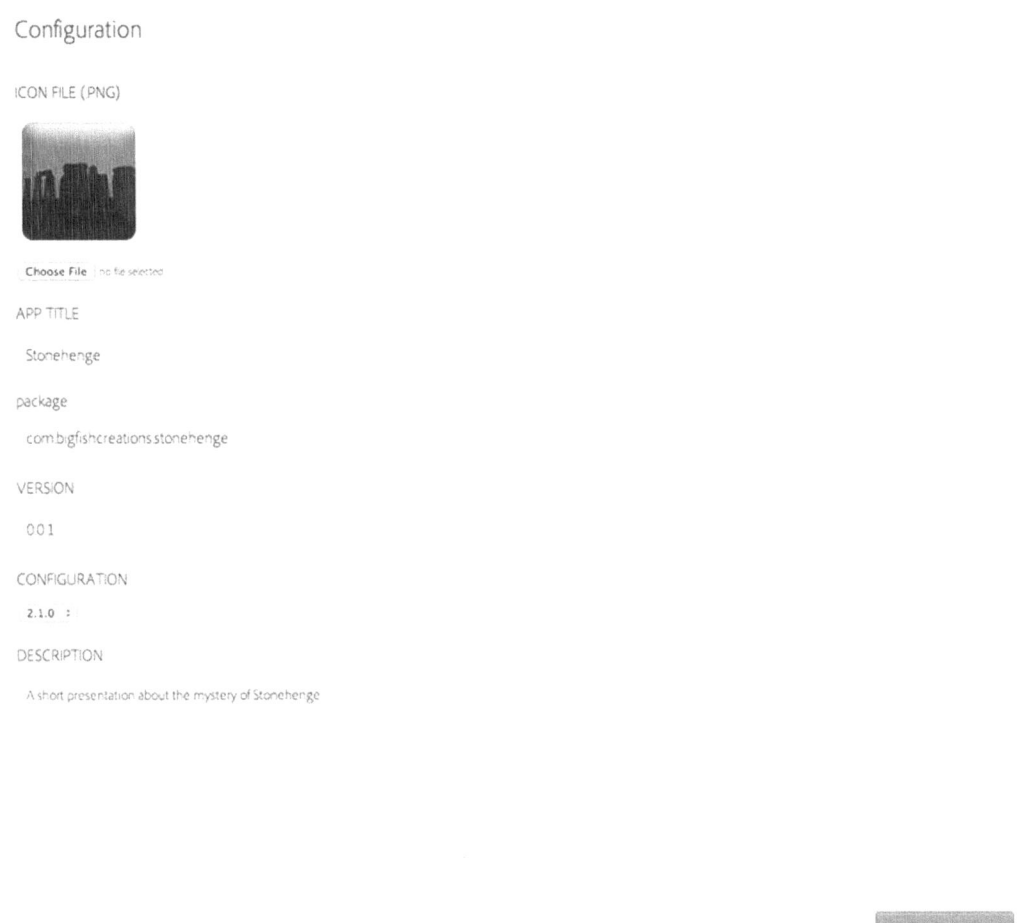

**Figure 10-8.** Further customizing our application in PhoneGap's Configuration section.

# Downloading and Testing Your PhoneGap App

With our PhoneGap build complete, we can set out to test our application on an available mobile device. As we mentioned earlier, PhoneGap makes it very easy to distribute your apps by providing download links to the various builds, or you can scan the QR code that was generated using a QR reader like Google Goggles or RedLaser. Or, if you obtained an Apple iOS developer certificate, you will be able to use iTunes to transfer the iOS build to your iOS device.

We are going to use RedLaser to scan the code and load it in our Android testing device.

1. If you don't have the free RedLaser QR code reader app, you can download it from the Google Play store at http://play.google.com.

2. In the Settings menu of your Android device, make sure under Applications you select Unknown Sources. This allows you to install nonmarket applications.

3. Launch RedLaser.

4. If you are not logged in to the PhoneGap Build service, log in and open the Stonehenge app under your App tab.

5. In RedLaser, click the scan button, and then hold your Android device in front of the QR code, which will take a moment, and scan the code, which opens a link that just happens to be a direct link to our Android build since we are scanning the code from an Android device (Figure 10-9). If we were scanning from another device, the QR code would redirect us to the correct build for our device.

6. When the code is scanned in your Android device, click Open browser. This will begin the download process of our PhoneGap APK file, which is an Android application package file—a file that contains all the necessary compiled code, assets, and resources to run on an Android device.

7. Once you have downloaded the APK file, swipe from the top of your device and locate the Stonehenge.apk file and click it. You will be asked if you want to install the app. Click OK.

8. Once the application is installed, you will have the option to open and test it.

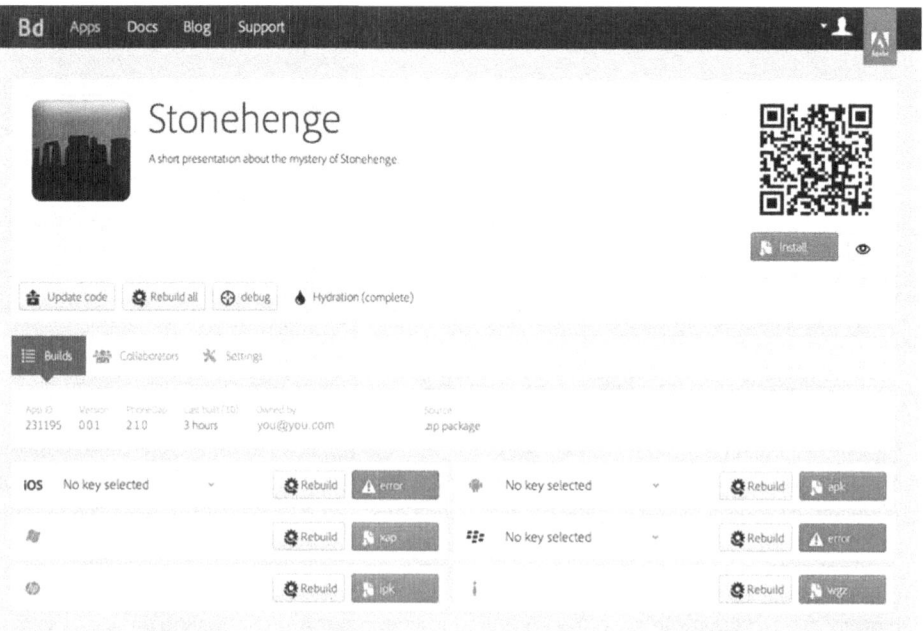

**Figure 10-9.** Our QR code for our Stonehenge app is in the upper right-hand corner of our app detail page, and it is ready for scanning by our QR Reader application. This is the easy way to download and install our application.

# Using Edge Inspect with Edge Animate

In the previous exercise, we created a mobile application for multiple devices using Adobe PhoneGap Build. We targeted our Edge Animate design to a screen resolution of 320 by 480 pixels, which is the standard for Apple's iPhone. However, in the world as we now know it, there are numerous resolutions for numerous mobile devices. The challenge for any aspiring Edge Animate designer is how to deal with variable screen sizes while designing and testing your creations. Fortunately, Edge Animate has included several features to help you deal with multiple screen sizes and devices. We plan to get to that in the next section, but first, we want to highlight a new tool from Adobe aimed squarely at the ever-growing device market. The tool, Adobe Edge Inspect, is an application that runs only in Google Chrome and allows you to connect and synchronize practically any mobile device with a development computer. Once you connect your devices to your development computer, when you view the Web in your desktop browser, what you see on the screen is essentially mirrored to your connected devices. We say "essentially mirrored" because what you see on your development computer is not what is on the desktop computer's screen, but rather the actual HTML content files. This means that if you include device-specific code in your files, like CSS media queries, for example, each device will deal with that code based on what that code tells the device to do. What does this mean? In simpler terms, Edge Inspect shows you what your web content looks like on multiple devices at the same time so you are able to make real-time changes to it, further enhancing your productivity.

But Edge Inspect doesn't just view online web content; it also supports localhost content, which are the URLs that Edge Animate generates when you choose `Preview in Browser`. Do you see where we are going with this? Exactly. Edge Inspect is a perfect companion to Edge Animate, and we'll show you why.

## Setting Up Your Edge Inspect Environment

The first thing we need to do is set up Edge Inspect to work with Edge Animate. We first want to install Edge Inspect.

1. Launch Adobe Creative Cloud.

2. Click the `Apps` tab and locate `Edge Inspect` under `Edge Tools & Services` and select the `Learn More` link.

3. The first step is to install Edge Inspect on your desktop (development) computer. Click the `Download` link to download and install Edge Inspect for desktop.

4. The second step is to install the `Google Chrome` browser extension. Of course, before you do that, you'll need to make sure you have Google Chrome installed. If you don't have it installed, you can download it for free from `Google.com`.

5. Click the link to the `Google Chrome` browser extension located on the Edge Inspect `Learn More` page. Install the extension in Chrome.

6. The last step is to install the Edge Inspect mobile clients on your devices. Click the links on the Edge Inspect `Learn More` page to download and install the specific mobile client for your devices.

7. Once you have everything installed, open Chrome and click the Edge Inspect icon in the top right corner to begin pairing your devices to your development computer (Figure 10-10).

**Figure 10-10.** Pairing a mobile device with Adobe Edge Inspect.

8. Launch the Edge Inspect mobile client on your device and click the + sign in the top right corner of the dialog to add a new connection (pairing).

9. In the connection box, enter the HostName or IP address that appears in the Edge Inspect menu in your desktop browser. Click Join.

10. When the Edge Inspect mobile client finds your desktop computer, it will produce a PIN (personal identification number) code. This is the code you will use to pair the two devices.

11. In the Edge Inspect dialog box on your desktop computer, enter the PIN code to pair your devices.

12. Once you have paired the two devices, test the connection by loading a web page in Chrome. If everything is working correctly, you should see the same web page appear in your mobile device.

## Configuring Edge Animate to Preview in Edge Inspect

Now that we have created our Edge Inspect network, we are ready to incorporate that into our Edge Animate workflow. In order to do that, we must set up our default browser. Typically with Mac OS X, the default browser is Safari. Likewise, in Microsoft Windows, the default browser is usually Internet Explorer. In Windows, you can set the default browser by going to `Control Panel > Programs > Set your default programs`. From there you can set Chrome to open web documents by default. We'll also quickly walk you through the steps on how to set up Chrome as your default browser in Mac OS X.

1. Open Safari.

2. In the Safari menu, choose Preferences.

3. Click the General tab.

4. In the Default web browser tab, select Google Chrome (Figure 10-11). Now you are ready to use Edge Inspect with Edge Animate.

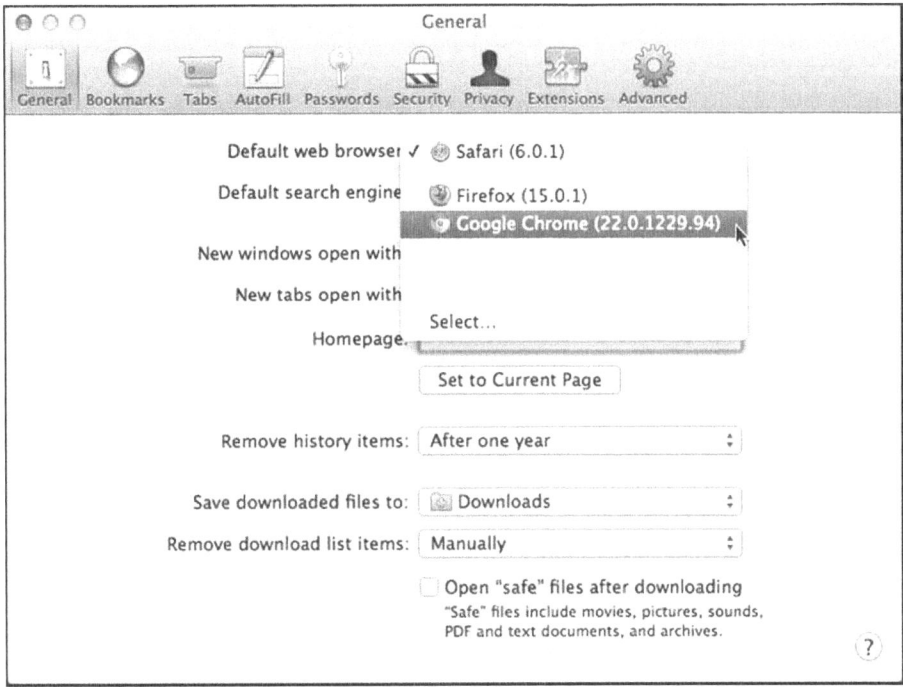

**Figure 10-11.** Setting Google Chrome as our default browser in Mac OS X.

# Using Edge Inspect with Edge Animate

With our workflow set up, we can start using Edge Inspect with Edge Animate. For the purpose of this exercise, we are going to keep it simple and just demonstrate the workflow and point out the value of using Edge Inspect during the development process.

We have prepared a simple interactive Edge Animate presentation that we will use for our lesson.

1. Locate your Exercise folder and open the folder named Inspect.

2. Click the index.an file, which will open in Edge Animate. On the stage we see a fancy gift (Figure 10-12).

**Figure 10-12.** Looking at our fancy gift in Edge Animate.

3. Make sure you launch the Adobe Inspect mobile application on your mobile devices. For our testing example, we are using an iPad 2 and an iPhone 4s.

4. In the File menu, click Preview in Browser.

5. Notice when you preview your Edge Animate content, Adobe Inspect loads it in your devices using a local URL, which we set up in the previous exercise (Figure 10-13).

MacBook Pro Screen

iPad 2 Screen

iPhone 4s Screen

**Figure 10-13.** Our fancy gift displayed in our connected devices via Adobe Edge Inspect.

6. On your desktop computer, click the gift and it will jiggle. Click it again and it will jiggle again. Click it a third time and you get cake!

7. Notice on your connected devices, we still see the gift displayed. Remember what we explained earlier, Edge Inspect doesn't mirror the screen; it actually loads the remote content into each connected device's Edge Inspect browser. This is a very important aspect to remember when using Edge Inspect. It allows you to test your code as it is intended for each device.

8. Go ahead and tap the gift on your devices until you get cake.

## Swiping Power from Edge Inspect and Edge Animate

We have successfully learned a valuable lesson about how Adobe Edge Inspect works, in particular, how your Edge Animate code is loaded separately into each testing device for you to literally work with on the fly. Think about it, without Edge Inspect, we would have to upload our Edge Animate content to the Web and open and test it in our mobile devices. This is a huge time hog that will weigh us down during our design, development, and testing stages. With Edge Inspect, we can get immediate feedback as to how our Edge Animate design will behave in different devices.

To really understand this, we need to do another simple exercise. The plan here is to create an interactive function in our Edge Animate design that can only be accomplished in a mobile device. We are certain you have figured it out by now since we gave you a clue in this section's title: we are going to add a function to the cake that will slice it with the swipe of a finger. And, remember, you can't swipe on a desktop computer, so this method will only work on a mobile device.

1. If you closed the last exercise, go ahead and open up the Inspect folder in your Exercises folder and load the index.an file in Edge Animate.

2. Move the playhead to the last frame on the timeline, which is at 0:02:089 seconds.

3. In the Elements panel on the left, click slice.

4. Make sure Autokeyframe is turned on. Under Position and Size add a keyframe to Left.

5. Move the playhead to the 0:02.50 mark.

6. Move the slice to L = 374 px.

7. Insert a trigger and enter: sym.play('Sliced'). When triggered, this will jump the playhead to a label we will create called Sliced. This will be the secondary state of our cake slice, which will be the same position of our first slice, but a new element.

8. Finish up by adding a label and name it 'Slice.' This is the first state of our slice.

9. With the slice element still selected, click the Actions button and choose touchmove.

10. In the box, click the Play button and enter the value 'Sliced' between the parentheses. This will jump to our 'Sliced' label, which we will create next.

11. Move the playhead to the 0:02.356 mark.

12. Add a label and name it 'Sliced.'

13. Add a trigger and insert a sym.stop(); code.

14. Drag a new instance of the Slice from the Library over the top of the original slice. Use the smart guides to line it up (Figure 10-14). Or, enter the values L = 374 and T = 69 under position and size, respectively.

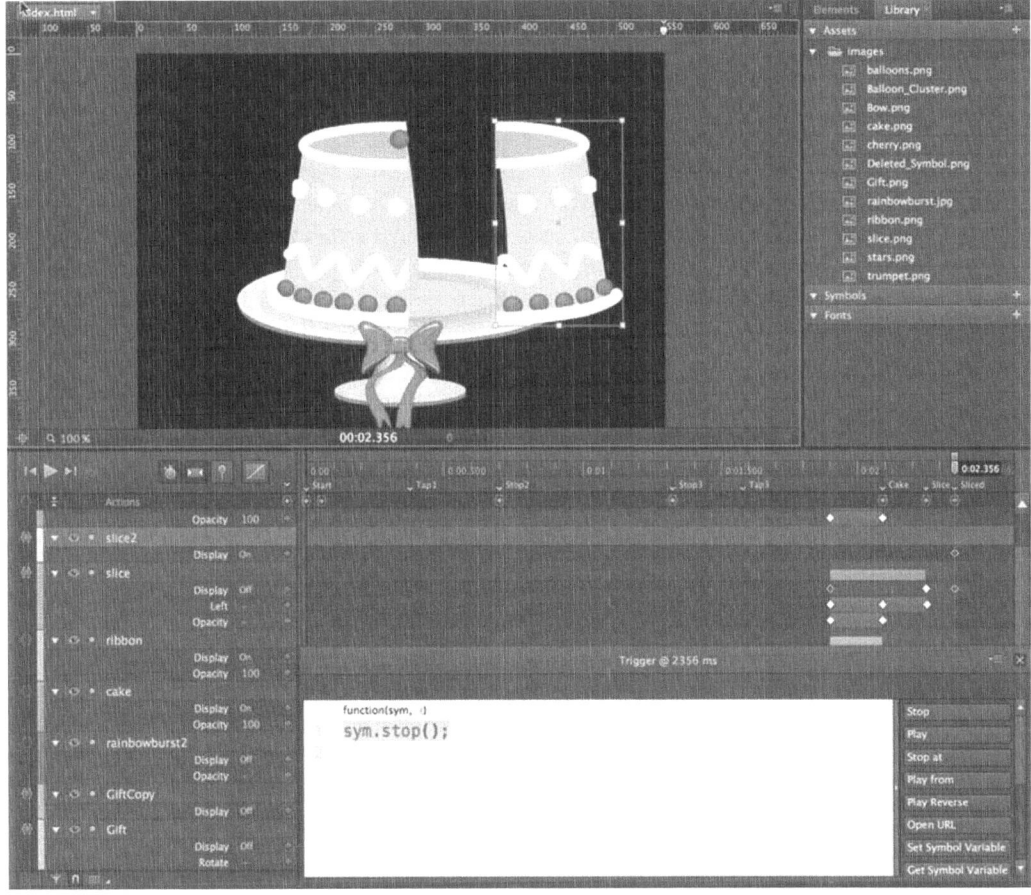

**Figure 10-14.** If we knew you were coming we would have swiped you a cake.

15. Make sure `Slice2` is set to Display `On` not `Always On`.

16. Choose `File: Preview in Browser` or press `Command/Ctrl + Return`.

17. On your desktop computer, click the gift three times until you see the cake. Try and click the cake to slice it. As you can see, you can't.

18. Now, on your mobile device, tap the gift twice until you see the cake. Tap the cake. Notice nothing happens.

19. Swipe the cake. Bingo! We've got cake!

# Responsive Design with Edge Animate

In the early days of the Web, designers were lucky in a sense and unlucky in another sense. The luck they had was the newness of the Web, the fact that it existed largely on the desktop, and that they could literally "hack" a web site together with basic coding and design tools. As the Web evolved, and mobile devices began to appear, it was clear that these folks had to be roped in since much of their code was rather difficult if not useless when experienced in nondesktop devices. At this point, web standards, which were essentially specific guidelines and best practices of how to code and design a web site, began to take hold and shape the Web. But it eventually became clear that experiencing a full-functioning web site on a mobile device was still challenging at best due in part to the size of the device viewport. To solve this dilemma, web designers began building two types of web sites simultaneously: a desktop version and a mobile version.

It was fairly recently that many web designers began to approach a mobile-first web design method, targeting the mobile presentation of their site's content first while understanding their desktop version could easily adapt to the mobile approach. But it took the realization of Ethan Marcotte, who coined the phrase "responsive design" in an article he wrote for *A List Apart* in 2010. Marcotte explained that mobile browsing would soon surpass desktop browsing, and as such, designers should focus on adaptive designs that had the ability to "respond" to the various capabilities of different viewing device. Thus, responsive design, in a nutshell, is the practice of designing web sites to be dynamic (fluid) in their adaptation to various screen types and devices rather than depending on the designer to code a site for the ever increasing number of mobile devices.

Why is this important? Simple. Edge Animate has features that allow you to create in a fluid and responsive manner. To understand how this comes together, let's design a responsive landing page in Edge Animate for a fictitious movie site.

1.  In your `Exercise` folder, open the `Responsive` folder and click the `index.an` file to open Edge Animate.

2.  Using what you have learned from the previous exercises, open and launch Adobe Edge Inspect in your mobile devices. We will be using Edge Inspect to see the changes we make to our composition as we apply our responsive design techniques.

3.  Let's take a look at what our design currently looks like. In the file menu, select `Preview in Browser`.

4.  While the design looks fairly decent in our iPad, when we look at it in the desktop browser and the iPhone, we notice gaps of white, which is our browser's default background color. Also, some of our elements are chopped off on the right side in our iPhone view. That's because our design is 1,200 pixels wide, and although we can scroll by swiping to the right on our iPhone, our user has the potential of missing information (Figure 10-15).

**Figure 10-15.** Our design as it looks in Adobe Inspect before we add our responsive features.

5.  The first thing we want to do is adjust our stage size to scale 100%. In the Elements panel on the timeline, click Stage.

6.  In the Properties panel, click the Width Units button so it changes 1200 px to 100%.

7.  Repeat this for the Height Units button, changing the 800 px to 100% (Figure 10-16).

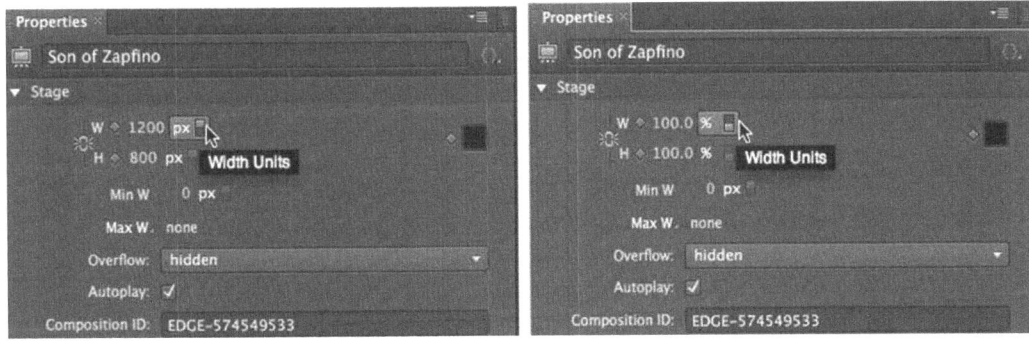

**Figure 10-16.** Setting our stage div to scale to 100%.

8. Let's take a look at our change. Under File, choose Preview in Browser or press Command/ Ctrl + Return.

9. Notice that our black background now scales correctly, but our background image is still 1,200 pixels by 800 pixels. We'll fix that next.

10. In the Timeline panel, click the element named background.

11. Under the Position and Size panel, click the Responsive Design Layout button, which is just above the 1,200 pixel unit width. This will open the Responsive Design templates that you can apply to elements on the Timeline.

12. We want our background image to scale both the width and height to 100%. So, in the template choices, choose Scale Background Image (Figure 10-17).

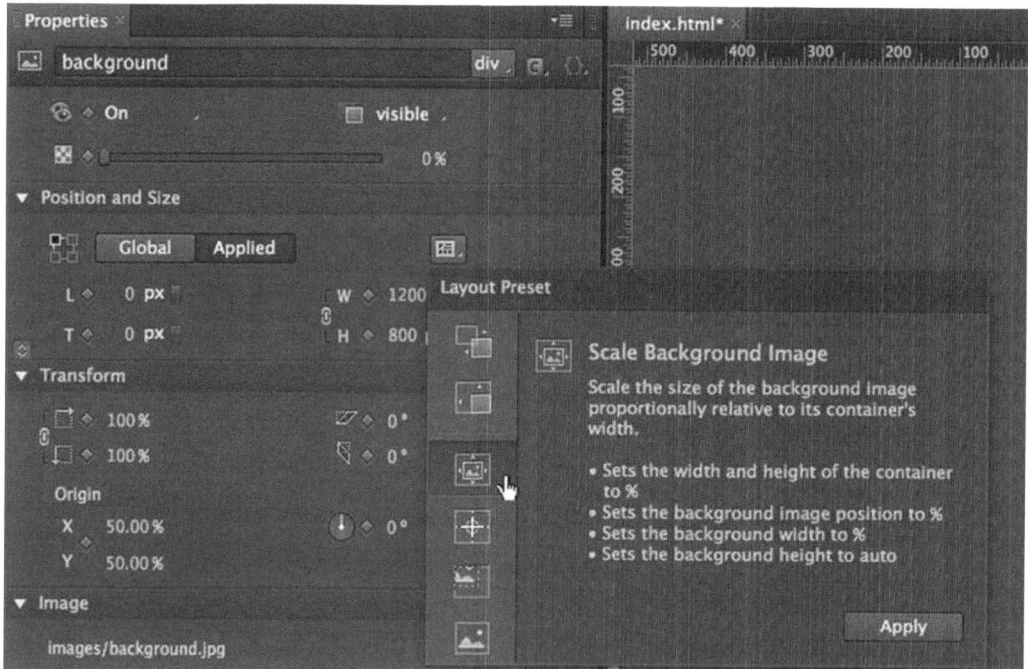

**Figure 10-17.** Choosing a responsive design Layout Preset to scale our background to 100%.

> The Scale Background Image preset will scale the background uniformly to fit the screen. That's fine for a desktop computer, which is set up largely to display a page horizontally. However, in a mobile device, when viewing a page in portrait orientation, our image will not stretch to the bottom. We fix that by changing the image size units under the Image tab from auto to 100%.

13. To make sure our background image scales 100%, even in portrait orientation on our smartphone, under the Image panel, change Auto to 100% (Figure 10-18).

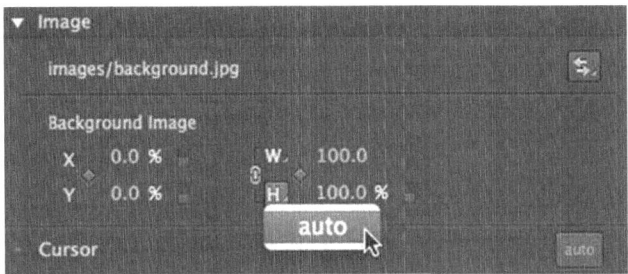

**Figure 10-18.** Fixing our background image to scale 100% by 100%.

14. Choose File: Preview in Browser. Our background is now correctly scaled 100%.

15. Choose File: Save to save your work.

## Adding the Finishing Touches to Our Responsive Design

Although we have our background and stage scaled correctly, we need to address some issues with our other elements. One of the things to keep in mind here when designing a responsive layout in Edge Animate is to plan somewhat ahead in terms of how you want your elements to behave when the viewport is different. If we were to code our design by hand, we would include breakpoints and media queries to tell our browser what to do when our viewport size is smaller (i.e., where to break, position, and scale our graphics and text). Although we can't add breakpoints to Edge Animate, we can set up our elements to scale and position appropriately within our design by utilizing a few options.

For example, when we scaled our stage and background, you may have noticed that on our mobile devices, our large spinning "Z" is cut off on the right side. What we need to do is tell Edge Animate to keep track of that element in terms of its relative position to the top right side of our design. Here's how we do that.

1. If you closed the previous exercise, locate your Exercise folder and open index.an inside the Responsive folder.

2. Move the playhead to the Zbig label.

3. In the Timeline panel, click the element Zbig.

4. Under Position and Size, click the small gray square next to the Global button to align the element Relative to top and right (Figure 10-19). Global allows you to see the computed position of an element, whereas Applied allows you to see the values that Edge Animate assigns to the element. For this exercise, we will stick with Edge Animate's default of Applied.

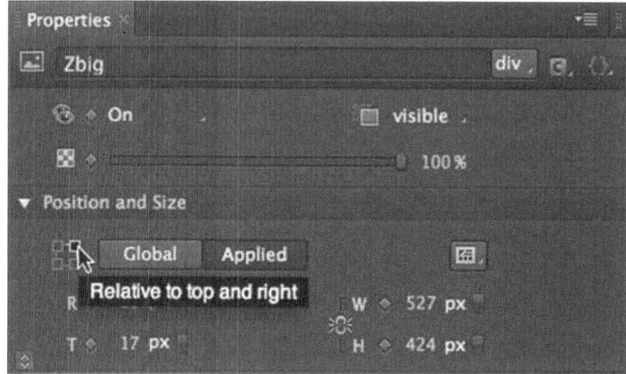

**Figure 10-19.** Aligning our Zbig element relative to the top and right.

5. Now we need to adjust our Text element to align on the bottom right of our design. To do that, we just follow step 4 but align our object to the Bottom and right (Figure 10-20).

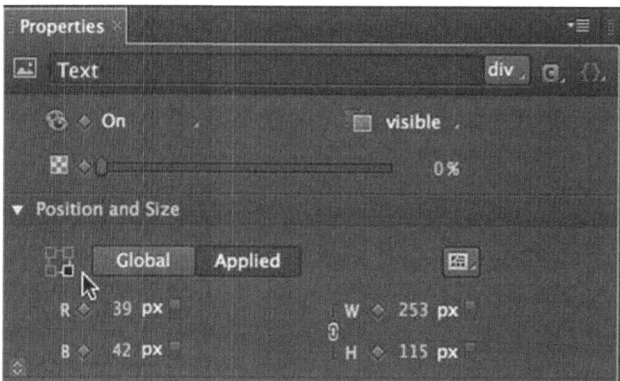

**Figure 10-20.** Setting our text element to position relative to the bottom right.

6. Choose File: Preview in Browser.

7. If you used Adobe Edge Inspect with your mobile devices and previewed changes, as you learned in the Edge Inspect exercise, you'll see your design responsively adapts in the viewport of your connected devices.

8. If you don't have Edge Inspect running, you can test the responsiveness of your design by resizing your browser window.

9. With our responsive design options set, your screens should look similar to Figure 10-21.

MacBook Pro Screen

iPhone 4s Screen

iPad 2 Screen

**Figure 10-21.** Screenshots from our final responsive designed Edge Animate composition.

> By the time our book reaches you, it is possible Adobe will have released Edge Reflow, which allows you to design responsive layouts, including breakpoints, and then integrate those layouts within your HTML designs. If you have an Adobe Creative Cloud membership, you will have access to Edge Reflow once it is publically released. For now, we can achieve much of what we need in terms of responsiveness by using the built-in tools in Edge Animate.

## Utilizing Responsive Design for PhoneGap Build

Remember we mentioned earlier that the current PhoneGap Build does not support tablet resolutions. In our PhoneGap exercise, we designed our Stonehenge application based on the specs of the iPhone screen of 320 by 420 pixels. However, our design did not scale completely when viewed on our Android device because our Android device's screen resolution was different from the iPhone's. This is the inherent problem of designing for multiple screens, a problem that is easily solved by employing Edge Animate's responsive design capabilities.

Some things to keep in mind when responsively designing mobile applications with Edge Animate version 1.0 and PhoneGap Build:

1.  Edge Animate symbols do not correctly scale in percentages. Avoid them in your responsive designs.

2.  Plan the layering of your elements wisely, making sure they don't overlap (i.e., hide important data or buttons when the viewport is resized).

3.  Use the KISS principle—keep it simple, stupid! When all else fails, don't overthink your design and use a simple, straightforward interface.

By utilizing what you have learned from the previous exercise, you can create a responsive Edge Animate design and utilize it for your PhoneGap Build application, supporting multiple devices in a single build. Feel free to try it out with the movie trailer presentation we created in the last exercise by publishing to the Web, then compressing the files as a ZIP archive and uploading it to PhoneGap Build. The results will speak for themselves.

# You Have Learned

In this chapter you've learned about Edge Animate's mobile capabilities and built a mobile app with Adobe PhoneGap Build. As you've discovered, Edge Animate is a powerful tool for mobile and responsive design.

Combined with the skills you have learned throughout this book, you are ready to go forth and create some powerful Edge Animate creations. With Edge Animate, the evolution of the Web and mobile apps will certainly expand as you begin to explore the power of Edge Animate's toolset.

Which brings us to the end of this book. We love to end our classes by asking our students a simple question: "Did you learn anything?" We hope you have learned how to start using Edge Animate in ways you may have never considered and that Edge Animate is an incredibly powerful motion graphics and interactivity tool aimed squarely at the modern Web.

We also like to end our classes with one final question: "Did you have fun?" We hope you did and that you have learned that the amount of fun you can have with Edge Animate should be illegal. If you agree, then we will end this book by saying: "We'll see you in jail."

# Index